HYPER POLICE™

ハイパーポリス

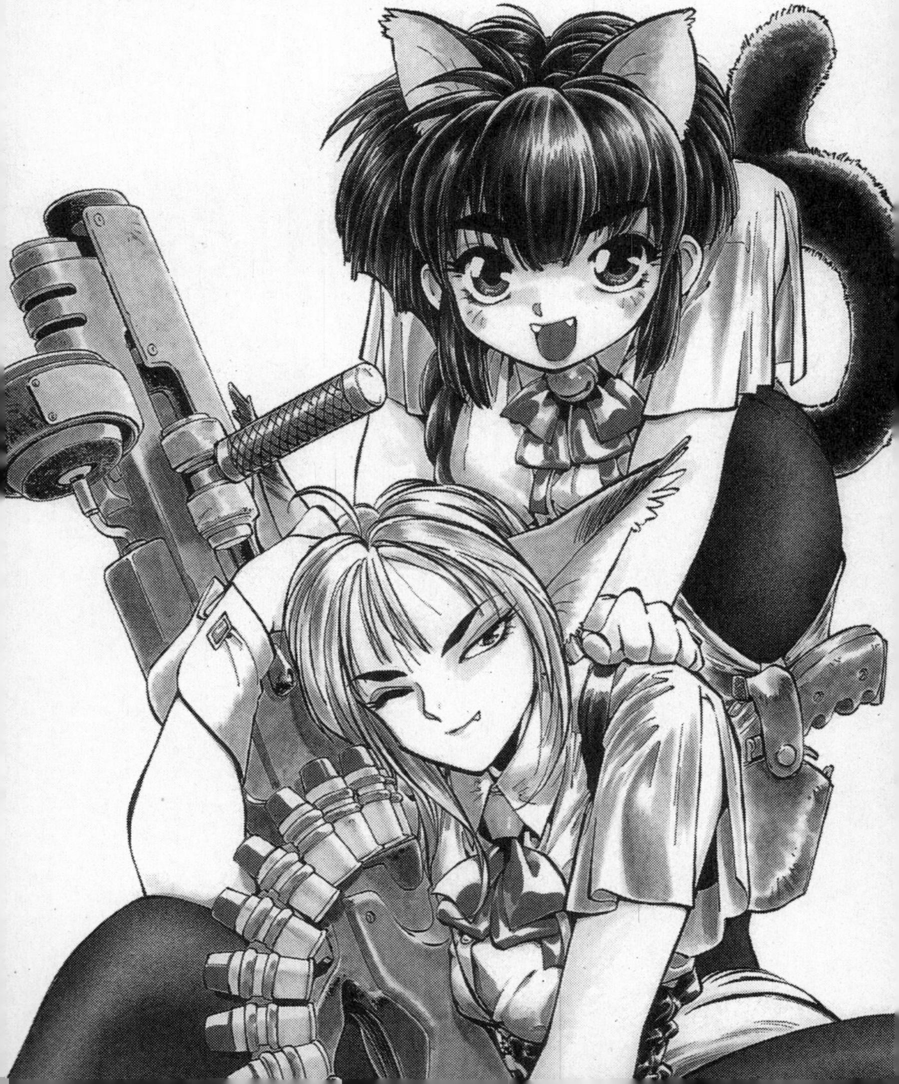

HYPER
ハイパーポリス
POLICE™

Hyper Police Vol. 4
Created by MEE

Translation - David Ury
English Adaptation - Aaron Sparrow
Retouch and Lettering - James Dashiell
Production Artist - Gloria Wu
Cover Design - Kyle Plummer

Editor - Tim Beedle
Digital Imaging Manager - Chris Buford
Production Managers - Jennifer Miller and Mutsumi Miyazaki
Managing Editor - Jill Freshney
VP of Production - Ron Klamert
Publisher and E.I.C. - Mike Kiley
President and C.O.O. - John Parker
C.E.O. - Stuart Levy

A  Manga

TOKYOPOP Inc.
5900 Wilshire Blvd. Suite 2000
Los Angeles, CA 90036

E-mail: info@TOKYOPOP.com
Come visit us online at www.TOKYOPOP.com

ISBN: 1-59532-297-3

First TOKYOPOP printing: September 2005
10 9 8 7 6 5 4 3 2 1
Printed in Canada

HYPER POLICE

ハイパーポリス™

by

MEE

Volume 4

HAMBURG // LONDON // LOS ANGELES // TOKYO

HYPER POLICE™

ハイパーポリス

The Story So Far...

It is the year 22 H.C. (Holy Century), and the human race has all but disappeared. The Japanese city of Shinjuku has become a haven for "monsters"—intelligent creatures that possess human-like anatomy with distinctly animal features. While most monsters are benevolent, all possess the ability to cause destruction, due largely to an internal struggle that is both constant and unwavering. Their evolved minds recognize the necessity for order and respect the sanctity of life, but the animal inside each of them is never too far beneath the surface...

Natsuki Sasahara is one such monster. A rookie at Police Company, a private police organization, she makes her living as a bounty hunter. She was scouted for the position by Batanen Fujioka, a werewolf who harbors a secret attraction for the young cat girl. Cool under pressure and stunningly efficient, Batanen is a seasoned veteran of the hunter trade. With his partner Tomy, Batanen always tops the list of monthly arrests. Recently, Police Company welcomed a new officer to their ranks. Sakura is part nine-tailed fox—or rather she WOULD be if her ninth tail would finish growing in. Partnered with Natsuki, Sakura has formed an uneasy friendship with the young cat girl. While Sakura has come to depend on Natsuki as a partner and roommate, she also hides a vicious desire to eat her. It is her hope that the strong magical essence Natsuki possesses will finally allow Sakura's stumpy tail to grow.

All four of our fearless hunters have learned to deal with budget cutbacks and faulty, obsolete equipment. However, none of them were prepared for the recent bankruptcy of Police Company. Times are tough, and when Sakura's litter of young children accidentally burn Natsuki's house down, Natsuki loses it, running Sakura and her boy toy samurai Sakunoshin out of town. Batanen offers her a room at his house, but when a misunderstanding and a mountain of sexual tension causes the situation to implode, Natsuki flees for parts unknown. Making matters even worse, Batanen receives a call informing him that Tomy has been wrongly arrested for attempted rape.

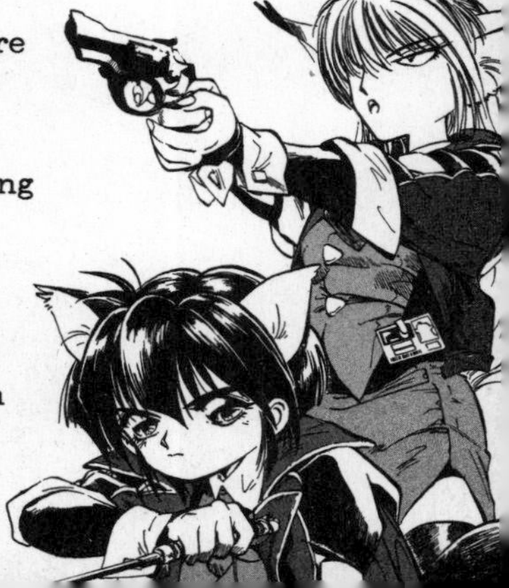

CHARACTERS

Natsuki

A rookie bounty hunter with magical powers and wicked sword skills. Her magic manifests itself as electrical energy capable of frying anything in sight, and is further amplified through the assistance of her two pet parasites: Raijin and Fujin.

Natsuki's partner and a fellow rookie, Sakura is a nine-tailed fox whose ninth tail has yet to grow in. To trigger its growth, Sakura plans to eat the highly magical Natsuki...as soon as she can figure out how.

Sakura

Batanen

A clean shot and a brutal brawler, Batanen is one of the best hunters in the biz. He was Police Company's pride and joy, and has been equally successful as a freelancer, largely due to his possession of something the others lack: a license.

Resourceful, quiet and clever, Tomy prefers to keep busy behind the scenes. He's proven to be an efficient yin to Batanen's yang, often accompanying the great hunter on some of his greatest hunts.

Tomy

CONTENTS

HYPER POLICE
MEE

Report #22

Grand Larceny Killed the Cat Part 1

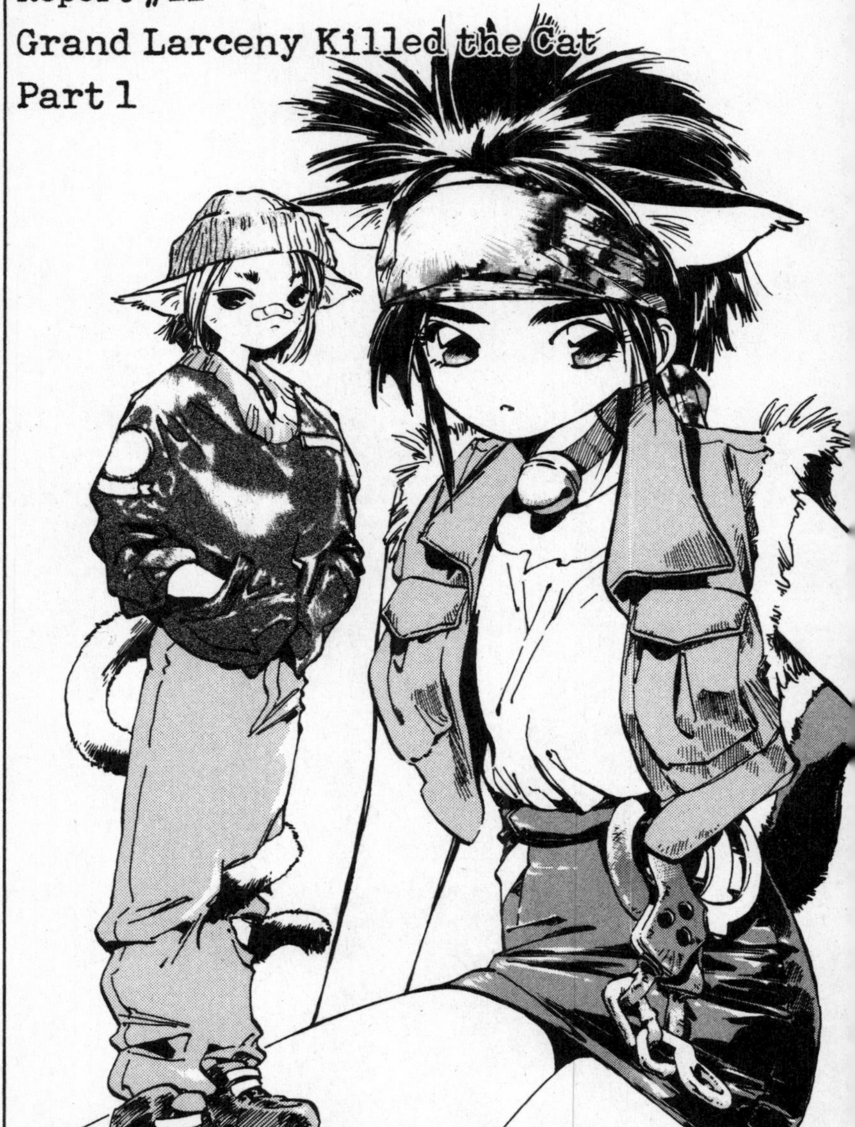

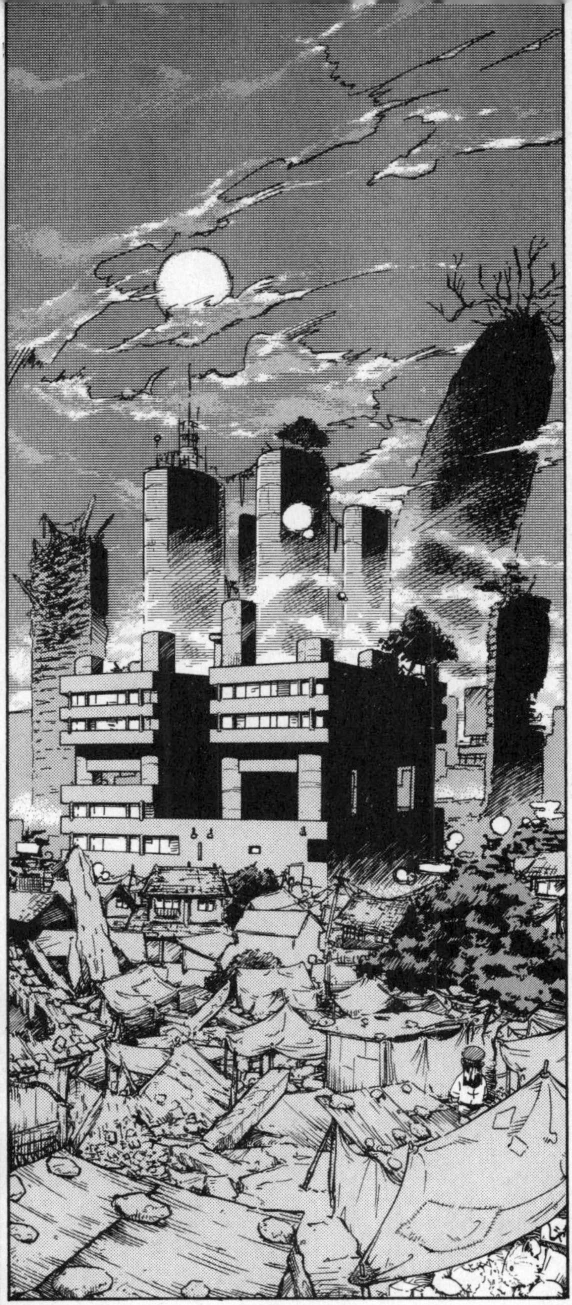
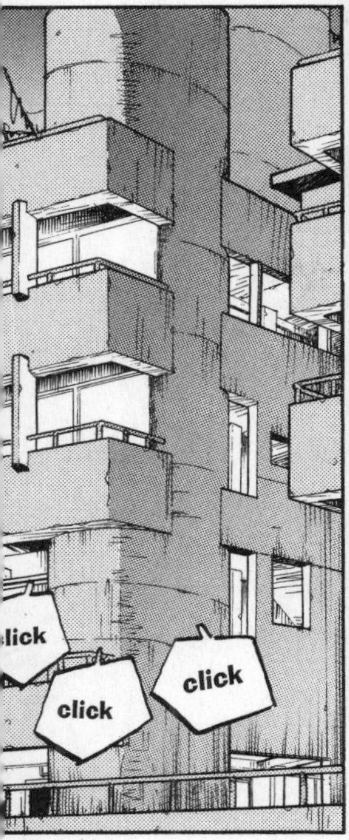
click
lick
click
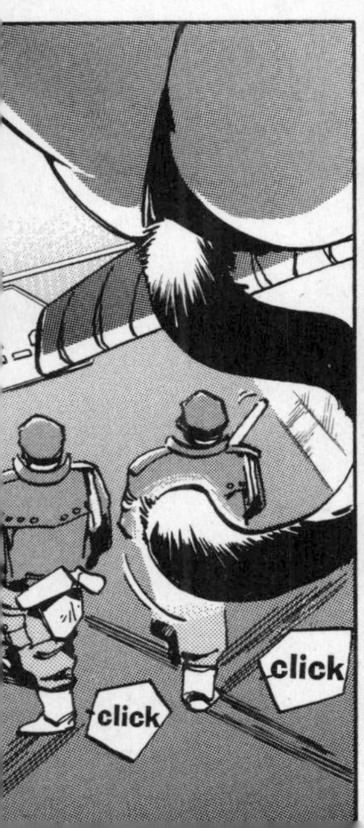
click
click

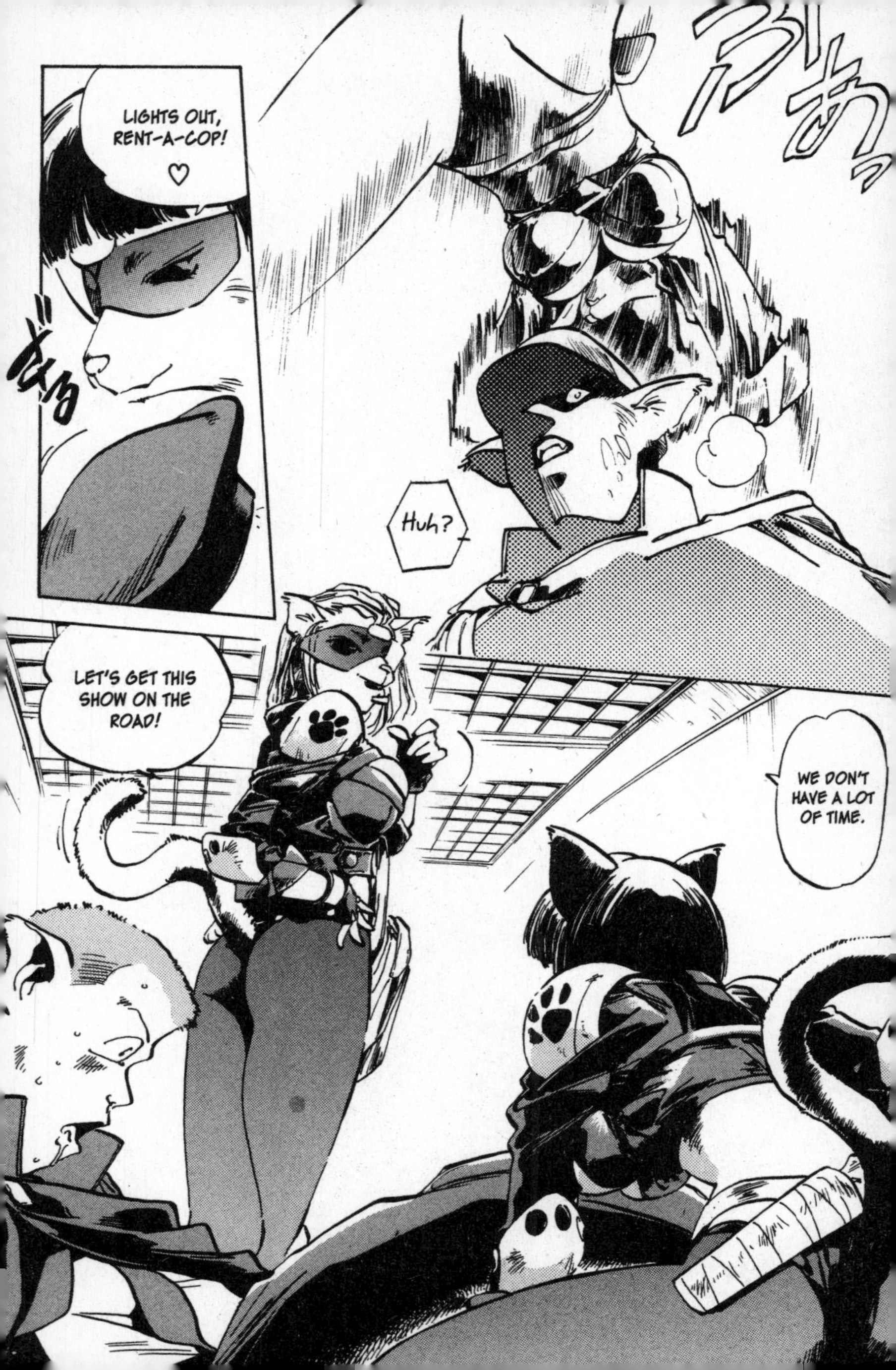

うあっ
Huh?
LIGHTS OUT, RENT-A-COP! ♡
WE DON'T HAVE A LOT OF TIME.
LET'S GET THIS SHOW ON THE ROAD!

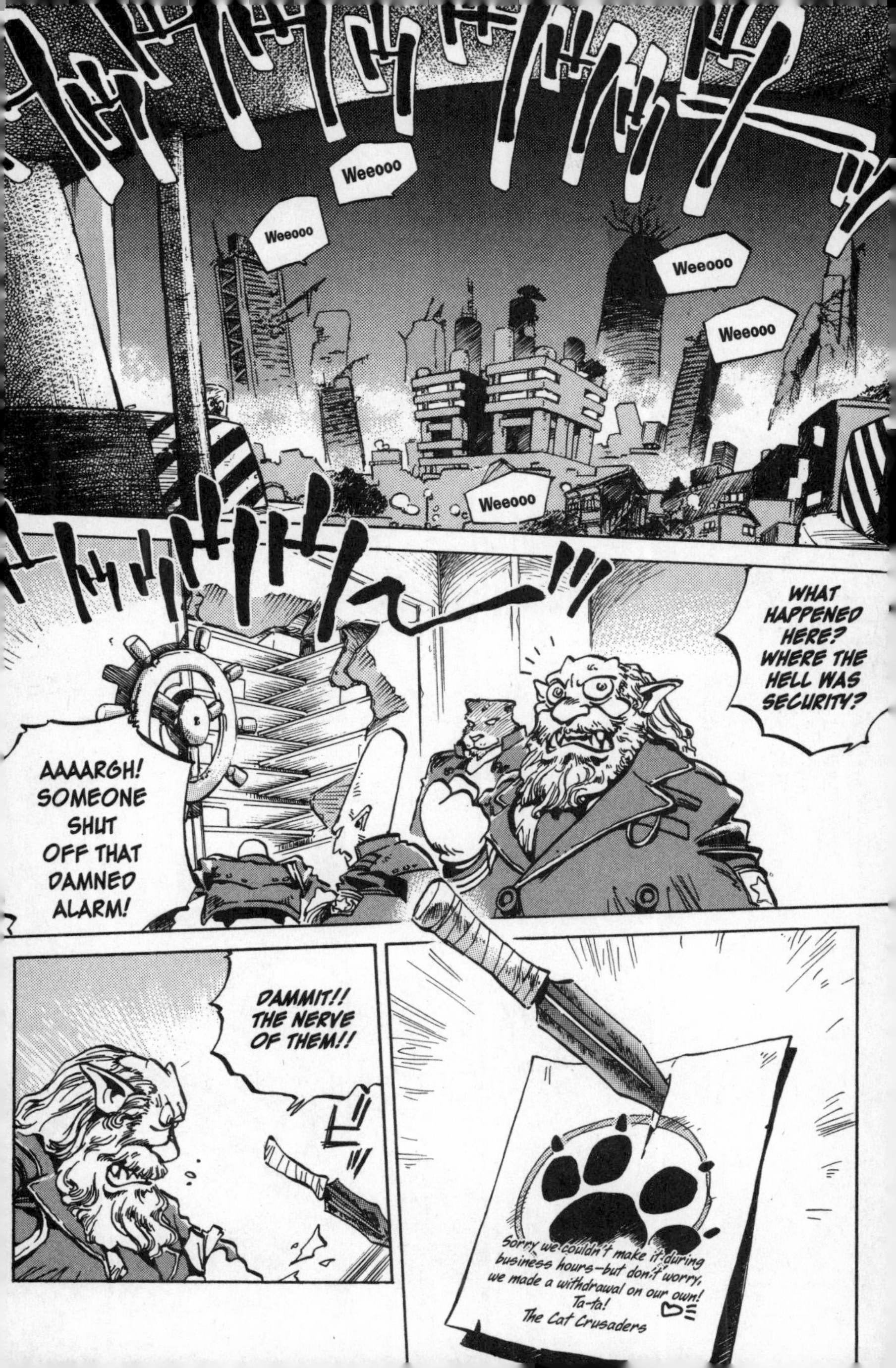
Weeooo
Weeooo
Weeooo
Weeooo
Weeooo
WHAT HAPPENED HERE? WHERE THE HELL WAS SECURITY?
AAAARGH! SOMEONE SHUT OFF THAT DAMNED ALARM!
Sorry we couldn't make it during business hours—but don't worry, we made a withdrawal on our own! Ta-ta! The Cat Crusaders
DAMMIT!! THE NERVE OF THEM!!

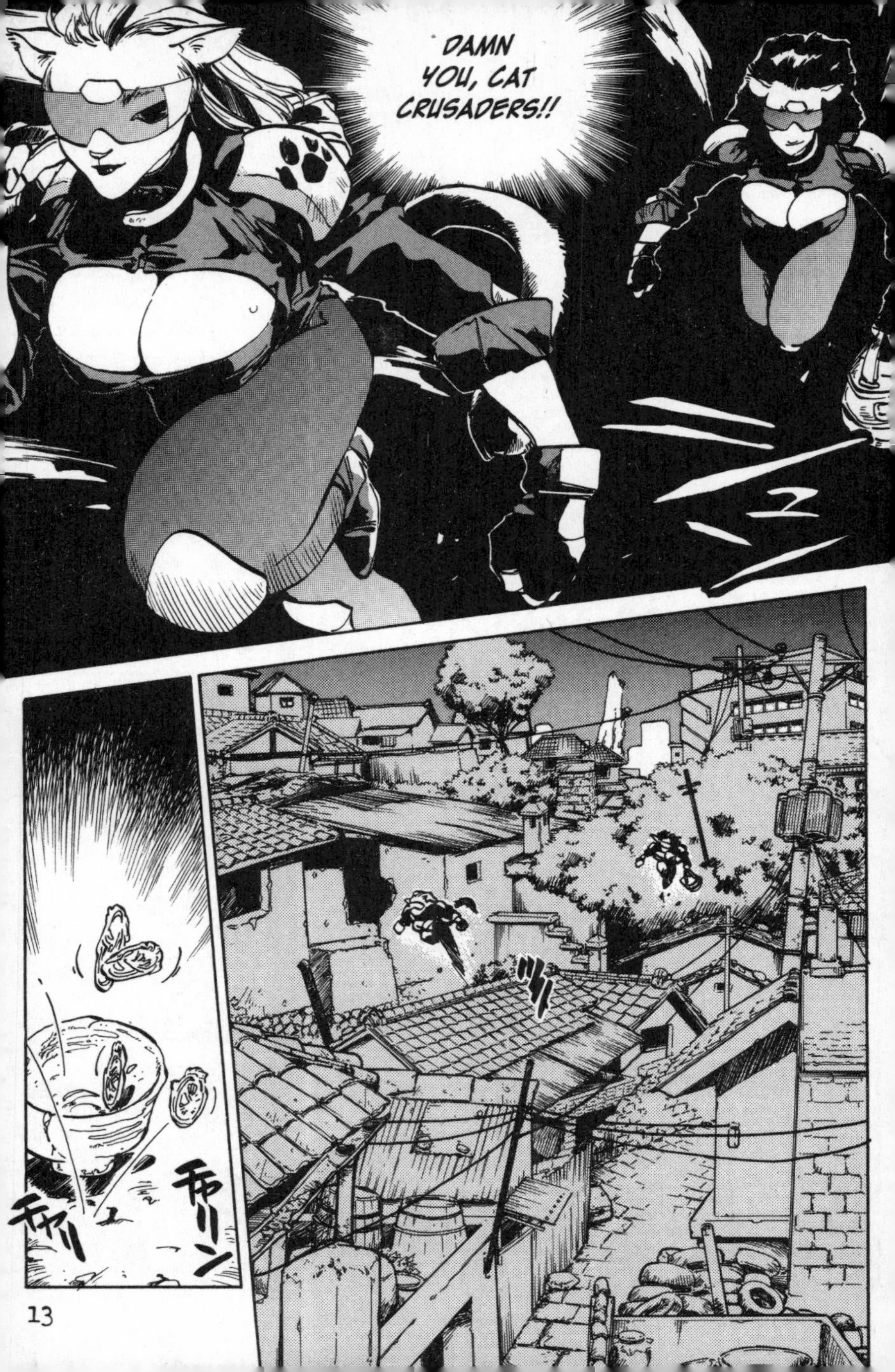
DAMN YOU, CAT CRUSADERS!!
チャリーン
チャリ

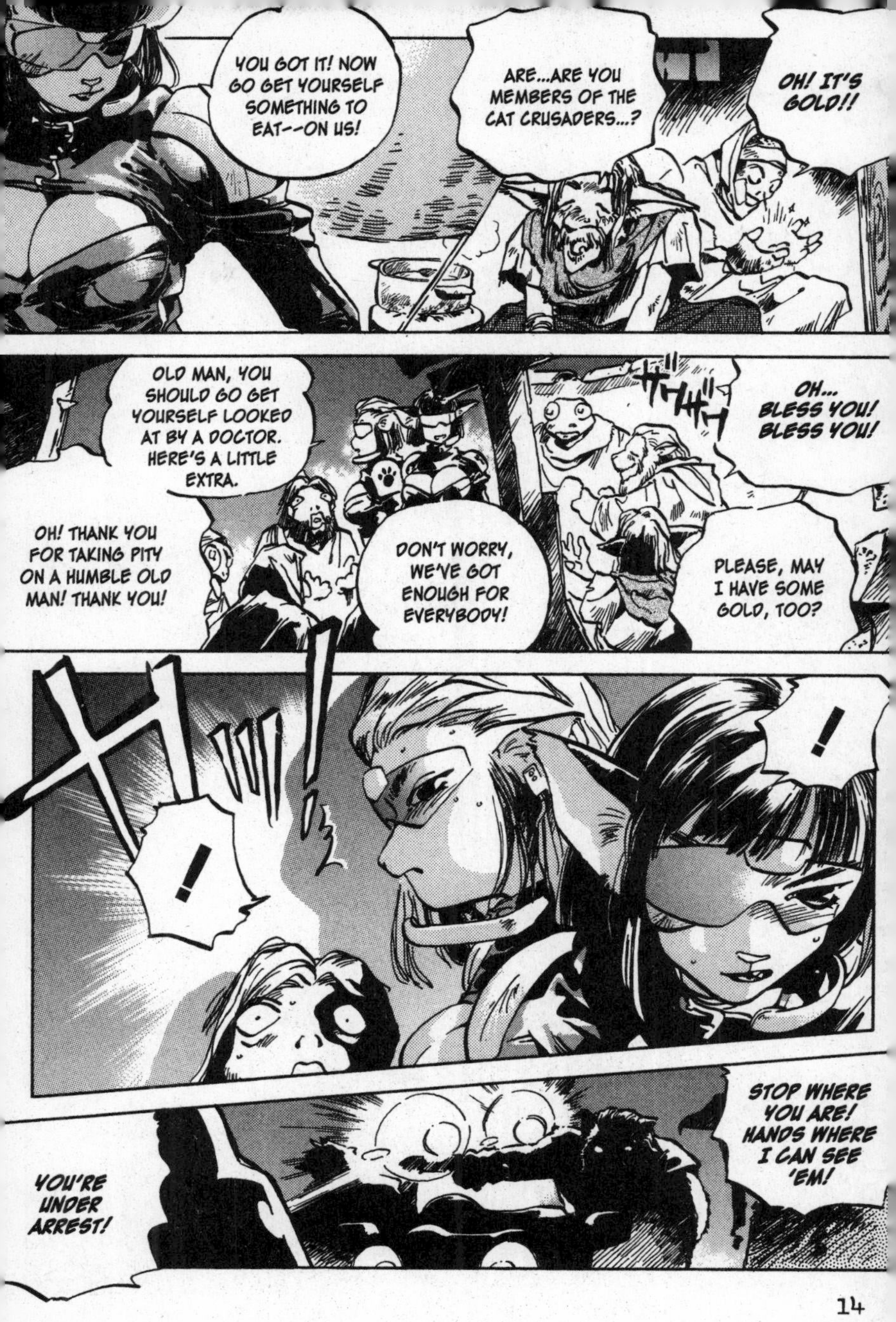

OH! IT'S GOLD!!
ARE...ARE YOU MEMBERS OF THE CAT CRUSADERS...?
YOU GOT IT! NOW GO GET YOURSELF SOMETHING TO EAT--ON US!
OH... BLESS YOU! BLESS YOU!
PLEASE, MAY I HAVE SOME GOLD, TOO?
DON'T WORRY, WE'VE GOT ENOUGH FOR EVERYBODY!
OLD MAN, YOU SHOULD GO GET YOURSELF LOOKED AT BY A DOCTOR. HERE'S A LITTLE EXTRA.
OH! THANK YOU FOR TAKING PITY ON A HUMBLE OLD MAN! THANK YOU!
!
!
!
STOP WHERE YOU ARE! HANDS WHERE I CAN SEE 'EM!
YOU'RE UNDER ARREST!

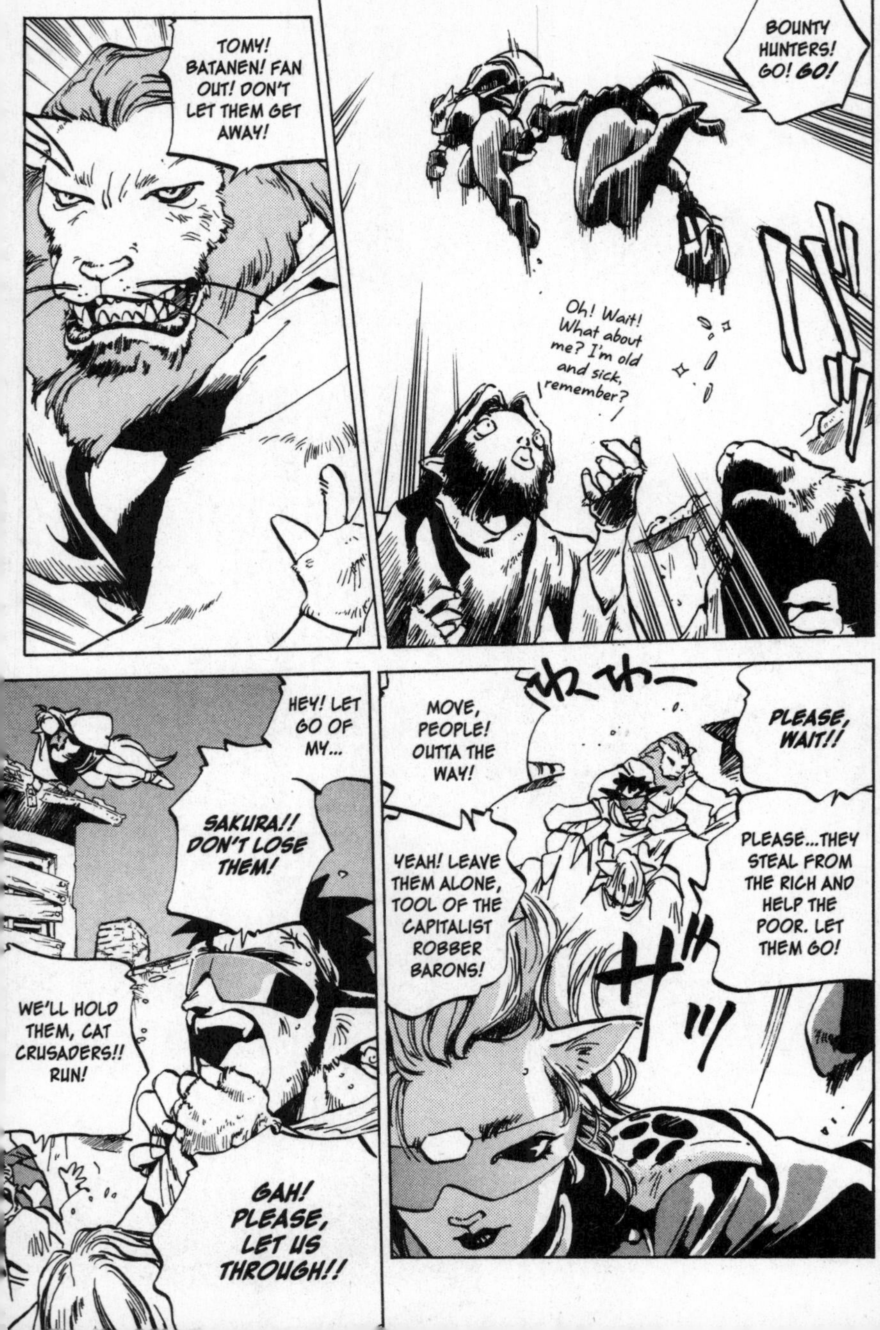
BOUNTY HUNTERS! GO! GO!
Oh! Wait! What about me? I'm old and sick, remember?
TOMY! BATANEN! FAN OUT! DON'T LET THEM GET AWAY!
PLEASE, WAIT!!
MOVE, PEOPLE! OUTTA THE WAY!
PLEASE...THEY STEAL FROM THE RICH AND HELP THE POOR. LET THEM GO!
YEAH! LEAVE THEM ALONE, TOOL OF THE CAPITALIST ROBBER BARONS!
HEY! LET GO OF MY...
SAKURA!! DON'T LOSE THEM!
WE'LL HOLD THEM, CAT CRUSADERS!! RUN!
GAH! PLEASE, LET US THROUGH!!

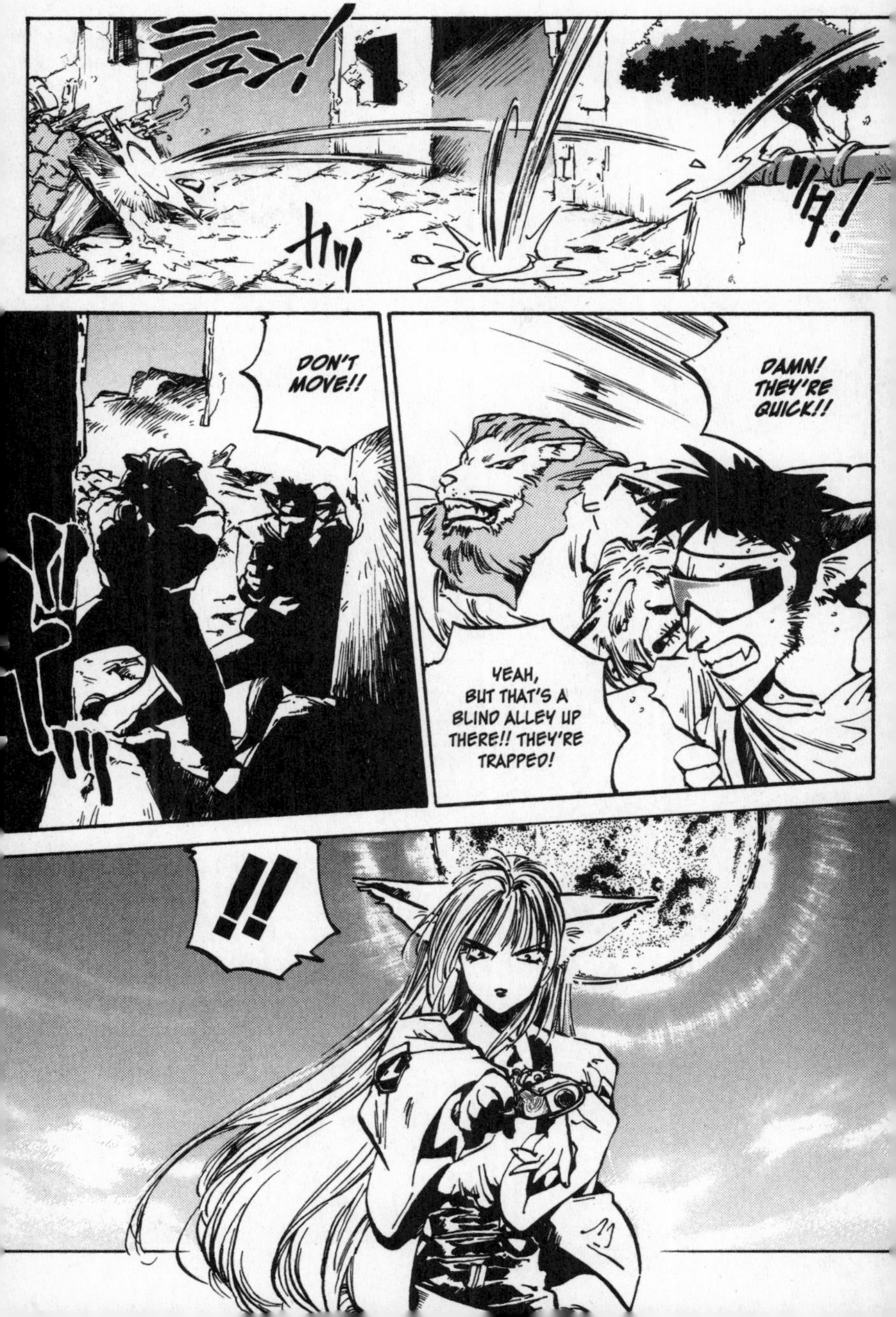
DAMN! THEY'RE QUICK!!
YEAH, BUT THAT'S A BLIND ALLEY UP THERE!! THEY'RE TRAPPED!
DON'T MOVE!!
!!

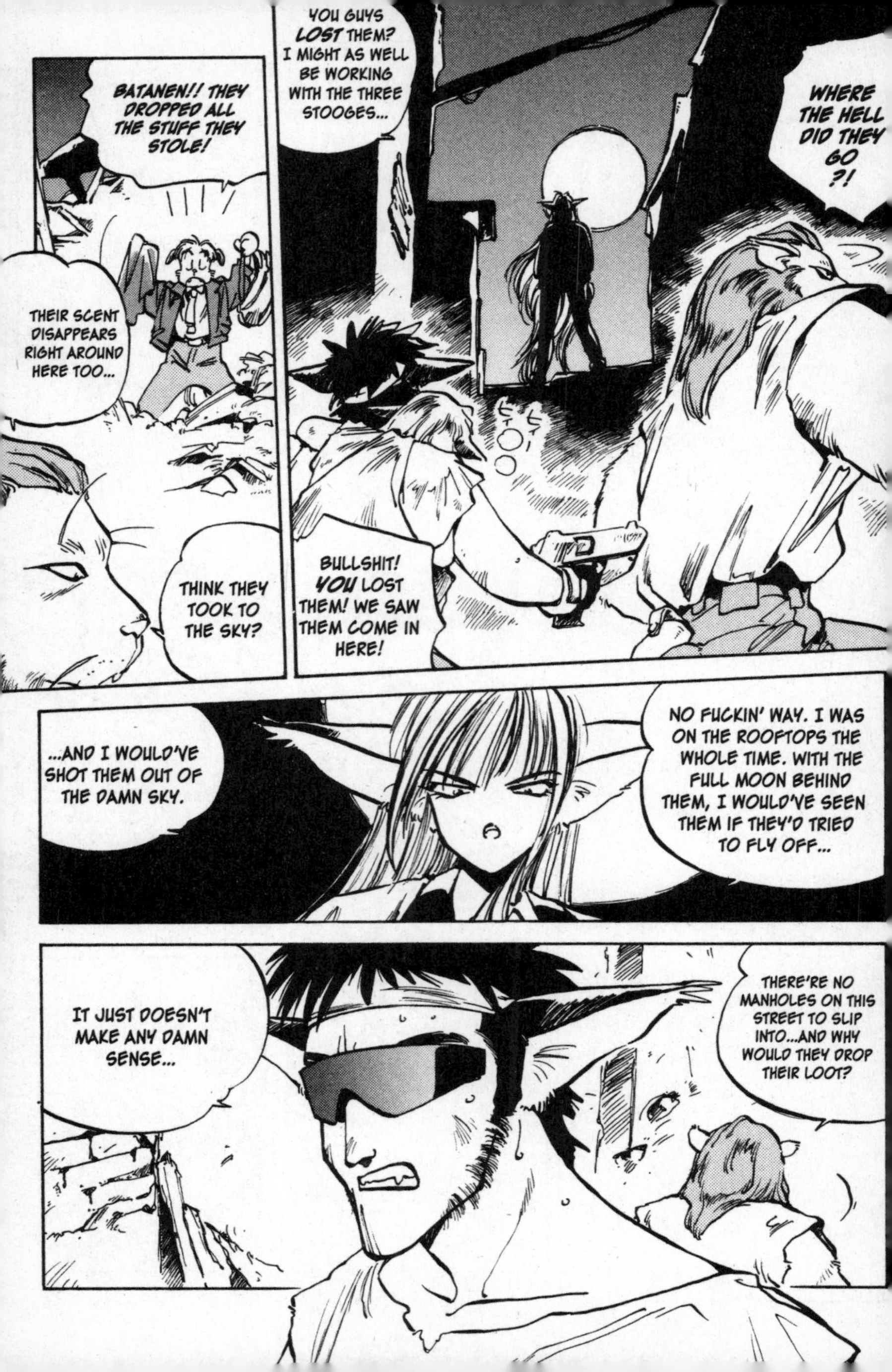
WHERE THE HELL DID THEY GO?!
YOU GUYS LOST THEM? I MIGHT AS WELL BE WORKING WITH THE THREE STOOGES...
BULLSHIT! YOU LOST THEM! WE SAW THEM COME IN HERE!
BATANEN!! THEY DROPPED ALL THE STUFF THEY STOLE!
THEIR SCENT DISAPPEARS RIGHT AROUND HERE TOO...
THINK THEY TOOK TO THE SKY?
NO FUCKIN' WAY. I WAS ON THE ROOFTOPS THE WHOLE TIME. WITH THE FULL MOON BEHIND THEM, I WOULD'VE SEEN THEM IF THEY'D TRIED TO FLY OFF...
...AND I WOULD'VE SHOT THEM OUT OF THE DAMN SKY.
THERE'RE NO MANHOLES ON THIS STREET TO SLIP INTO...AND WHY WOULD THEY DROP THEIR LOOT?
IT JUST DOESN'T MAKE ANY DAMN SENSE...

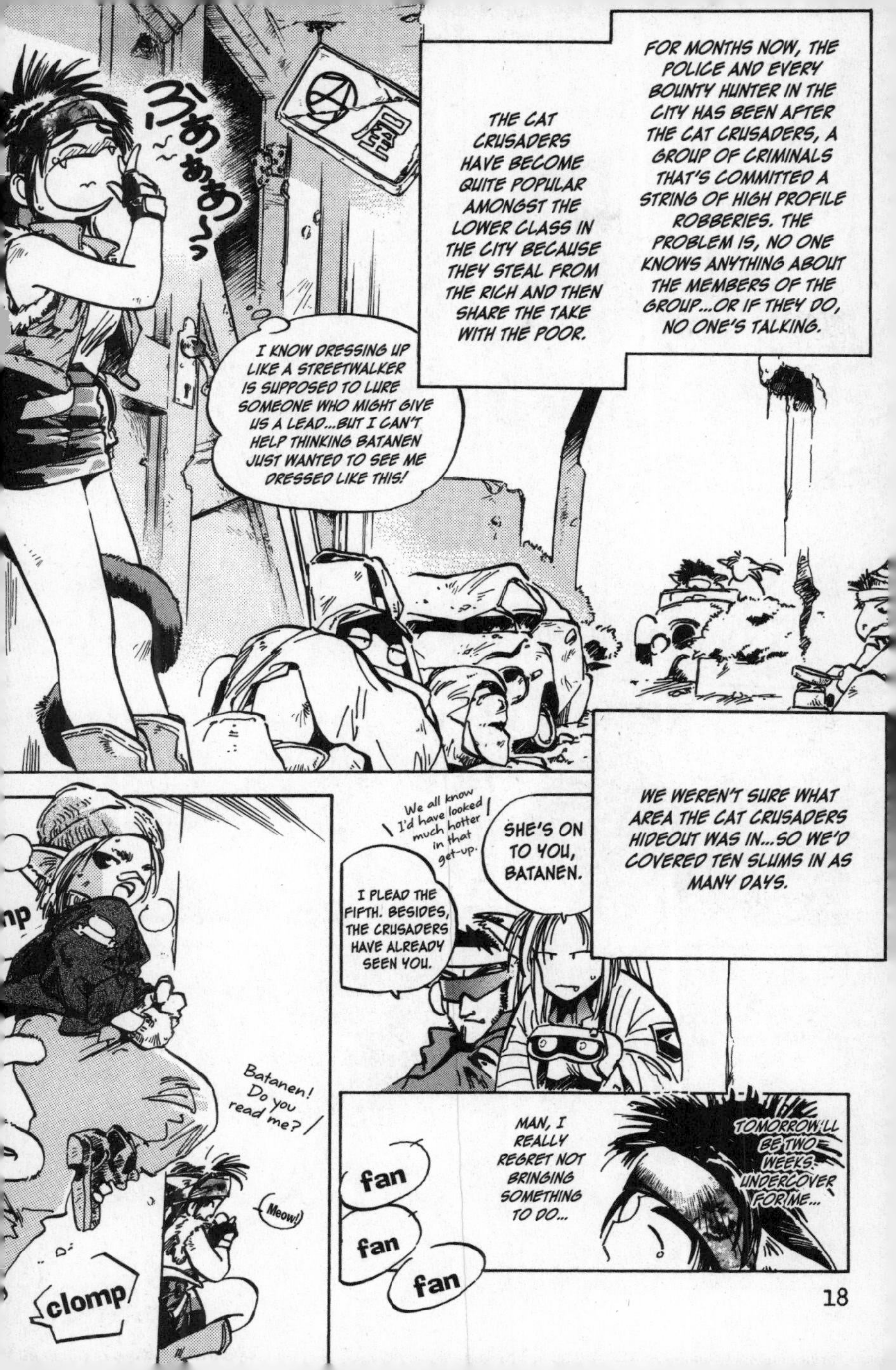
FOR MONTHS NOW, THE POLICE AND EVERY BOUNTY HUNTER IN THE CITY HAS BEEN AFTER THE CAT CRUSADERS, A GROUP OF CRIMINALS THAT'S COMMITTED A STRING OF HIGH PROFILE ROBBERIES. THE PROBLEM IS, NO ONE KNOWS ANYTHING ABOUT THE MEMBERS OF THE GROUP...OR IF THEY DO, NO ONE'S TALKING.
THE CAT CRUSADERS HAVE BECOME QUITE POPULAR AMONGST THE LOWER CLASS IN THE CITY BECAUSE THEY STEAL FROM THE RICH AND THEN SHARE THE TAKE WITH THE POOR.
ふあぁあ〜っ
I KNOW DRESSING UP LIKE A STREETWALKER IS SUPPOSED TO LURE SOMEONE WHO MIGHT GIVE US A LEAD...BUT I CAN'T HELP THINKING BATANEN JUST WANTED TO SEE ME DRESSED LIKE THIS!
WE WEREN'T SURE WHAT AREA THE CAT CRUSADERS HIDEOUT WAS IN...SO WE'D COVERED TEN SLUMS IN AS MANY DAYS.
SHE'S ON TO YOU, BATANEN.
We all know I'd have looked much hotter in that get-up.
I PLEAD THE FIFTH. BESIDES, THE CRUSADERS HAVE ALREADY SEEN YOU.
TOMORROW'LL BE TWO WEEKS UNDERCOVER FOR ME...
MAN, I REALLY REGRET NOT BRINGING SOMETHING TO DO...
fan
fan
fan
Batanen! Do you read me?
Meow!
clomp

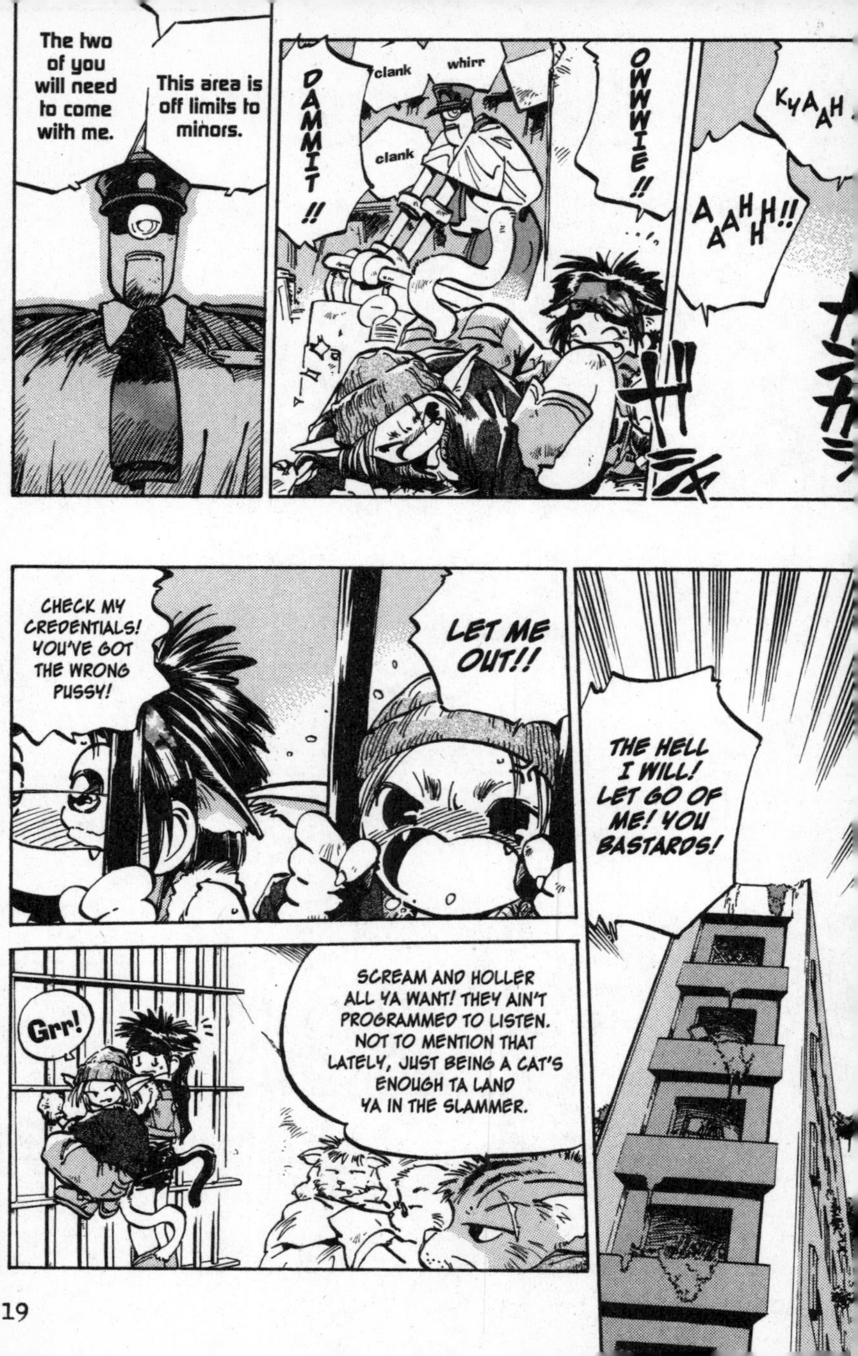
KYAAH AAAHHH!!
OWWWIE!!
whirr
clank
DAMMIT!!
clank
This area is off limits to minors.
The two of you will need to come with me.
THE HELL I WILL! LET GO OF ME! YOU BASTARDS!
LET ME OUT!!
CHECK MY CREDENTIALS! YOU'VE GOT THE WRONG PUSSY!
SCREAM AND HOLLER ALL YA WANT! THEY AIN'T PROGRAMMED TO LISTEN. NOT TO MENTION THAT LATELY, JUST BEING A CAT'S ENOUGH TA LAND YA IN THE SLAMMER.
Grr!

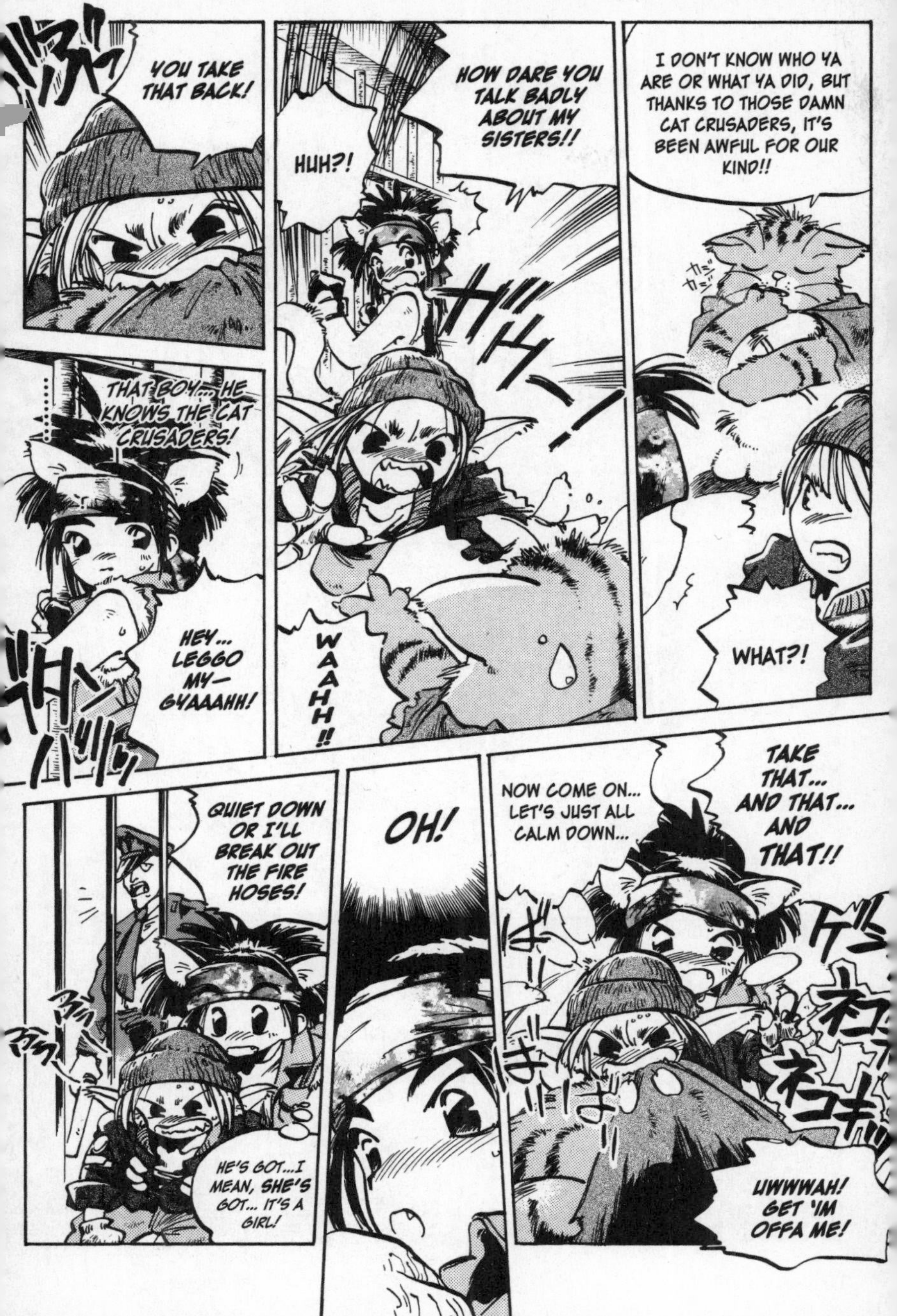

I DON'T KNOW WHO YA ARE OR WHAT YA DID, BUT THANKS TO THOSE DAMN CAT CRUSADERS, IT'S BEEN AWFUL FOR OUR KIND!!
WHAT?!
HOW DARE YOU TALK BADLY ABOUT MY SISTERS!!
HUH?!
WAAAHH!!
YOU TAKE THAT BACK!
THAT BOY... HE KNOWS THE CAT CRUSADERS!
HEY... LEGGO MY— GYAAAHH!
TAKE THAT... AND THAT... AND THAT!!
NOW COME ON... LET'S JUST ALL CALM DOWN...
UWWWAH! GET 'IM OFFA ME!
OH!
QUIET DOWN OR I'LL BREAK OUT THE FIRE HOSES!
HE'S GOT...I MEAN, SHE'S GOT... IT'S A GIRL!

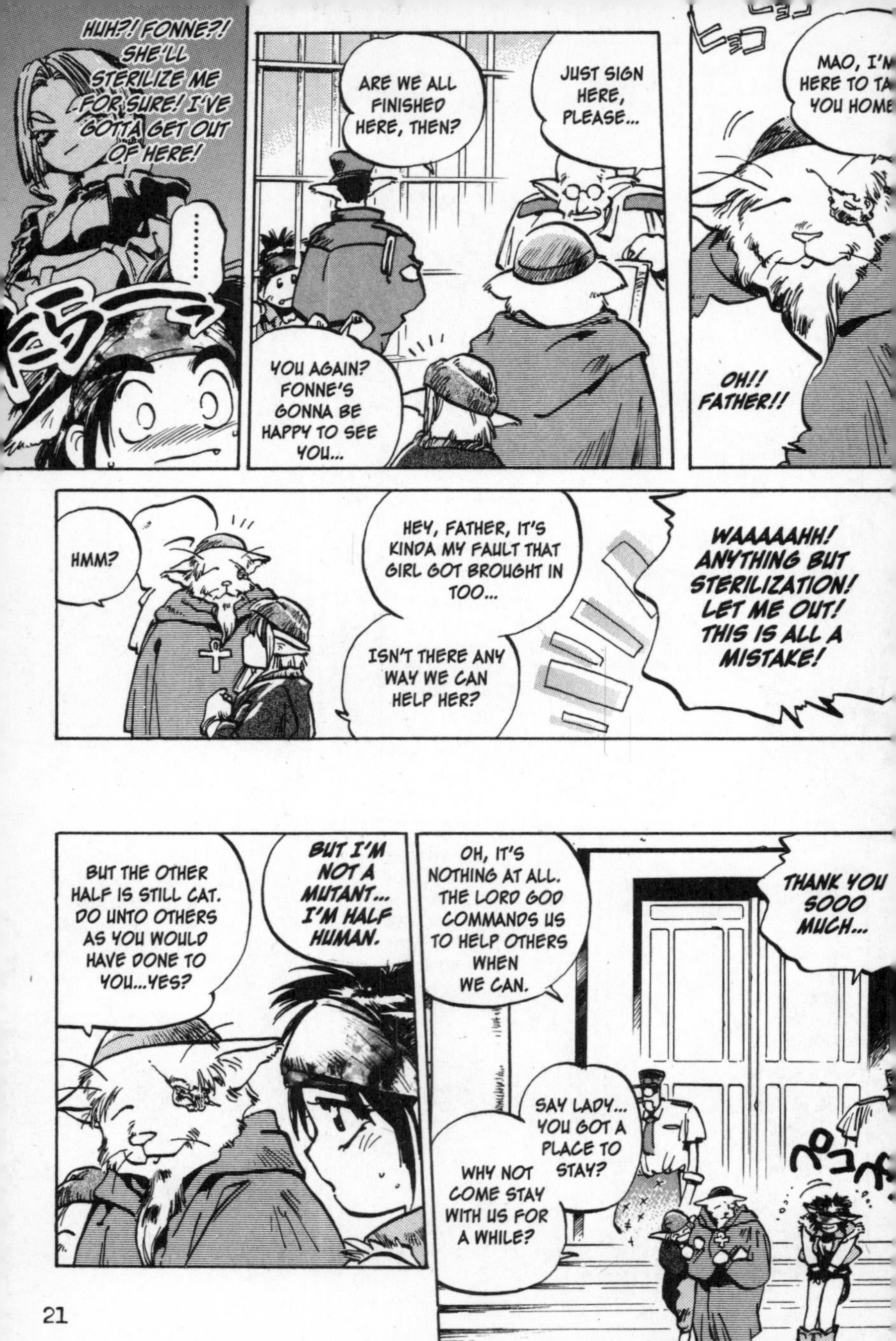
MAO, I'M HERE TO TA YOU HOME
OH!! FATHER!!
JUST SIGN HERE, PLEASE...
ARE WE ALL FINISHED HERE, THEN?
YOU AGAIN? FONNE'S GONNA BE HAPPY TO SEE YOU...
HUH?! FONNE?! SHE'LL STERILIZE ME FOR SURE! I'VE GOTTA GET OUT OF HERE!
......
WAAAAAHH! ANYTHING BUT STERILIZATION! LET ME OUT! THIS IS ALL A MISTAKE!
HEY, FATHER, IT'S KINDA MY FAULT THAT GIRL GOT BROUGHT IN TOO...
ISN'T THERE ANY WAY WE CAN HELP HER?
HMM?
THANK YOU SOOO MUCH...
OH, IT'S NOTHING AT ALL. THE LORD GOD COMMANDS US TO HELP OTHERS WHEN WE CAN.
SAY LADY... YOU GOT A PLACE TO STAY?
WHY NOT COME STAY WITH US FOR A WHILE?
BUT I'M NOT A MUTANT... I'M HALF HUMAN.
BUT THE OTHER HALF IS STILL CAT. DO UNTO OTHERS AS YOU WOULD HAVE DONE TO YOU...YES?

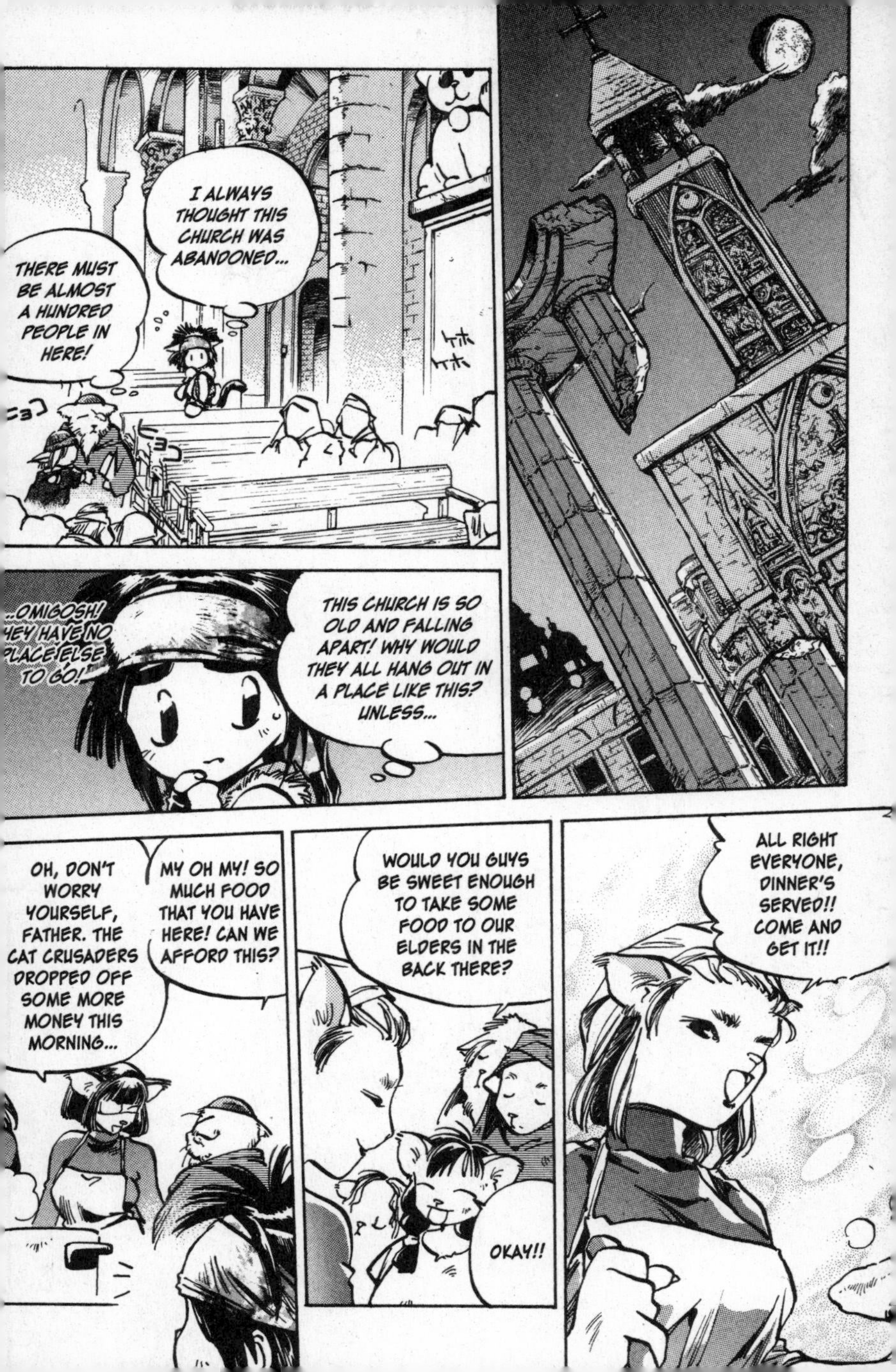
I ALWAYS THOUGHT THIS CHURCH WAS ABANDONED...
THERE MUST BE ALMOST A HUNDRED PEOPLE IN HERE!
ケホ ケホ
THIS CHURCH IS SO OLD AND FALLING APART! WHY WOULD THEY ALL HANG OUT IN A PLACE LIKE THIS? UNLESS...
..OMIGOSH! HEY HAVE NO PLACE ELSE TO GO!
ALL RIGHT EVERYONE, DINNER'S SERVED!! COME AND GET IT!!
WOULD YOU GUYS BE SWEET ENOUGH TO TAKE SOME FOOD TO OUR ELDERS IN THE BACK THERE?
OKAY!!
MY OH MY! SO MUCH FOOD THAT YOU HAVE HERE! CAN WE AFFORD THIS?
OH, DON'T WORRY YOURSELF, FATHER. THE CAT CRUSADERS DROPPED OFF SOME MORE MONEY THIS MORNING...

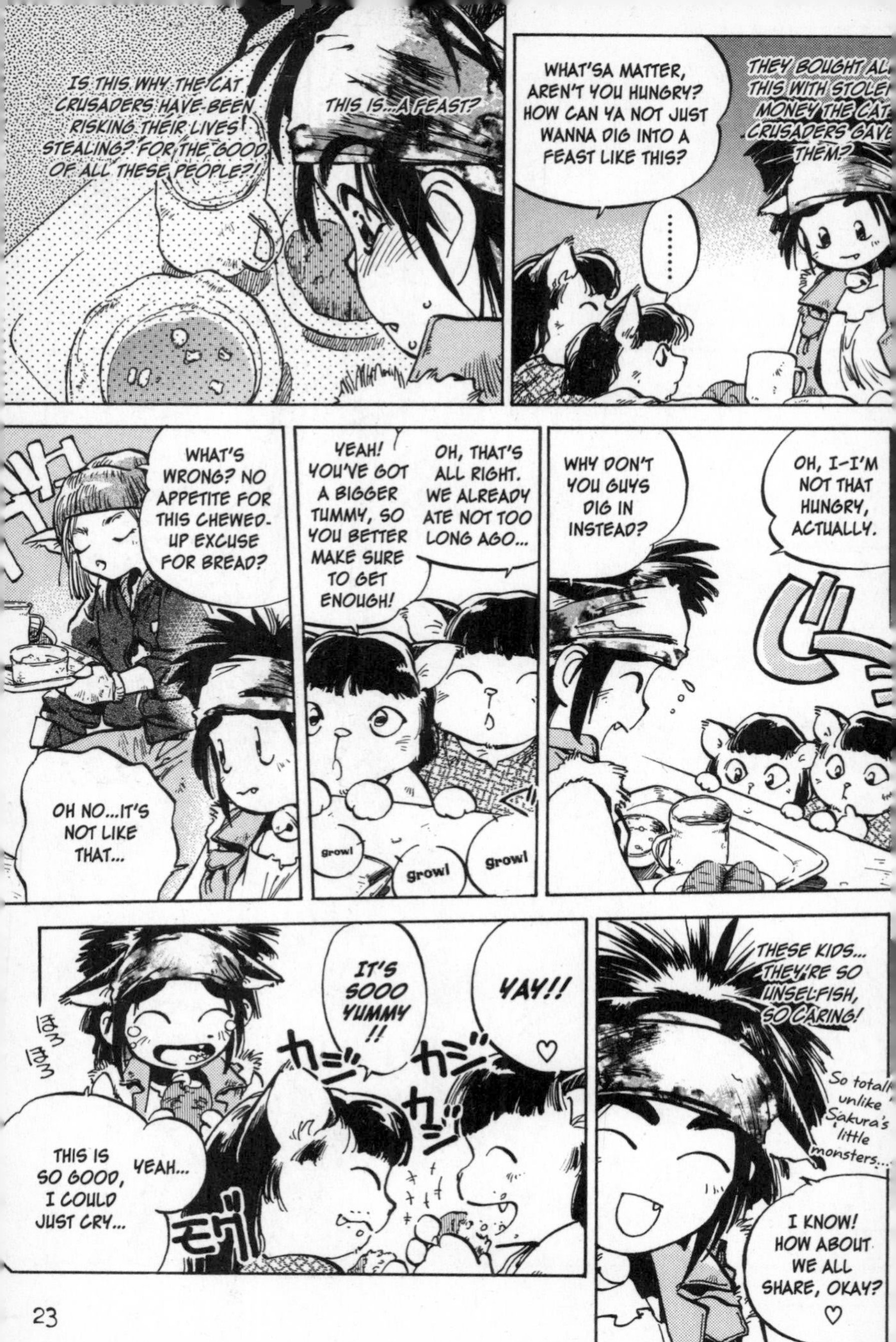
THEY BOUGHT AL THIS WITH STOLE MONEY THE CAT CRUSADERS GAVE THEM?
WHAT'SA MATTER, AREN'T YOU HUNGRY? HOW CAN YA NOT JUST WANNA DIG INTO A FEAST LIKE THIS?
....
THIS IS...A FEAST?
IS THIS WHY THE CAT CRUSADERS HAVE BEEN RISKING THEIR LIVES STEALING? FOR THE GOOD OF ALL THESE PEOPLE?!
OH, I-I'M NOT THAT HUNGRY, ACTUALLY.
WHY DON'T YOU GUYS DIG IN INSTEAD?
OH, THAT'S ALL RIGHT. WE ALREADY ATE NOT TOO LONG AGO...
YEAH! YOU'VE GOT A BIGGER TUMMY, SO YOU BETTER MAKE SURE TO GET ENOUGH!
growl
growl
growl
WHAT'S WRONG? NO APPETITE FOR THIS CHEWED-UP EXCUSE FOR BREAD?
OH NO...IT'S NOT LIKE THAT...
THESE KIDS... THEY'RE SO UNSELFISH, SO CARING!
So totall unlike Sakura's little monsters...
I KNOW! HOW ABOUT WE ALL SHARE, OKAY? ♡
YAY!! ♡
IT'S SOOO YUMMY!!
カジ
カジ
カジ
ほろ ほろ
THIS IS SO GOOD, I COULD JUST CRY...
YEAH...
モグ

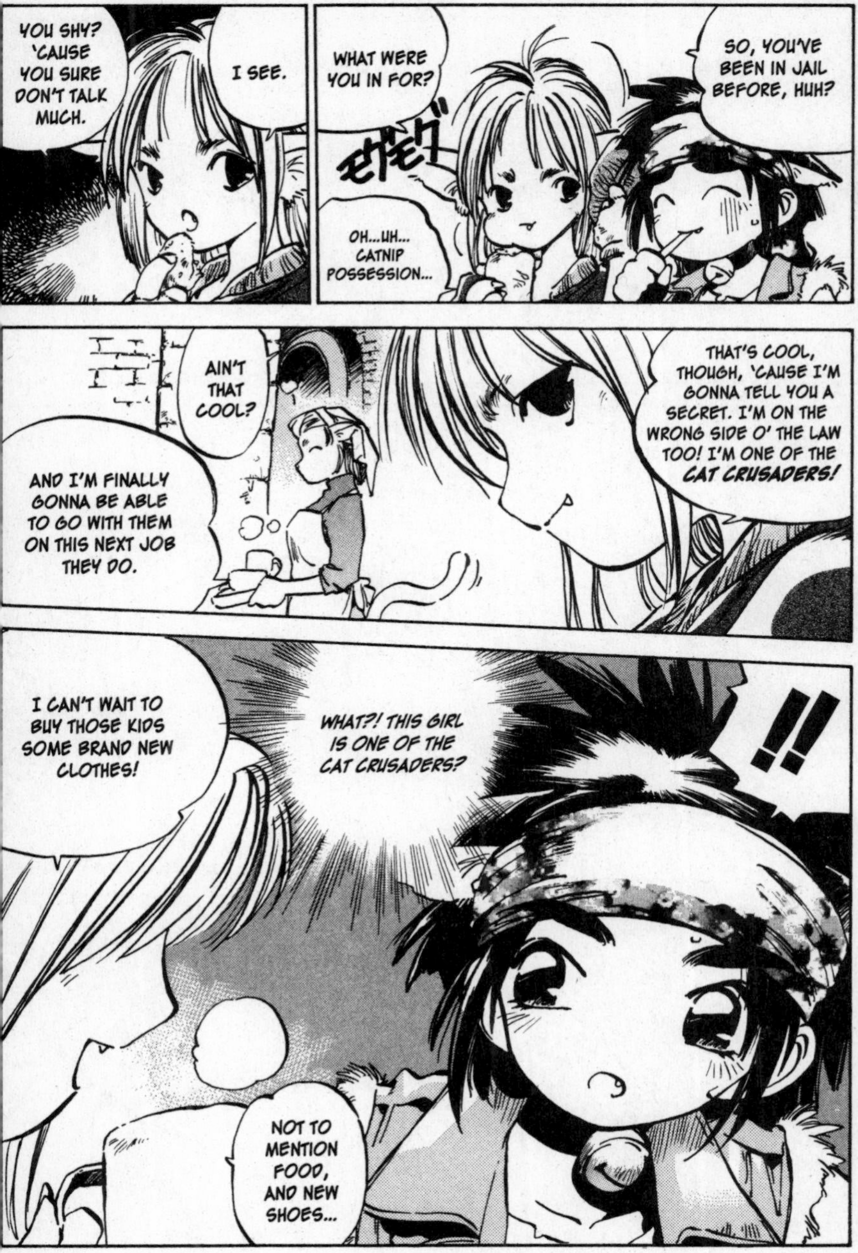
SO, YOU'VE BEEN IN JAIL BEFORE, HUH?
WHAT WERE YOU IN FOR?
OH...UH... CATNIP POSSESSION...
I SEE.
YOU SHY? 'CAUSE YOU SURE DON'T TALK MUCH.
THAT'S COOL, THOUGH, 'CAUSE I'M GONNA TELL YOU A SECRET. I'M ON THE WRONG SIDE O' THE LAW TOO! I'M ONE OF THE CAT CRUSADERS!
AIN'T THAT COOL?
AND I'M FINALLY GONNA BE ABLE TO GO WITH THEM ON THIS NEXT JOB THEY DO.
!!
WHAT?! THIS GIRL IS ONE OF THE CAT CRUSADERS?
I CAN'T WAIT TO BUY THOSE KIDS SOME BRAND NEW CLOTHES!
NOT TO MENTION FOOD, AND NEW SHOES...

Report #23

Grand Larceny Killed the Cat

Part 2

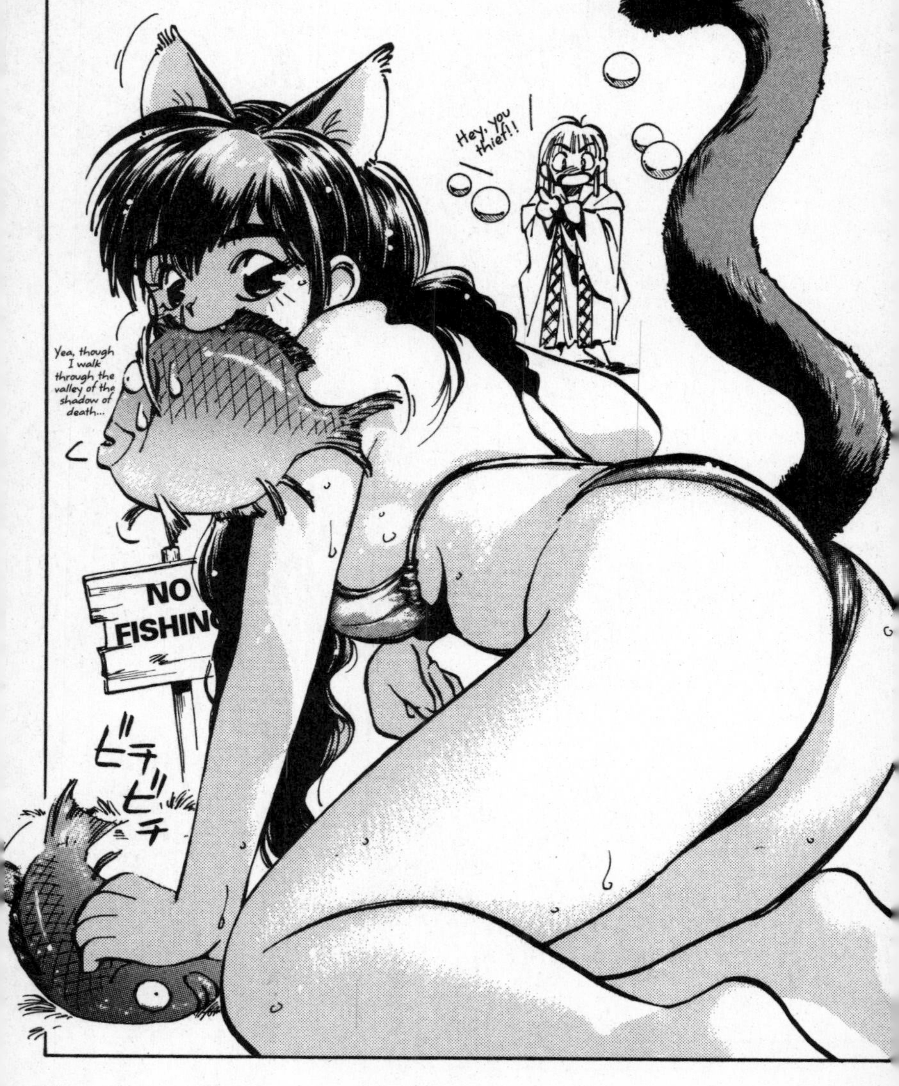
Hey, you thief!!
Yea, though I walk through the valley of the shadow of death...
NO FISHING
ビチビチ

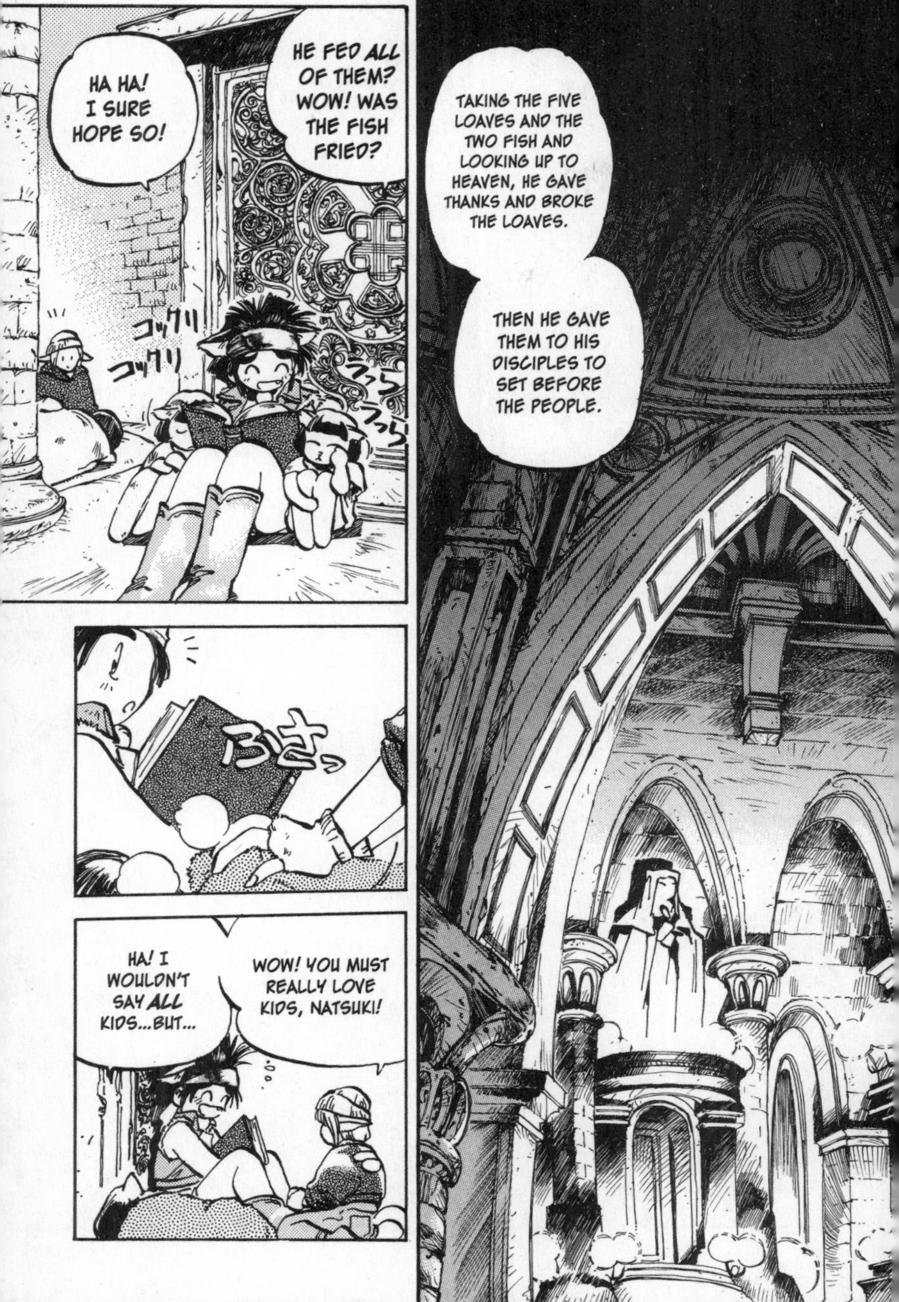
TAKING THE FIVE LOAVES AND THE TWO FISH AND LOOKING UP TO HEAVEN, HE GAVE THANKS AND BROKE THE LOAVES.
THEN HE GAVE THEM TO HIS DISCIPLES TO SET BEFORE THE PEOPLE.
HE FED ALL OF THEM? WOW! WAS THE FISH FRIED?
HA HA! I SURE HOPE SO!
うっら うっら
ゴックリ ゴックリ
ふさっ
WOW! YOU MUST REALLY LOVE KIDS, NATSUKI!
HA! I WOULDN'T SAY ALL KIDS...BUT...

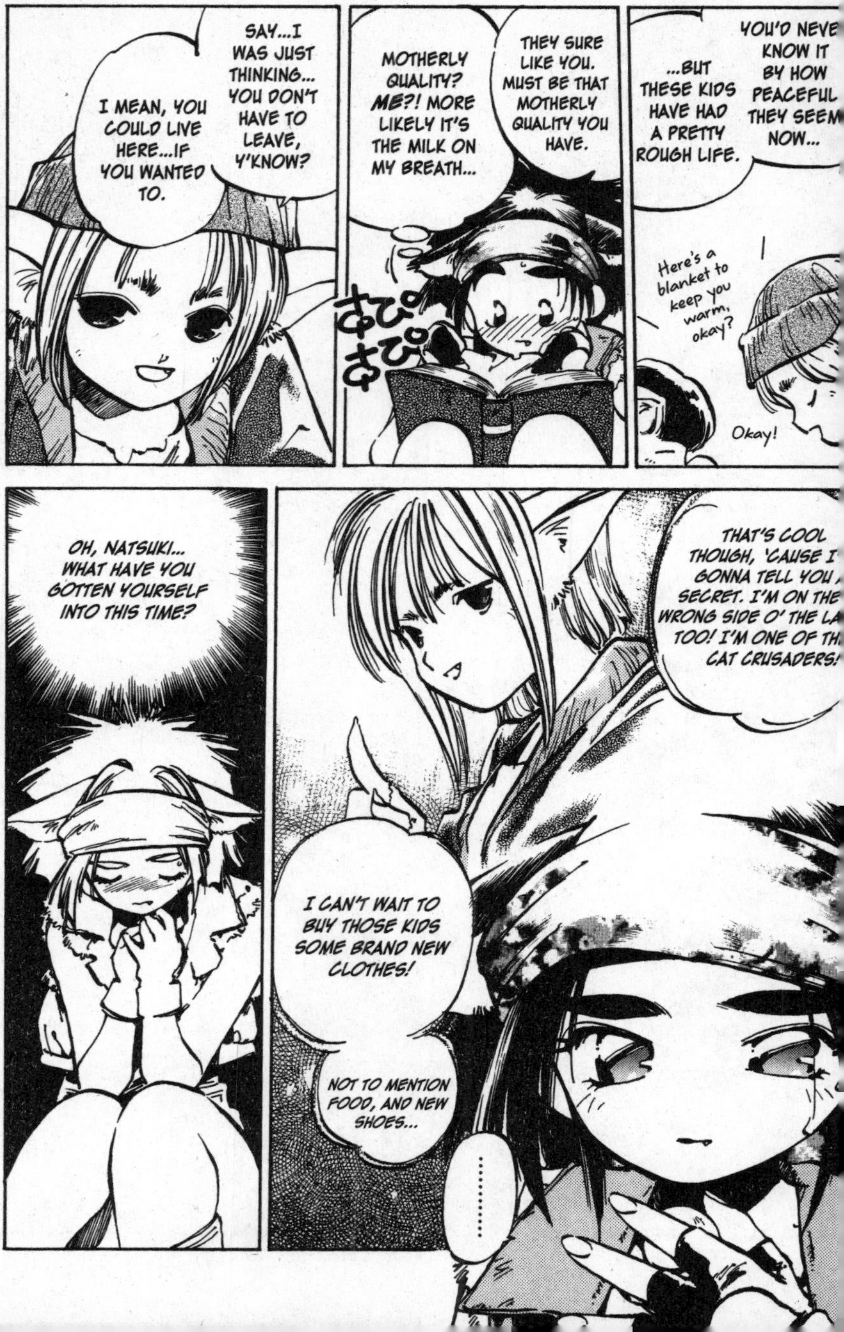
YOU'D NEVE KNOW IT BY HOW PEACEFUL THEY SEEM NOW...
...BUT THESE KIDS HAVE HAD A PRETTY ROUGH LIFE.
Here's a blanket to keep you warm, okay?
Okay!
THEY SURE LIKE YOU. MUST BE THAT MOTHERLY QUALITY YOU HAVE.
MOTHERLY QUALITY? ME?! MORE LIKELY IT'S THE MILK ON MY BREATH...
すぴ すぴ
SAY...I WAS JUST THINKING... YOU DON'T HAVE TO LEAVE, Y'KNOW?
I MEAN, YOU COULD LIVE HERE...IF YOU WANTED TO.
THAT'S COOL THOUGH, 'CAUSE I GONNA TELL YOU SECRET. I'M ON THE WRONG SIDE O' THE LA TOO! I'M ONE OF TH CAT CRUSADERS!
I CAN'T WAIT TO BUY THOSE KIDS SOME BRAND NEW CLOTHES!
NOT TO MENTION FOOD, AND NEW SHOES...
....
OH, NATSUKI... WHAT HAVE YOU GOTTEN YOURSELF INTO THIS TIME?

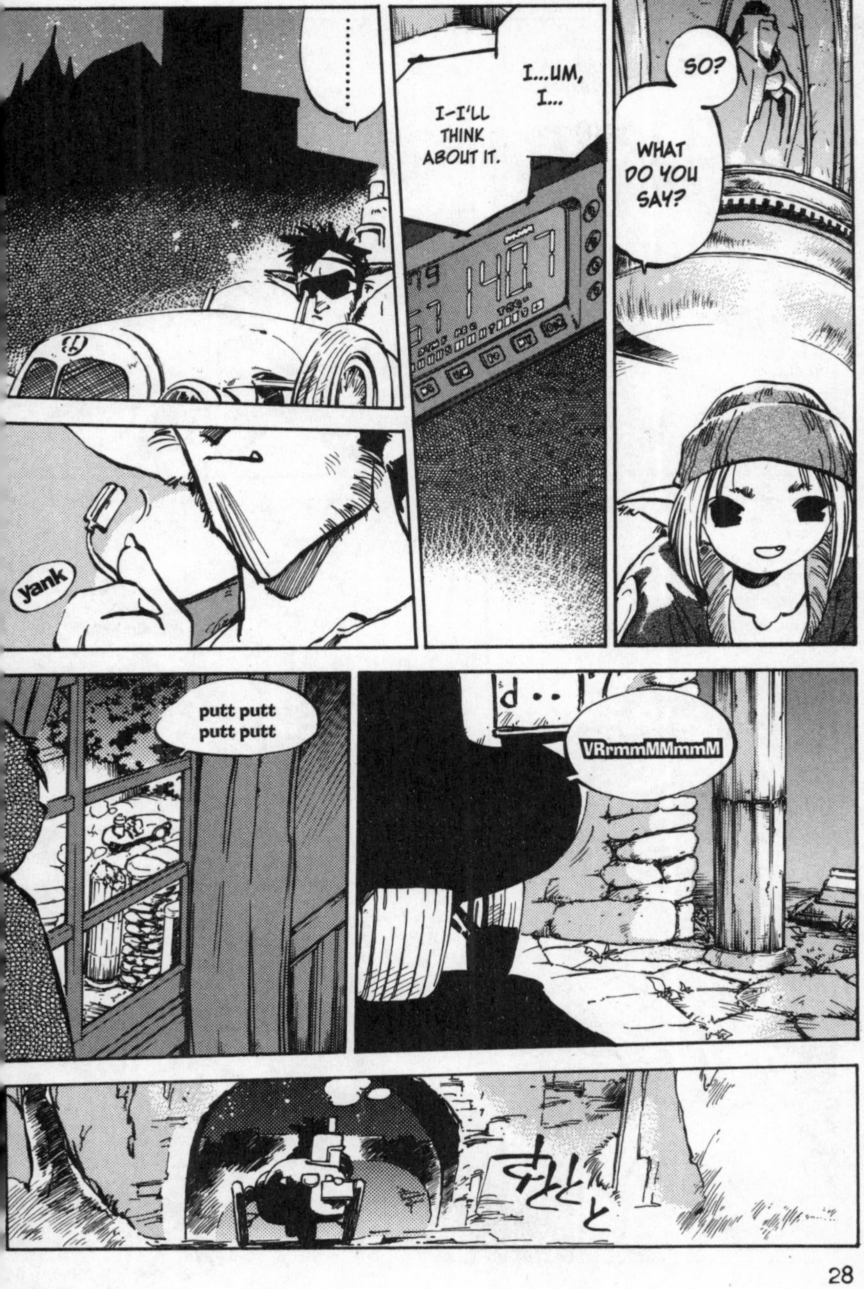
SO?
WHAT DO YOU SAY?
I...UM, I...
I-I'LL THINK ABOUT IT.
......
yank
VRrmmMMmmM
putt putt putt putt
すととと

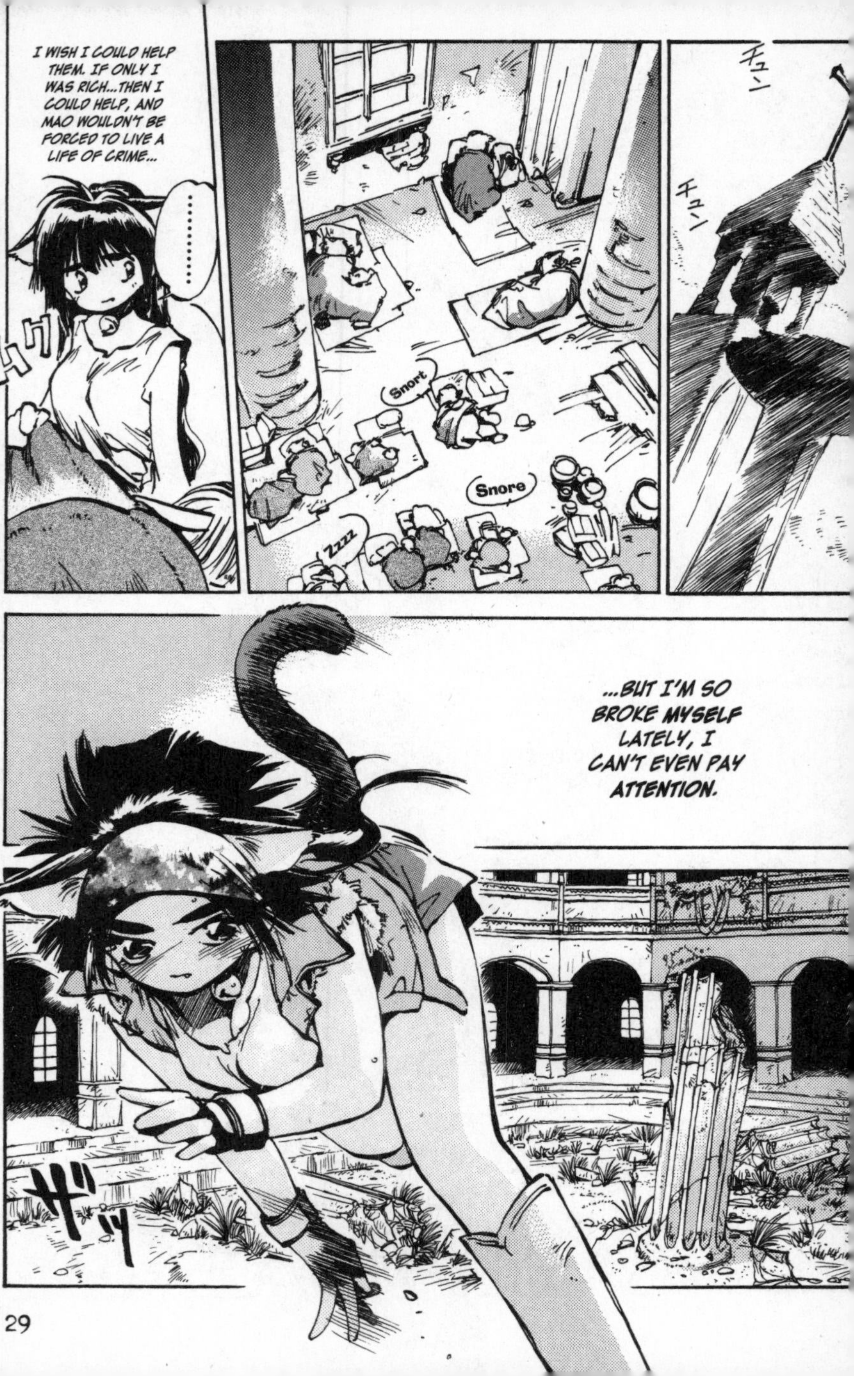
チュン
チュン
Snort
Snore
Zzzz
I WISH I COULD HELP THEM. IF ONLY I WAS RICH...THEN I COULD HELP, AND MAO WOULDN'T BE FORCED TO LIVE A LIFE OF CRIME...
......
ムク
...BUT I'M SO BROKE MYSELF LATELY, I CAN'T EVEN PAY ATTENTION.
ザリッ

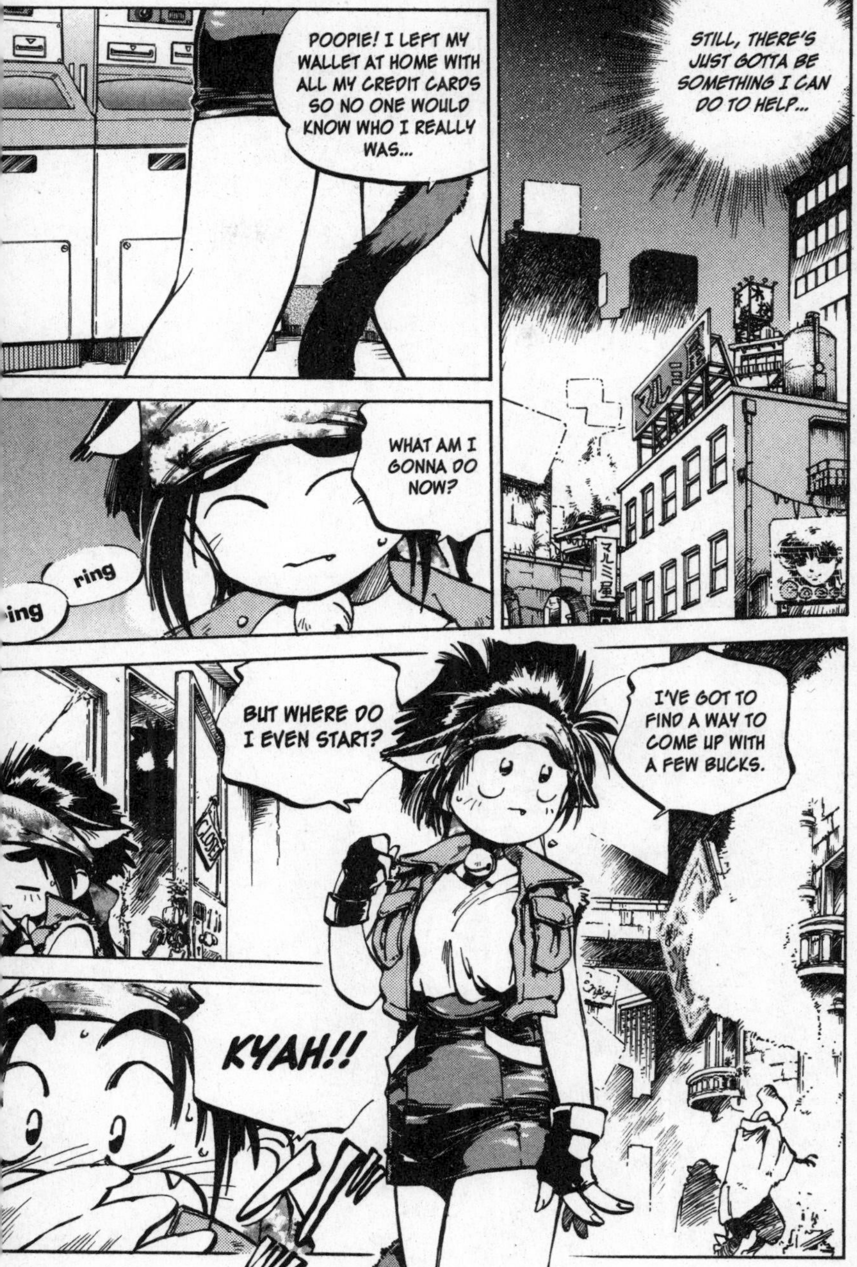
STILL, THERE'S JUST GOTTA BE SOMETHING I CAN DO TO HELP...
マルミ屋
POOPIE! I LEFT MY WALLET AT HOME WITH ALL MY CREDIT CARDS SO NO ONE WOULD KNOW WHO I REALLY WAS...
WHAT AM I GONNA DO NOW?
ring
ring
I'VE GOT TO FIND A WAY TO COME UP WITH A FEW BUCKS.
BUT WHERE DO I EVEN START?
KYAH!!

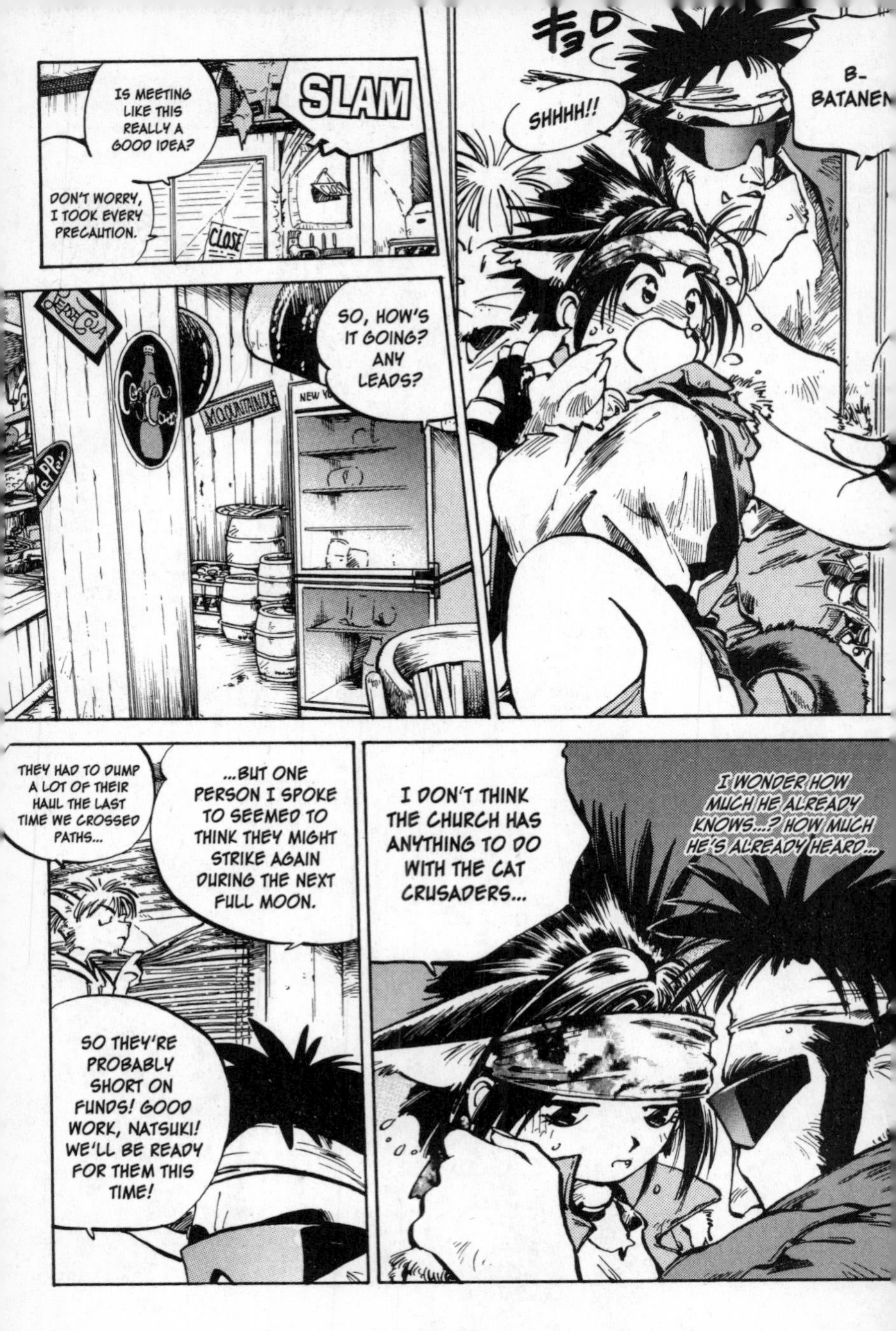
B-
BATANEN
キョロ
SHHHH!!
SLAM
IS MEETING LIKE THIS REALLY A GOOD IDEA?
DON'T WORRY, I TOOK EVERY PRECAUTION.
CLOSE
SO, HOW'S IT GOING? ANY LEADS?
I WONDER HOW MUCH HE ALREADY KNOWS...? HOW MUCH HE'S ALREADY HEARD...
I DON'T THINK THE CHURCH HAS ANYTHING TO DO WITH THE CAT CRUSADERS...
...BUT ONE PERSON I SPOKE TO SEEMED TO THINK THEY MIGHT STRIKE AGAIN DURING THE NEXT FULL MOON.
THEY HAD TO DUMP A LOT OF THEIR HAUL THE LAST TIME WE CROSSED PATHS...
SO THEY'RE PROBABLY SHORT ON FUNDS! GOOD WORK, NATSUKI! WE'LL BE READY FOR THEM THIS TIME!

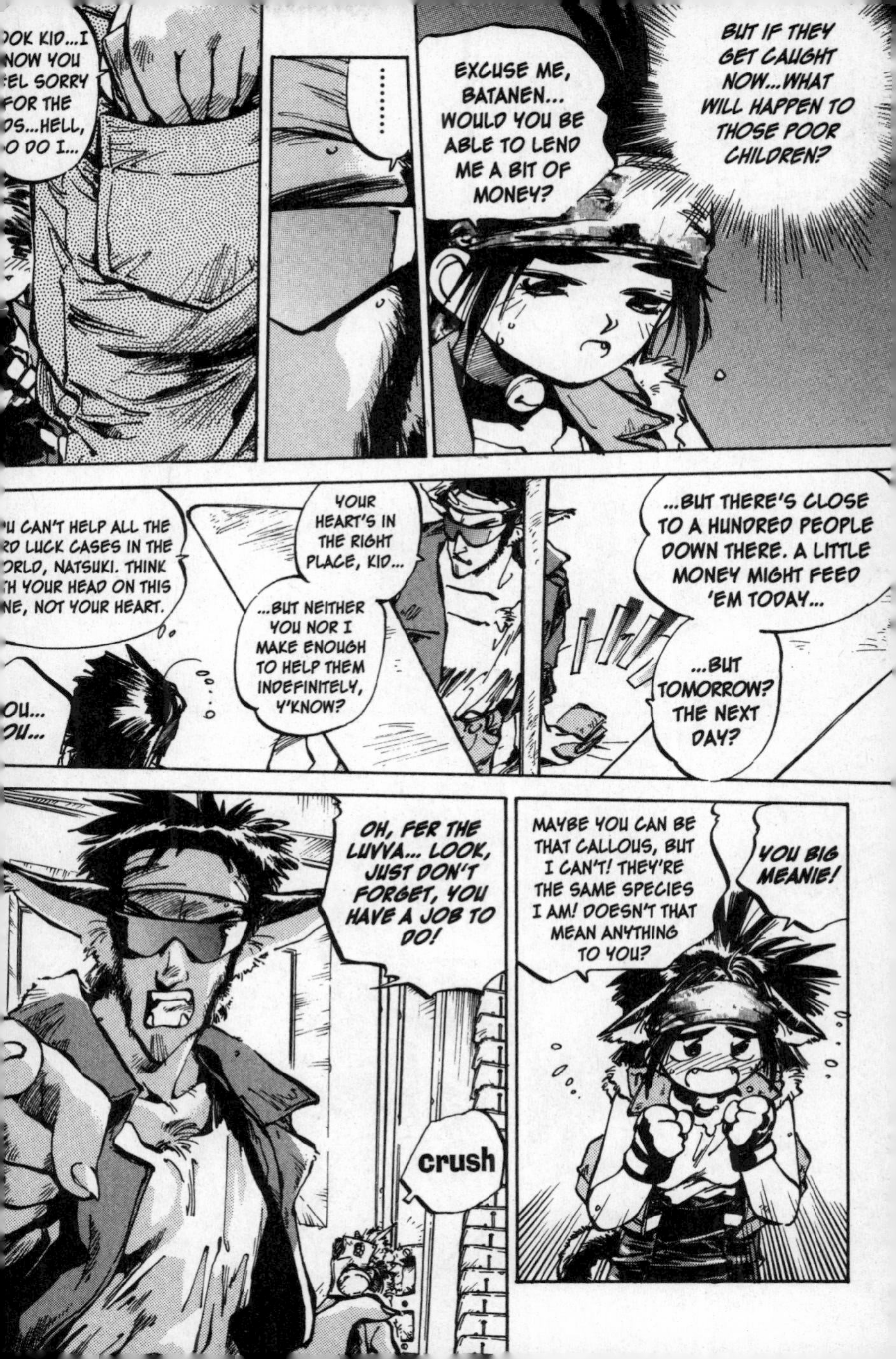
BUT IF THEY GET CAUGHT NOW...WHAT WILL HAPPEN TO THOSE POOR CHILDREN?
EXCUSE ME, BATANEN... WOULD YOU BE ABLE TO LEND ME A BIT OF MONEY?
......
OOK KID...I NOW YOU EEL SORRY FOR THE DS...HELL, O DO I...
...BUT THERE'S CLOSE TO A HUNDRED PEOPLE DOWN THERE. A LITTLE MONEY MIGHT FEED 'EM TODAY...
...BUT TOMORROW? THE NEXT DAY?
YOUR HEART'S IN THE RIGHT PLACE, KID...
...BUT NEITHER YOU NOR I MAKE ENOUGH TO HELP THEM INDEFINITELY, Y'KNOW?
U CAN'T HELP ALL THE RD LUCK CASES IN THE ORLD, NATSUKI. THINK TH YOUR HEAD ON THIS NE, NOT YOUR HEART.
OU... OU...
YOU BIG MEANIE!
MAYBE YOU CAN BE THAT CALLOUS, BUT I CAN'T! THEY'RE THE SAME SPECIES I AM! DOESN'T THAT MEAN ANYTHING TO YOU?
OH, FER THE LUVVA... LOOK, JUST DON'T FORGET, YOU HAVE A JOB TO DO!
crush

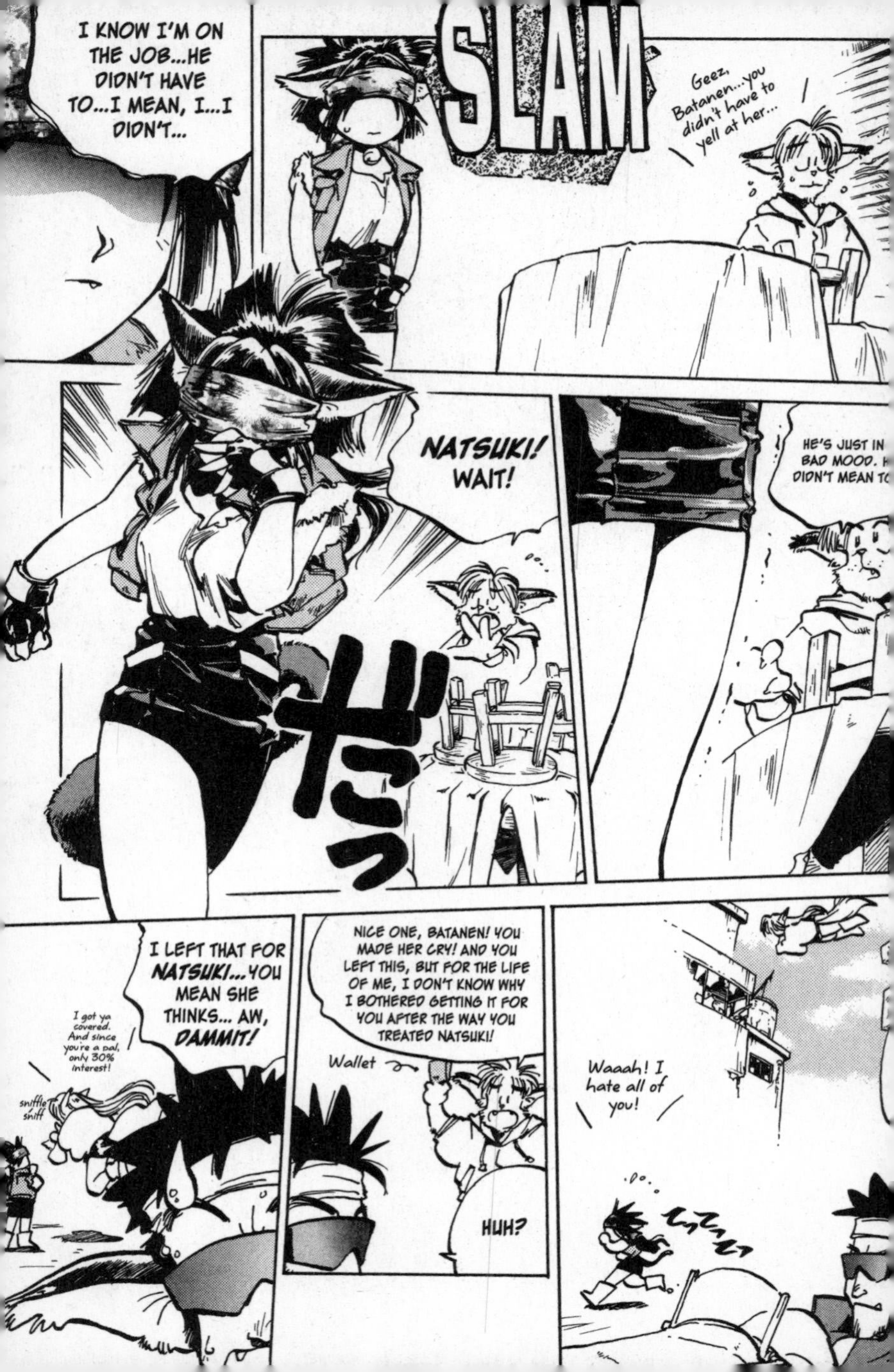
Geez, Batanen...you didn't have to yell at her...
SLAM
I KNOW I'M ON THE JOB...HE DIDN'T HAVE TO...I MEAN, I...I DIDN'T...
HE'S JUST IN BAD MOOD. H DIDN'T MEAN TO
NATSUKI! WAIT!
だっ
Waaah! I hate all of you!
NICE ONE, BATANEN! YOU MADE HER CRY! AND YOU LEFT THIS, BUT FOR THE LIFE OF ME, I DON'T KNOW WHY I BOTHERED GETTING IT FOR YOU AFTER THE WAY YOU TREATED NATSUKI!
Wallet
HUH?
I LEFT THAT FOR NATSUKI...YOU MEAN SHE THINKS... AW, DAMMIT!
I got ya covered. And since you're a pal, only 30% interest!
sniffle sniff

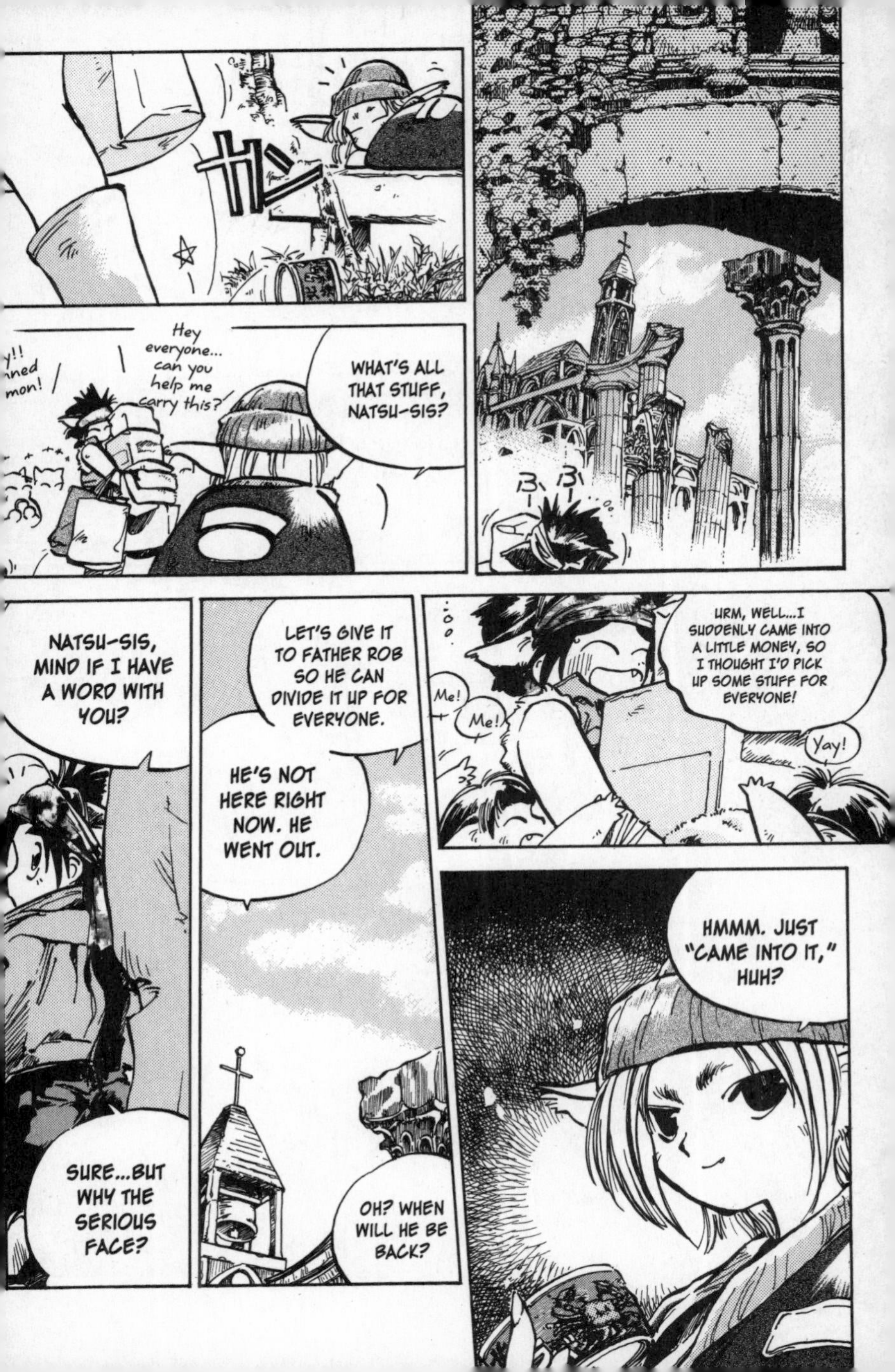
WHAT'S ALL THAT STUFF, NATSU-SIS?
Hey everyone... can you help me carry this?
URM, WELL...I SUDDENLY CAME INTO A LITTLE MONEY, SO I THOUGHT I'D PICK UP SOME STUFF FOR EVERYONE!
Yay!
Me!
Me!
HMMM. JUST "CAME INTO IT," HUH?
LET'S GIVE IT TO FATHER ROB SO HE CAN DIVIDE IT UP FOR EVERYONE.
HE'S NOT HERE RIGHT NOW. HE WENT OUT.
OH? WHEN WILL HE BE BACK?
NATSU-SIS, MIND IF I HAVE A WORD WITH YOU?
SURE...BUT WHY THE SERIOUS FACE?

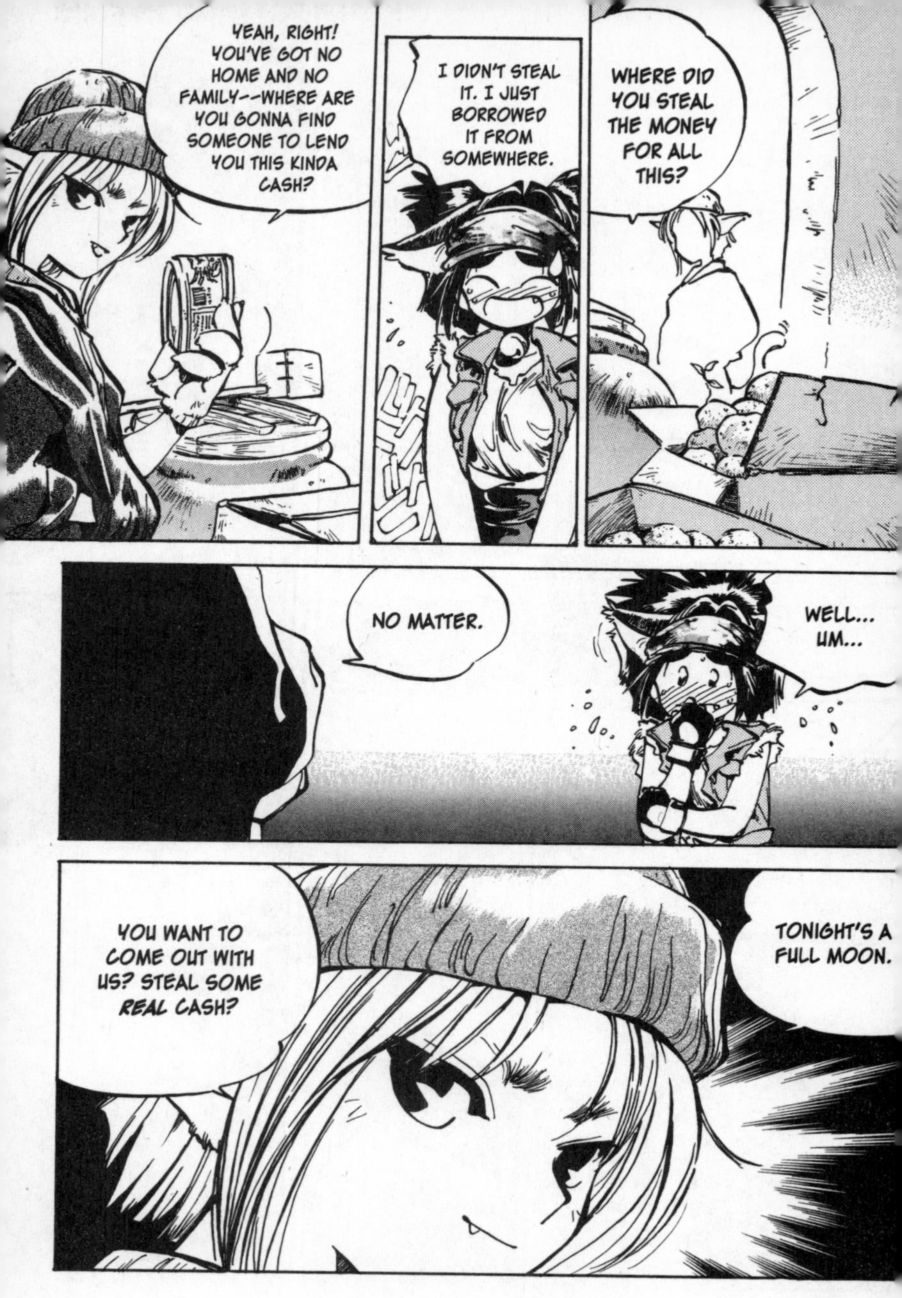

WHERE DID YOU STEAL THE MONEY FOR ALL THIS?
I DIDN'T STEAL IT. I JUST BORROWED IT FROM SOMEWHERE.
YEAH, RIGHT! YOU'VE GOT NO HOME AND NO FAMILY--WHERE ARE YOU GONNA FIND SOMEONE TO LEND YOU THIS KINDA CASH?
WELL... UM...
NO MATTER.
TONIGHT'S A FULL MOON.
YOU WANT TO COME OUT WITH US? STEAL SOME *REAL* CASH?

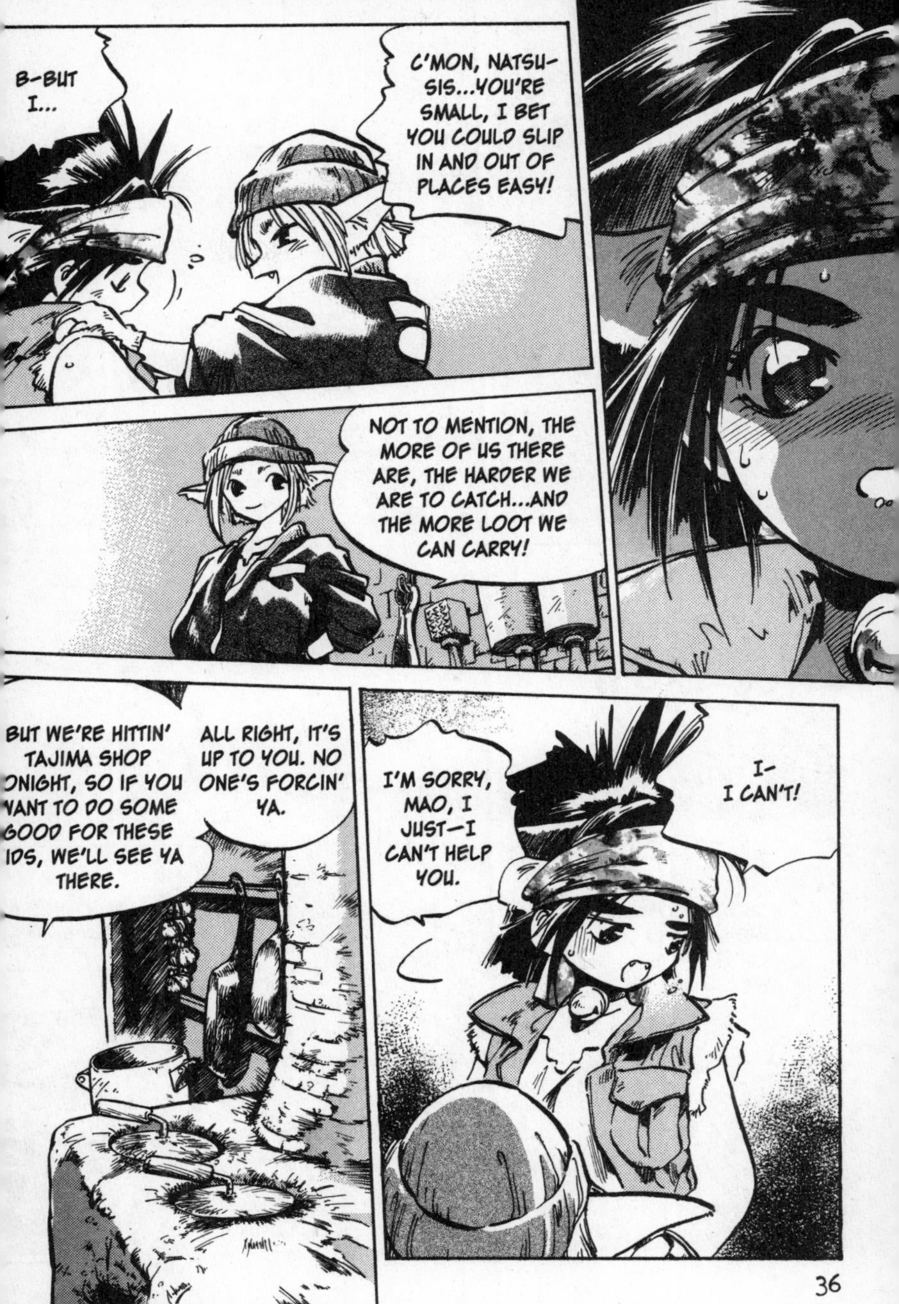
C'MON, NATSU-SIS...YOU'RE SMALL, I BET YOU COULD SLIP IN AND OUT OF PLACES EASY!
B-BUT I...
NOT TO MENTION, THE MORE OF US THERE ARE, THE HARDER WE ARE TO CATCH...AND THE MORE LOOT WE CAN CARRY!
I- I CAN'T!
I'M SORRY, MAO, I JUST—I CAN'T HELP YOU.
ALL RIGHT, IT'S UP TO YOU. NO ONE'S FORCIN' YA.
BUT WE'RE HITTIN' TAJIMA SHOP ONIGHT, SO IF YOU VANT TO DO SOME GOOD FOR THESE IDS, WE'LL SEE YA THERE.

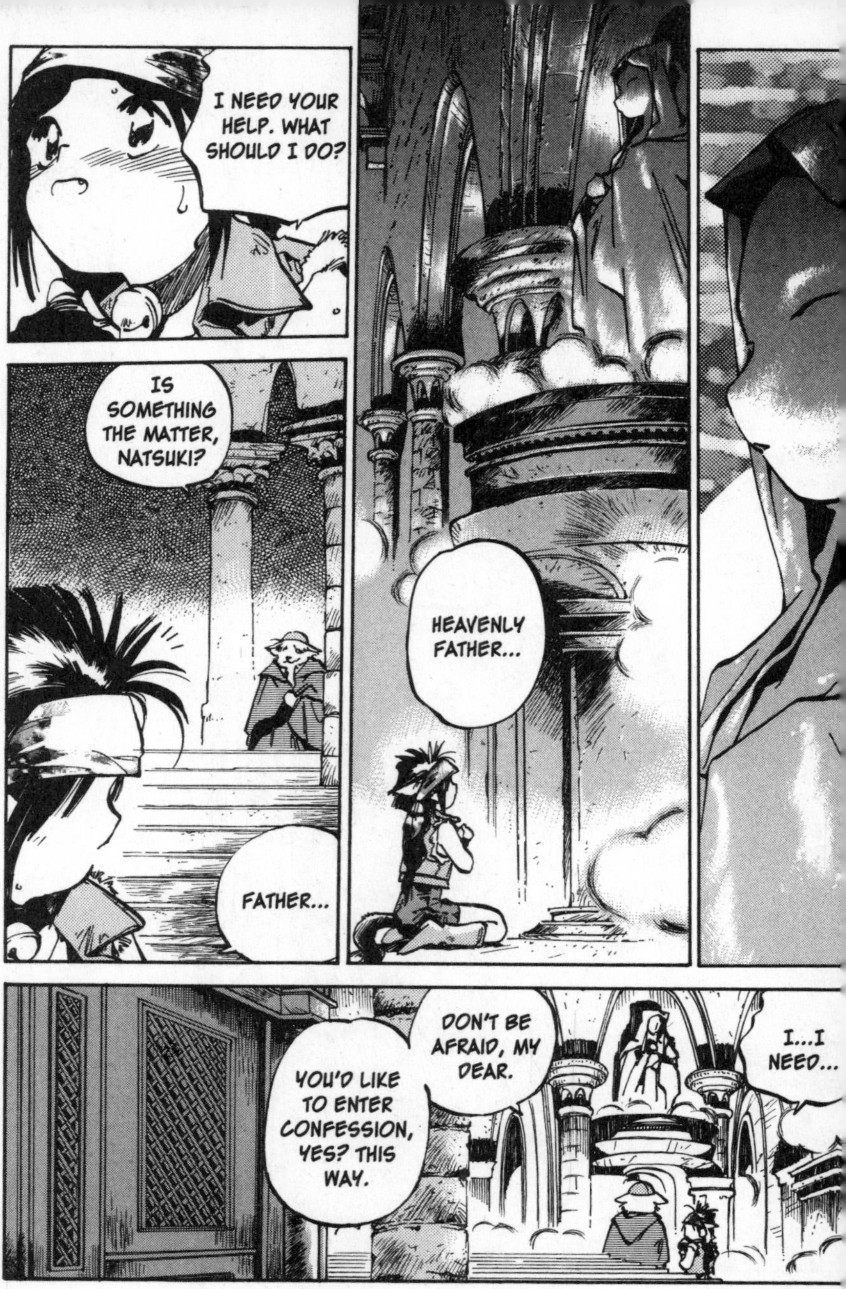
HEAVENLY FATHER...
I NEED YOUR HELP. WHAT SHOULD I DO?
IS SOMETHING THE MATTER, NATSUKI?
FATHER...
I...I NEED...
DON'T BE AFRAID, MY DEAR.
YOU'D LIKE TO ENTER CONFESSION, YES? THIS WAY.

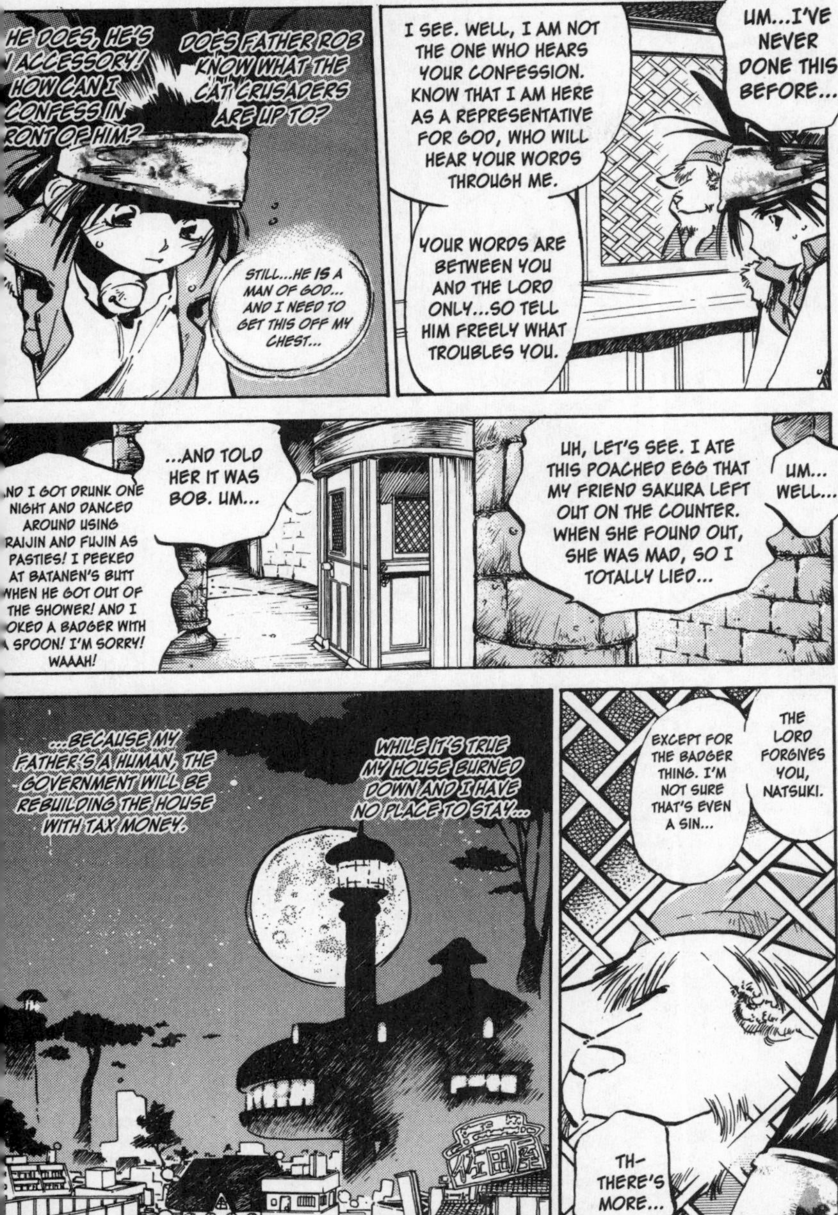
UM...I'VE NEVER DONE THIS BEFORE...
I SEE. WELL, I AM NOT THE ONE WHO HEARS YOUR CONFESSION. KNOW THAT I AM HERE AS A REPRESENTATIVE FOR GOD, WHO WILL HEAR YOUR WORDS THROUGH ME.
YOUR WORDS ARE BETWEEN YOU AND THE LORD ONLY...SO TELL HIM FREELY WHAT TROUBLES YOU.
DOES FATHER ROB KNOW WHAT THE CAT CRUSADERS ARE UP TO?
HE DOES, HE'S ACCESSORY! HOW CAN I CONFESS IN RONT OF HIM?
STILL...HE IS A MAN OF GOD... AND I NEED TO GET THIS OFF MY CHEST...
UM... WELL...
UH, LET'S SEE. I ATE THIS POACHED EGG THAT MY FRIEND SAKURA LEFT OUT ON THE COUNTER. WHEN SHE FOUND OUT, SHE WAS MAD, SO I TOTALLY LIED...
...AND TOLD HER IT WAS BOB. UM...
ND I GOT DRUNK ONE NIGHT AND DANCED AROUND USING RAIJIN AND FUJIN AS PASTIES! I PEEKED AT BATANEN'S BUTT WHEN HE GOT OUT OF THE SHOWER! AND I OKED A BADGER WITH SPOON! I'M SORRY! WAAAH!
THE LORD FORGIVES YOU, NATSUKI.
EXCEPT FOR THE BADGER THING. I'M NOT SURE THAT'S EVEN A SIN...
TH- THERE'S MORE...
WHILE IT'S TRUE MY HOUSE BURNED DOWN AND I HAVE NO PLACE TO STAY...
...BECAUSE MY FATHER'S A HUMAN, THE GOVERNMENT WILL BE REBUILDING THE HOUSE WITH TAX MONEY.

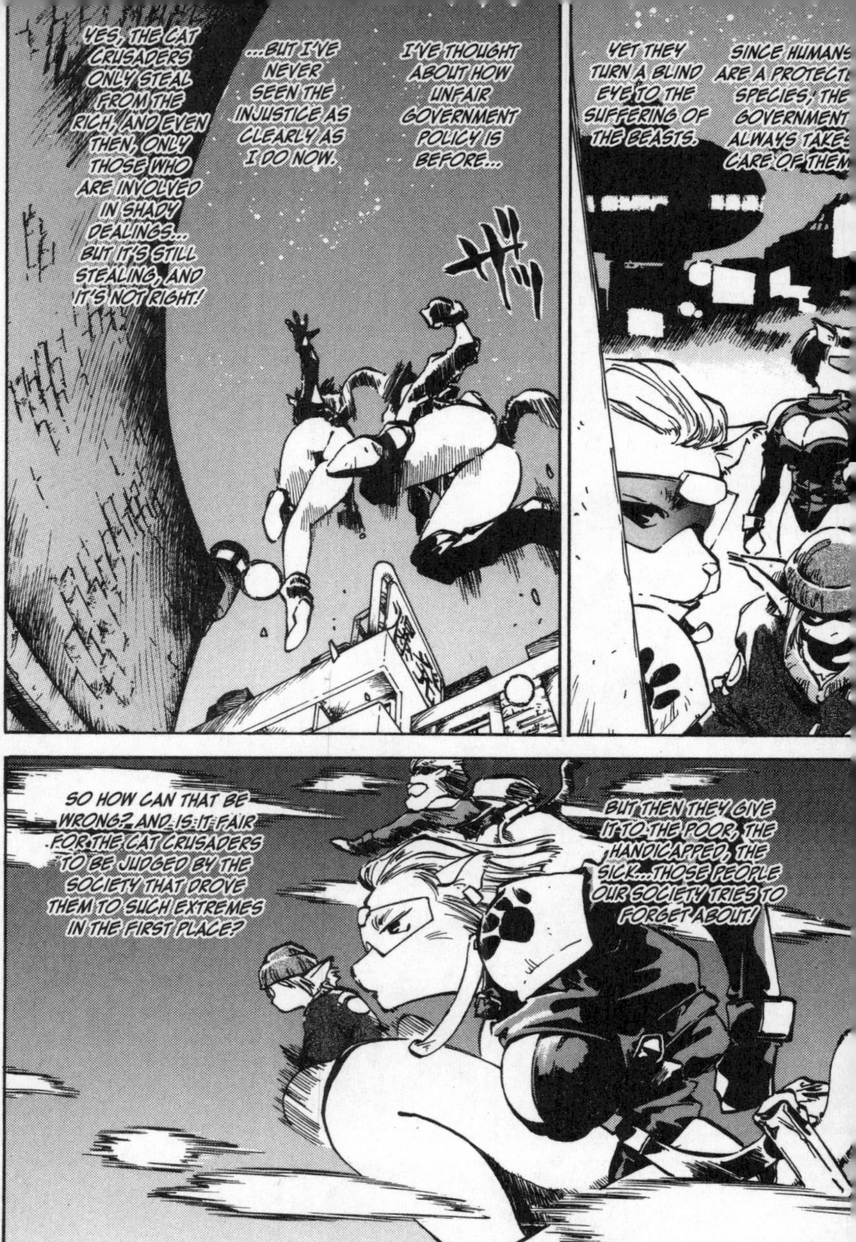
SINCE HUMANS ARE A PROTECTE SPECIES, THE GOVERNMENT ALWAYS TAKES CARE OF THEM
YET THEY TURN A BLIND EYE TO THE SUFFERING OF THE BEASTS.
I'VE THOUGHT ABOUT HOW UNFAIR GOVERNMENT POLICY IS BEFORE...
...BUT I'VE NEVER SEEN THE INJUSTICE AS CLEARLY AS I DO NOW.
YES, THE CAT CRUSADERS ONLY STEAL FROM THE RICH, AND EVEN THEN, ONLY THOSE WHO ARE INVOLVED IN SHADY DEALINGS... BUT IT'S STILL STEALING, AND IT'S NOT RIGHT!
BUT THEN THEY GIVE IT TO THE POOR, THE HANDICAPPED, THE SICK...THOSE PEOPLE OUR SOCIETY TRIES TO FORGET ABOUT!
SO HOW CAN THAT BE WRONG? AND IS IT FAIR FOR THE CAT CRUSADERS TO BE JUDGED BY THE SOCIETY THAT DROVE THEM TO SUCH EXTREMES IN THE FIRST PLACE?

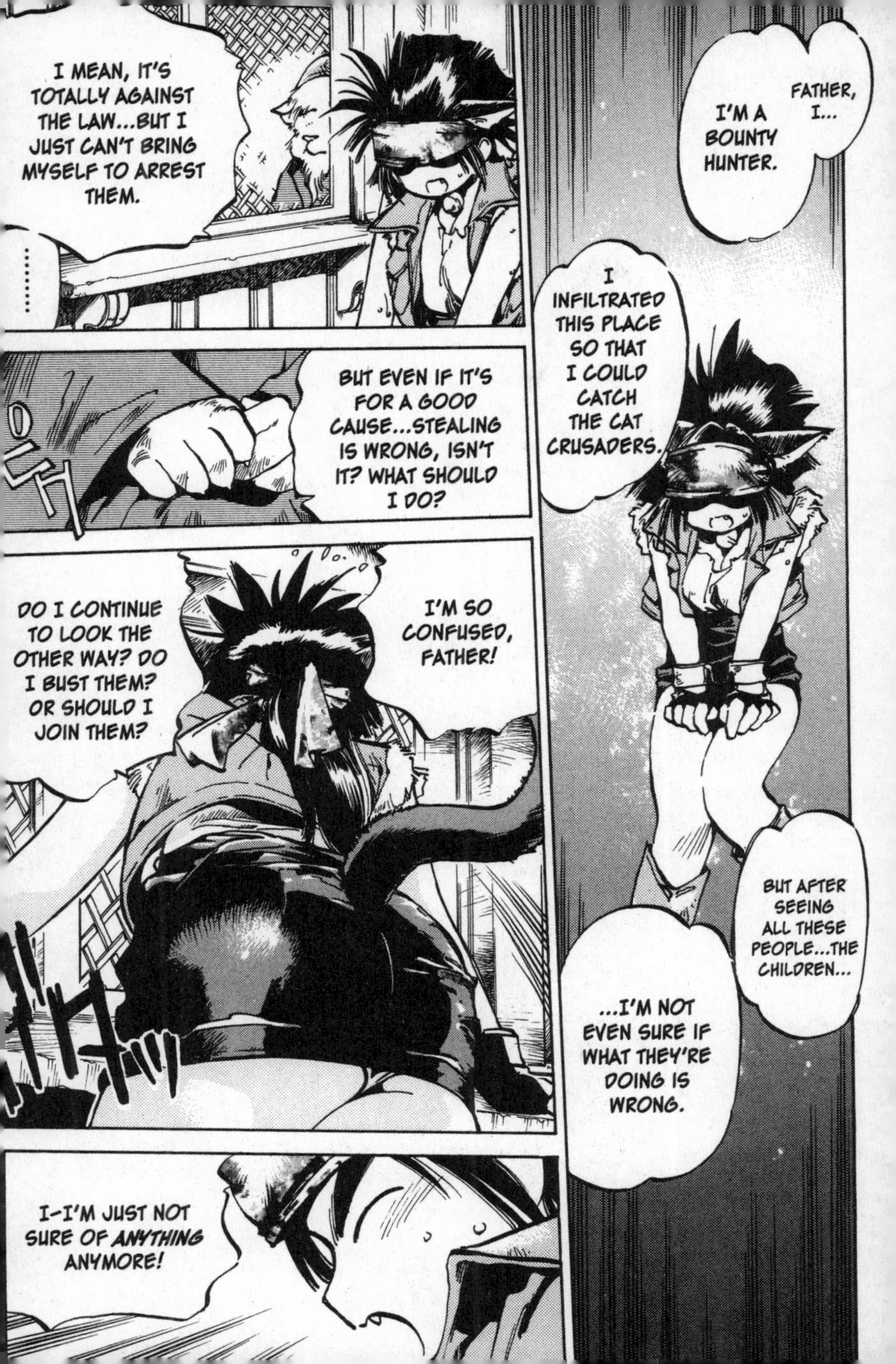
FATHER, I...
I'M A BOUNTY HUNTER.
I INFILTRATED THIS PLACE SO THAT I COULD CATCH THE CAT CRUSADERS.
BUT AFTER SEEING ALL THESE PEOPLE...THE CHILDREN...
...I'M NOT EVEN SURE IF WHAT THEY'RE DOING IS WRONG.
I MEAN, IT'S TOTALLY AGAINST THE LAW...BUT I JUST CAN'T BRING MYSELF TO ARREST THEM.
......
BUT EVEN IF IT'S FOR A GOOD CAUSE...STEALING IS WRONG, ISN'T IT? WHAT SHOULD I DO?
I'M SO CONFUSED, FATHER!
DO I CONTINUE TO LOOK THE OTHER WAY? DO I BUST THEM? OR SHOULD I JOIN THEM?
I-I'M JUST NOT SURE OF ANYTHING ANYMORE!

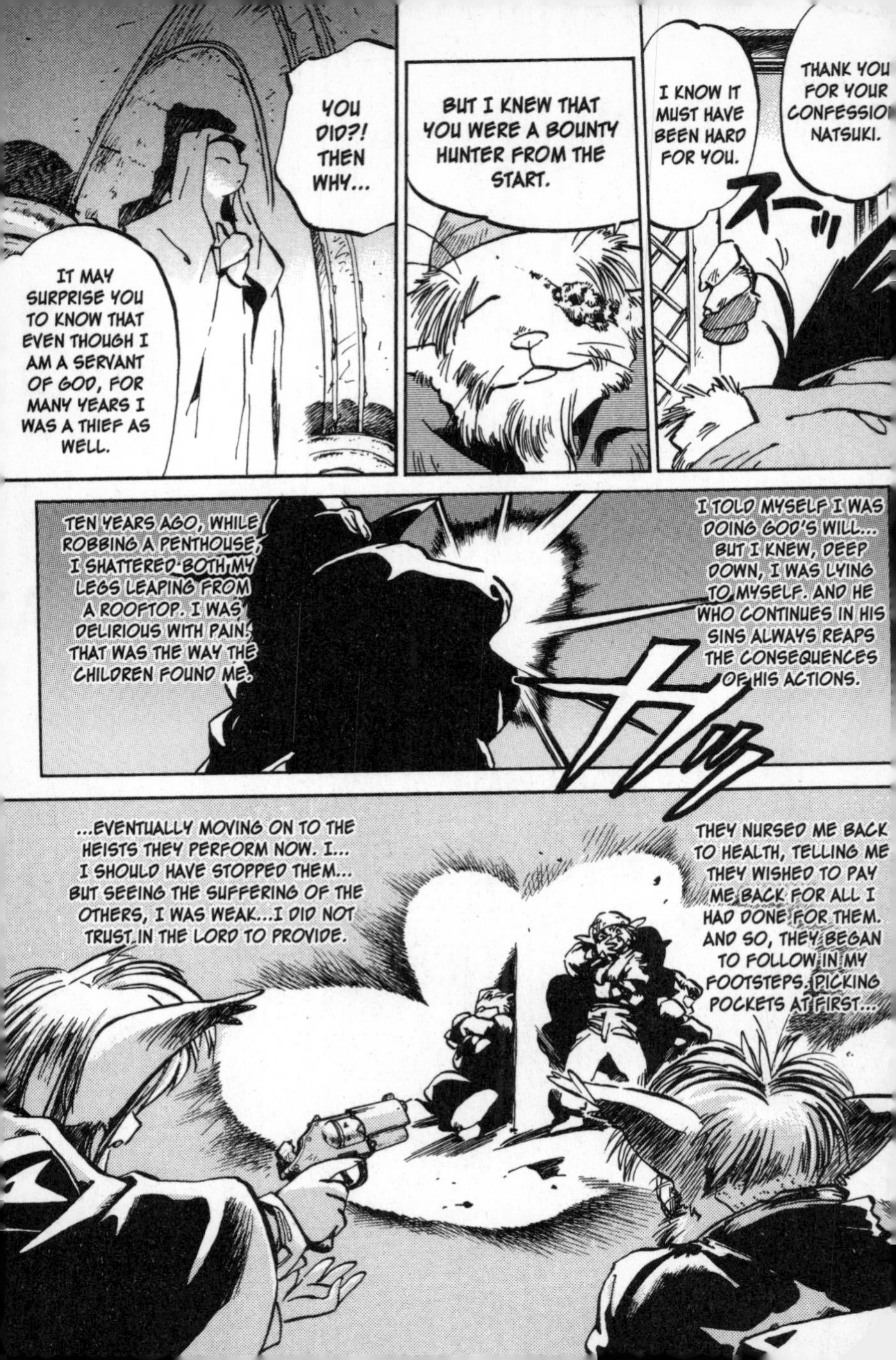
THANK YOU FOR YOUR CONFESSIO NATSUKI.
I KNOW IT MUST HAVE BEEN HARD FOR YOU.
スーッ
BUT I KNEW THAT YOU WERE A BOUNTY HUNTER FROM THE START.
YOU DID?! THEN WHY...
IT MAY SURPRISE YOU TO KNOW THAT EVEN THOUGH I AM A SERVANT OF GOD, FOR MANY YEARS I WAS A THIEF AS WELL.
I TOLD MYSELF I WAS DOING GOD'S WILL... BUT I KNEW, DEEP DOWN, I WAS LYING TO MYSELF. AND HE WHO CONTINUES IN HIS SINS ALWAYS REAPS THE CONSEQUENCES OF HIS ACTIONS.
TEN YEARS AGO, WHILE ROBBING A PENTHOUSE, I SHATTERED BOTH MY LEGS LEAPING FROM A ROOFTOP. I WAS DELIRIOUS WITH PAIN. THAT WAS THE WAY THE CHILDREN FOUND ME.
ザッ
THEY NURSED ME BACK TO HEALTH, TELLING ME THEY WISHED TO PAY ME BACK FOR ALL I HAD DONE FOR THEM. AND SO, THEY BEGAN TO FOLLOW IN MY FOOTSTEPS. PICKING POCKETS AT FIRST...
...EVENTUALLY MOVING ON TO THE HEISTS THEY PERFORM NOW. I... I SHOULD HAVE STOPPED THEM... BUT SEEING THE SUFFERING OF THE OTHERS, I WAS WEAK...I DID NOT TRUST IN THE LORD TO PROVIDE.

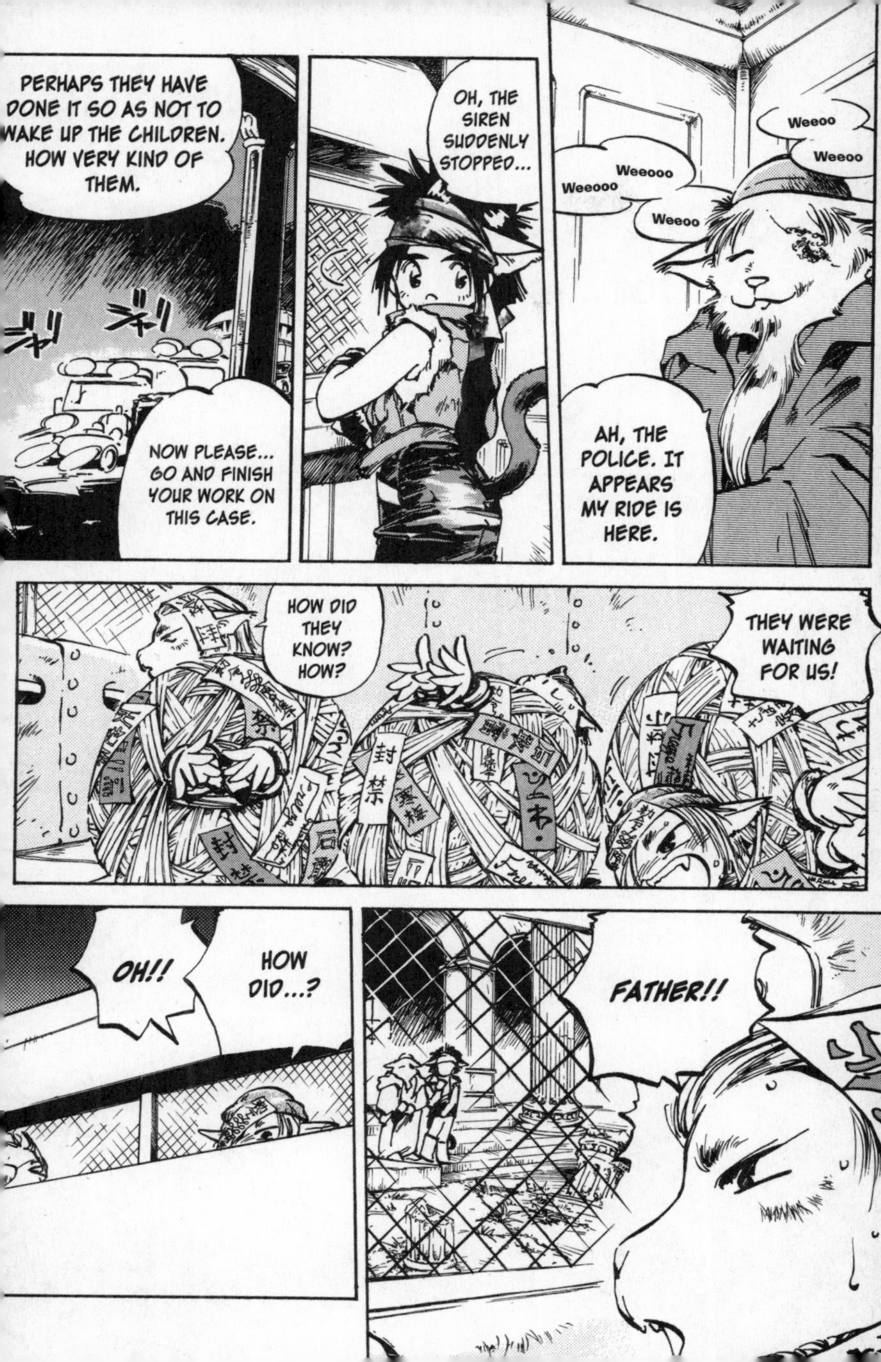
Weeoo
Weeoo
Weeooo
Weeooo
Weeoo
AH, THE POLICE. IT APPEARS MY RIDE IS HERE.
OH, THE SIREN SUDDENLY STOPPED...
PERHAPS THEY HAVE DONE IT SO AS NOT TO WAKE UP THE CHILDREN. HOW VERY KIND OF THEM.
ジャリ
ジャリ
NOW PLEASE... GO AND FINISH YOUR WORK ON THIS CASE.
THEY WERE WAITING FOR US!
HOW DID THEY KNOW? HOW?
FATHER!!
HOW DID...?
OH!!

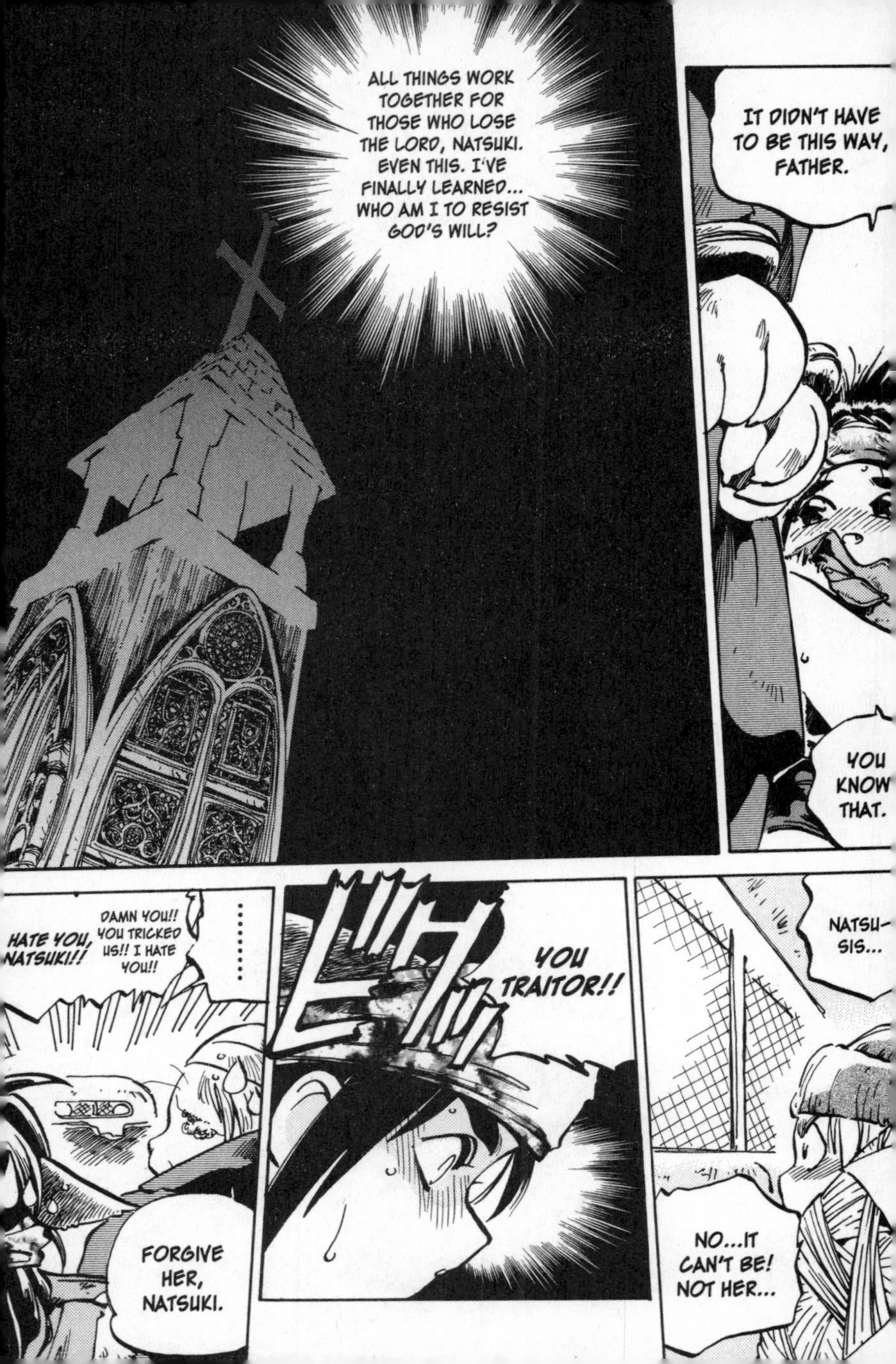
IT DIDN'T HAVE TO BE THIS WAY, FATHER.
YOU KNOW THAT.
ALL THINGS WORK TOGETHER FOR THOSE WHO LOSE THE LORD, NATSUKI. EVEN THIS. I'VE FINALLY LEARNED... WHO AM I TO RESIST GOD'S WILL?
NATSU-SIS...
NO...IT CAN'T BE! NOT HER...
YOU TRAITOR!!
......
DAMN YOU!! YOU TRICKED US!! I HATE YOU!!
HATE YOU, NATSUKI!!
FORGIVE HER, NATSUKI.

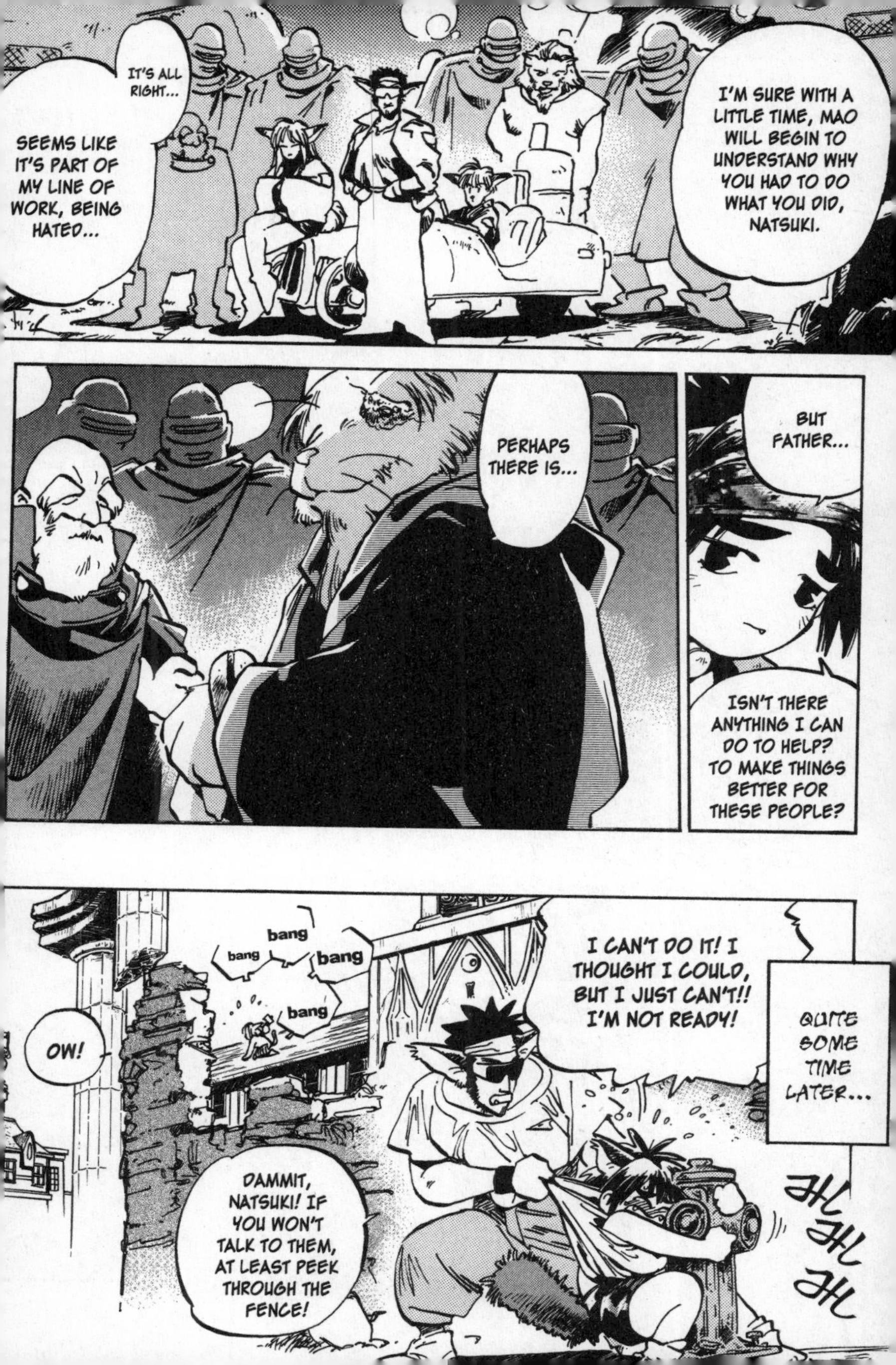
I'M SURE WITH A LITTLE TIME, MAO WILL BEGIN TO UNDERSTAND WHY YOU HAD TO DO WHAT YOU DID, NATSUKI.
IT'S ALL RIGHT...
SEEMS LIKE IT'S PART OF MY LINE OF WORK, BEING HATED...
BUT FATHER...
ISN'T THERE ANYTHING I CAN DO TO HELP? TO MAKE THINGS BETTER FOR THESE PEOPLE?
PERHAPS THERE IS...
QUITE SOME TIME LATER...
I CAN'T DO IT! I THOUGHT I COULD, BUT I JUST CAN'T!! I'M NOT READY!
bang
bang
bang
bang
OW!
DAMMIT, NATSUKI! IF YOU WON'T TALK TO THEM, AT LEAST PEEK THROUGH THE FENCE!

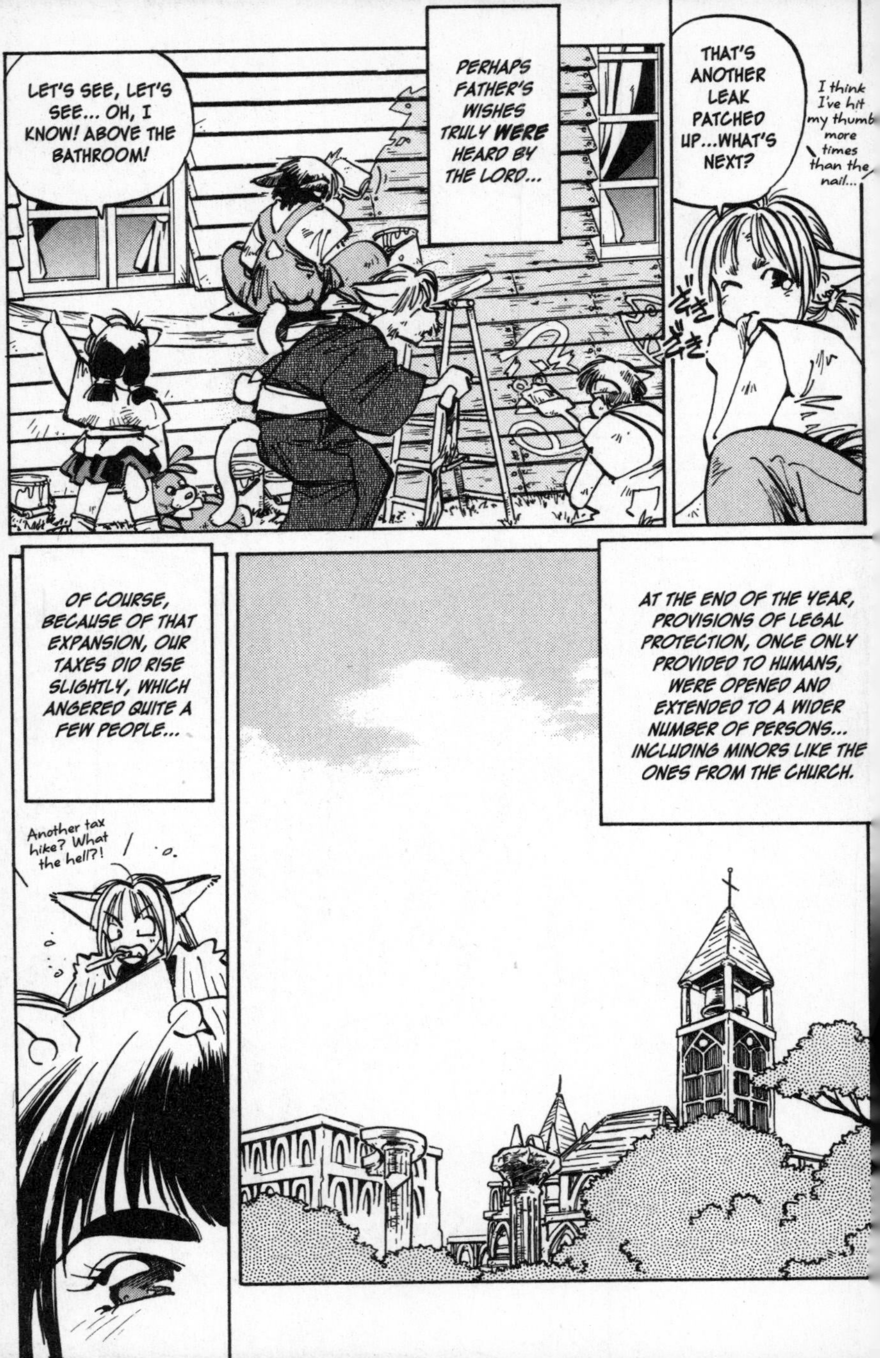
THAT'S ANOTHER LEAK PATCHED UP...WHAT'S NEXT?
I think I've hit my thumb more times than the nail...
PERHAPS FATHER'S WISHES TRULY **WERE** HEARD BY THE LORD...
LET'S SEE, LET'S SEE... OH, I KNOW! ABOVE THE BATHROOM!
AT THE END OF THE YEAR, PROVISIONS OF LEGAL PROTECTION, ONCE ONLY PROVIDED TO HUMANS, WERE OPENED AND EXTENDED TO A WIDER NUMBER OF PERSONS... INCLUDING MINORS LIKE THE ONES FROM THE CHURCH.
OF COURSE, BECAUSE OF THAT EXPANSION, OUR TAXES DID RISE SLIGHTLY, WHICH ANGERED QUITE A FEW PEOPLE...
Another tax hike? What the hell?!

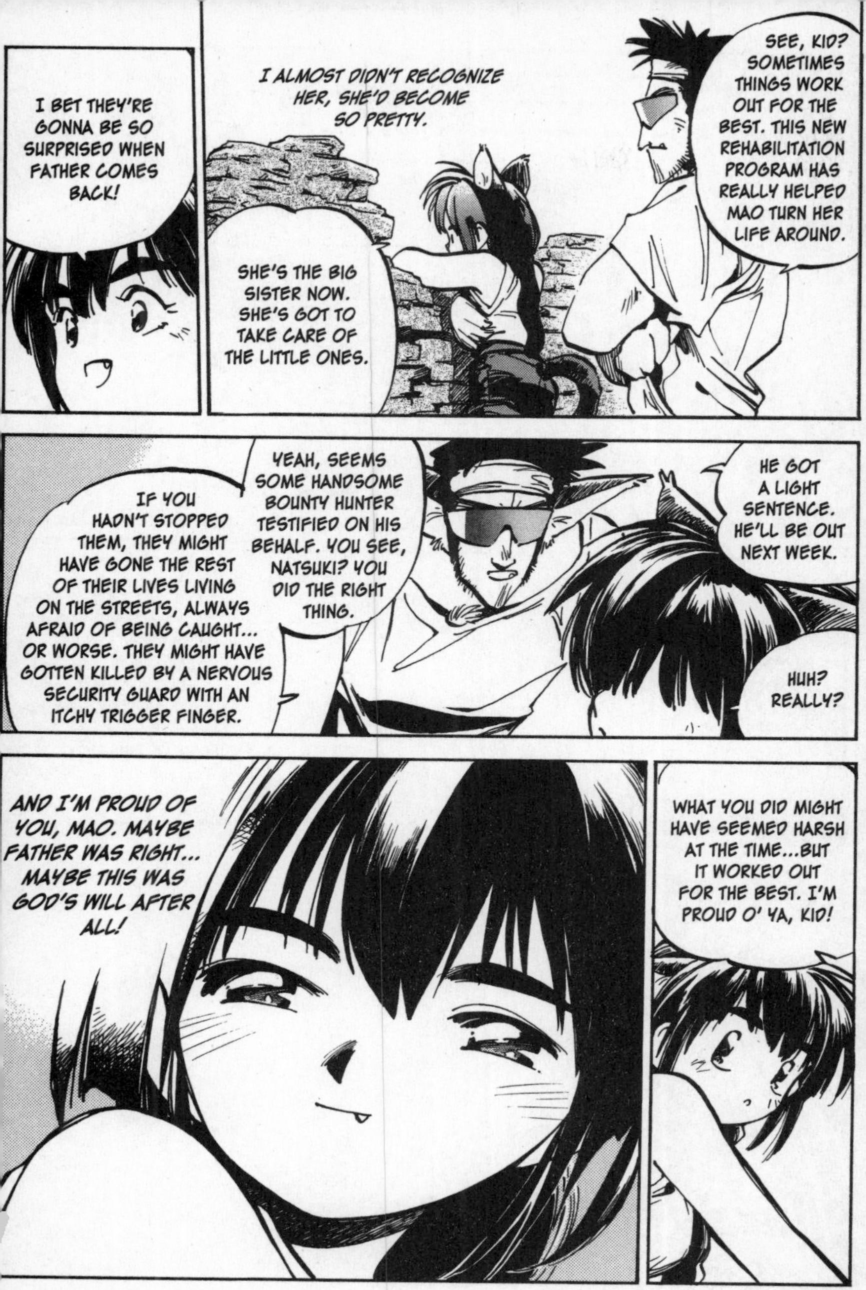

SEE, KID? SOMETIMES THINGS WORK OUT FOR THE BEST. THIS NEW REHABILITATION PROGRAM HAS REALLY HELPED MAO TURN HER LIFE AROUND.
I ALMOST DIDN'T RECOGNIZE HER, SHE'D BECOME SO PRETTY.
SHE'S THE BIG SISTER NOW. SHE'S GOT TO TAKE CARE OF THE LITTLE ONES.
I BET THEY'RE GONNA BE SO SURPRISED WHEN FATHER COMES BACK!
HE GOT A LIGHT SENTENCE. HE'LL BE OUT NEXT WEEK.
HUH? REALLY?
YEAH, SEEMS SOME HANDSOME BOUNTY HUNTER TESTIFIED ON HIS BEHALF. YOU SEE, NATSUKI? YOU DID THE RIGHT THING.
IF YOU HADN'T STOPPED THEM, THEY MIGHT HAVE GONE THE REST OF THEIR LIVES LIVING ON THE STREETS, ALWAYS AFRAID OF BEING CAUGHT... OR WORSE. THEY MIGHT HAVE GOTTEN KILLED BY A NERVOUS SECURITY GUARD WITH AN ITCHY TRIGGER FINGER.
WHAT YOU DID MIGHT HAVE SEEMED HARSH AT THE TIME...BUT IT WORKED OUT FOR THE BEST. I'M PROUD O' YA, KID!
AND I'M PROUD OF YOU, MAO. MAYBE FATHER WAS RIGHT... MAYBE THIS WAS GOD'S WILL AFTER ALL!

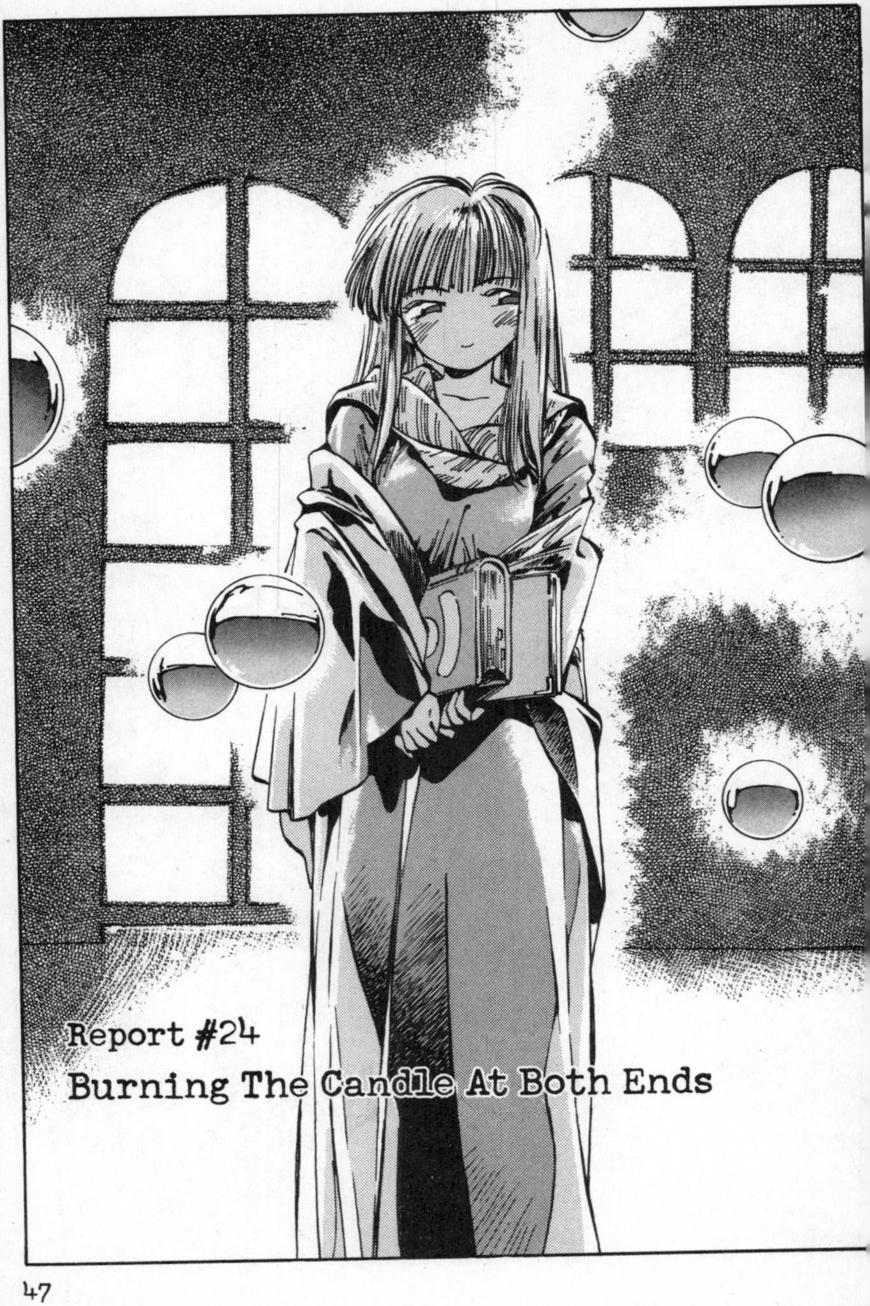
Report #24
Burning The Candle At Both Ends

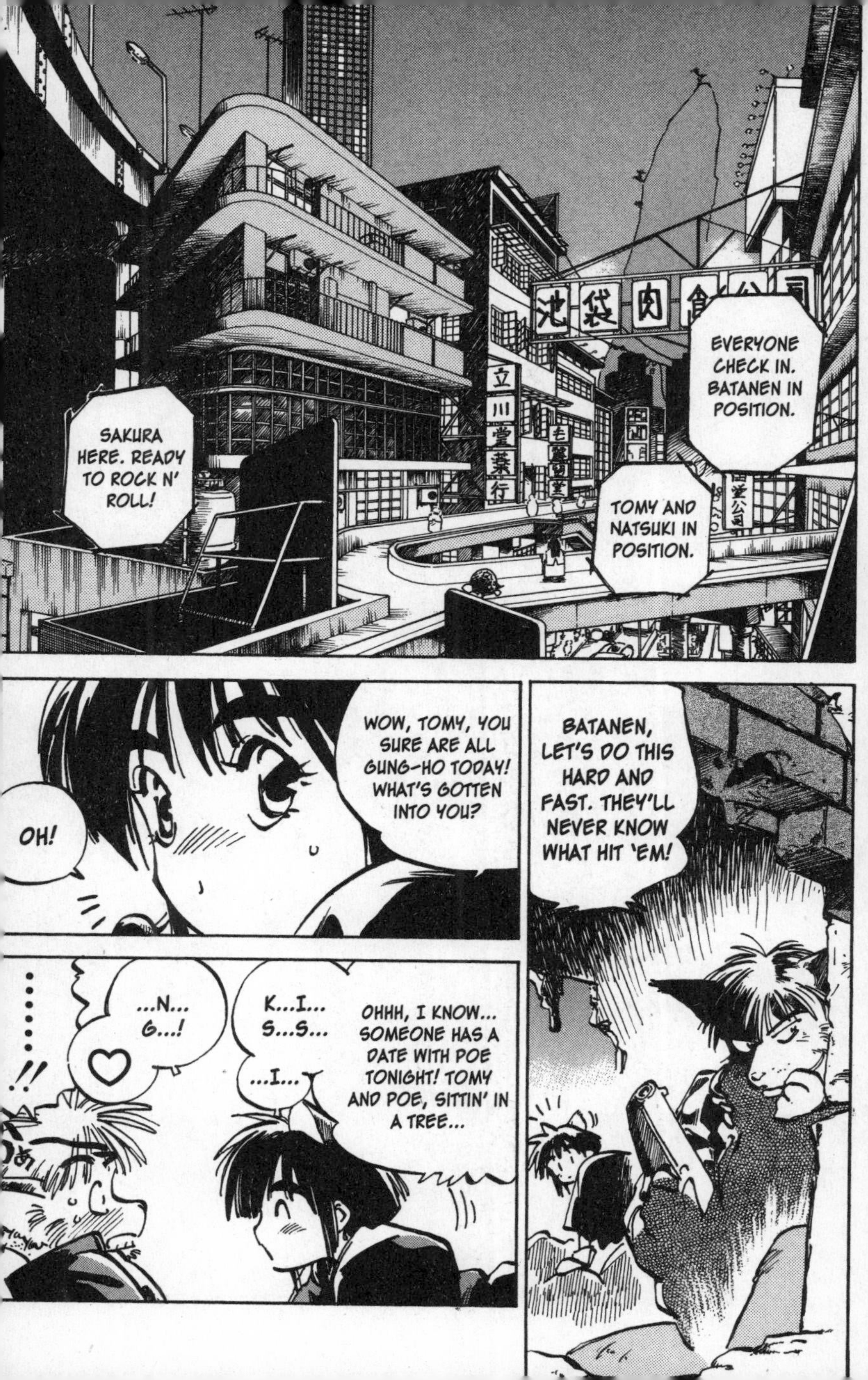
池袋肉食公司
EVERYONE CHECK IN. BATANEN IN POSITION.
TOMY AND NATSUKI IN POSITION.
SAKURA HERE. READY TO ROCK N' ROLL!
BATANEN, LET'S DO THIS HARD AND FAST. THEY'LL NEVER KNOW WHAT HIT 'EM!
WOW, TOMY, YOU SURE ARE ALL GUNG-HO TODAY! WHAT'S GOTTEN INTO YOU?
OH!
OHHH, I KNOW... SOMEONE HAS A DATE WITH POE TONIGHT! TOMY AND POE, SITTIN' IN A TREE...
K...I... S...S... ...I...
...N... G...!
......!!

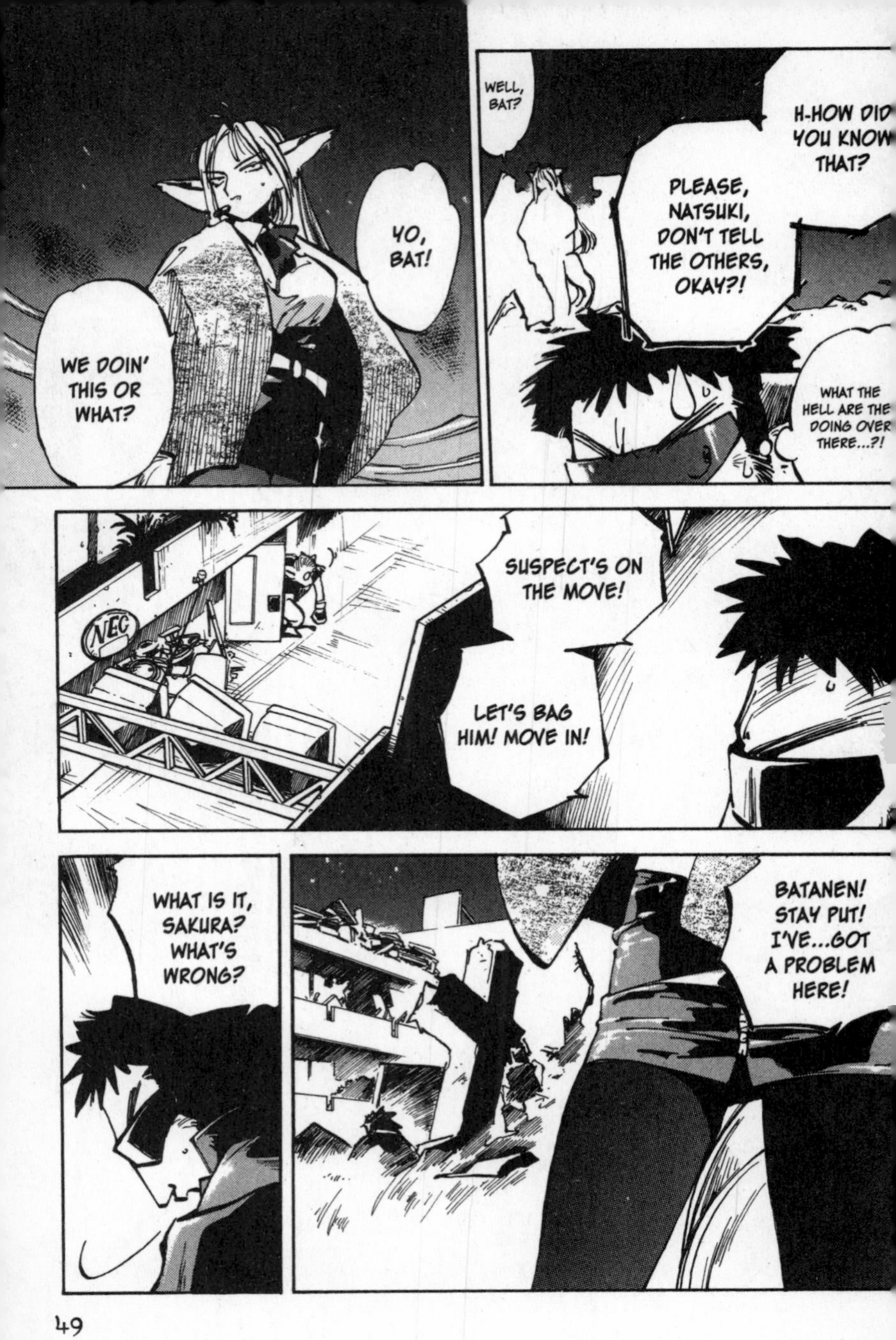
H-HOW DID YOU KNOW THAT?
WELL, BAT?
PLEASE, NATSUKI, DON'T TELL THE OTHERS, OKAY?!
WHAT THE HELL ARE THE DOING OVER THERE...?!
YO, BAT!
WE DOIN' THIS OR WHAT?
SUSPECT'S ON THE MOVE!
LET'S BAG HIM! MOVE IN!
BATANEN! STAY PUT! I'VE...GOT A PROBLEM HERE!
WHAT IS IT, SAKURA? WHAT'S WRONG?

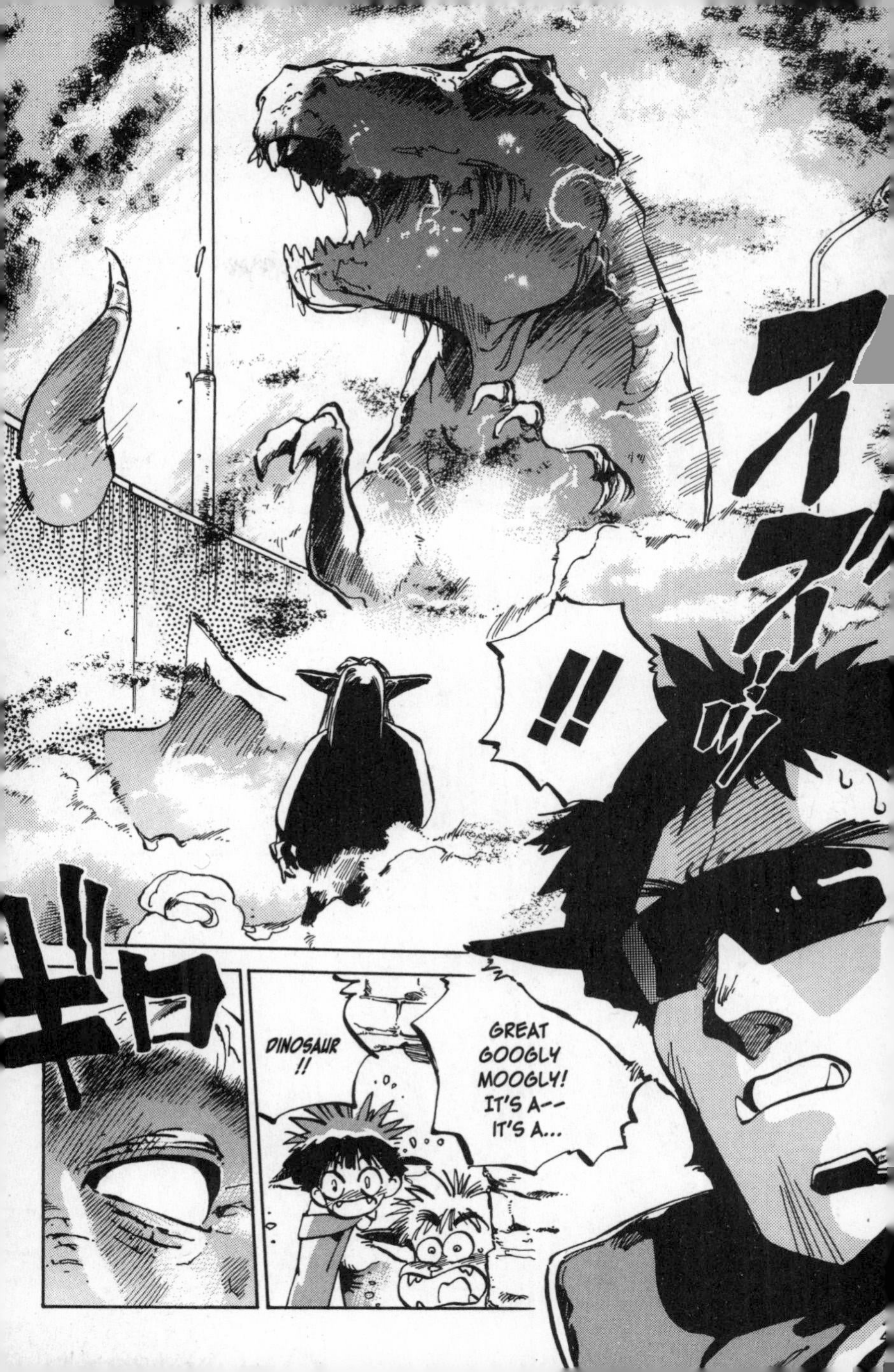
!!
GREAT GOOGLY MOOGLY! IT'S A-- IT'S A...
DINOSAUR !!
ギロ

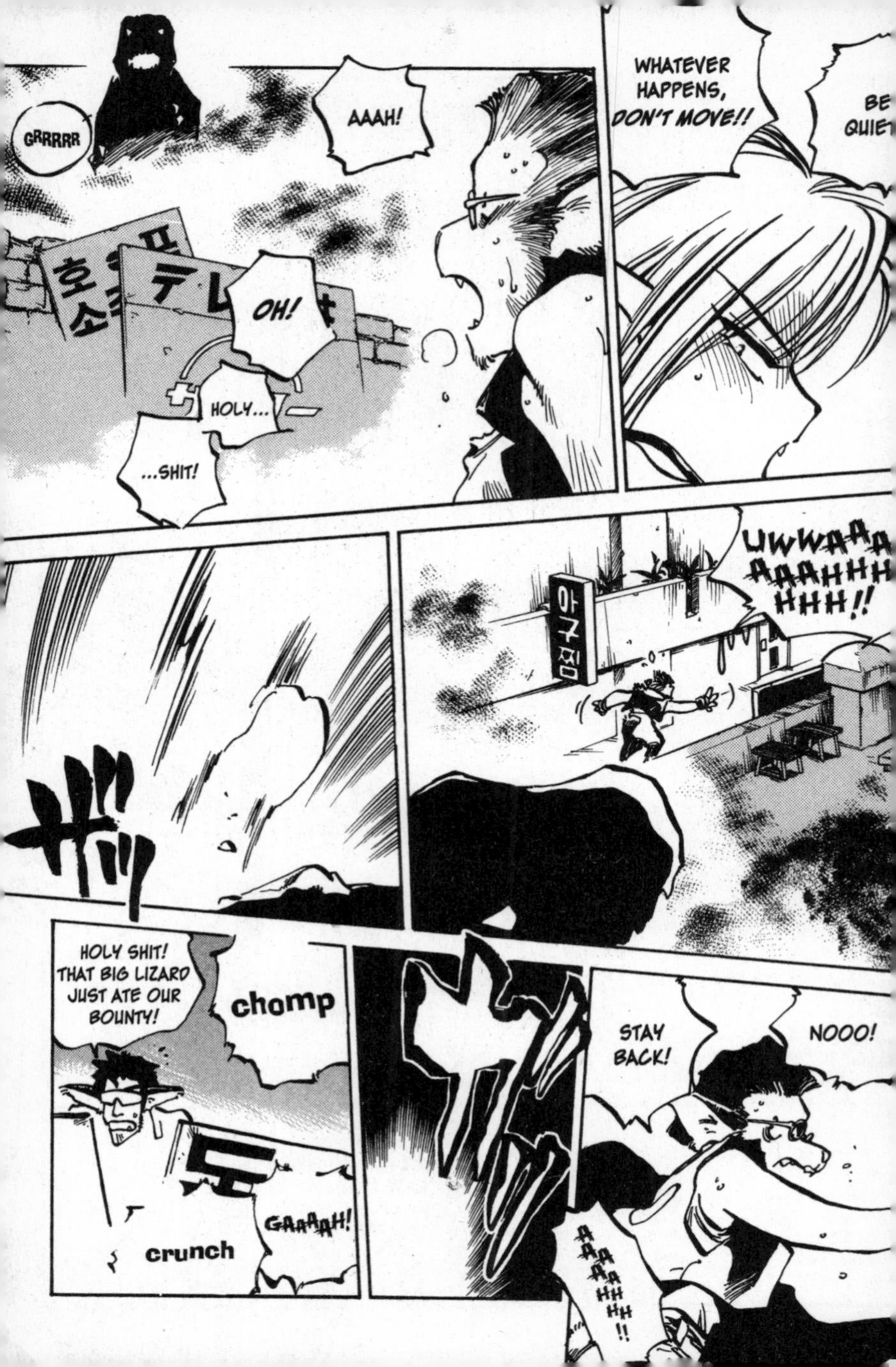
BE QUIET
WHATEVER HAPPENS, DON'T MOVE!!
AAAH!
GRRRRR
OH!
HOLY...
...SHIT!
UWWAAAAAAHHHHHH!!
아구찜
NOOO!
STAY BACK!
AAAAAHHHH!!
chomp
HOLY SHIT! THAT BIG LIZARD JUST ATE OUR BOUNTY!
GAAAAH!
crunch

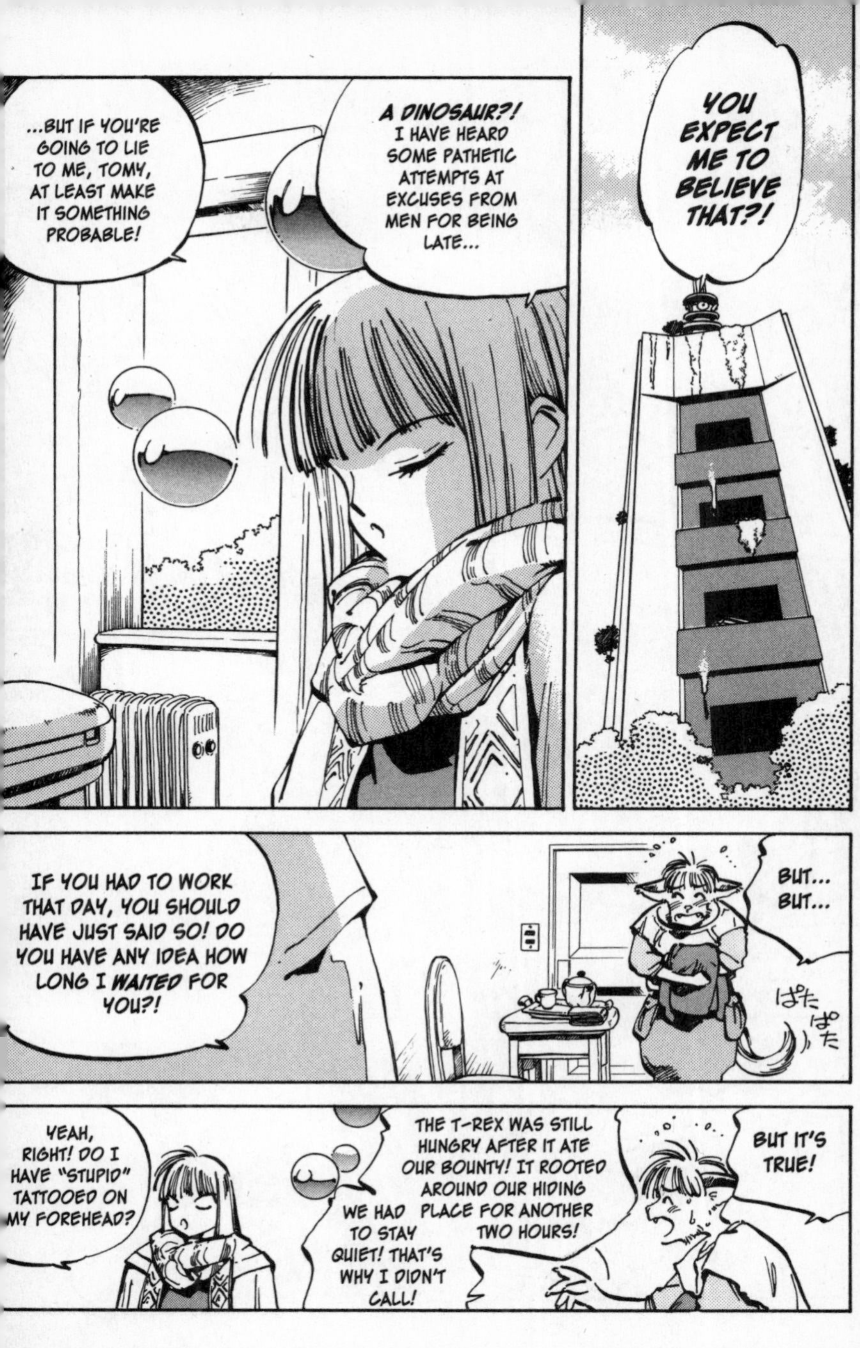
YOU EXPECT ME TO BELIEVE THAT?!
A DINOSAUR?! I HAVE HEARD SOME PATHETIC ATTEMPTS AT EXCUSES FROM MEN FOR BEING LATE...
...BUT IF YOU'RE GOING TO LIE TO ME, TOMY, AT LEAST MAKE IT SOMETHING PROBABLE!
BUT... BUT...
ぱたぱた
IF YOU HAD TO WORK THAT DAY, YOU SHOULD HAVE JUST SAID SO! DO YOU HAVE ANY IDEA HOW LONG I WAITED FOR YOU?!
BUT IT'S TRUE!
THE T-REX WAS STILL HUNGRY AFTER IT ATE OUR BOUNTY! IT ROOTED AROUND OUR HIDING PLACE FOR ANOTHER TWO HOURS!
WE HAD TO STAY QUIET! THAT'S WHY I DIDN'T CALL!
YEAH, RIGHT! DO I HAVE "STUPID" TATTOOED ON MY FOREHEAD?

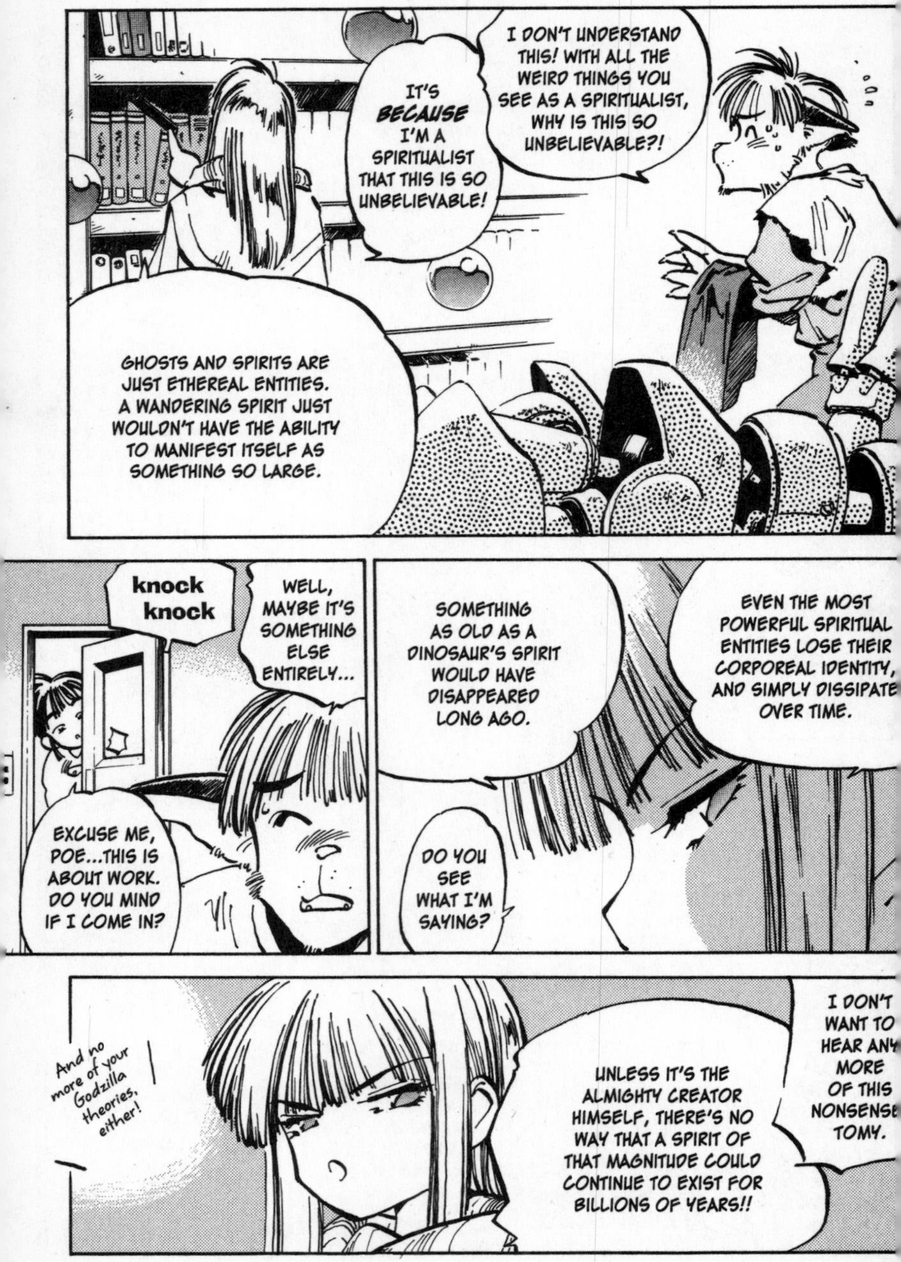
I DON'T UNDERSTAND THIS! WITH ALL THE WEIRD THINGS YOU SEE AS A SPIRITUALIST, WHY IS THIS SO UNBELIEVABLE?!
IT'S BECAUSE I'M A SPIRITUALIST THAT THIS IS SO UNBELIEVABLE!
GHOSTS AND SPIRITS ARE JUST ETHEREAL ENTITIES. A WANDERING SPIRIT JUST WOULDN'T HAVE THE ABILITY TO MANIFEST ITSELF AS SOMETHING SO LARGE.
EVEN THE MOST POWERFUL SPIRITUAL ENTITIES LOSE THEIR CORPOREAL IDENTITY, AND SIMPLY DISSIPATE OVER TIME.
SOMETHING AS OLD AS A DINOSAUR'S SPIRIT WOULD HAVE DISAPPEARED LONG AGO.
DO YOU SEE WHAT I'M SAYING?
WELL, MAYBE IT'S SOMETHING ELSE ENTIRELY...
knock knock
EXCUSE ME, POE...THIS IS ABOUT WORK. DO YOU MIND IF I COME IN?
I DON'T WANT TO HEAR ANY MORE OF THIS NONSENSE, TOMY.
UNLESS IT'S THE ALMIGHTY CREATOR HIMSELF, THERE'S NO WAY THAT A SPIRIT OF THAT MAGNITUDE COULD CONTINUE TO EXIST FOR BILLIONS OF YEARS!!
And no more of your Godzilla theories, either!

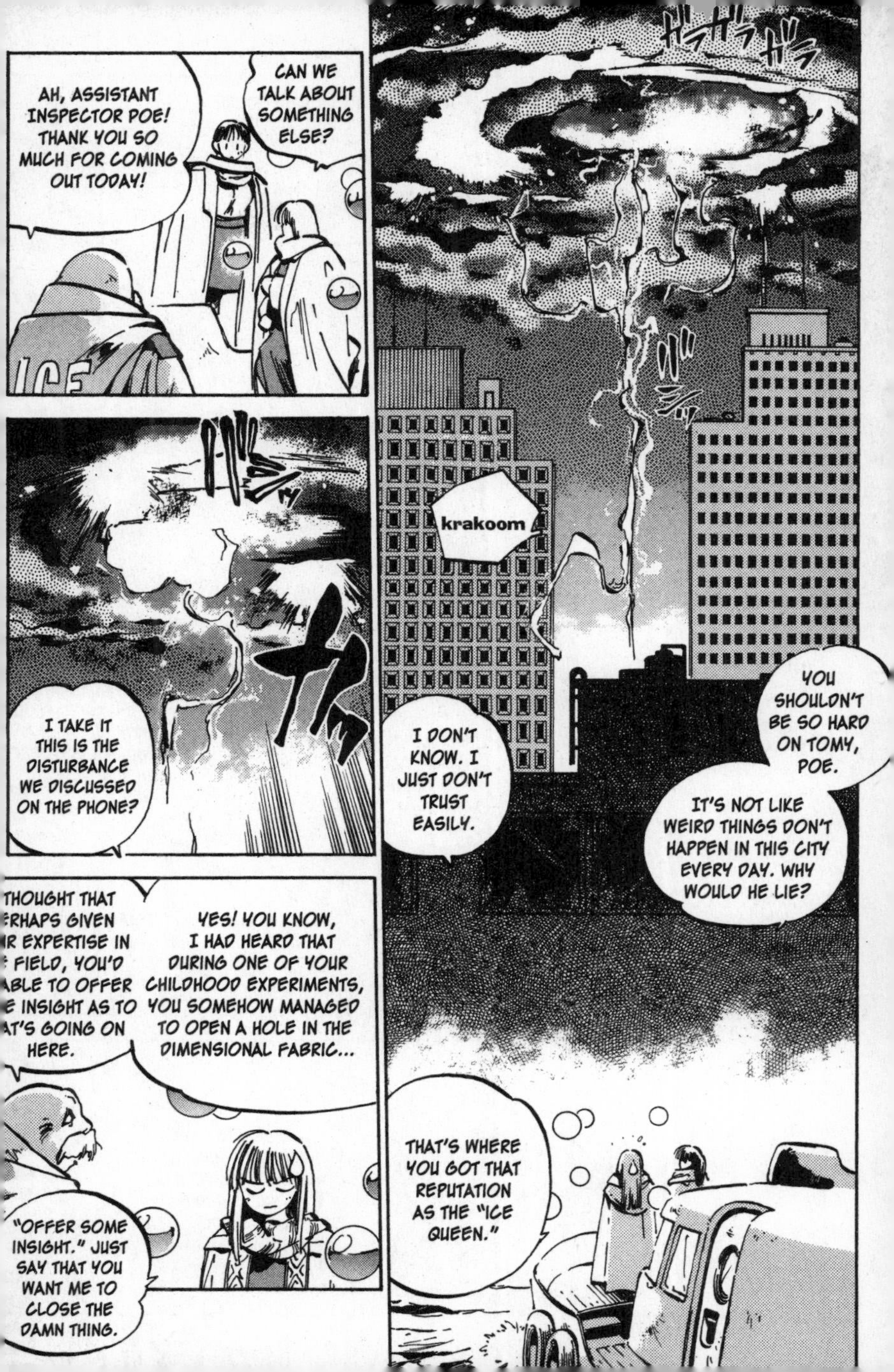
ガラガラガラ
krakoom
YOU SHOULDN'T BE SO HARD ON TOMY, POE.
IT'S NOT LIKE WEIRD THINGS DON'T HAPPEN IN THIS CITY EVERY DAY. WHY WOULD HE LIE?
I DON'T KNOW. I JUST DON'T TRUST EASILY.
THAT'S WHERE YOU GOT THAT REPUTATION AS THE "ICE QUEEN."
CAN WE TALK ABOUT SOMETHING ELSE?
AH, ASSISTANT INSPECTOR POE! THANK YOU SO MUCH FOR COMING OUT TODAY!
I TAKE IT THIS IS THE DISTURBANCE WE DISCUSSED ON THE PHONE?
YES! YOU KNOW, I HAD HEARD THAT DURING ONE OF YOUR CHILDHOOD EXPERIMENTS, YOU SOMEHOW MANAGED TO OPEN A HOLE IN THE DIMENSIONAL FABRIC...
THOUGHT THAT ERHAPS GIVEN IR EXPERTISE IN FIELD, YOU'D ABLE TO OFFER E INSIGHT AS TO AT'S GOING ON HERE.
"OFFER SOME INSIGHT." JUST SAY THAT YOU WANT ME TO CLOSE THE DAMN THING.

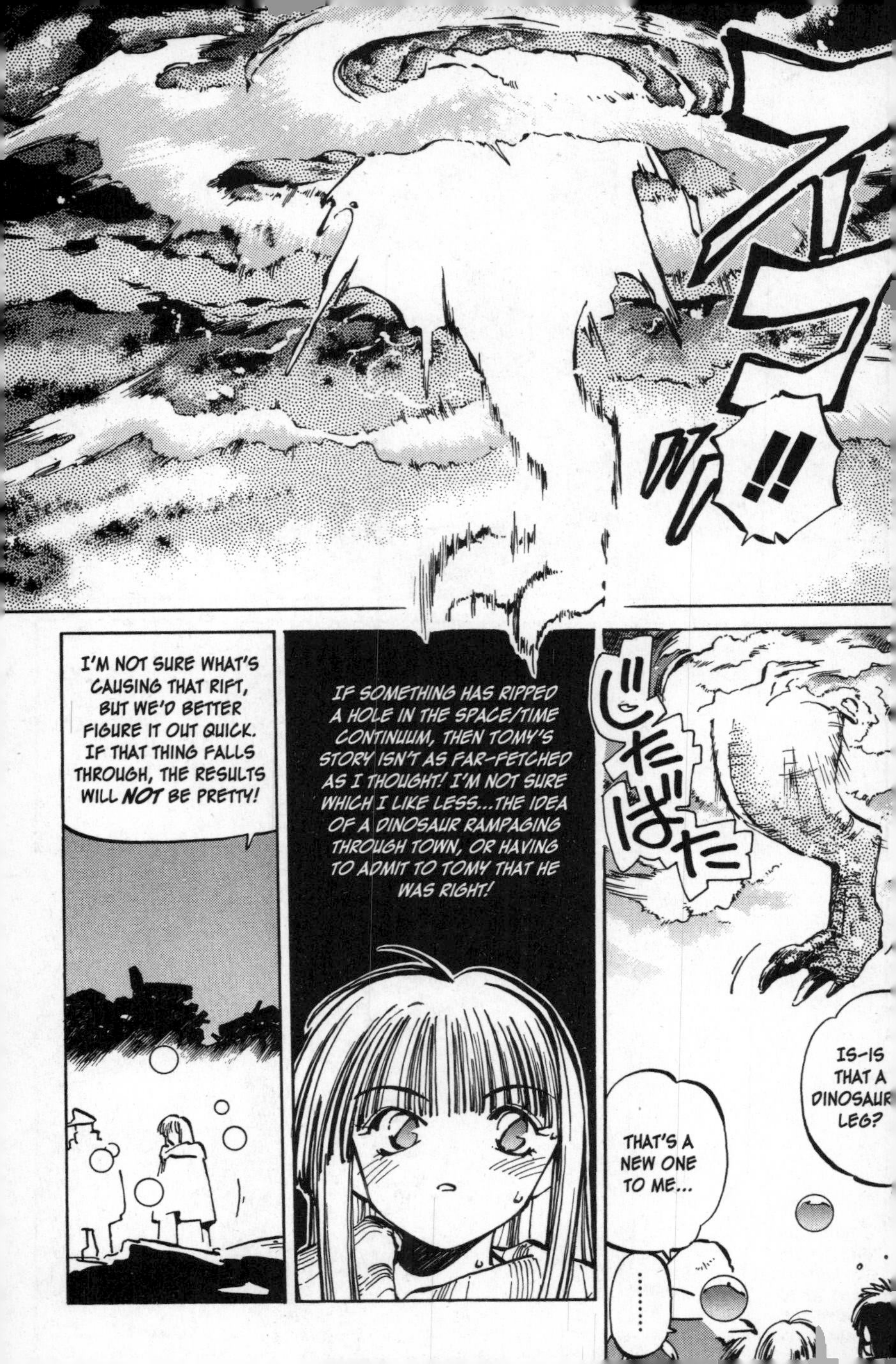

じたばた
IS-IS THAT A DINOSAUR LEG?
THAT'S A NEW ONE TO ME...
......
IF SOMETHING HAS RIPPED A HOLE IN THE SPACE/TIME CONTINUUM, THEN TOMY'S STORY ISN'T AS FAR-FETCHED AS I THOUGHT! I'M NOT SURE WHICH I LIKE LESS...THE IDEA OF A DINOSAUR RAMPAGING THROUGH TOWN, OR HAVING TO ADMIT TO TOMY THAT HE WAS RIGHT!
I'M NOT SURE WHAT'S CAUSING THAT RIFT, BUT WE'D BETTER FIGURE IT OUT QUICK. IF THAT THING FALLS THROUGH, THE RESULTS WILL NOT BE PRETTY!

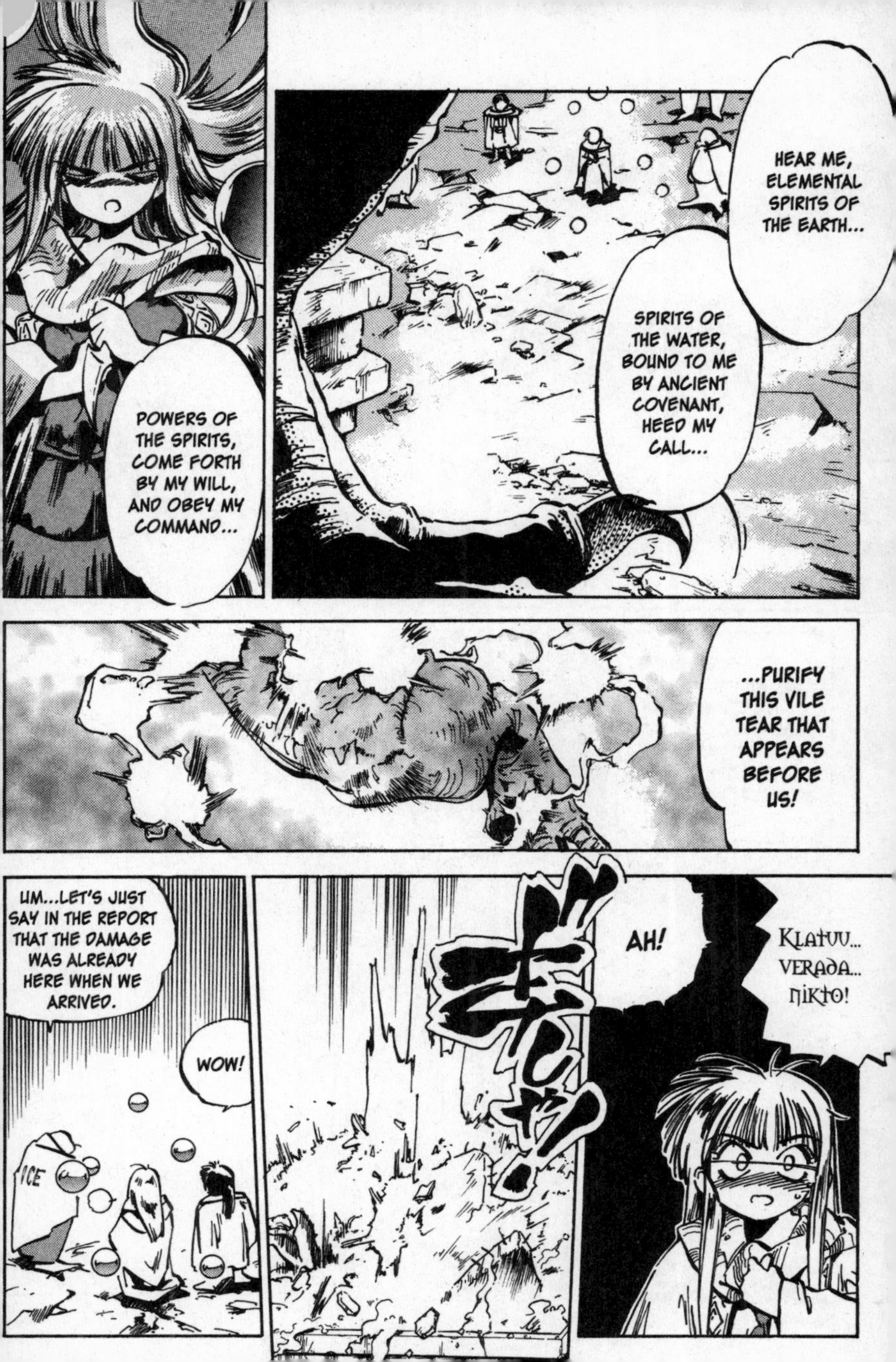
HEAR ME, ELEMENTAL SPIRITS OF THE EARTH...
SPIRITS OF THE WATER, BOUND TO ME BY ANCIENT COVENANT, HEED MY CALL...
POWERS OF THE SPIRITS, COME FORTH BY MY WILL, AND OBEY MY COMMAND...
...PURIFY THIS VILE TEAR THAT APPEARS BEFORE US!
KLATUU... VERADA... NIKTO!
AH!
UM...LET'S JUST SAY IN THE REPORT THAT THE DAMAGE WAS ALREADY HERE WHEN WE ARRIVED.
WOW!
ICE

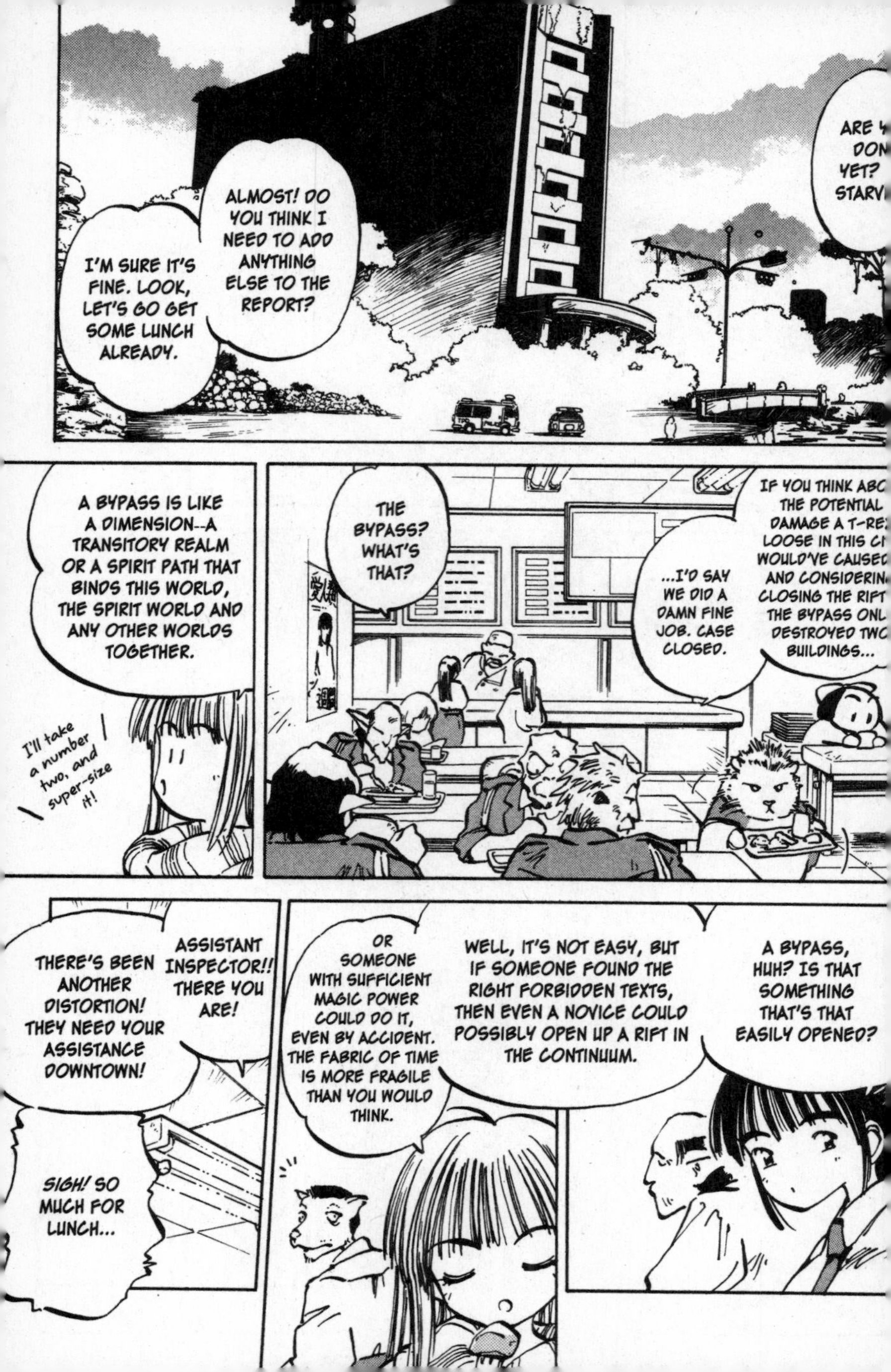
ARE Y DON YET? STARV
ALMOST! DO YOU THINK I NEED TO ADD ANYTHING ELSE TO THE REPORT?
I'M SURE IT'S FINE. LOOK, LET'S GO GET SOME LUNCH ALREADY.
IF YOU THINK ABO THE POTENTIAL DAMAGE A T-RE LOOSE IN THIS CI WOULD'VE CAUSE AND CONSIDERIN CLOSING THE RIFT THE BYPASS ONL DESTROYED TWO BUILDINGS...
...I'D SAY WE DID A DAMN FINE JOB. CASE CLOSED.
THE BYPASS? WHAT'S THAT?
A BYPASS IS LIKE A DIMENSION--A TRANSITORY REALM OR A SPIRIT PATH THAT BINDS THIS WORLD, THE SPIRIT WORLD AND ANY OTHER WORLDS TOGETHER.
I'll take a number two, and super-size it!
A BYPASS, HUH? IS THAT SOMETHING THAT'S THAT EASILY OPENED?
WELL, IT'S NOT EASY, BUT IF SOMEONE FOUND THE RIGHT FORBIDDEN TEXTS, THEN EVEN A NOVICE COULD POSSIBLY OPEN UP A RIFT IN THE CONTINUUM.
OR SOMEONE WITH SUFFICIENT MAGIC POWER COULD DO IT, EVEN BY ACCIDENT. THE FABRIC OF TIME IS MORE FRAGILE THAN YOU WOULD THINK.
ASSISTANT INSPECTOR!! THERE YOU ARE!
THERE'S BEEN ANOTHER DISTORTION! THEY NEED YOUR ASSISTANCE DOWNTOWN!
SIGH! SO MUCH FOR LUNCH...

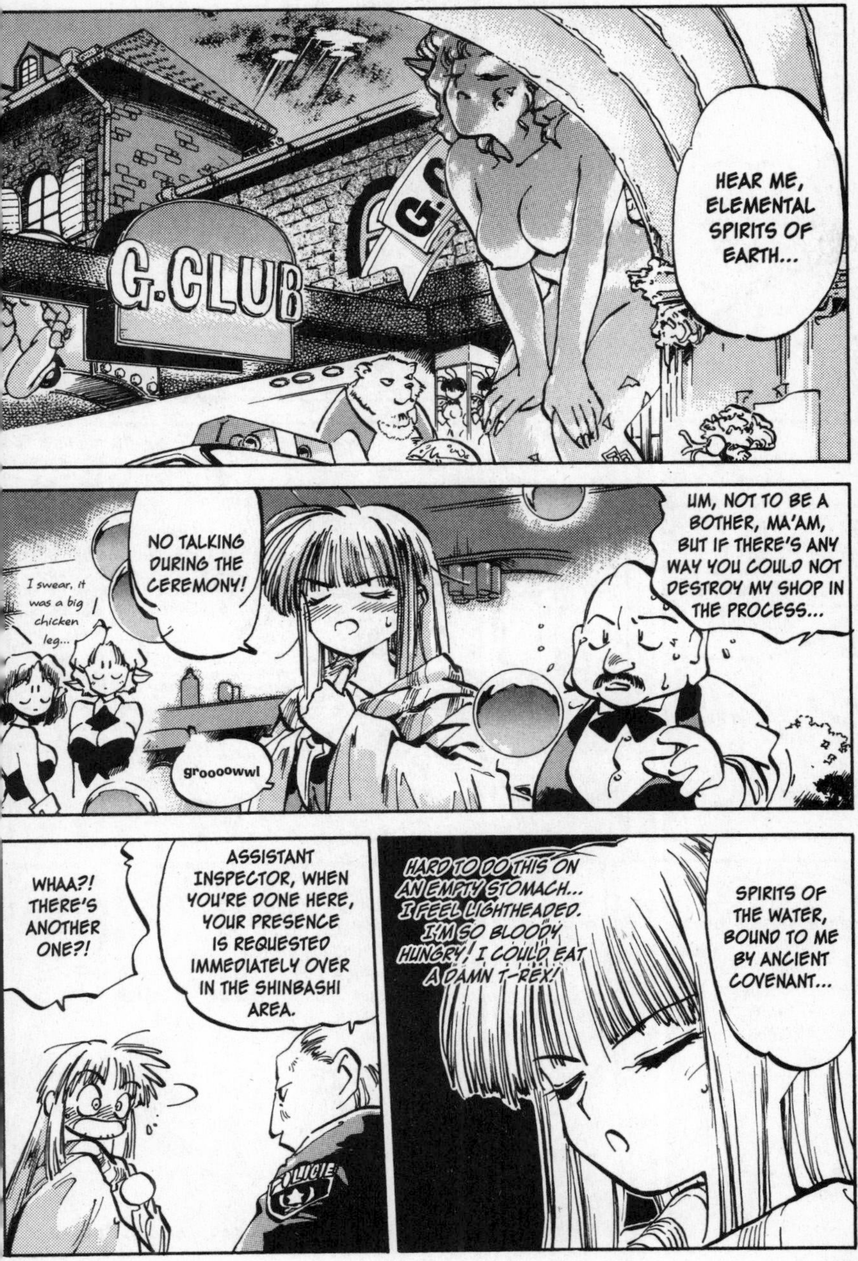
HEAR ME, ELEMENTAL SPIRITS OF EARTH...
G.CLUB
UM, NOT TO BE A BOTHER, MA'AM, BUT IF THERE'S ANY WAY YOU COULD NOT DESTROY MY SHOP IN THE PROCESS...
NO TALKING DURING THE CEREMONY!
I swear, it was a big chicken leg...
groooowwl
SPIRITS OF THE WATER, BOUND TO ME BY ANCIENT COVENANT...
HARD TO DO THIS ON AN EMPTY STOMACH... I FEEL LIGHTHEADED. I'M SO BLOODY HUNGRY, I COULD EAT A DAMN T-REX!
ASSISTANT INSPECTOR, WHEN YOU'RE DONE HERE, YOUR PRESENCE IS REQUESTED IMMEDIATELY OVER IN THE SHINBASHI AREA.
WHAA?! THERE'S ANOTHER ONE?!
POLICIE

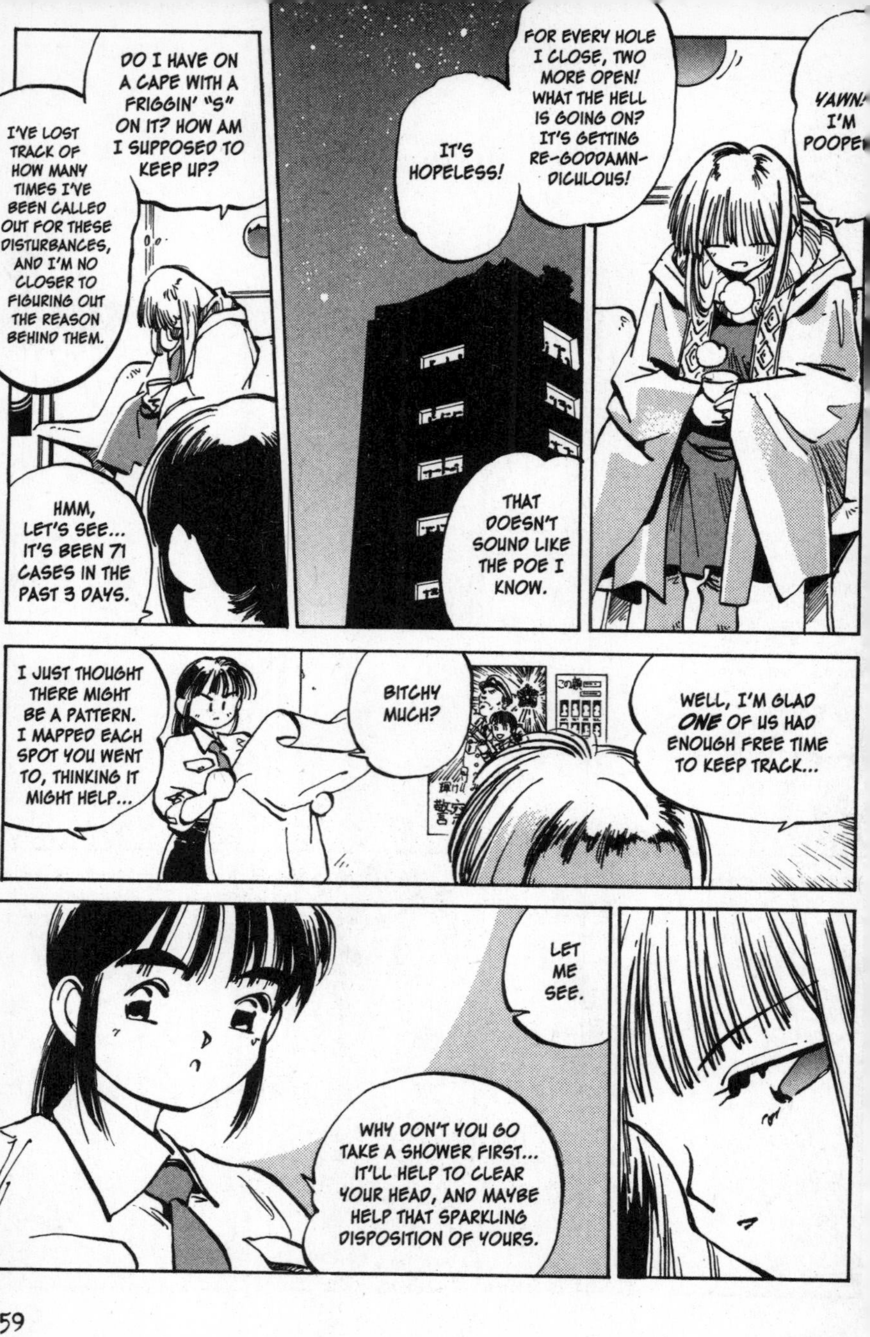

YAWN! I'M POOPE
FOR EVERY HOLE I CLOSE, TWO MORE OPEN! WHAT THE HELL IS GOING ON? IT'S GETTING RE-GODDAMN-DICULOUS!
IT'S HOPELESS!
THAT DOESN'T SOUND LIKE THE POE I KNOW.
DO I HAVE ON A CAPE WITH A FRIGGIN' "S" ON IT? HOW AM I SUPPOSED TO KEEP UP?
I'VE LOST TRACK OF HOW MANY TIMES I'VE BEEN CALLED OUT FOR THESE DISTURBANCES, AND I'M NO CLOSER TO FIGURING OUT THE REASON BEHIND THEM.
HMM, LET'S SEE... IT'S BEEN 71 CASES IN THE PAST 3 DAYS.
WELL, I'M GLAD ONE OF US HAD ENOUGH FREE TIME TO KEEP TRACK...
BITCHY MUCH?
I JUST THOUGHT THERE MIGHT BE A PATTERN. I MAPPED EACH SPOT YOU WENT TO, THINKING IT MIGHT HELP...
LET ME SEE.
WHY DON'T YOU GO TAKE A SHOWER FIRST... IT'LL HELP TO CLEAR YOUR HEAD, AND MAYBE HELP THAT SPARKLING DISPOSITION OF YOURS.

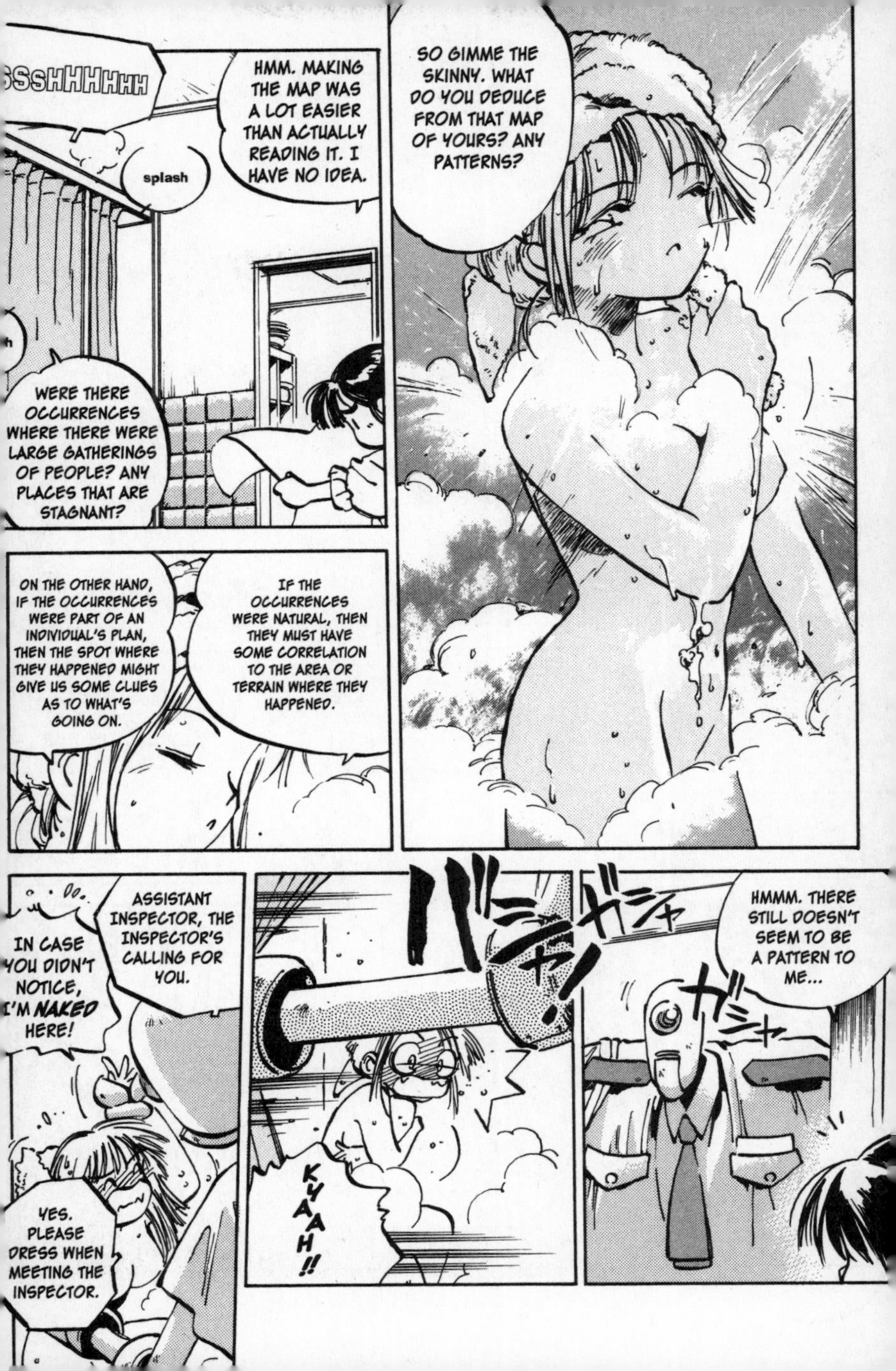
SO GIMME THE SKINNY. WHAT DO YOU DEDUCE FROM THAT MAP OF YOURS? ANY PATTERNS?
HMM. MAKING THE MAP WAS A LOT EASIER THAN ACTUALLY READING IT. I HAVE NO IDEA.
SSSHHHHHH
splash
WERE THERE OCCURRENCES WHERE THERE WERE LARGE GATHERINGS OF PEOPLE? ANY PLACES THAT ARE STAGNANT?
IF THE OCCURRENCES WERE NATURAL, THEN THEY MUST HAVE SOME CORRELATION TO THE AREA OR TERRAIN WHERE THEY HAPPENED.
ON THE OTHER HAND, IF THE OCCURRENCES WERE PART OF AN INDIVIDUAL'S PLAN, THEN THE SPOT WHERE THEY HAPPENED MIGHT GIVE US SOME CLUES AS TO WHAT'S GOING ON.
HMMM. THERE STILL DOESN'T SEEM TO BE A PATTERN TO ME...
KYAAAH!!
ASSISTANT INSPECTOR, THE INSPECTOR'S CALLING FOR YOU.
IN CASE YOU DIDN'T NOTICE, I'M ***NAKED*** HERE!
YES. PLEASE DRESS WHEN MEETING THE INSPECTOR.

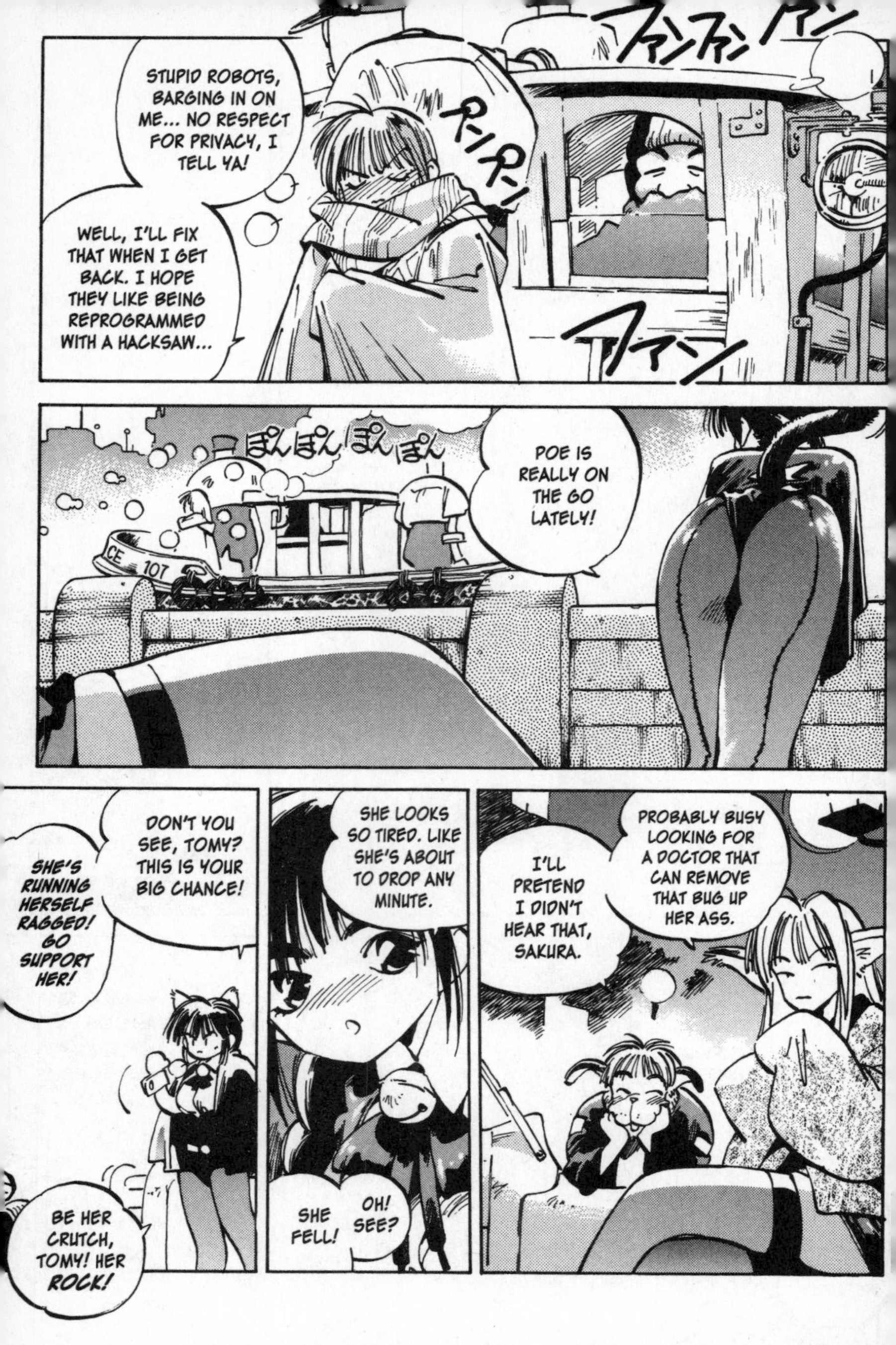

STUPID ROBOTS, BARGING IN ON ME... NO RESPECT FOR PRIVACY, I TELL YA!
WELL, I'LL FIX THAT WHEN I GET BACK. I HOPE THEY LIKE BEING REPROGRAMMED WITH A HACKSAW...
POE IS REALLY ON THE GO LATELY!
ぽんぽん ぽんぽん
CE 107
PROBABLY BUSY LOOKING FOR A DOCTOR THAT CAN REMOVE THAT BUG UP HER ASS.
I'LL PRETEND I DIDN'T HEAR THAT, SAKURA.
SHE LOOKS SO TIRED. LIKE SHE'S ABOUT TO DROP ANY MINUTE.
OH! SEE?
SHE FELL!
DON'T YOU SEE, TOMY? THIS IS YOUR BIG CHANCE!
SHE'S RUNNING HERSELF RAGGED! GO SUPPORT HER!
BE HER CRUTCH, TOMY! HER ROCK!

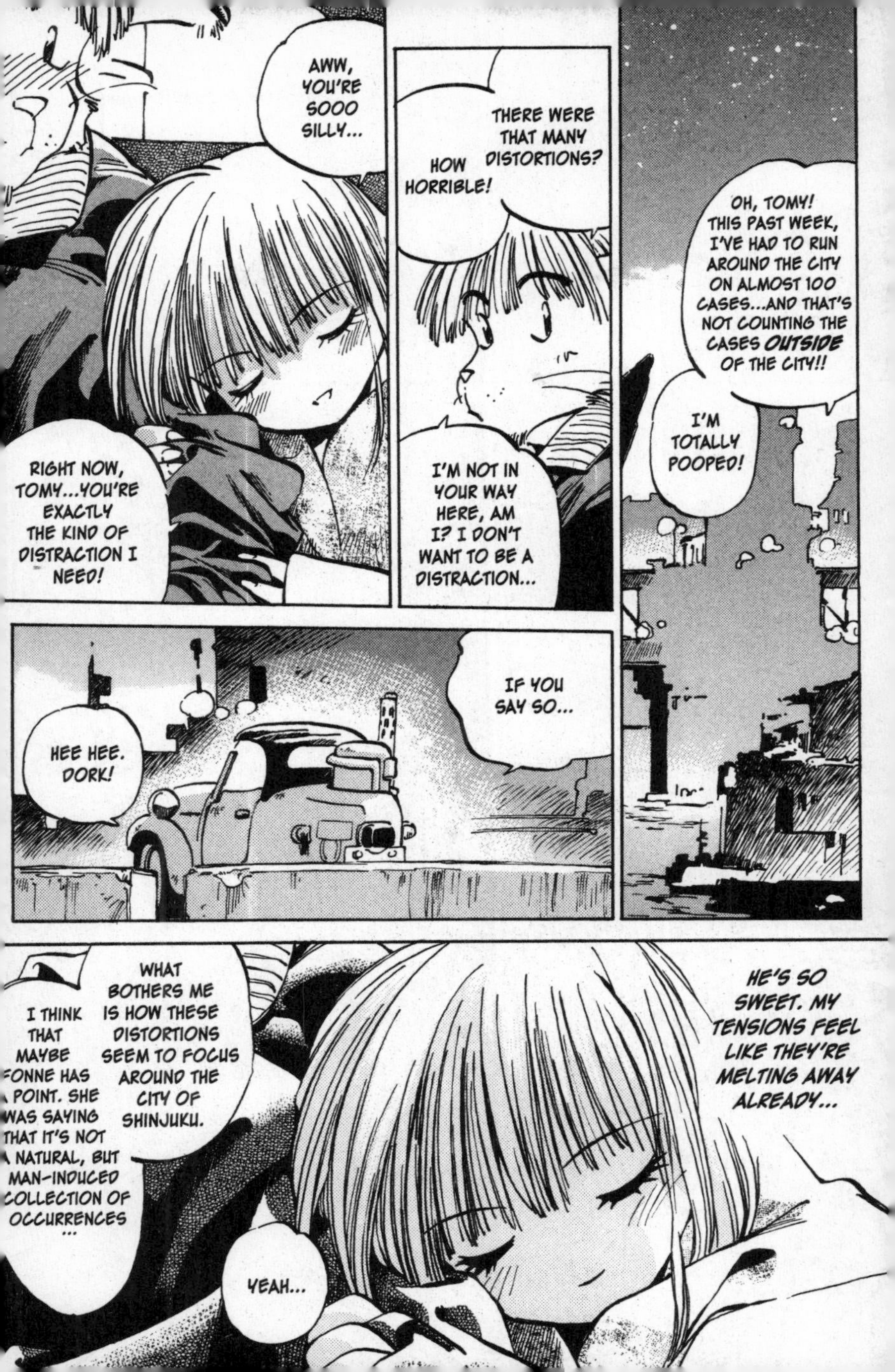
OH, TOMY! THIS PAST WEEK, I'VE HAD TO RUN AROUND THE CITY ON ALMOST 100 CASES...AND THAT'S NOT COUNTING THE CASES *OUTSIDE* OF THE CITY!!
I'M TOTALLY POOPED!
THERE WERE THAT MANY DISTORTIONS?
HOW HORRIBLE!
I'M NOT IN YOUR WAY HERE, AM I? I DON'T WANT TO BE A DISTRACTION...
AWW, YOU'RE SOOO SILLY...
RIGHT NOW, TOMY...YOU'RE EXACTLY THE KIND OF DISTRACTION I NEED!
IF YOU SAY SO...
HEE HEE. DORK!
HE'S SO SWEET. MY TENSIONS FEEL LIKE THEY'RE MELTING AWAY ALREADY...
WHAT BOTHERS ME IS HOW THESE DISTORTIONS SEEM TO FOCUS AROUND THE CITY OF SHINJUKU.
I THINK THAT MAYBE ONNE HAS A POINT. SHE WAS SAYING THAT IT'S NOT A NATURAL, BUT MAN-INDUCED COLLECTION OF OCCURRENCES...
YEAH...

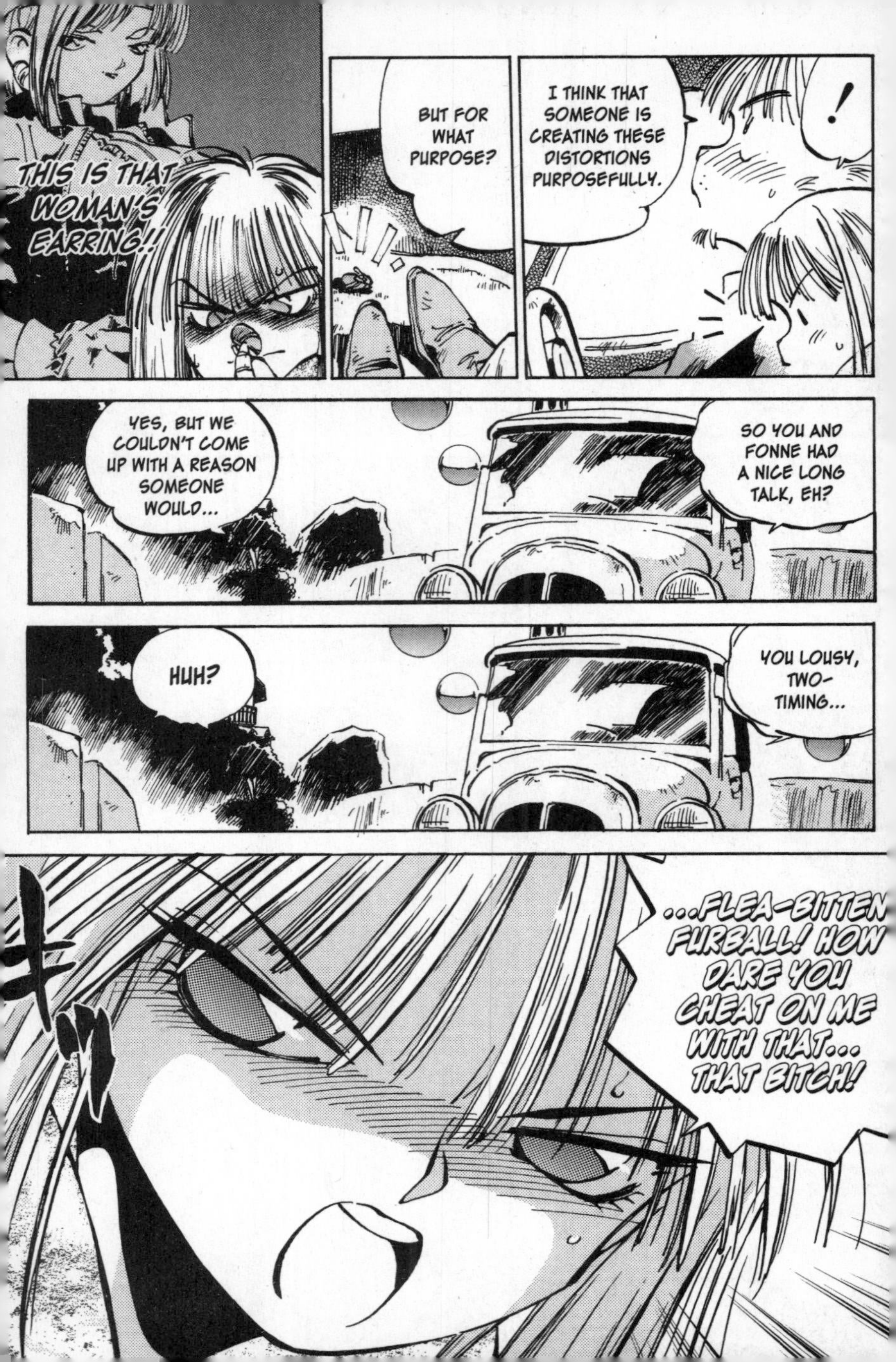
!
I THINK THAT SOMEONE IS CREATING THESE DISTORTIONS PURPOSEFULLY.
BUT FOR WHAT PURPOSE?
THIS IS THAT WOMAN'S EARRING!!
SO YOU AND FONNE HAD A NICE LONG TALK, EH?
YES, BUT WE COULDN'T COME UP WITH A REASON SOMEONE WOULD...
YOU LOUSY, TWO-TIMING...
HUH?
...FLEA-BITTEN FURBALL! HOW DARE YOU CHEAT ON ME WITH THAT... THAT BITCH!

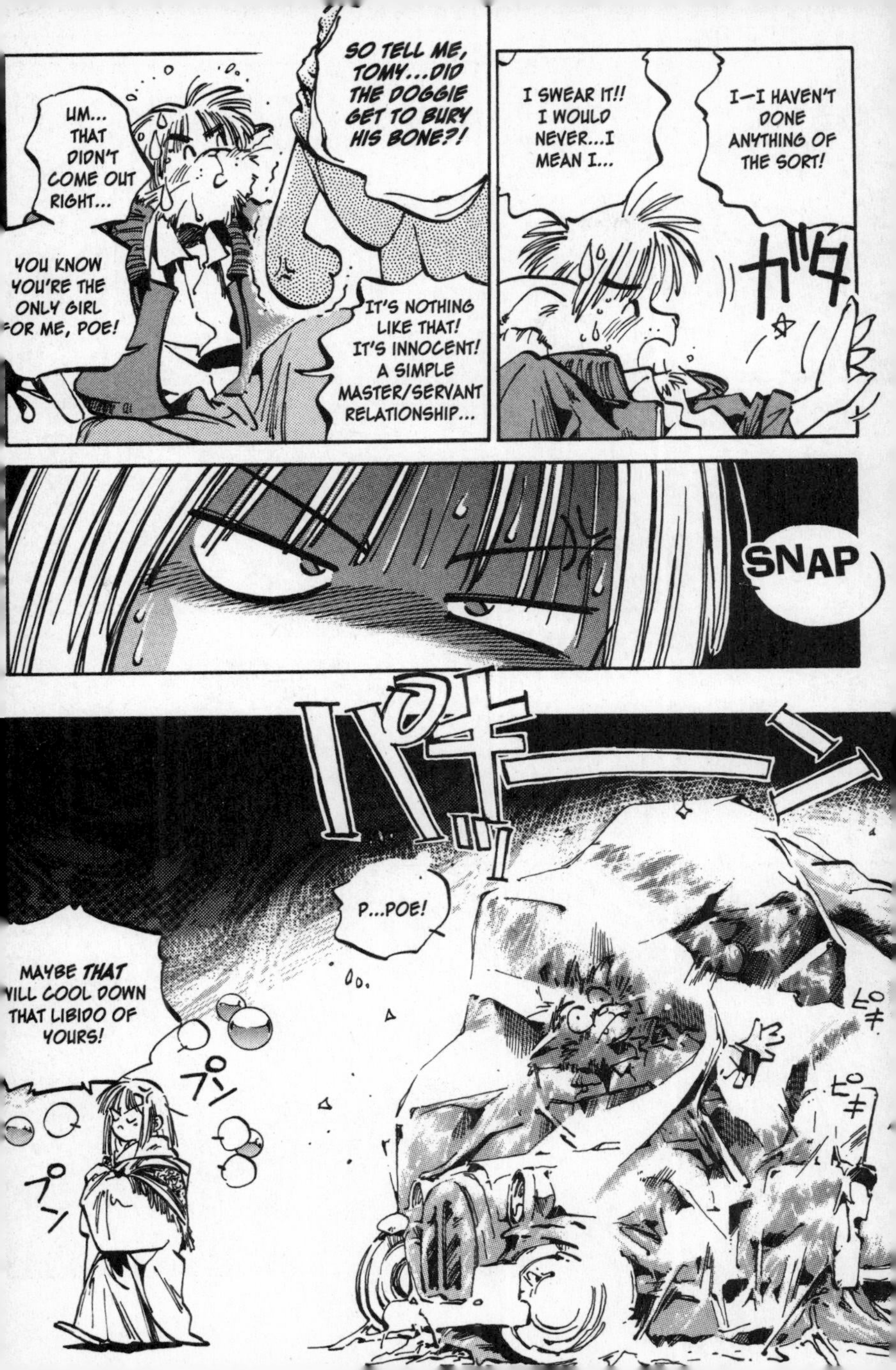
I—I HAVEN'T DONE ANYTHING OF THE SORT!
I SWEAR IT!! I WOULD NEVER...I MEAN I...
SO TELL ME, TOMY...DID THE DOGGIE GET TO BURY HIS BONE?!
IT'S NOTHING LIKE THAT! IT'S INNOCENT! A SIMPLE MASTER/SERVANT RELATIONSHIP...
UM... THAT DIDN'T COME OUT RIGHT...
YOU KNOW YOU'RE THE ONLY GIRL FOR ME, POE!
SNAP
P...POE!
MAYBE *THAT* WILL COOL DOWN THAT LIBIDO OF YOURS!

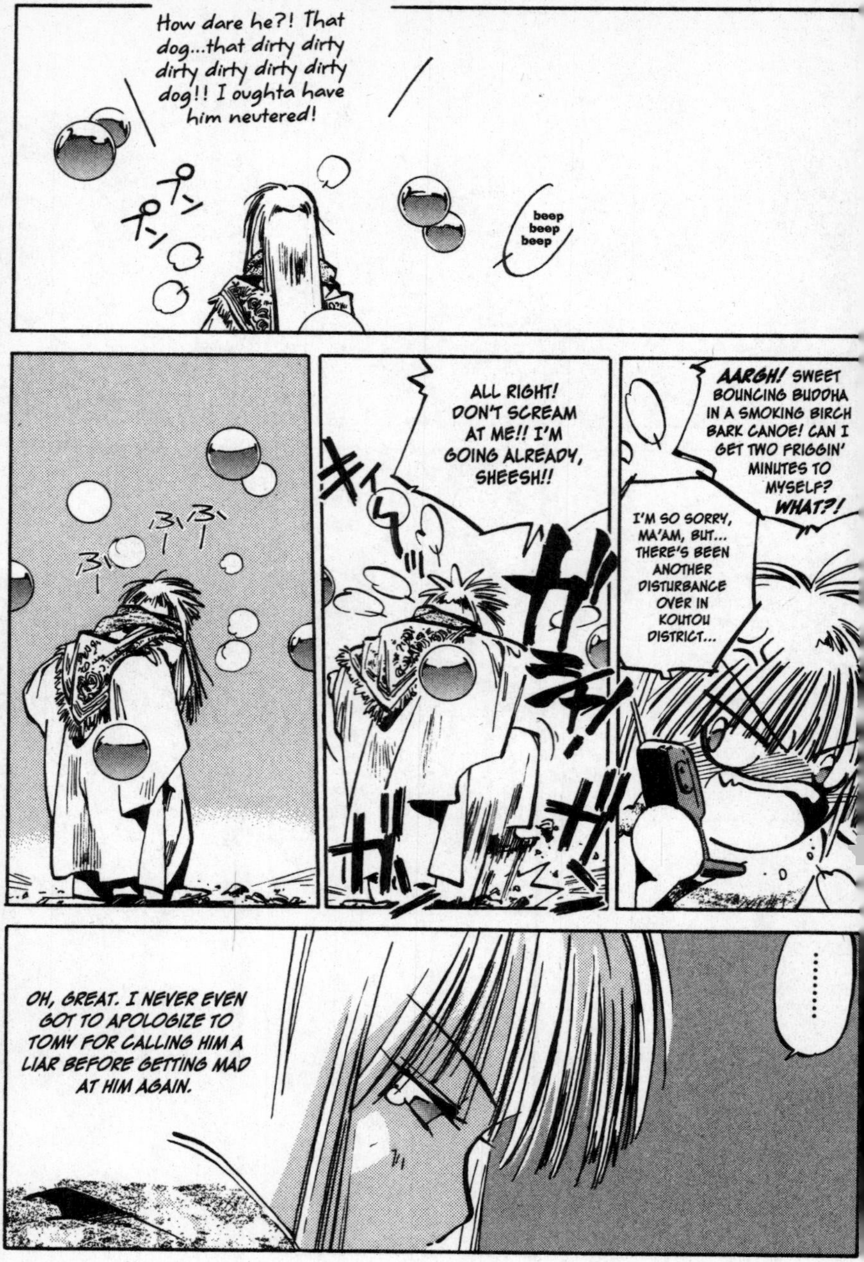

How dare he?! That dog...that dirty dirty dirty dirty dirty dirty dog!! I oughta have him neutered!
beep beep beep
AARGH! SWEET BOUNCING BUDDHA IN A SMOKING BIRCH BARK CANOE! CAN I GET TWO FRIGGIN' MINUTES TO MYSELF? WHAT?!
I'M SO SORRY, MA'AM, BUT... THERE'S BEEN ANOTHER DISTURBANCE OVER IN KOUTOU DISTRICT...
ALL RIGHT! DON'T SCREAM AT ME!! I'M GOING ALREADY, SHEESH!!
......
OH, GREAT. I NEVER EVEN GOT TO APOLOGIZE TO TOMY FOR CALLING HIM A LIAR BEFORE GETTING MAD AT HIM AGAIN.

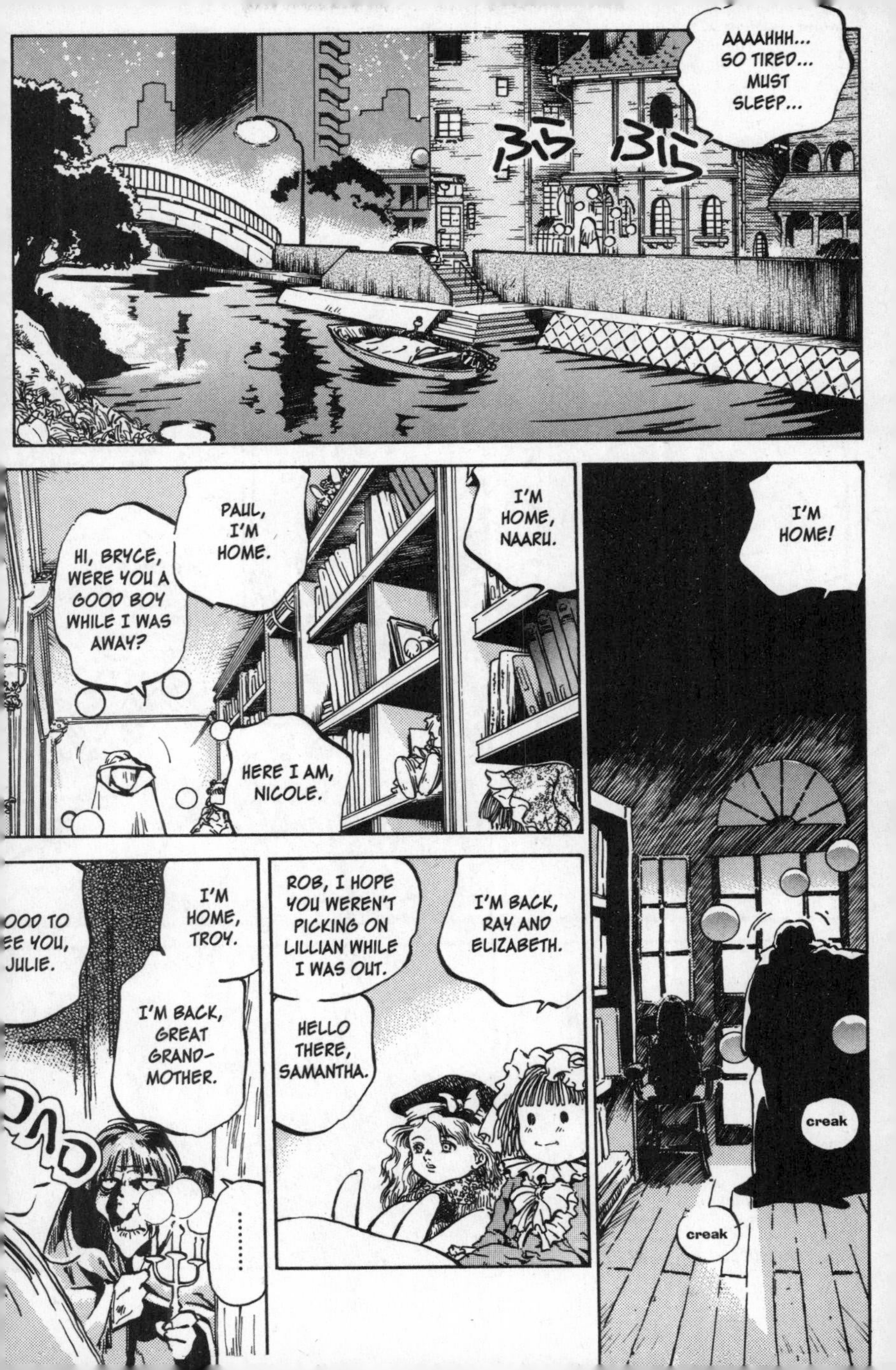
AAAAHHH... SO TIRED... MUST SLEEP...
I'M HOME!
creak
creak
I'M HOME, NAARU.
PAUL, I'M HOME.
HI, BRYCE, WERE YOU A GOOD BOY WHILE I WAS AWAY?
HERE I AM, NICOLE.
I'M BACK, RAY AND ELIZABETH.
ROB, I HOPE YOU WEREN'T PICKING ON LILLIAN WHILE I WAS OUT.
HELLO THERE, SAMANTHA.
I'M HOME, TROY.
OOD TO EE YOU, JULIE.
I'M BACK, GREAT GRAND-MOTHER.
......

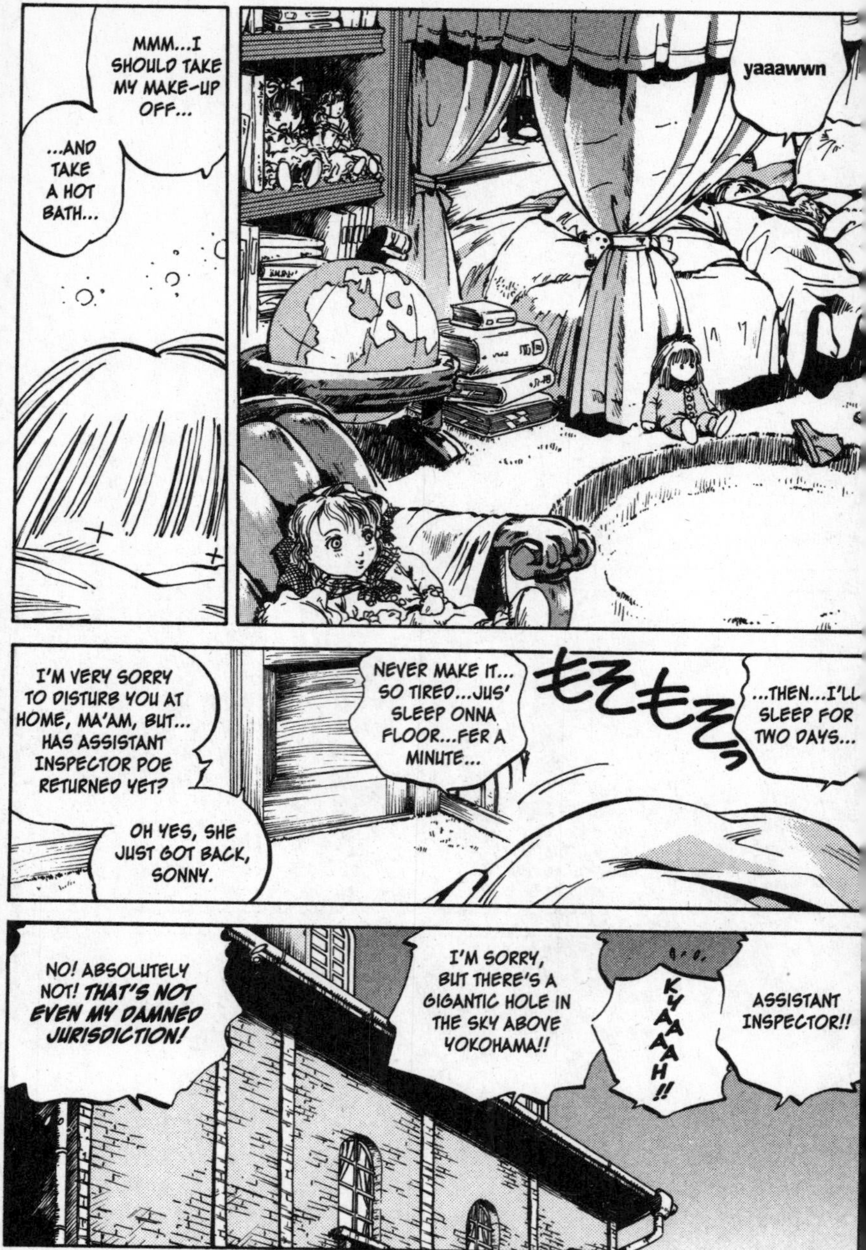
yaaawwn
MMM...I SHOULD TAKE MY MAKE-UP OFF...
...AND TAKE A HOT BATH...
...THEN...I'LL SLEEP FOR TWO DAYS...
もそもそ
NEVER MAKE IT... SO TIRED...JUS' SLEEP ONNA FLOOR...FER A MINUTE...
I'M VERY SORRY TO DISTURB YOU AT HOME, MA'AM, BUT... HAS ASSISTANT INSPECTOR POE RETURNED YET?
OH YES, SHE JUST GOT BACK, SONNY.
ASSISTANT INSPECTOR!!
KYAAAAH!!
I'M SORRY, BUT THERE'S A GIGANTIC HOLE IN THE SKY ABOVE YOKOHAMA!!
NO! ABSOLUTELY NOT! THAT'S NOT EVEN MY DAMNED JURISDICTION!

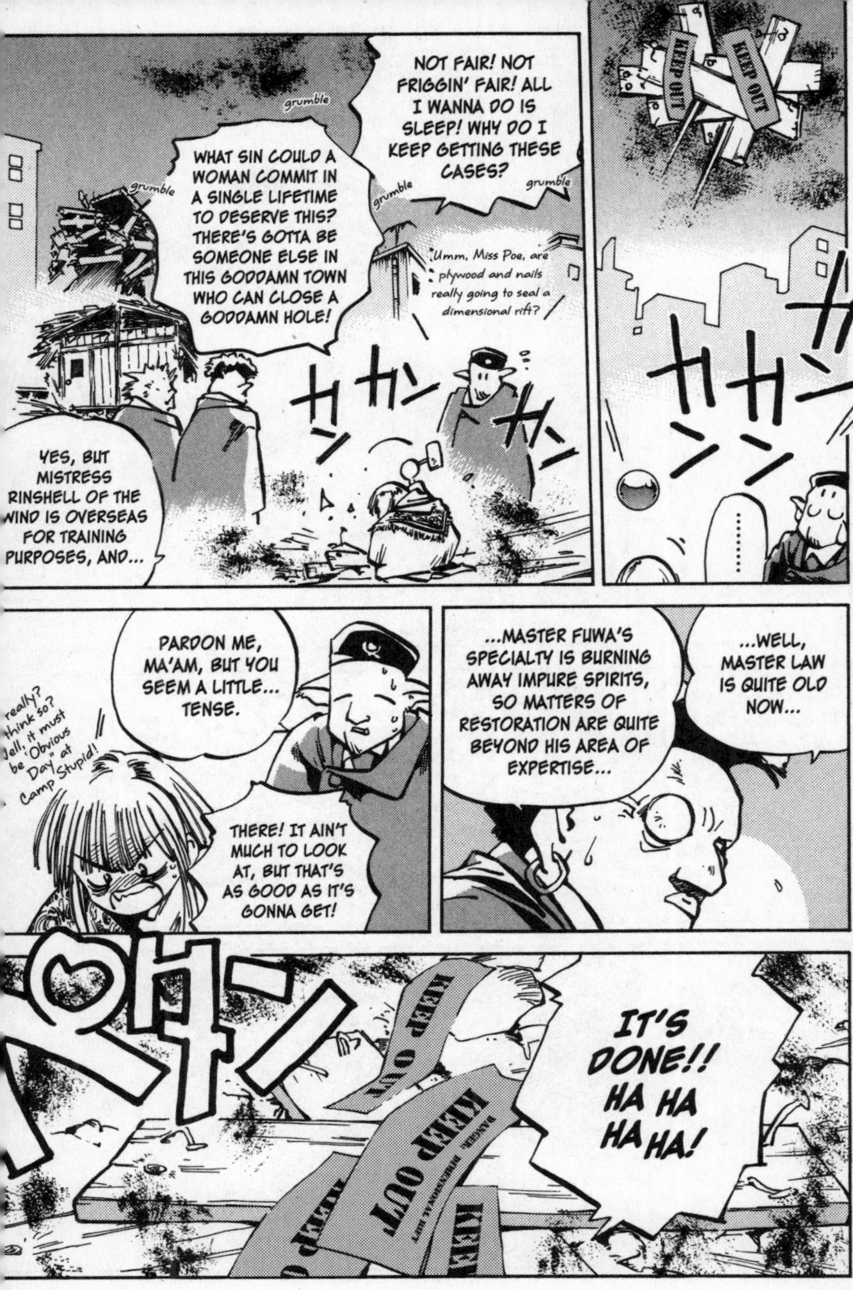
KEEP OUT
KEEP OUT
......
NOT FAIR! NOT FRIGGIN' FAIR! ALL I WANNA DO IS SLEEP! WHY DO I KEEP GETTING THESE CASES?
grumble
grumble
WHAT SIN COULD A WOMAN COMMIT IN A SINGLE LIFETIME TO DESERVE THIS? THERE'S GOTTA BE SOMEONE ELSE IN THIS GODDAMN TOWN WHO CAN CLOSE A GODDAMN HOLE!
grumble
grumble
Umm, Miss Poe, are plywood and nails really going to seal a dimensional rift?
YES, BUT MISTRESS RINSHELL OF THE WIND IS OVERSEAS FOR TRAINING PURPOSES, AND...
...WELL, MASTER LAW IS QUITE OLD NOW...
...MASTER FUWA'S SPECIALTY IS BURNING AWAY IMPURE SPIRITS, SO MATTERS OF RESTORATION ARE QUITE BEYOND HIS AREA OF EXPERTISE...
PARDON ME, MA'AM, BUT YOU SEEM A LITTLE... TENSE.
really? think so? Well, it must be 'Obvious Day' at Camp Stupid!
THERE! IT AIN'T MUCH TO LOOK AT, BUT THAT'S AS GOOD AS IT'S GONNA GET!
IT'S DONE!! HA HA HA HA!
KEEP OUT
KEEP OUT

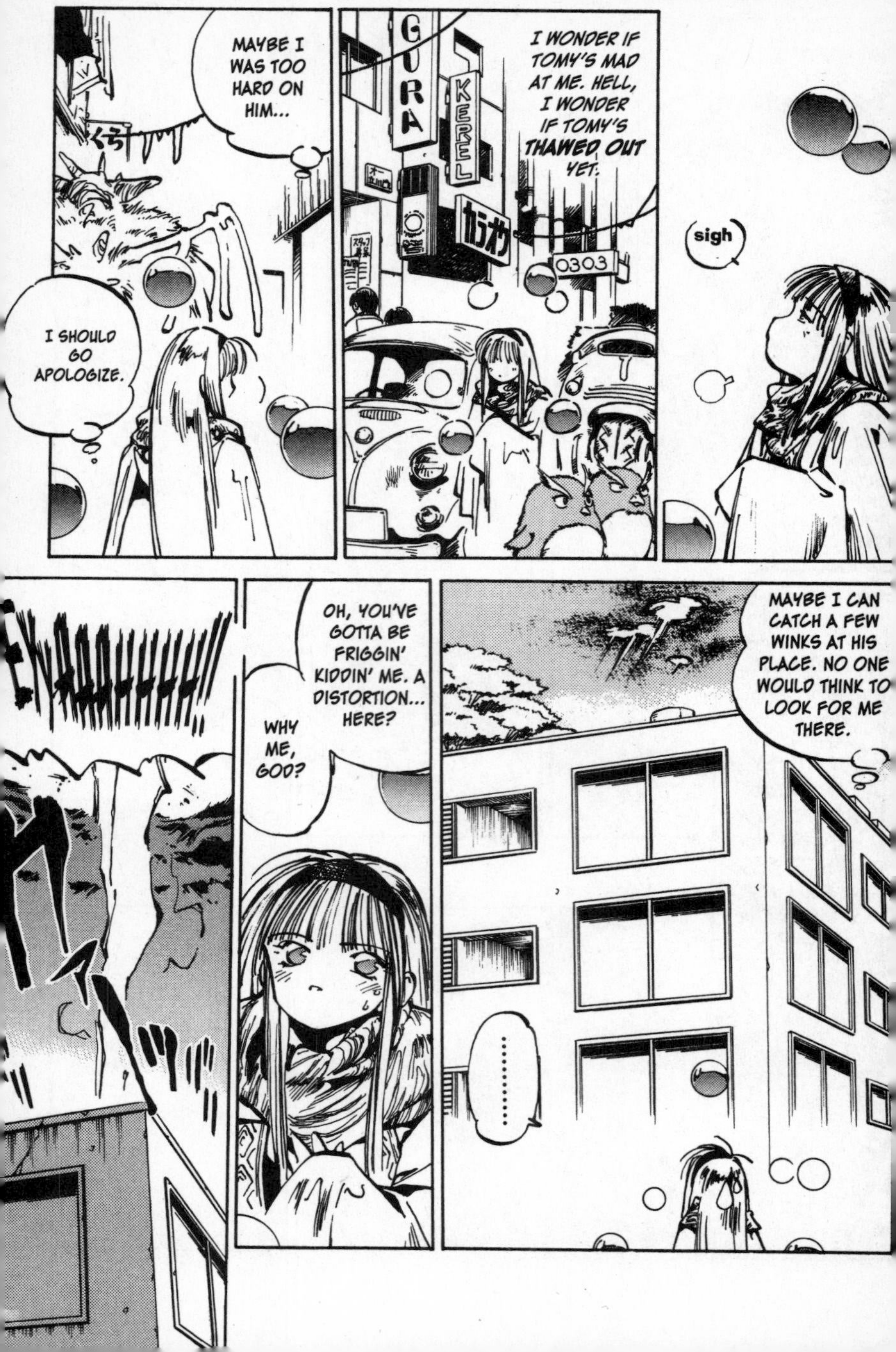
sigh
I WONDER IF TOMY'S MAD AT ME. HELL, I WONDER IF TOMY'S THAWED OUT YET.
MAYBE I WAS TOO HARD ON HIM...
I SHOULD GO APOLOGIZE.
MAYBE I CAN CATCH A FEW WINKS AT HIS PLACE. NO ONE WOULD THINK TO LOOK FOR ME THERE.
......
OH, YOU'VE GOTTA BE FRIGGIN' KIDDIN' ME. A DISTORTION... HERE?
WHY ME, GOD?
EYAAAHHHH!!

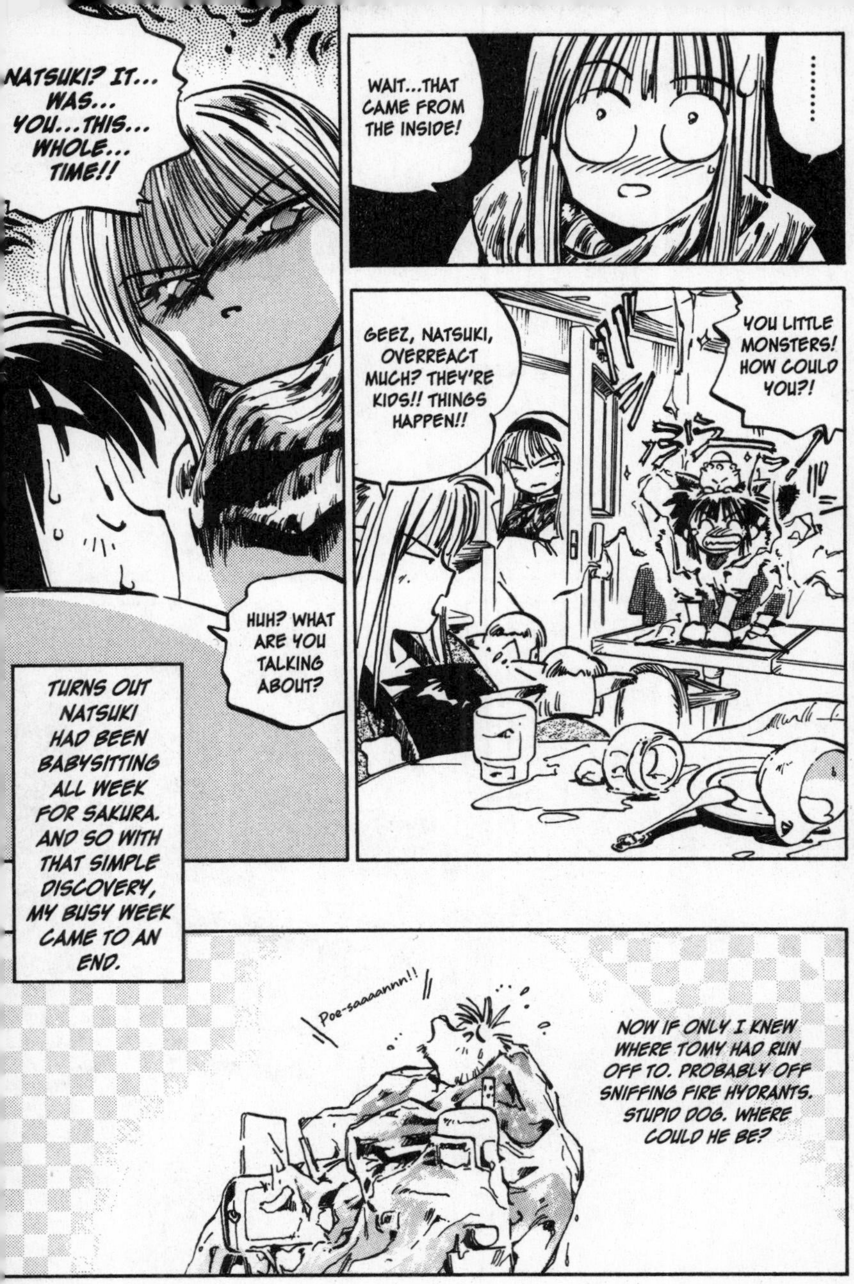
....
WAIT...THAT CAME FROM THE INSIDE!
YOU LITTLE MONSTERS! HOW COULD YOU?!
GEEZ, NATSUKI, OVERREACT MUCH? THEY'RE KIDS!! THINGS HAPPEN!!
NATSUKI? IT... WAS... YOU...THIS... WHOLE... TIME!!
HUH? WHAT ARE YOU TALKING ABOUT?
TURNS OUT NATSUKI HAD BEEN BABYSITTING ALL WEEK FOR SAKURA. AND SO WITH THAT SIMPLE DISCOVERY, MY BUSY WEEK CAME TO AN END.
NOW IF ONLY I KNEW WHERE TOMY HAD RUN OFF TO. PROBABLY OFF SNIFFING FIRE HYDRANTS. STUPID DOG. WHERE COULD HE BE?
Poe-saaaannn!!

Report #25
A Balcony Where The Sun Shines Brightest
Part 1

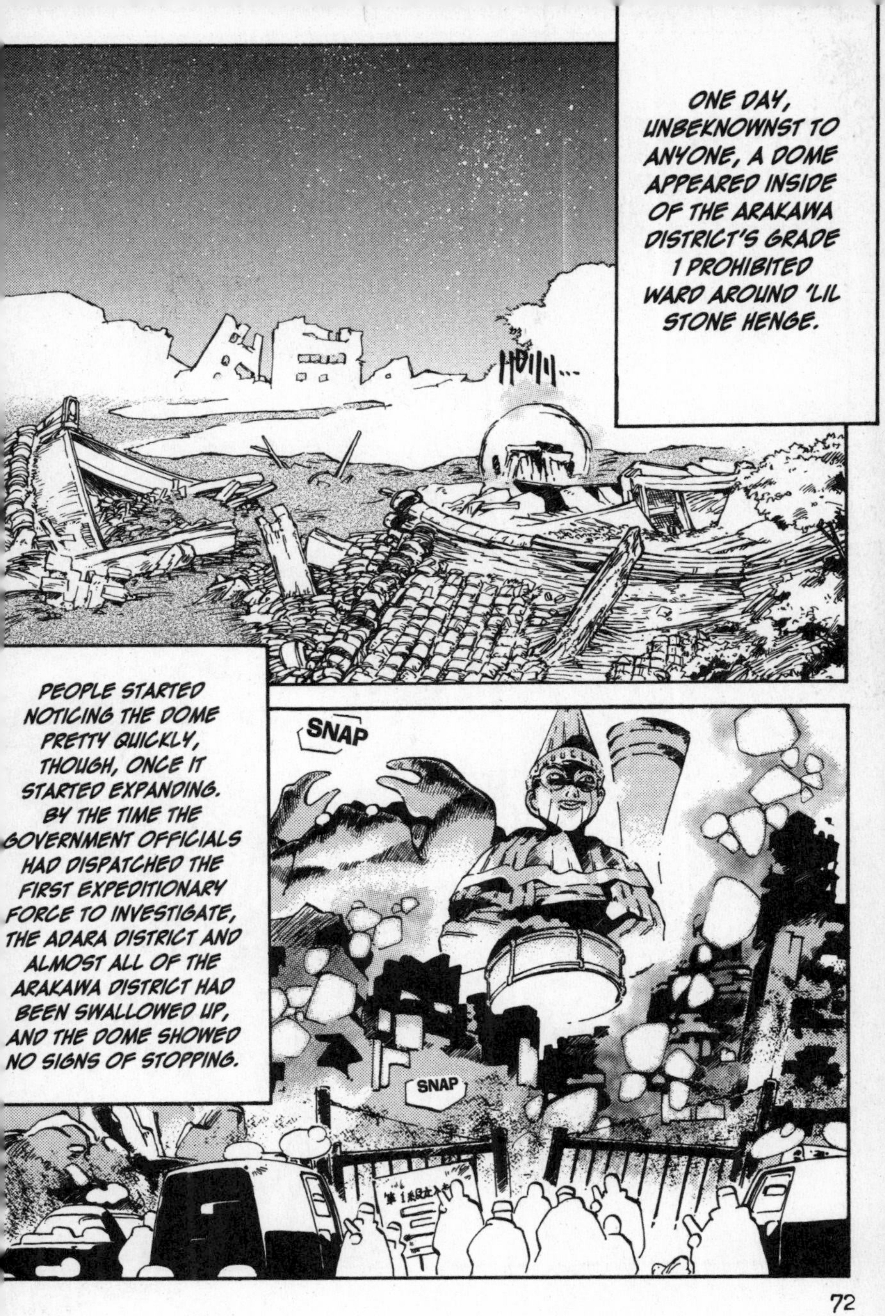
ONE DAY, UNBEKNOWNST TO ANYONE, A DOME APPEARED INSIDE OF THE ARAKAWA DISTRICT'S GRADE 1 PROHIBITED WARD AROUND 'LIL STONE HENGE.
PEOPLE STARTED NOTICING THE DOME PRETTY QUICKLY, THOUGH, ONCE IT STARTED EXPANDING. BY THE TIME THE GOVERNMENT OFFICIALS HAD DISPATCHED THE FIRST EXPEDITIONARY FORCE TO INVESTIGATE, THE ADARA DISTRICT AND ALMOST ALL OF THE ARAKAWA DISTRICT HAD BEEN SWALLOWED UP, AND THE DOME SHOWED NO SIGNS OF STOPPING.
SNAP
SNAP

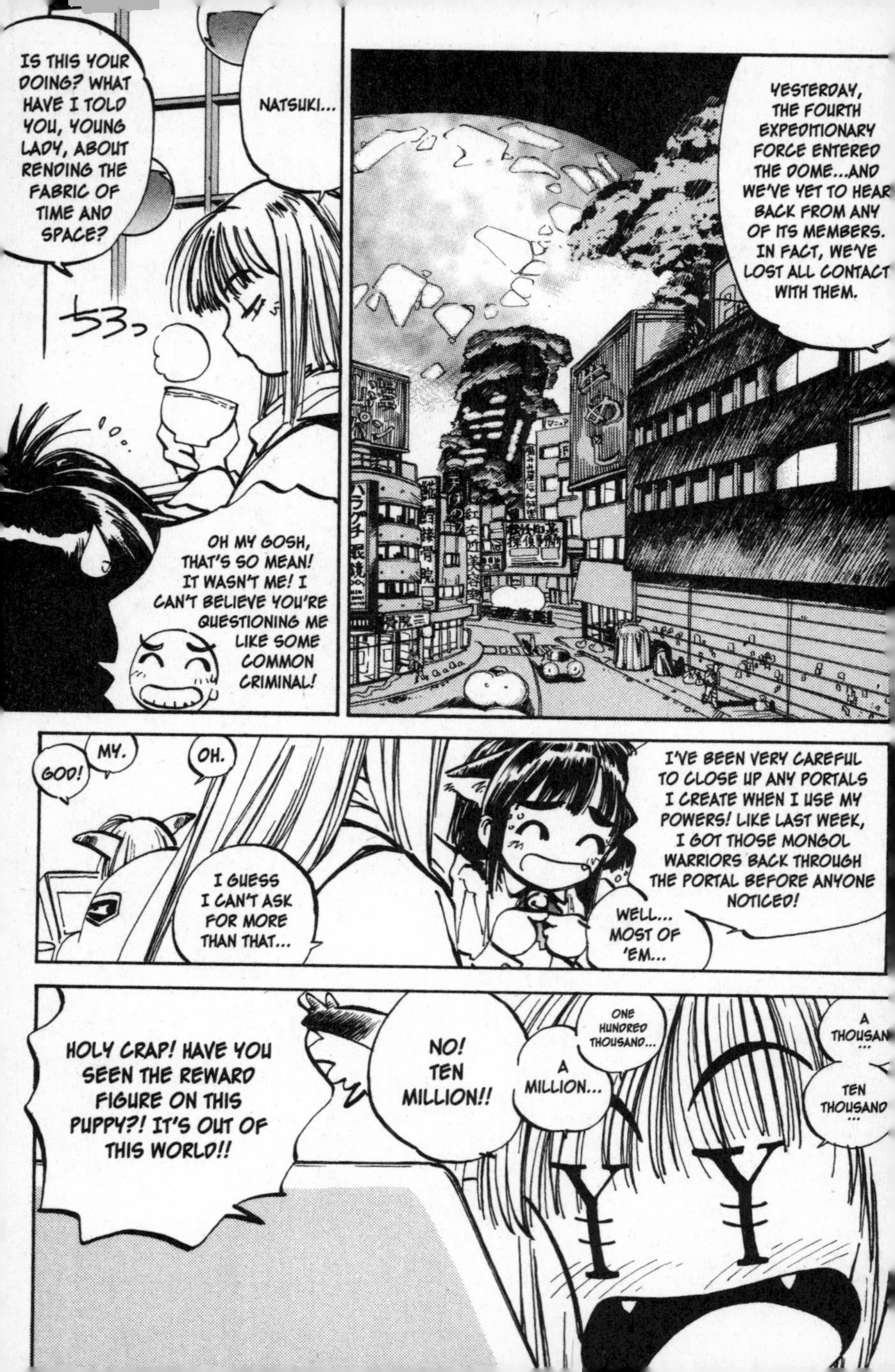
YESTERDAY, THE FOURTH EXPEDITIONARY FORCE ENTERED THE DOME...AND WE'VE YET TO HEAR BACK FROM ANY OF ITS MEMBERS. IN FACT, WE'VE LOST ALL CONTACT WITH THEM.
NATSUKI...
IS THIS YOUR DOING? WHAT HAVE I TOLD YOU, YOUNG LADY, ABOUT RENDING THE FABRIC OF TIME AND SPACE?
ちろっ
OH MY GOSH, THAT'S SO MEAN! IT WASN'T ME! I CAN'T BELIEVE YOU'RE QUESTIONING ME LIKE SOME COMMON CRIMINAL!
I'VE BEEN VERY CAREFUL TO CLOSE UP ANY PORTALS I CREATE WHEN I USE MY POWERS! LIKE LAST WEEK, I GOT THOSE MONGOL WARRIORS BACK THROUGH THE PORTAL BEFORE ANYONE NOTICED!
WELL... MOST OF 'EM...
I GUESS I CAN'T ASK FOR MORE THAN THAT...
OH.
MY.
GOD!
A THOUSAN...
TEN THOUSAND...
ONE HUNDRED THOUSAND...
A MILLION...
NO! TEN MILLION!!
HOLY CRAP! HAVE YOU SEEN THE REWARD FIGURE ON THIS PUPPY?! IT'S OUT OF THIS WORLD!!

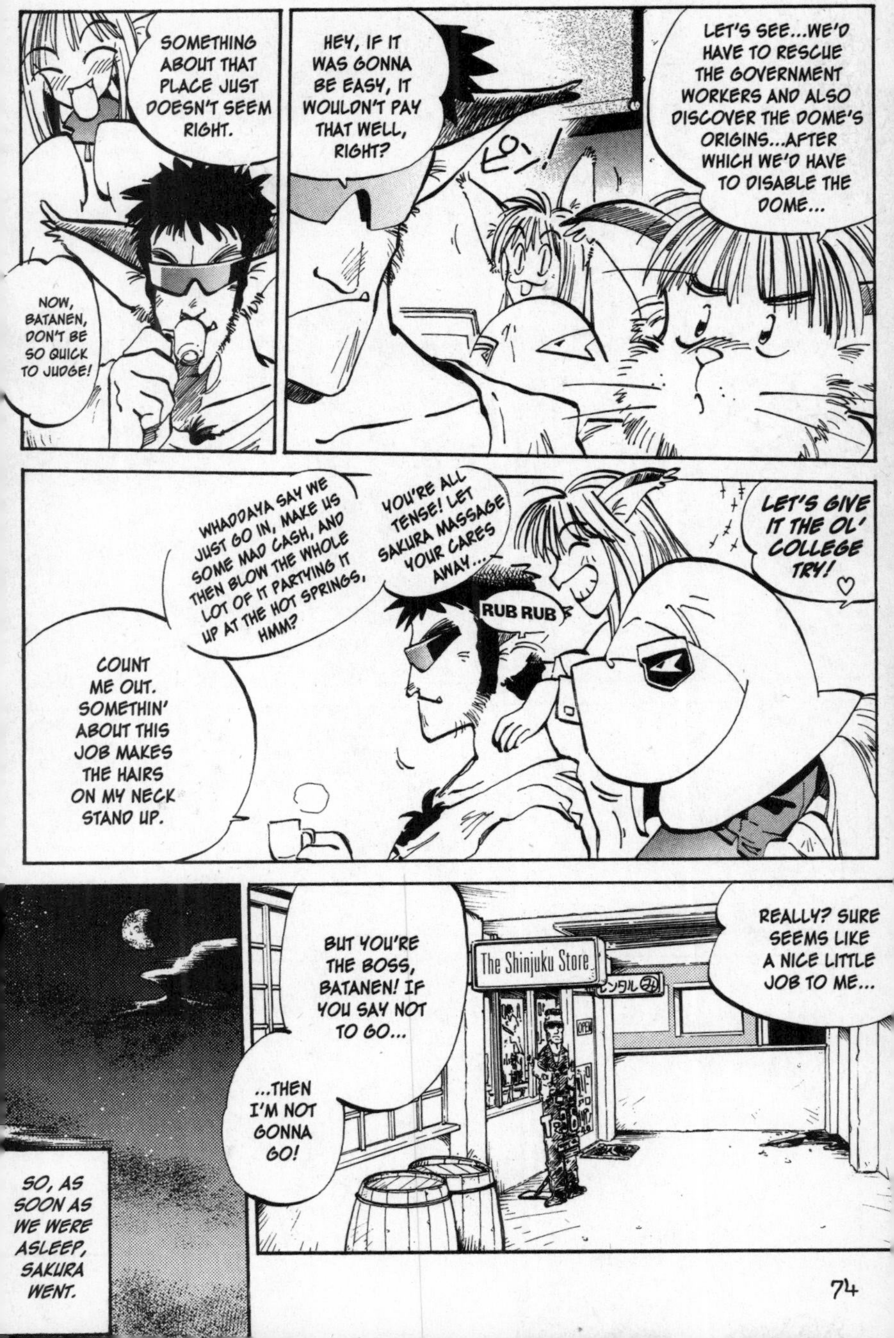
LET'S SEE...WE'D HAVE TO RESCUE THE GOVERNMENT WORKERS AND ALSO DISCOVER THE DOME'S ORIGINS...AFTER WHICH WE'D HAVE TO DISABLE THE DOME...
HEY, IF IT WAS GONNA BE EASY, IT WOULDN'T PAY THAT WELL, RIGHT?
SOMETHING ABOUT THAT PLACE JUST DOESN'T SEEM RIGHT.
NOW, BATANEN, DON'T BE SO QUICK TO JUDGE!
LET'S GIVE IT THE OL' COLLEGE TRY! ♡
YOU'RE ALL TENSE! LET SAKURA MASSAGE YOUR CARES AWAY...
RUB RUB
WHADDAYA SAY WE JUST GO IN, MAKE US SOME MAD CASH, AND THEN BLOW THE WHOLE LOT OF IT PARTYING IT UP AT THE HOT SPRINGS, HMM?
COUNT ME OUT. SOMETHIN' ABOUT THIS JOB MAKES THE HAIRS ON MY NECK STAND UP.
REALLY? SURE SEEMS LIKE A NICE LITTLE JOB TO ME...
The Shinjuku Store
BUT YOU'RE THE BOSS, BATANEN! IF YOU SAY NOT TO GO...
...THEN I'M NOT GONNA GO!
SO, AS SOON AS WE WERE ASLEEP, SAKURA WENT.

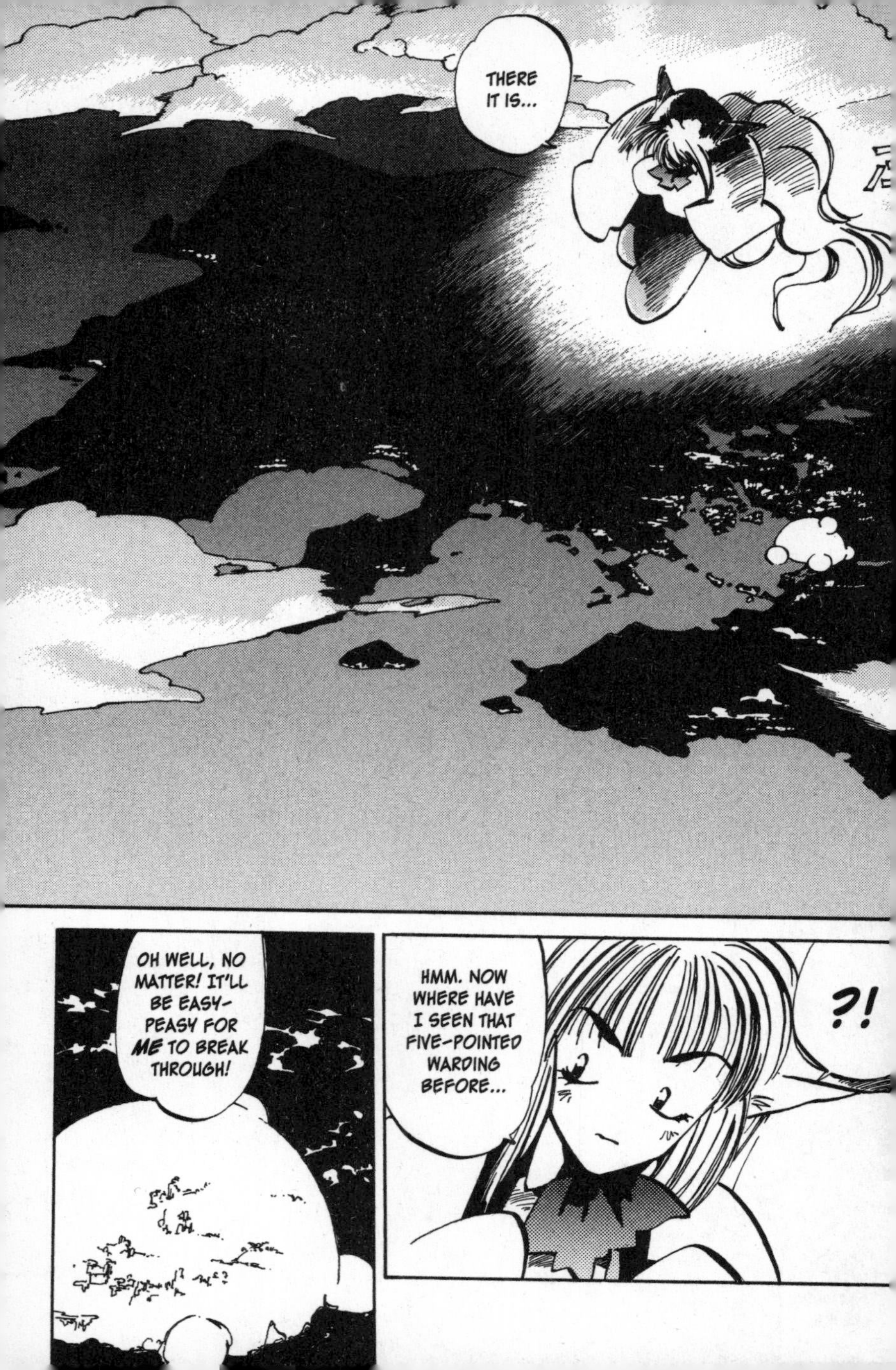
THERE IT IS...
?!
HMM. NOW WHERE HAVE I SEEN THAT FIVE-POINTED WARDING BEFORE...
OH WELL, NO MATTER! IT'LL BE EASY-PEASY FOR *ME* TO BREAK THROUGH!

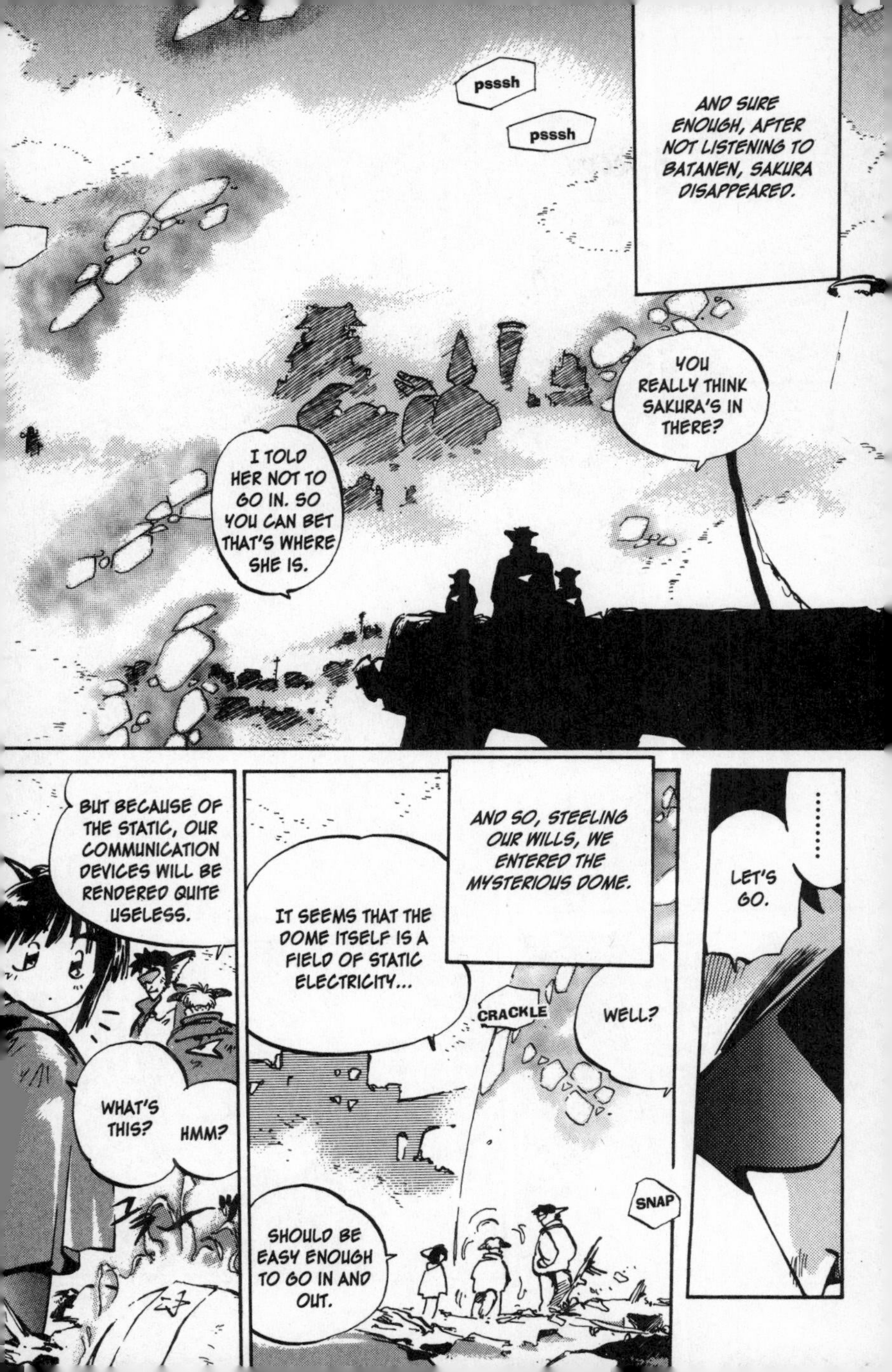
AND SURE ENOUGH, AFTER NOT LISTENING TO BATANEN, SAKURA DISAPPEARED.
psssh
psssh
YOU REALLY THINK SAKURA'S IN THERE?
I TOLD HER NOT TO GO IN. SO YOU CAN BET THAT'S WHERE SHE IS.
......
LET'S GO.
AND SO, STEELING OUR WILLS, WE ENTERED THE MYSTERIOUS DOME.
WELL?
CRACKLE
IT SEEMS THAT THE DOME ITSELF IS A FIELD OF STATIC ELECTRICITY...
SNAP
SHOULD BE EASY ENOUGH TO GO IN AND OUT.
BUT BECAUSE OF THE STATIC, OUR COMMUNICATION DEVICES WILL BE RENDERED QUITE USELESS.
WHAT'S THIS?
HMM?

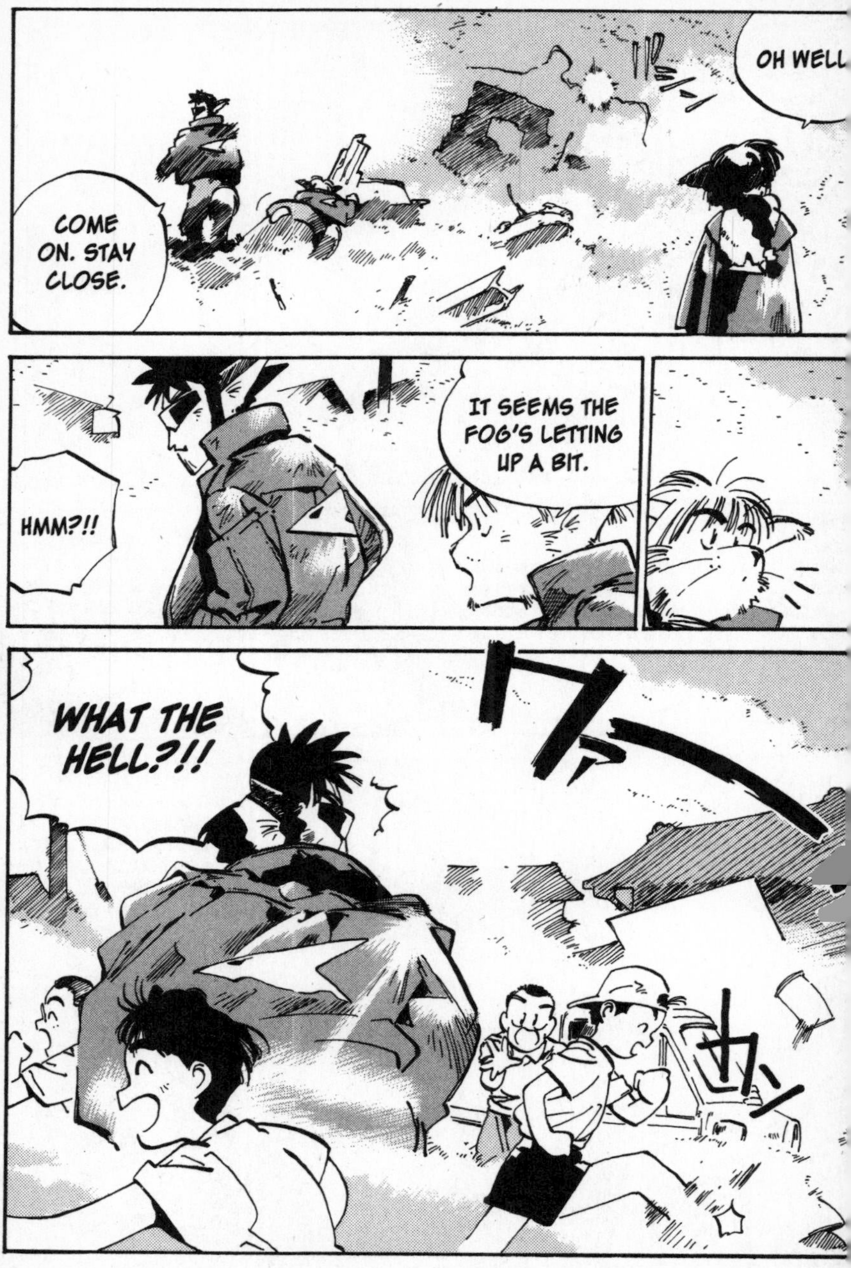
OH WELL
COME ON. STAY CLOSE.
IT SEEMS THE FOG'S LETTING UP A BIT.
HMM?!!
ワァー
WHAT THE HELL?!!
カン

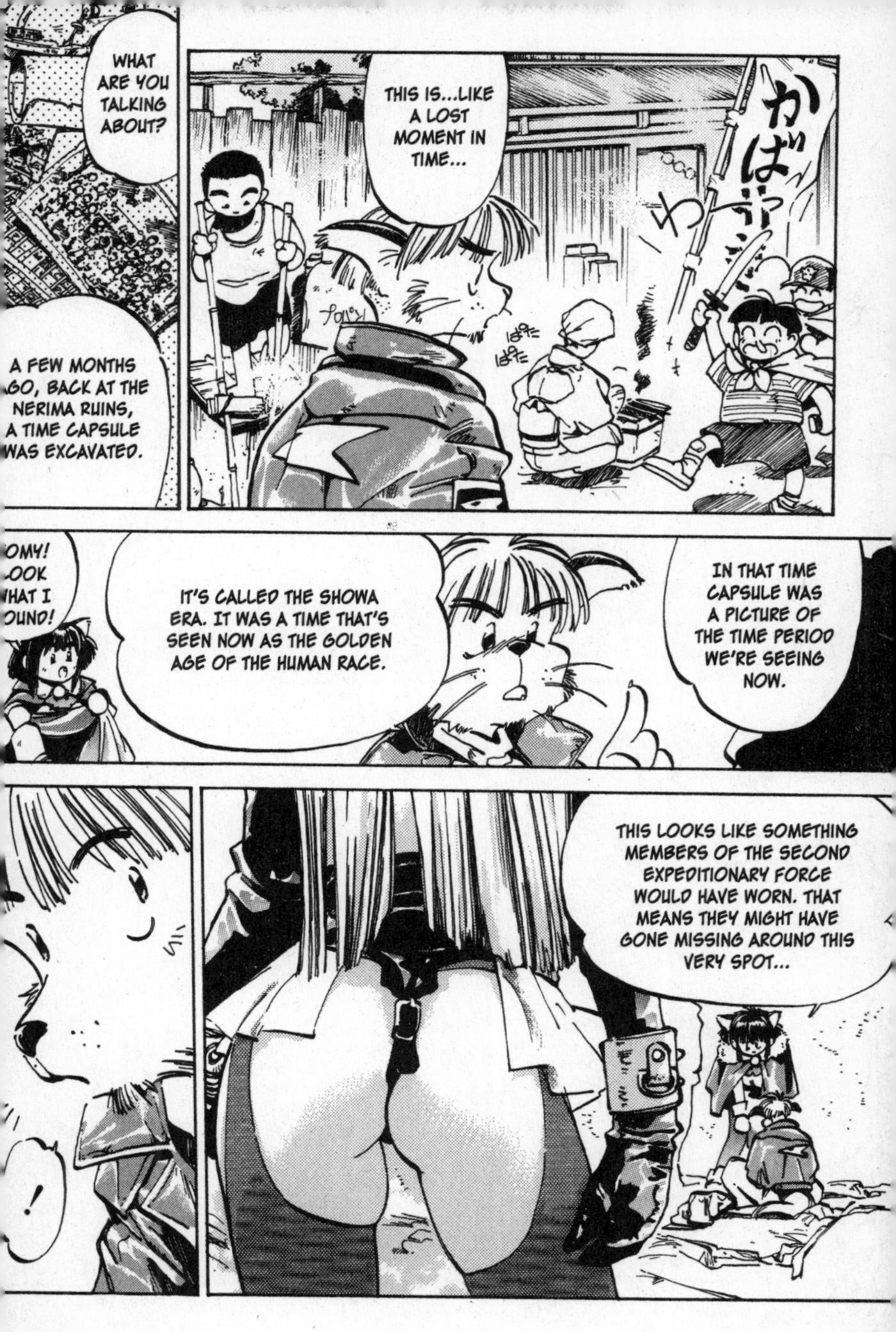
THIS IS...LIKE A LOST MOMENT IN TIME...
WHAT ARE YOU TALKING ABOUT?
A FEW MONTHS AGO, BACK AT THE NERIMA RUINS, A TIME CAPSULE WAS EXCAVATED.
IN THAT TIME CAPSULE WAS A PICTURE OF THE TIME PERIOD WE'RE SEEING NOW.
IT'S CALLED THE SHOWA ERA. IT WAS A TIME THAT'S SEEN NOW AS THE GOLDEN AGE OF THE HUMAN RACE.
OMY! OOK HAT I OUND!
THIS LOOKS LIKE SOMETHING MEMBERS OF THE SECOND EXPEDITIONARY FORCE WOULD HAVE WORN. THAT MEANS THEY MIGHT HAVE GONE MISSING AROUND THIS VERY SPOT...
!

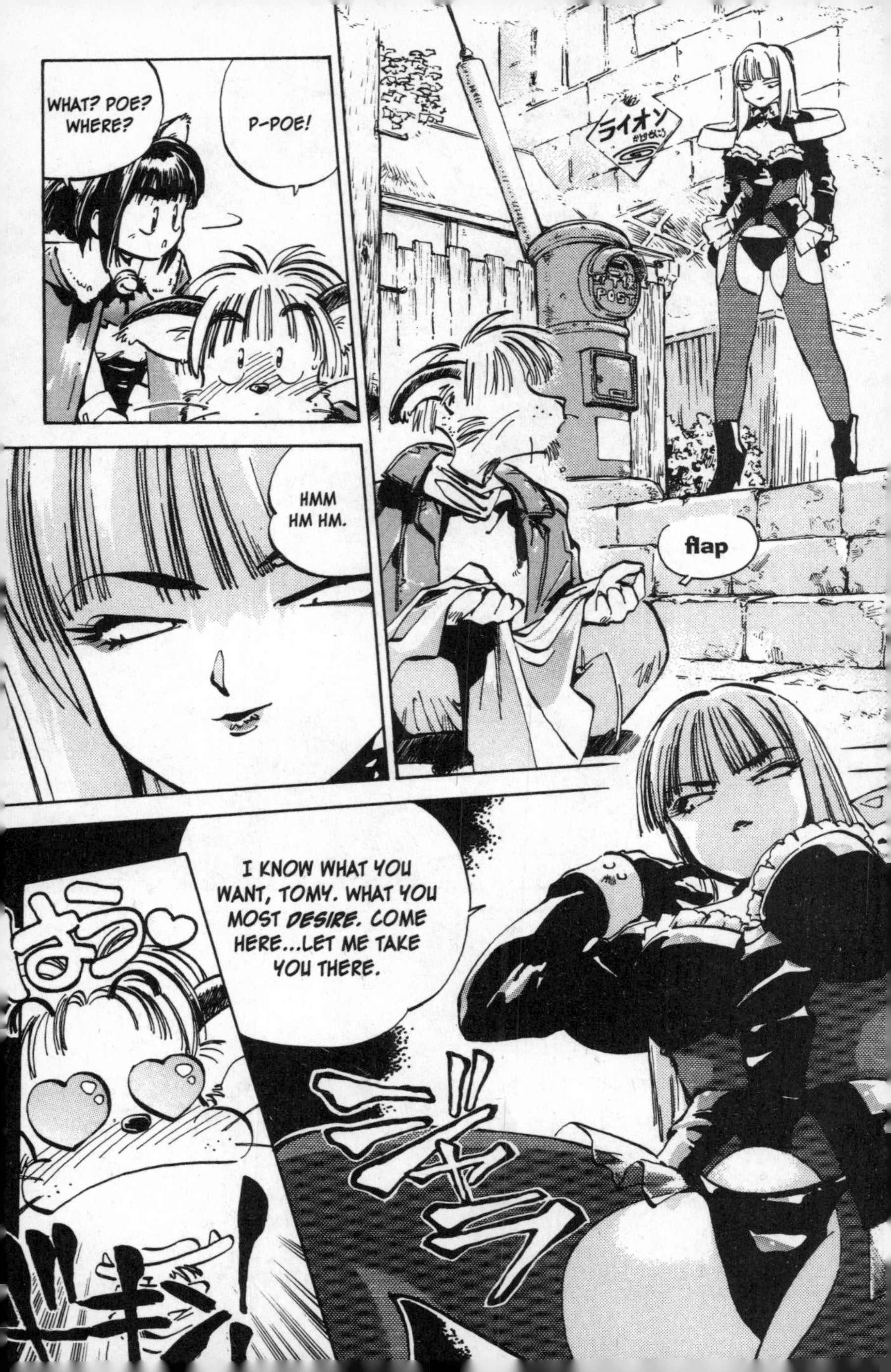
ライオン
flap
P-POE!
WHAT? POE? WHERE?
HMM HM HM.
I KNOW WHAT YOU WANT, TOMY. WHAT YOU MOST *DESIRE*. COME HERE...LET ME TAKE YOU THERE.

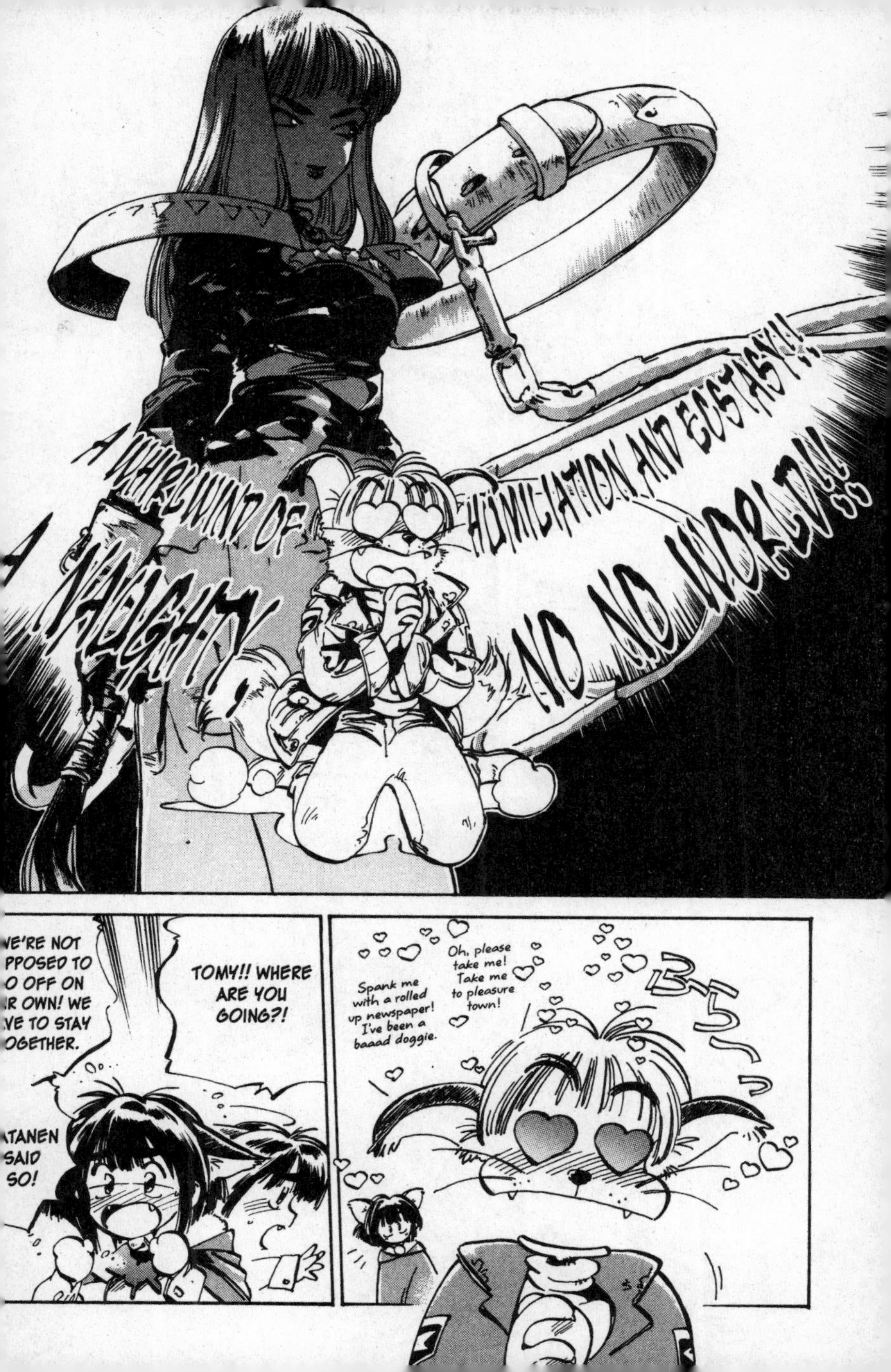
A WHIRLWIND OF HUMILIATION AND ECSTASY!!
A NAUGHTY NO NO WORLD!!
Oh, please take me! Take me to pleasure town!
Spank me with a rolled up newspaper! I've been a baaad doggie.
TOMY!! WHERE ARE YOU GOING?!
E'RE NOT PPOSED TO O OFF ON R OWN! WE VE TO STAY OGETHER.
ATANEN SAID SO!

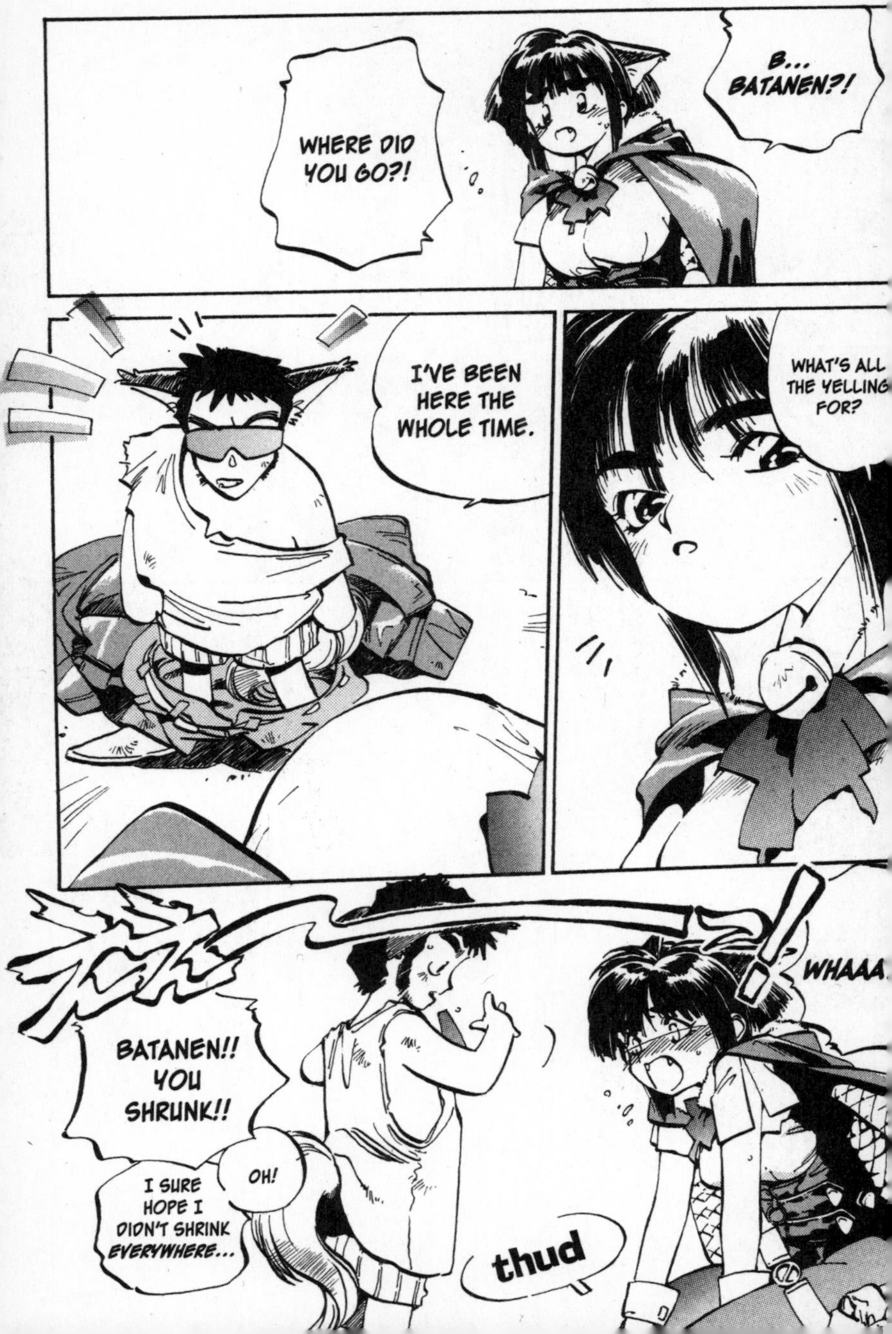
B... BATANEN?!
WHERE DID YOU GO?!
WHAT'S ALL THE YELLING FOR?
I'VE BEEN HERE THE WHOLE TIME.
WHAAA
BATANEN!! YOU SHRUNK!!
OH!
I SURE HOPE I DIDN'T SHRINK *EVERYWHERE*...
thud

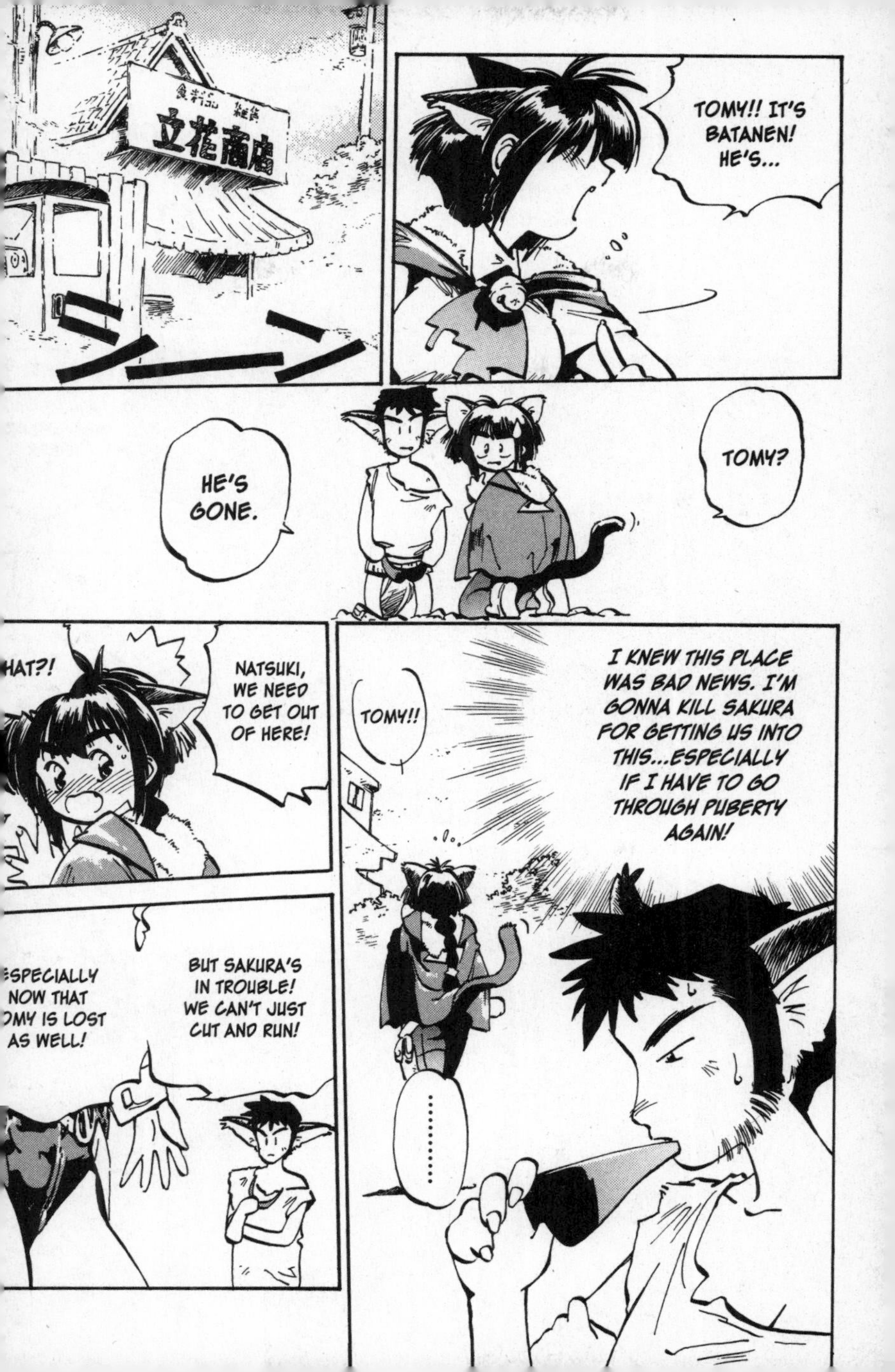
TOMY!! IT'S BATANEN! HE'S...
立花商店
TOMY?
HE'S GONE.
I KNEW THIS PLACE WAS BAD NEWS. I'M GONNA KILL SAKURA FOR GETTING US INTO THIS...ESPECIALLY IF I HAVE TO GO THROUGH PUBERTY AGAIN!
TOMY!!
......
NATSUKI, WE NEED TO GET OUT OF HERE!
HAT?!
BUT SAKURA'S IN TROUBLE! WE CAN'T JUST CUT AND RUN!
SPECIALLY NOW THAT OMY IS LOST AS WELL!

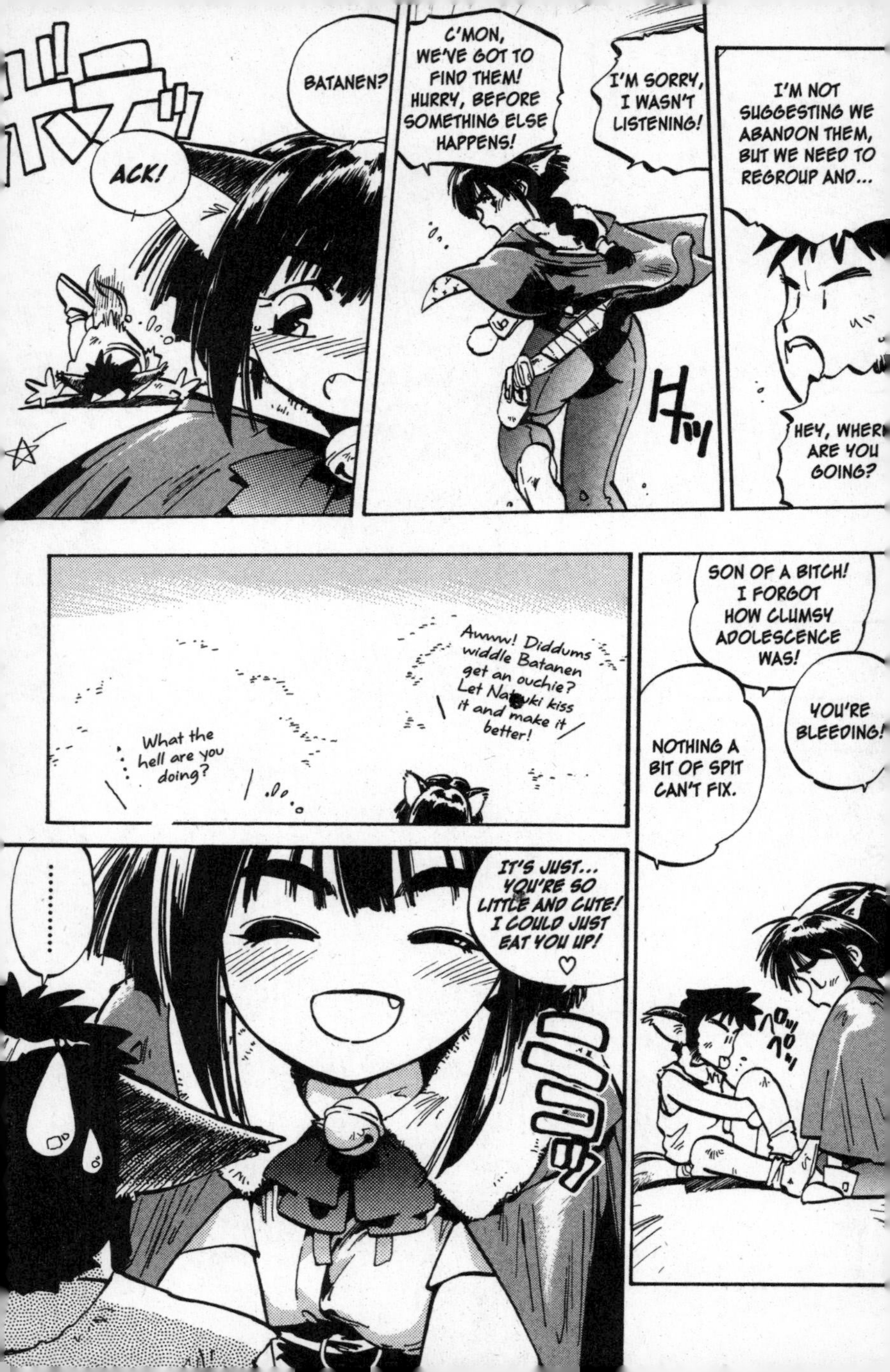
I'M NOT SUGGESTING WE ABANDON THEM, BUT WE NEED TO REGROUP AND...
HEY, WHER ARE YOU GOING?
I'M SORRY, I WASN'T LISTENING!
C'MON, WE'VE GOT TO FIND THEM! HURRY, BEFORE SOMETHING ELSE HAPPENS!
BATANEN?
ACK!
SON OF A BITCH! I FORGOT HOW CLUMSY ADOLESCENCE WAS!
YOU'RE BLEEDING!
NOTHING A BIT OF SPIT CAN'T FIX.
Awww! Diddums widdle Batanen get an ouchie? Let Natsuki kiss it and make it better!
What the hell are you doing?
IT'S JUST... YOU'RE SO LITTLE AND CUTE! I COULD JUST EAT YOU UP! ♡
......

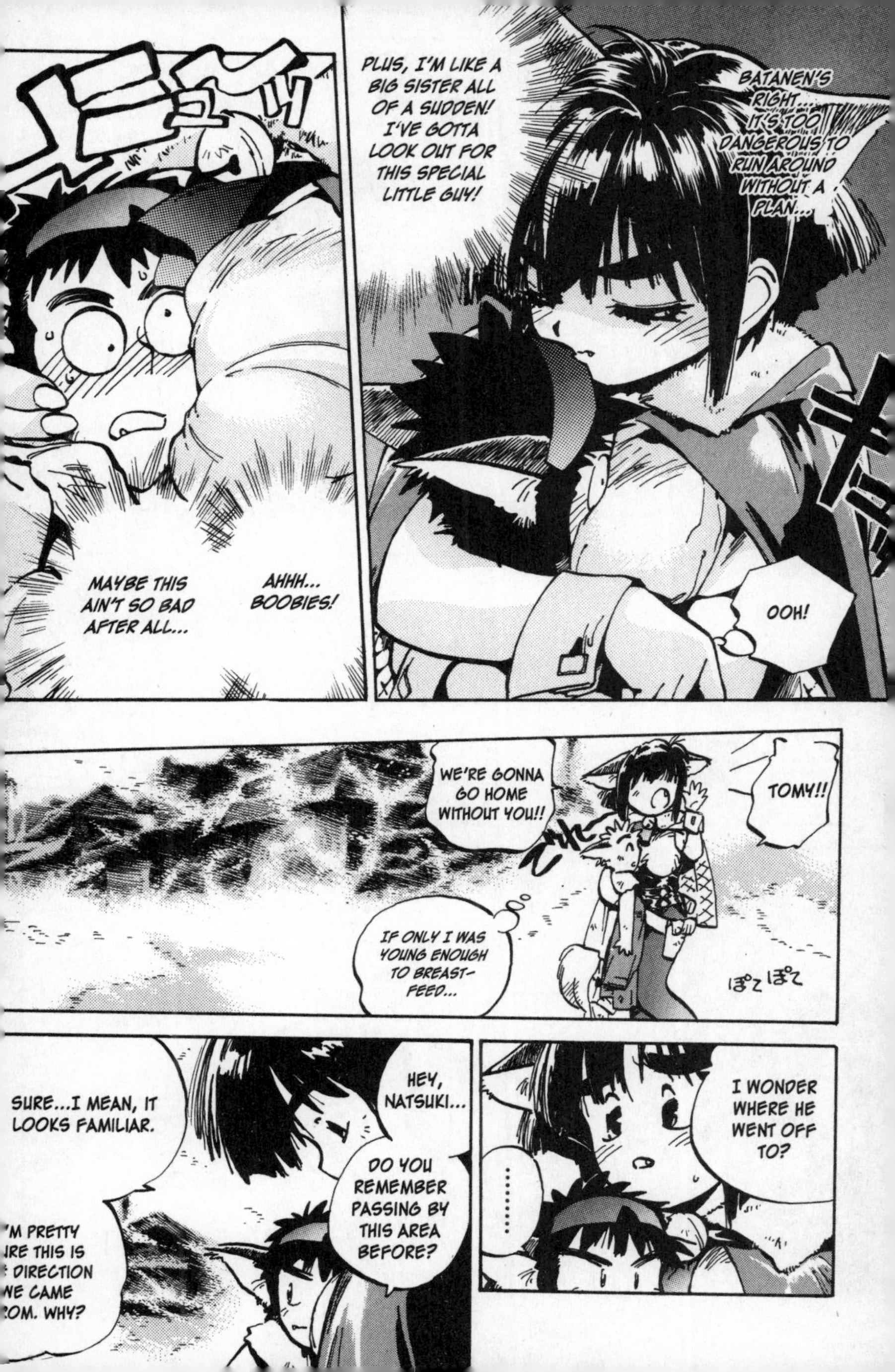

BATANEN'S RIGHT... IT'S TOO DANGEROUS TO RUN AROUND WITHOUT A PLAN...
PLUS, I'M LIKE A BIG SISTER ALL OF A SUDDEN! I'VE GOTTA LOOK OUT FOR THIS SPECIAL LITTLE GUY!
OOH!
AHHH... BOOBIES!
MAYBE THIS AIN'T SO BAD AFTER ALL...
TOMY!!
WE'RE GONNA GO HOME WITHOUT YOU!!
IF ONLY I WAS YOUNG ENOUGH TO BREAST-FEED...
ぽてぽて
I WONDER WHERE HE WENT OFF TO?
......
HEY, NATSUKI...
DO YOU REMEMBER PASSING BY THIS AREA BEFORE?
SURE...I MEAN, IT LOOKS FAMILIAR.
'M PRETTY URE THIS IS E DIRECTION WE CAME ROM. WHY?

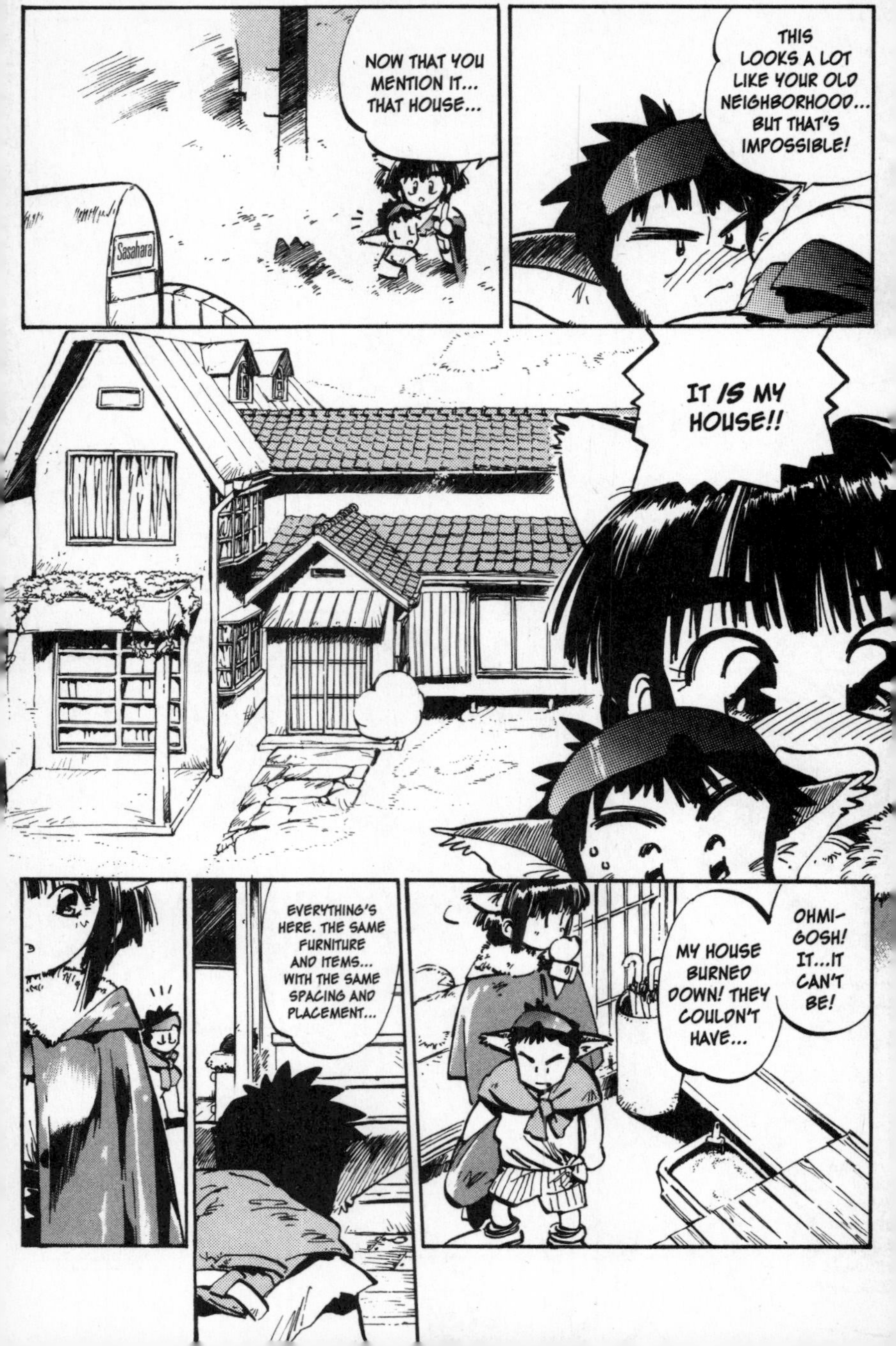
THIS LOOKS A LOT LIKE YOUR OLD NEIGHBORHOOD... BUT THAT'S IMPOSSIBLE!
NOW THAT YOU MENTION IT... THAT HOUSE...
Sasahara
IT *IS* MY HOUSE!!
OHMI-GOSH! IT...IT CAN'T BE!
MY HOUSE BURNED DOWN! THEY COULDN'T HAVE...
EVERYTHING'S HERE. THE SAME FURNITURE AND ITEMS... WITH THE SAME SPACING AND PLACEMENT...

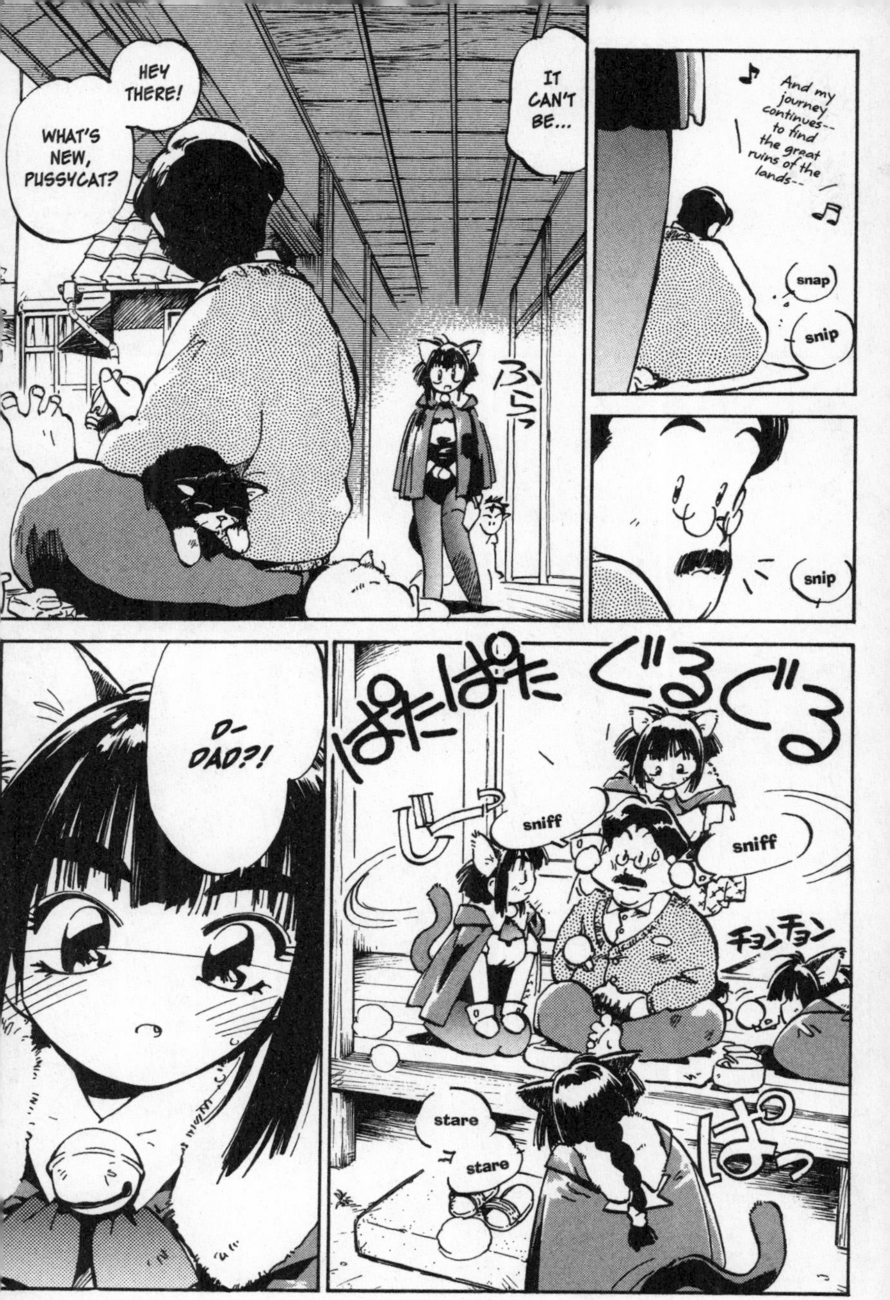
And my journey continues-- to find the great ruins of the lands--
snap
snip
snip
IT CAN'T BE...
HEY THERE!
WHAT'S NEW, PUSSYCAT?
ふらっ
ぱたぱた ぐるぐる
sniff
sniff
チョンチョン
stare
stare
ぱっ
D-DAD?!

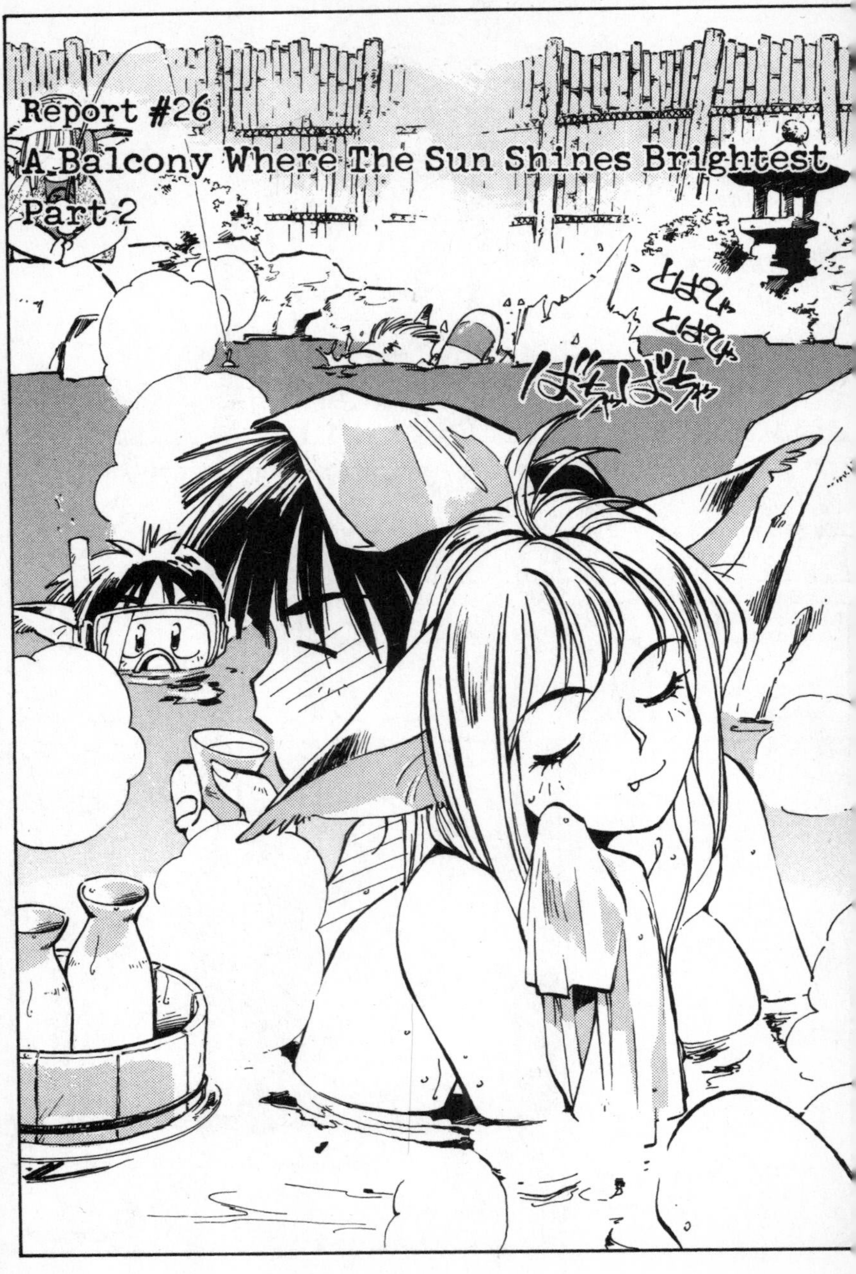
Report #26
A Balcony Where The Sun Shines Brightest
Part 2
とぱしゃ
とぱしゃ
ばちゃばちゃ

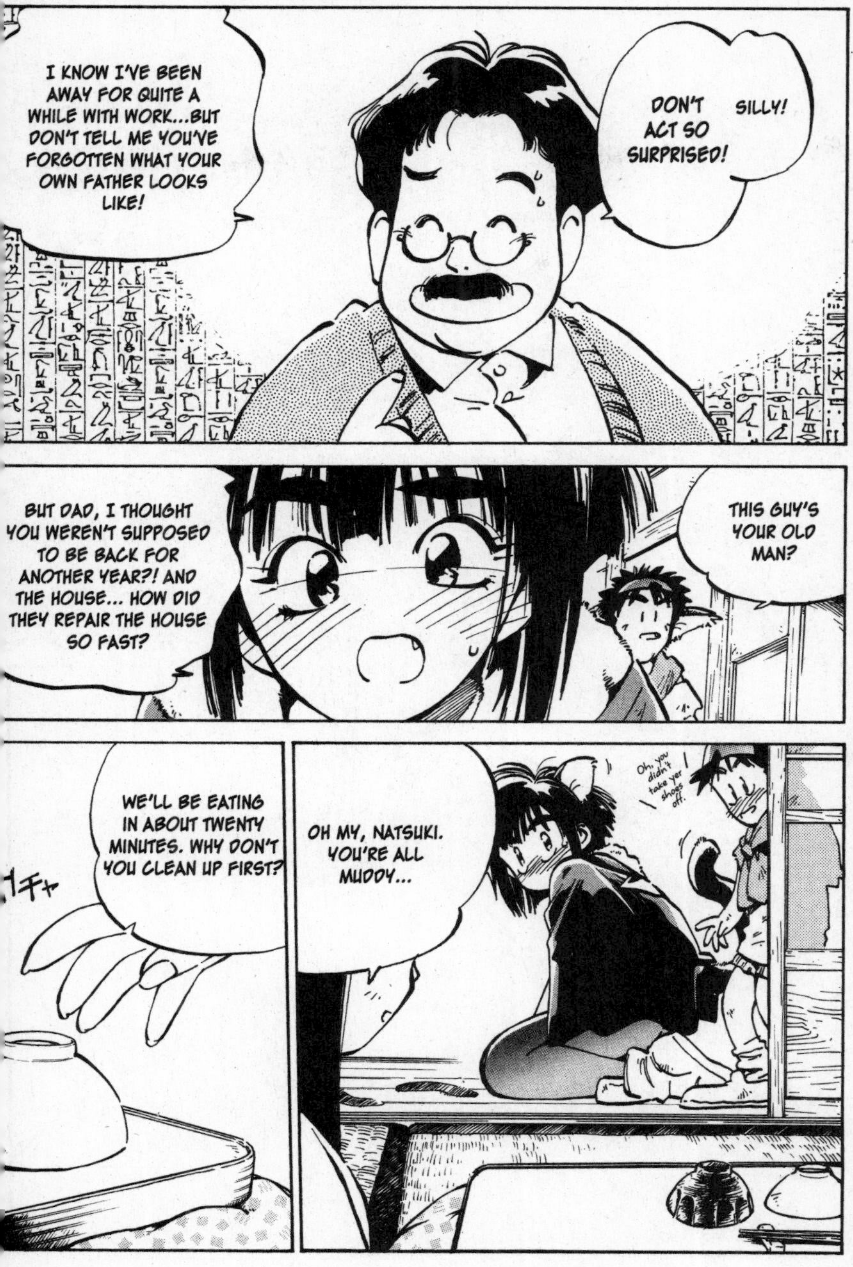
DON'T ACT SO SURPRISED! SILLY!
I KNOW I'VE BEEN AWAY FOR QUITE A WHILE WITH WORK...BUT DON'T TELL ME YOU'VE FORGOTTEN WHAT YOUR OWN FATHER LOOKS LIKE!
THIS GUY'S YOUR OLD MAN?
BUT DAD, I THOUGHT YOU WEREN'T SUPPOSED TO BE BACK FOR ANOTHER YEAR?! AND THE HOUSE... HOW DID THEY REPAIR THE HOUSE SO FAST?
Oh, you didn't take yer shoes off.
OH MY, NATSUKI. YOU'RE ALL MUDDY...
WE'LL BE EATING IN ABOUT TWENTY MINUTES. WHY DON'T YOU CLEAN UP FIRST?
チャ

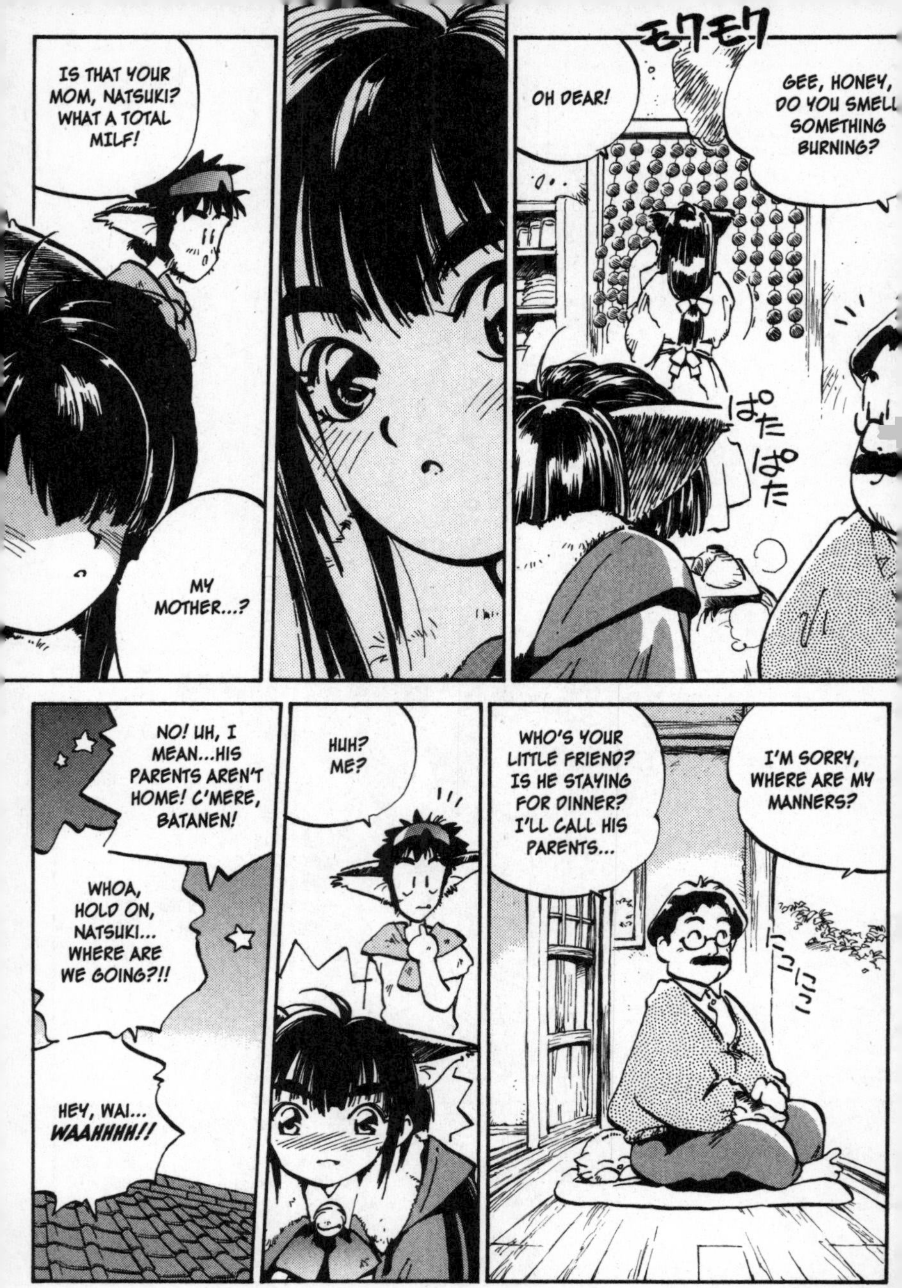
モクモク
GEE, HONEY, DO YOU SMELL SOMETHING BURNING?
OH DEAR!
ぱたぱた
IS THAT YOUR MOM, NATSUKI? WHAT A TOTAL MILF!
MY MOTHER...?
I'M SORRY, WHERE ARE MY MANNERS?
WHO'S YOUR LITTLE FRIEND? IS HE STAYING FOR DINNER? I'LL CALL HIS PARENTS...
にこにこ
HUH? ME?
NO! UH, I MEAN...HIS PARENTS AREN'T HOME! C'MERE, BATANEN!
WHOA, HOLD ON, NATSUKI... WHERE ARE WE GOING?!!
HEY, WAI... ***WAAHHHH!!***

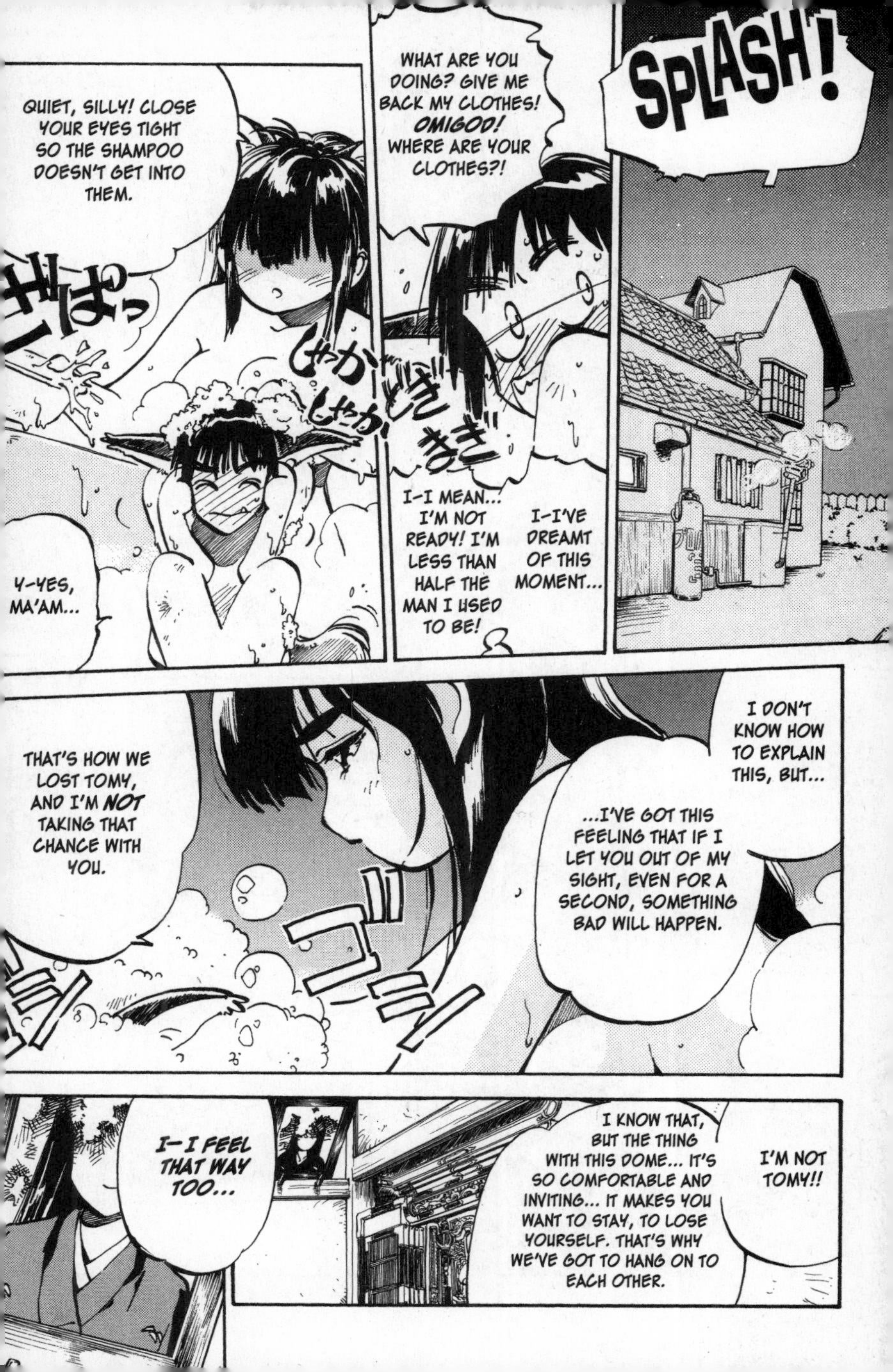
SPLASH!
WHAT ARE YOU DOING? GIVE ME BACK MY CLOTHES! *OMIGOD!* WHERE ARE YOUR CLOTHES?!
I-I'VE DREAMT OF THIS MOMENT...
I-I MEAN... I'M NOT READY! I'M LESS THAN HALF THE MAN I USED TO BE!
QUIET, SILLY! CLOSE YOUR EYES TIGHT SO THE SHAMPOO DOESN'T GET INTO THEM.
Y-YES, MA'AM...
I DON'T KNOW HOW TO EXPLAIN THIS, BUT...
...I'VE GOT THIS FEELING THAT IF I LET YOU OUT OF MY SIGHT, EVEN FOR A SECOND, SOMETHING BAD WILL HAPPEN.
THAT'S HOW WE LOST TOMY, AND I'M *NOT* TAKING THAT CHANCE WITH YOU.
I'M NOT TOMY!!
I KNOW THAT, BUT THE THING WITH THIS DOME... IT'S SO COMFORTABLE AND INVITING... IT MAKES YOU WANT TO STAY, TO LOSE YOURSELF. THAT'S WHY WE'VE GOT TO HANG ON TO EACH OTHER.
I-I FEEL THAT WAY TOO...

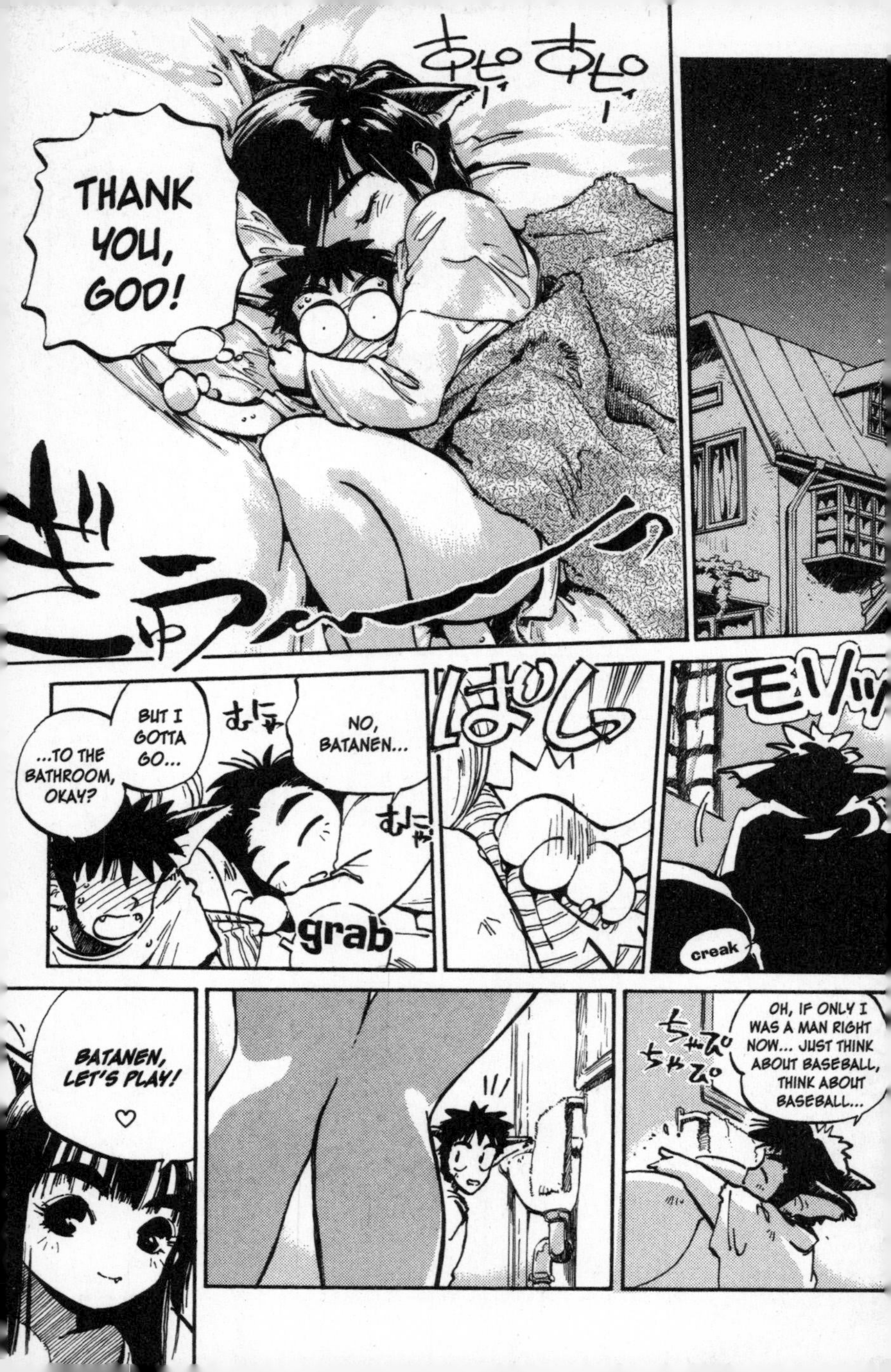
THANK YOU, GOD!
creak
NO, BATANEN...
BUT I GOTTA GO...
...TO THE BATHROOM, OKAY?
grab
OH, IF ONLY I WAS A MAN RIGHT NOW... JUST THINK ABOUT BASEBALL, THINK ABOUT BASEBALL...
BATANEN, LET'S PLAY! ♡

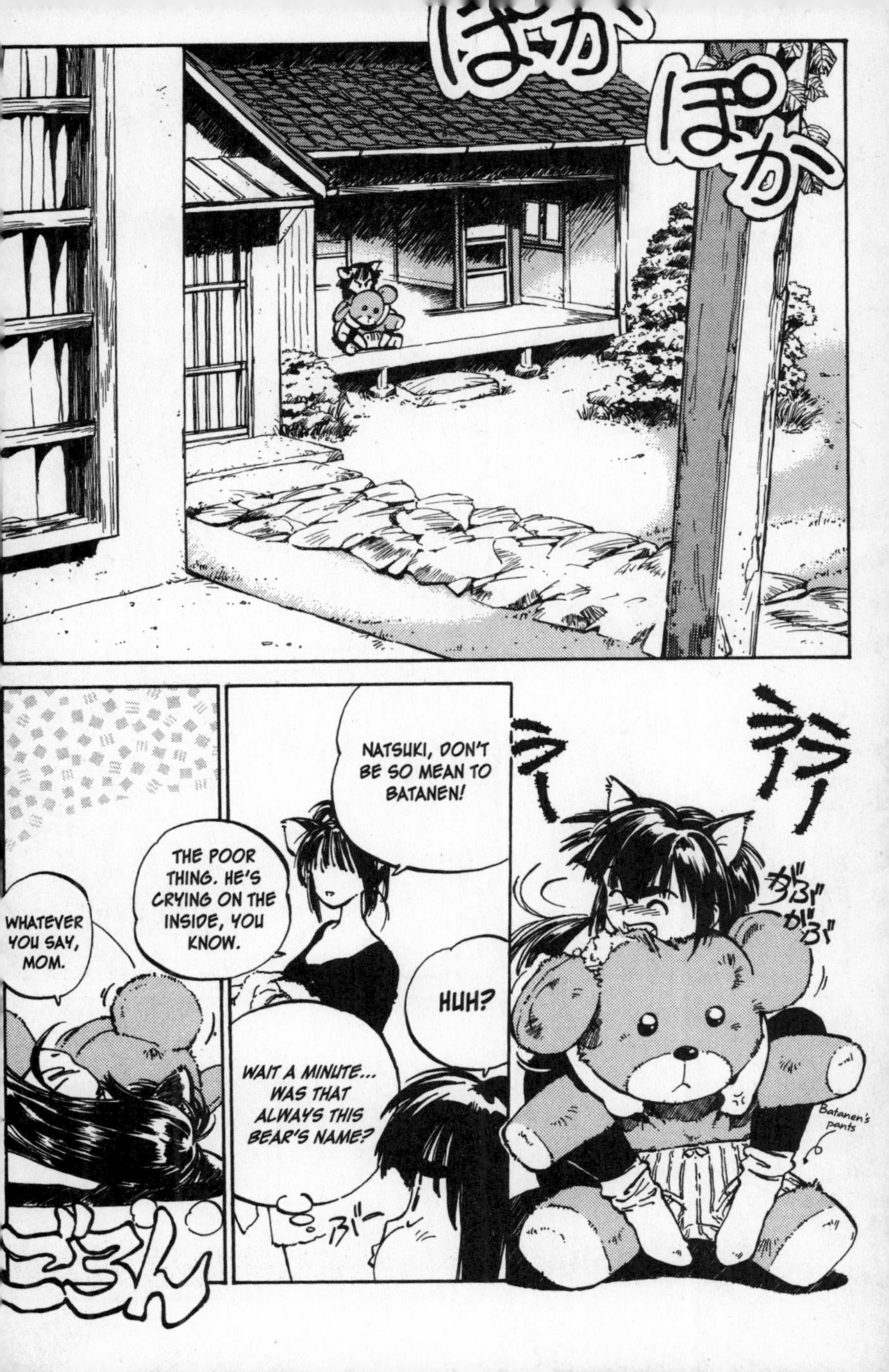
ぽか
ぽか
がぶ
がぶ
Batanen's pants
NATSUKI, DON'T BE SO MEAN TO BATANEN!
THE POOR THING. HE'S CRYING ON THE INSIDE, YOU KNOW.
HUH?
WAIT A MINUTE... WAS THAT ALWAYS THIS BEAR'S NAME?
WHATEVER YOU SAY, MOM.

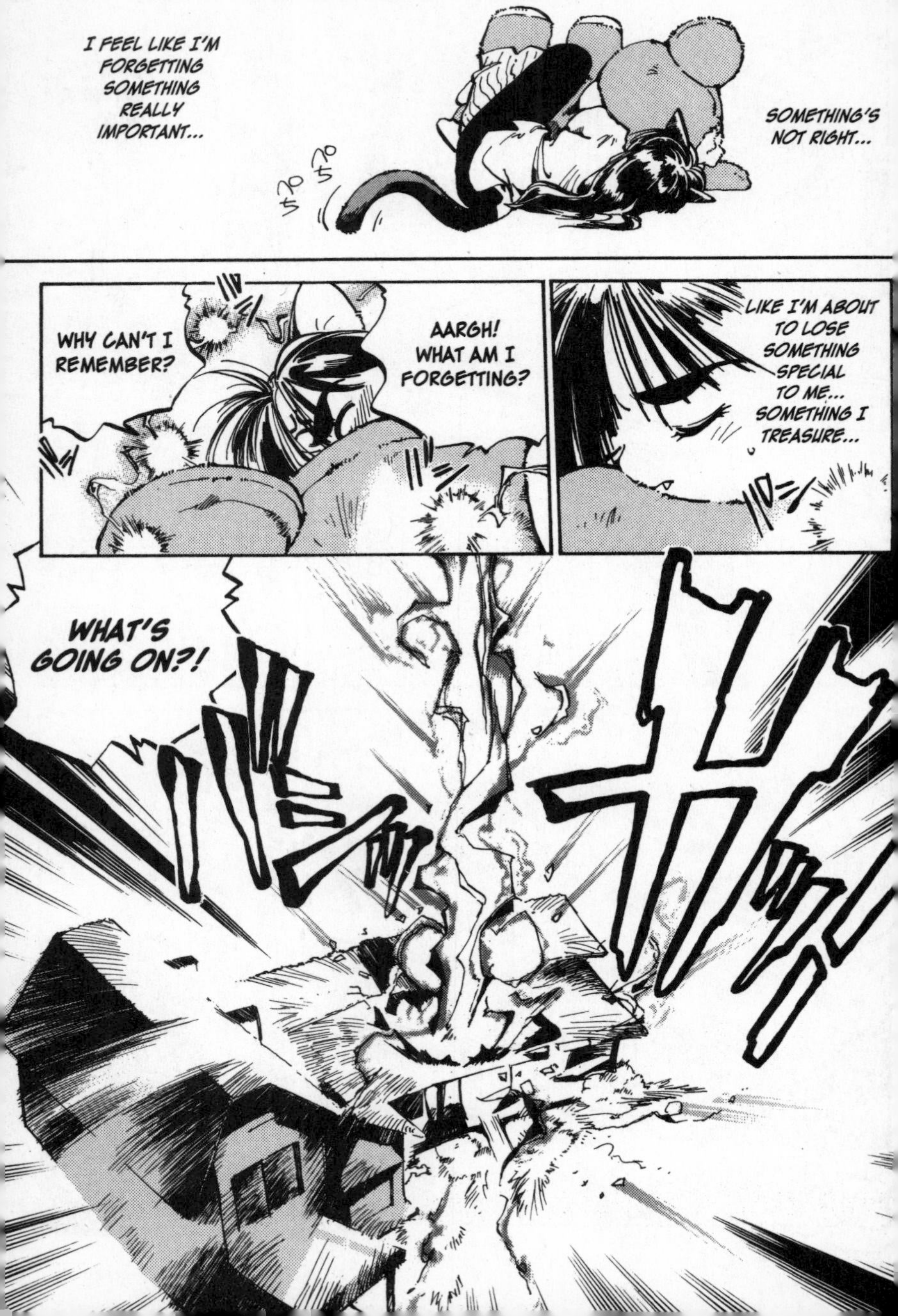
SOMETHING'S NOT RIGHT...
I FEEL LIKE I'M FORGETTING SOMETHING REALLY IMPORTANT...
LIKE I'M ABOUT TO LOSE SOMETHING SPECIAL TO ME... SOMETHING I TREASURE...
AARGH! WHAT AM I FORGETTING?
WHY CAN'T I REMEMBER?
WHAT'S GOING ON?!

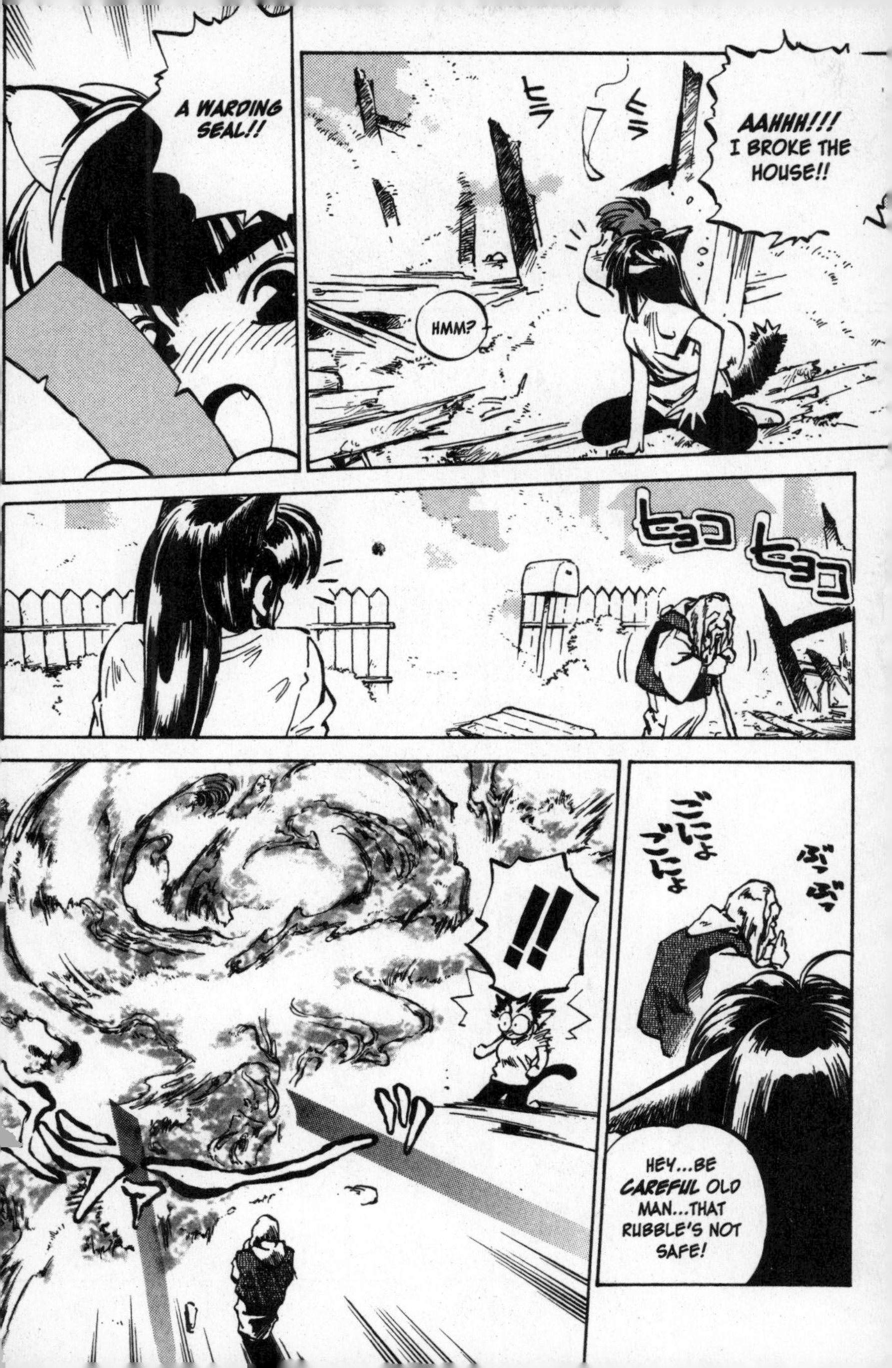
AAHHH!!! I BROKE THE HOUSE!!
ヒラ
ヒラ
HMM?
A WARDING SEAL!!
ヒョコ ヒョコ
ごにょごにょ
ぶっぶっ
HEY...BE CAREFUL OLD MAN...THAT RUBBLE'S NOT SAFE!
!!

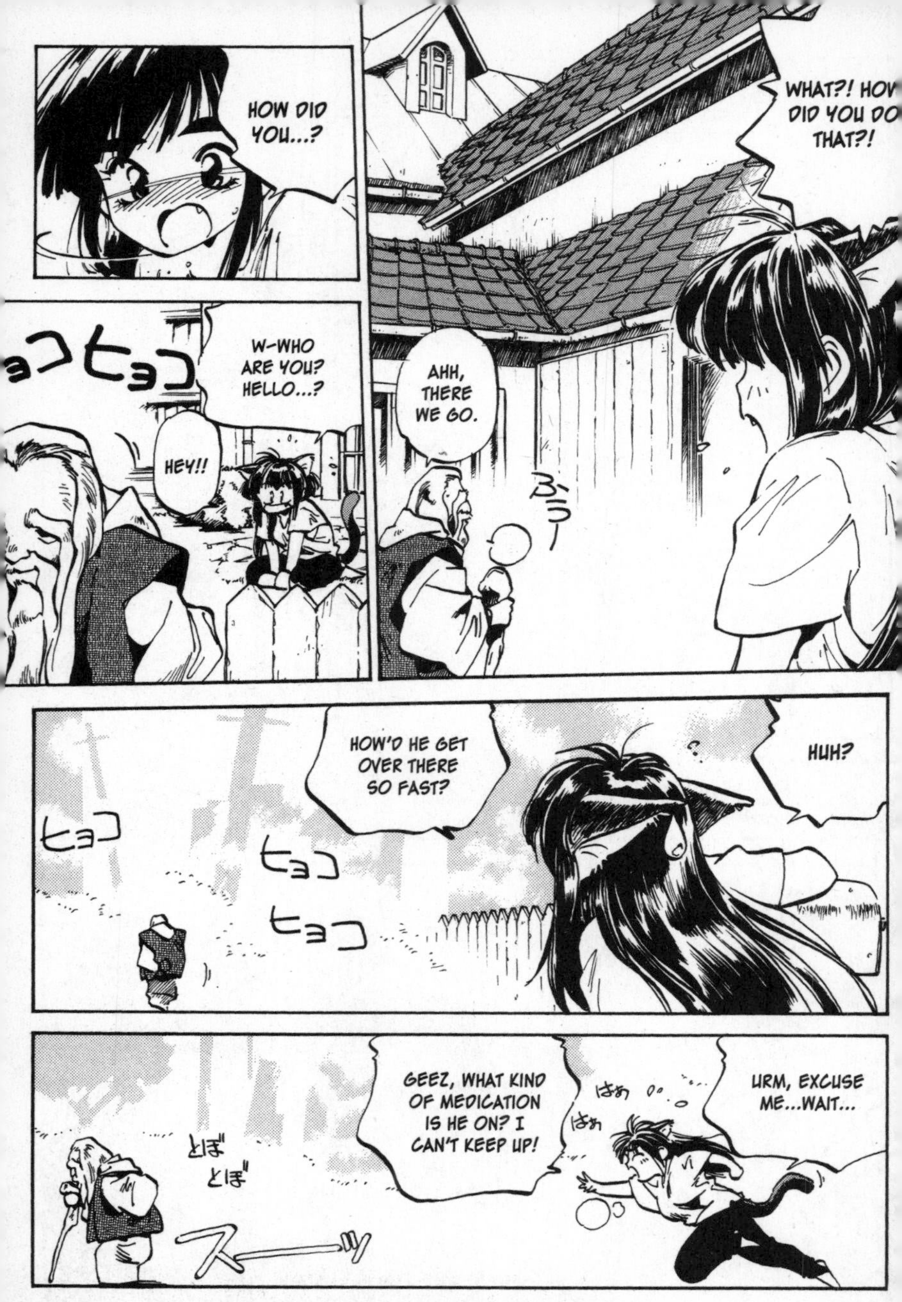
WHAT?! HOW DID YOU DO THAT?!
AHH, THERE WE GO.
HOW DID YOU...?
W-WHO ARE YOU? HELLO...?
HEY!!
HUH?
HOW'D HE GET OVER THERE SO FAST?
URM, EXCUSE ME...WAIT...
GEEZ, WHAT KIND OF MEDICATION IS HE ON? I CAN'T KEEP UP!

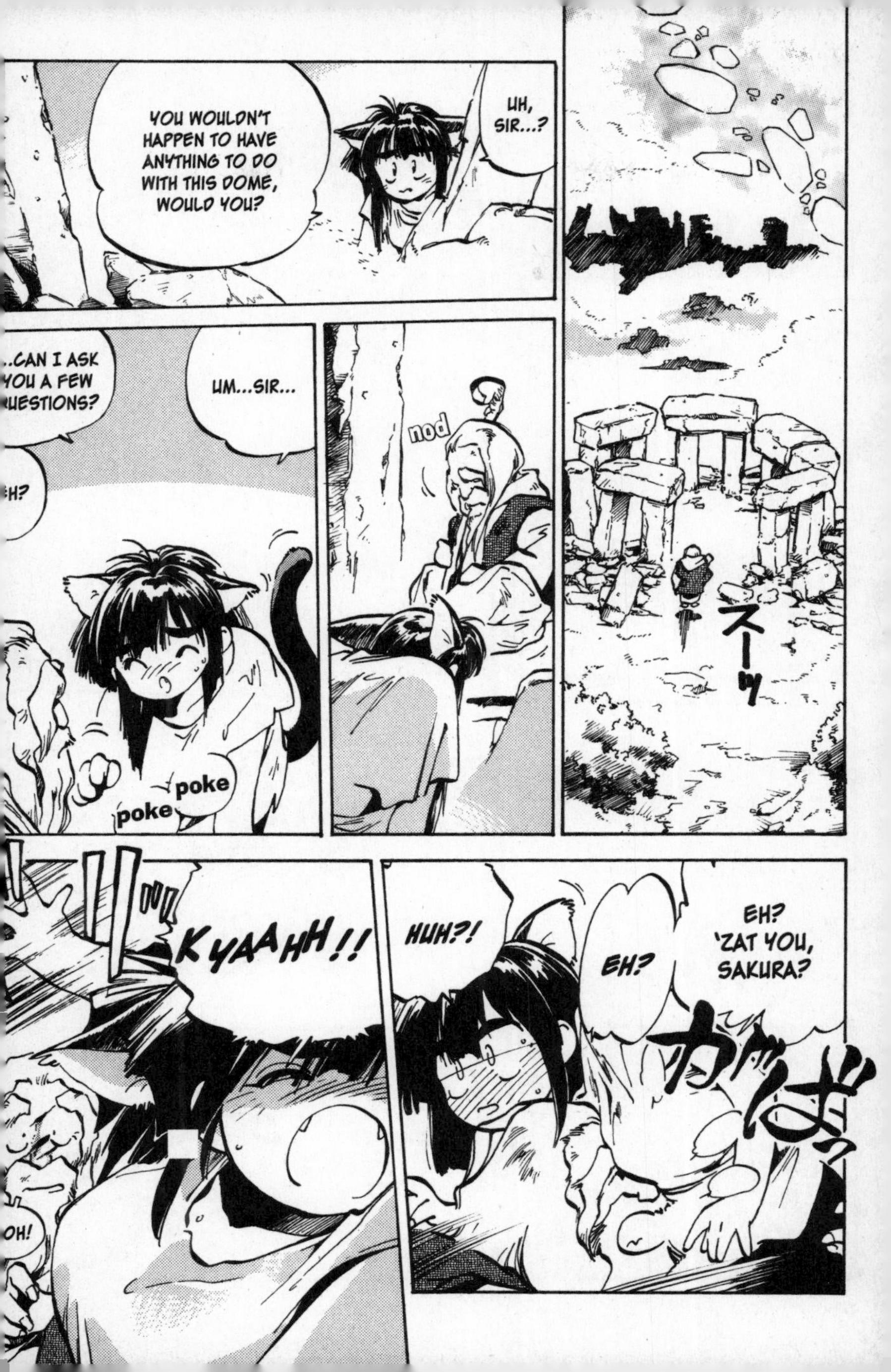
スーッ
UH, SIR...?
YOU WOULDN'T HAPPEN TO HAVE ANYTHING TO DO WITH THIS DOME, WOULD YOU?
nod
UM...SIR...
..CAN I ASK YOU A FEW UESTIONS?
H?
poke
poke
EH? 'ZAT YOU, SAKURA?
EH?
HUH?!
KYAAHH!!
OH!

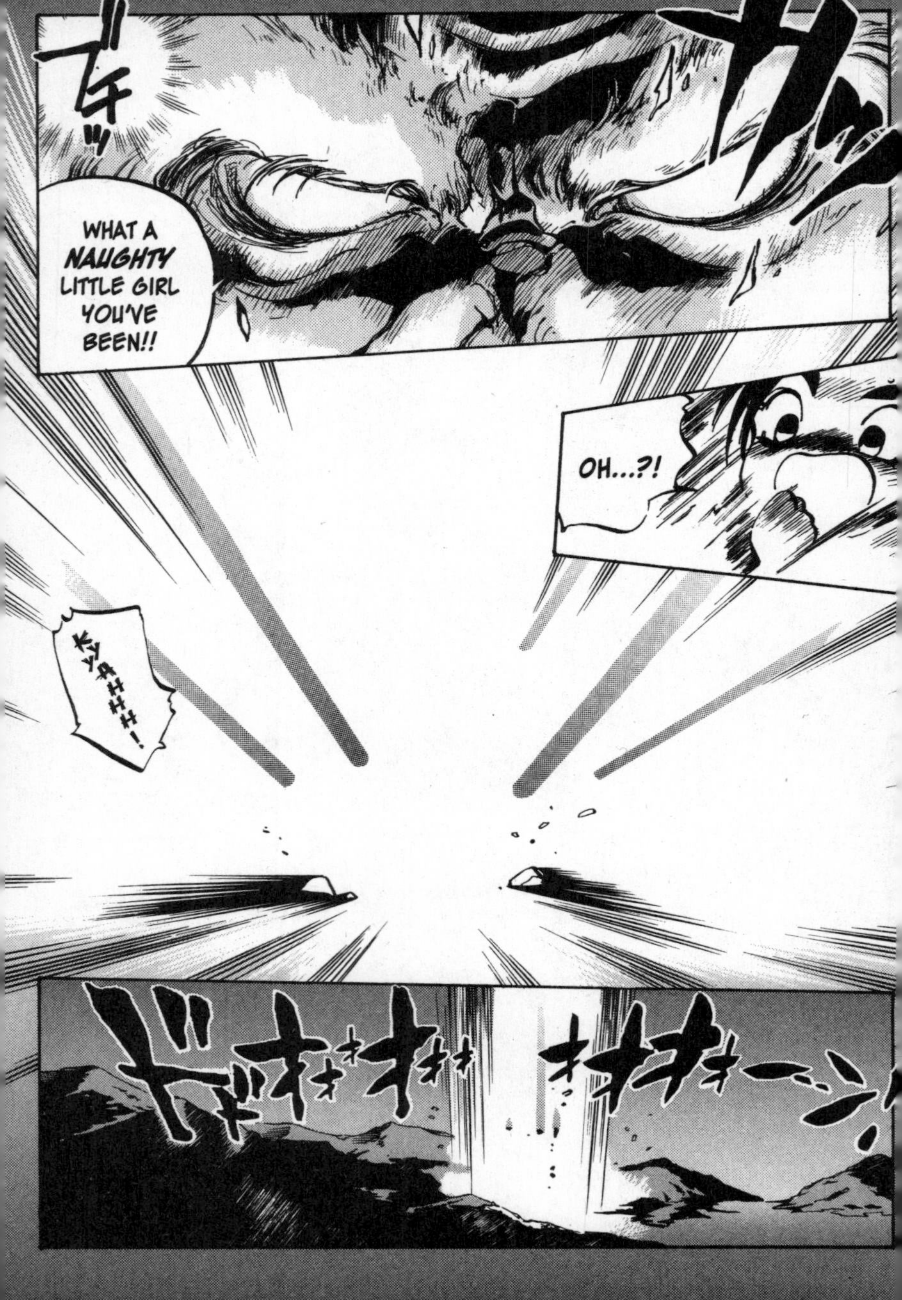
WHAT A NAUGHTY LITTLE GIRL YOU'VE BEEN!!
OH...?!
KYAHHHH!!

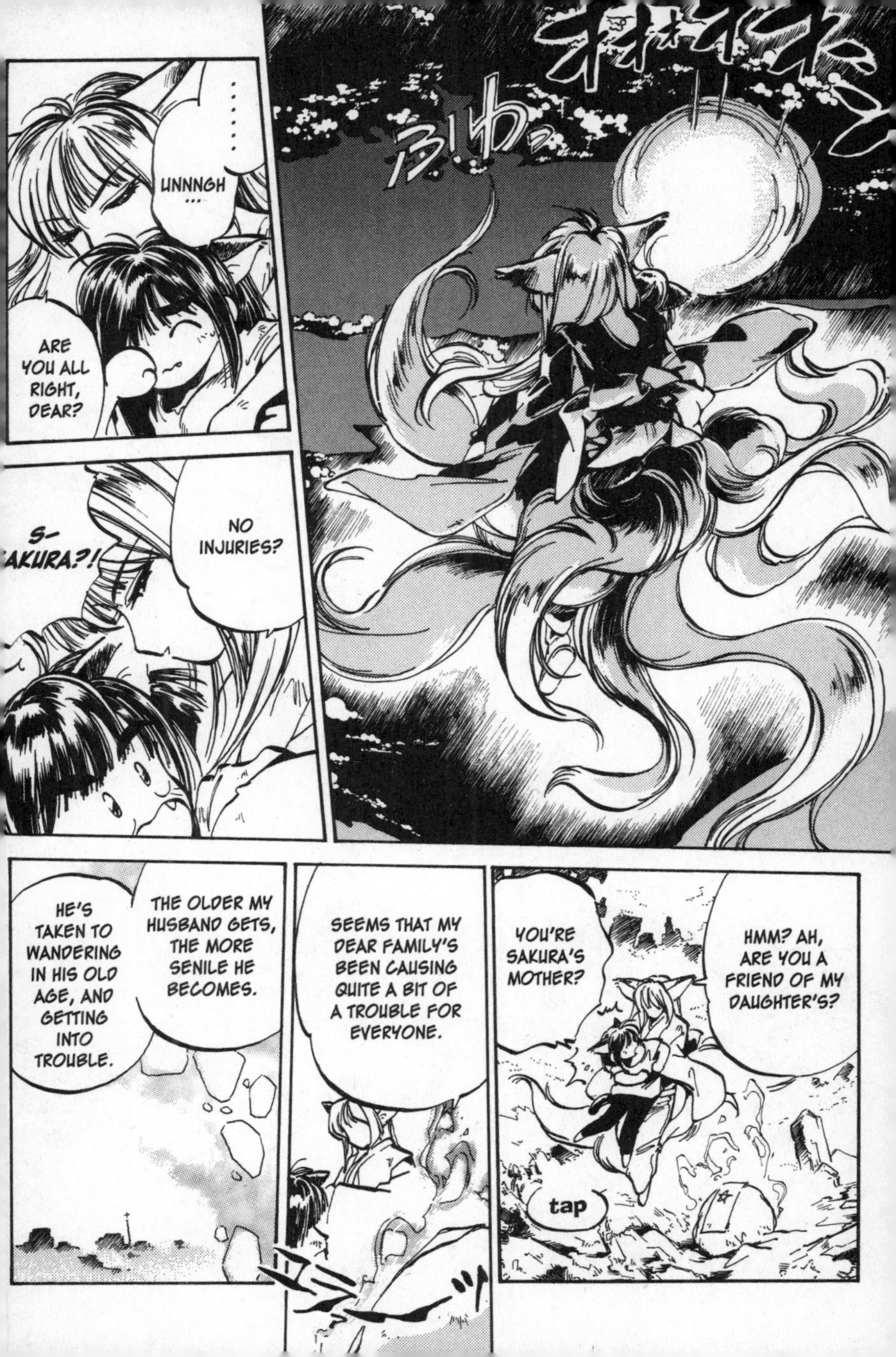
......
UNNNGH ...
ARE YOU ALL RIGHT, DEAR?
NO INJURIES?
S- AKURA?!
HMM? AH, ARE YOU A FRIEND OF MY DAUGHTER'S?
YOU'RE SAKURA'S MOTHER?
tap
SEEMS THAT MY DEAR FAMILY'S BEEN CAUSING QUITE A BIT OF A TROUBLE FOR EVERYONE.
THE OLDER MY HUSBAND GETS, THE MORE SENILE HE BECOMES.
HE'S TAKEN TO WANDERING IN HIS OLD AGE, AND GETTING INTO TROUBLE.

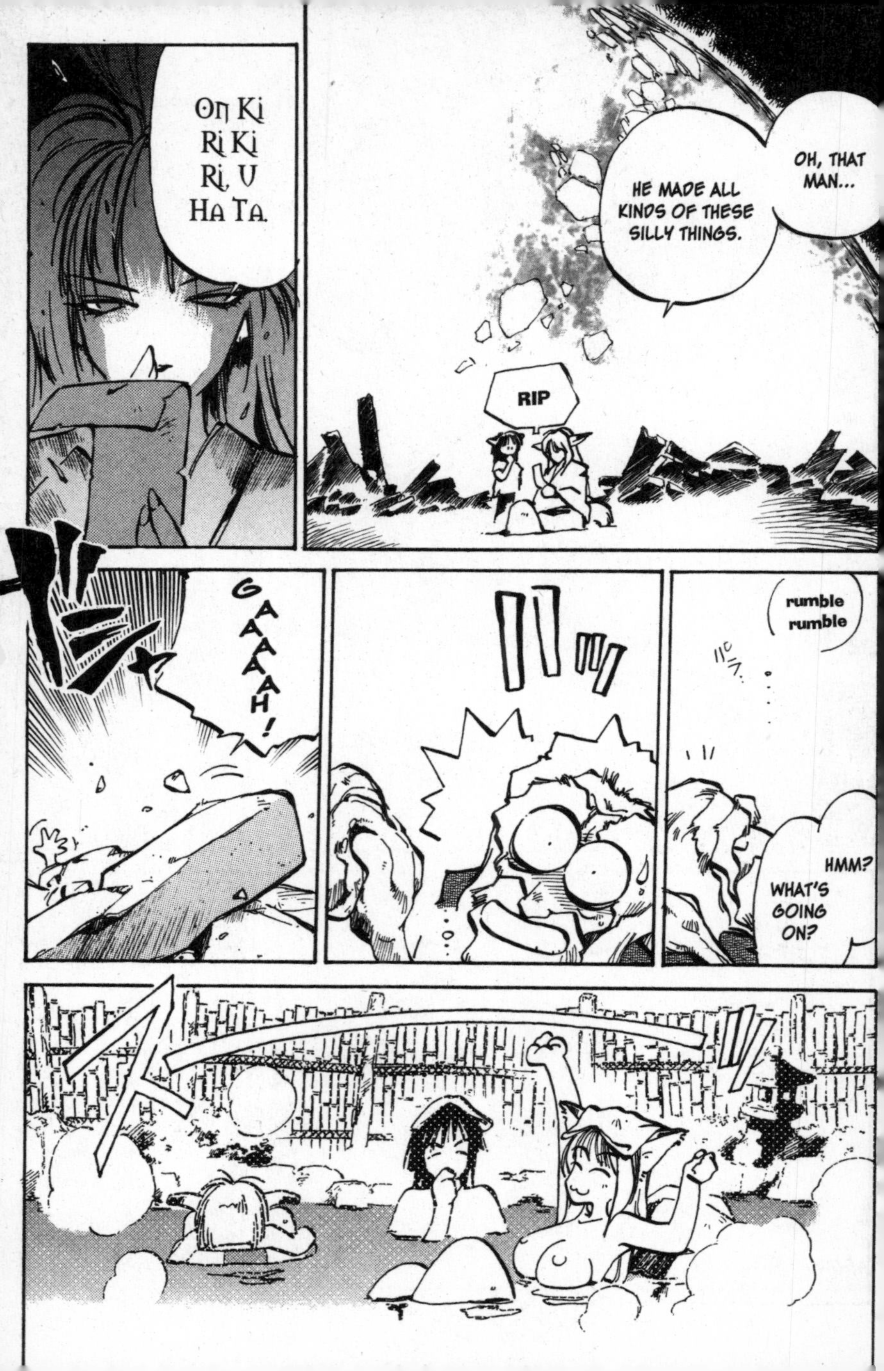
OH, THAT MAN...
HE MADE ALL KINDS OF THESE SILLY THINGS.
RIP
On Ki Ri Ki Ri, U Ha Ta.
rumble rumble
HMM? WHAT'S GOING ON?
GAAAAAH!

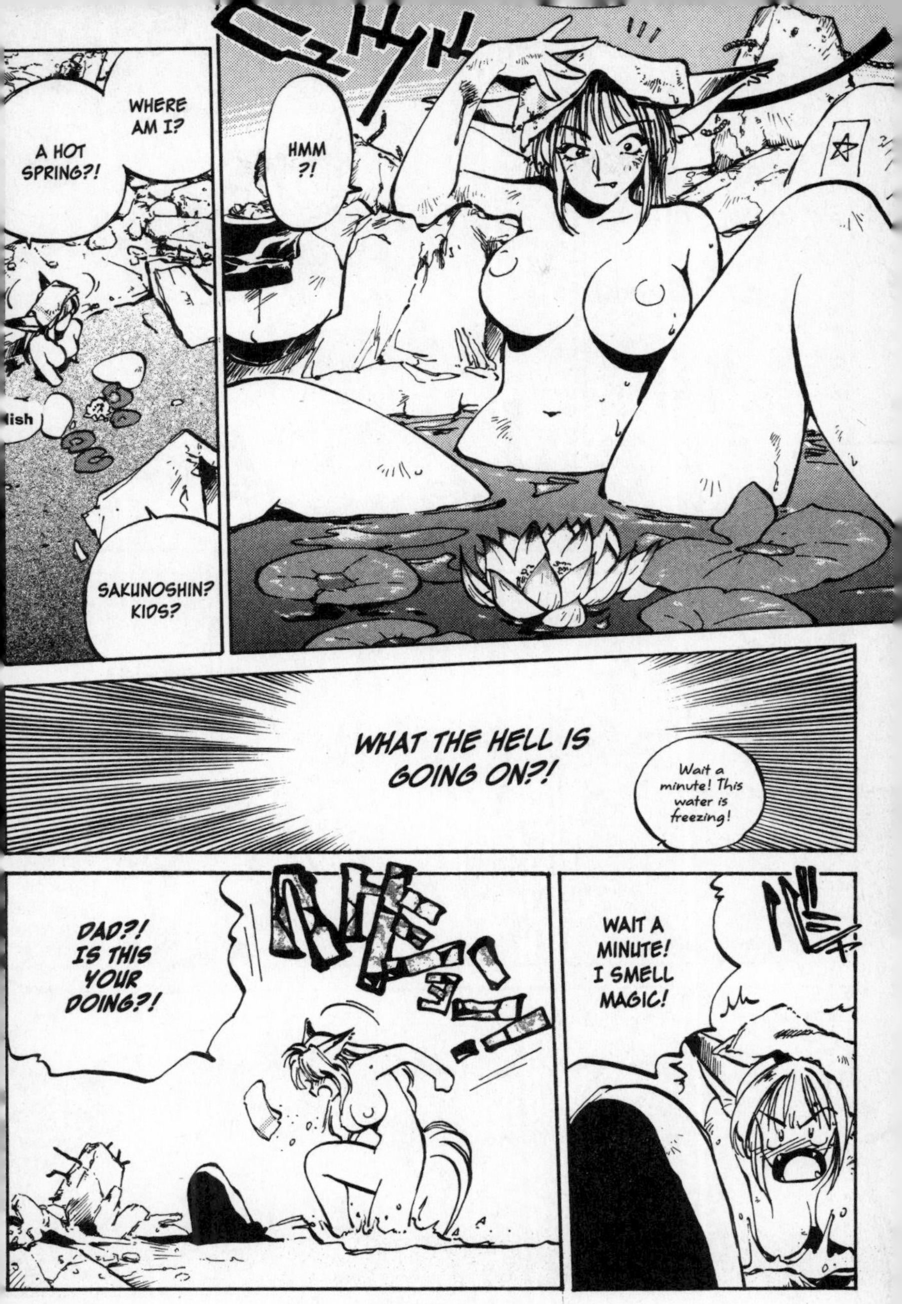
HMM ?!
WHERE AM I?
A HOT SPRING?!
SAKUNOSHIN? KIDS?
WHAT THE HELL IS GOING ON?!
Wait a minute! This water is freezing!
WAIT A MINUTE! I SMELL MAGIC!
DAD?! IS THIS YOUR DOING?!

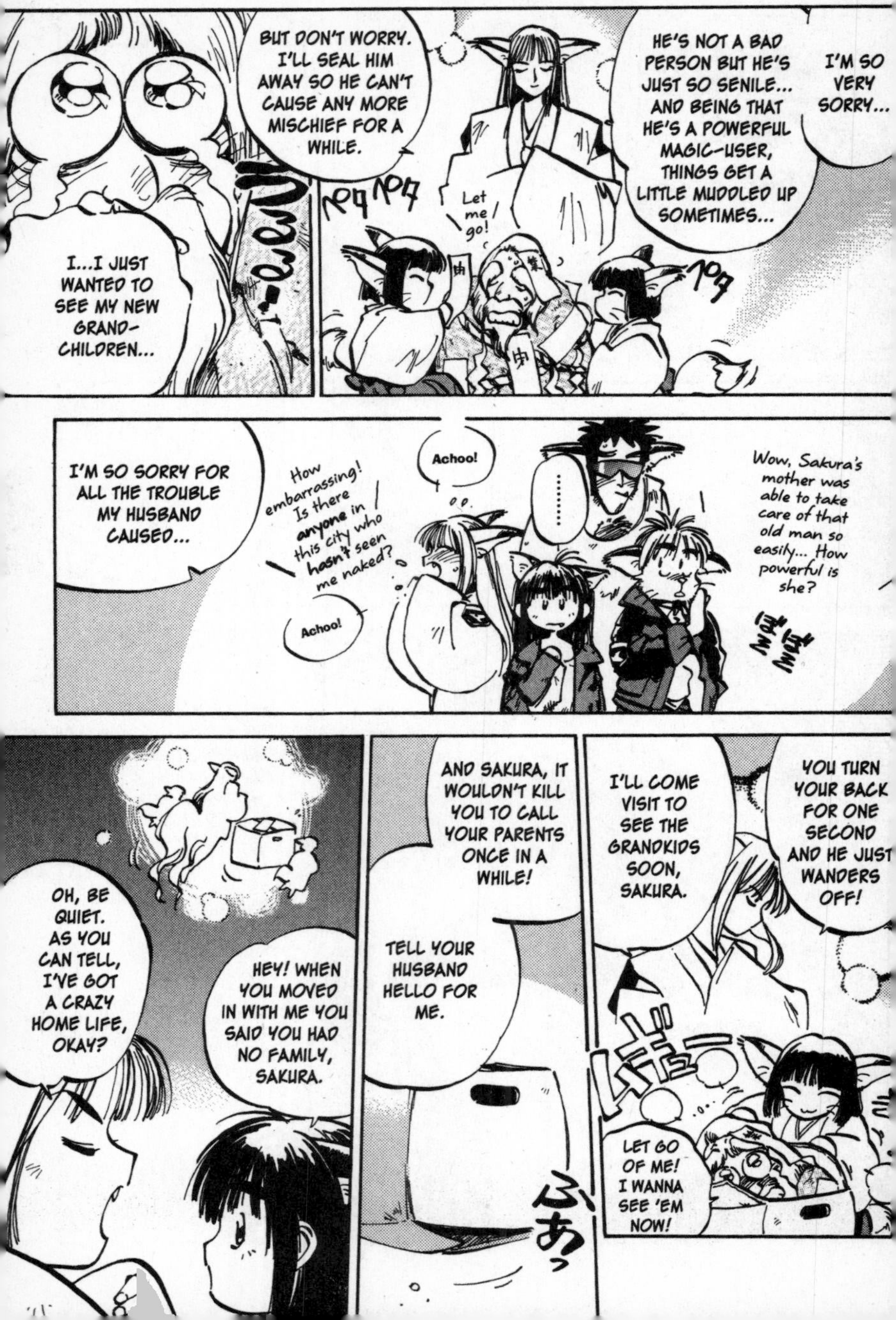
I'M SO VERY SORRY...
HE'S NOT A BAD PERSON BUT HE'S JUST SO SENILE... AND BEING THAT HE'S A POWERFUL MAGIC-USER, THINGS GET A LITTLE MUDDLED UP SOMETIMES...
BUT DON'T WORRY. I'LL SEAL HIM AWAY SO HE CAN'T CAUSE ANY MORE MISCHIEF FOR A WHILE.
Let me go!
I...I JUST WANTED TO SEE MY NEW GRAND-CHILDREN...
Wow, Sakura's mother was able to take care of that old man so easily... How powerful is she?
......
Achoo!
How embarrassing! Is there anyone in this city who hasn't seen me naked?
Achoo!
I'M SO SORRY FOR ALL THE TROUBLE MY HUSBAND CAUSED...
YOU TURN YOUR BACK FOR ONE SECOND AND HE JUST WANDERS OFF!
I'LL COME VISIT TO SEE THE GRANDKIDS SOON, SAKURA.
LET GO OF ME! I WANNA SEE 'EM NOW!
AND SAKURA, IT WOULDN'T KILL YOU TO CALL YOUR PARENTS ONCE IN A WHILE!
TELL YOUR HUSBAND HELLO FOR ME.
ふあっ
HEY! WHEN YOU MOVED IN WITH ME YOU SAID YOU HAD NO FAMILY, SAKURA.
OH, BE QUIET. AS YOU CAN TELL, I'VE GOT A CRAZY HOME LIFE, OKAY?

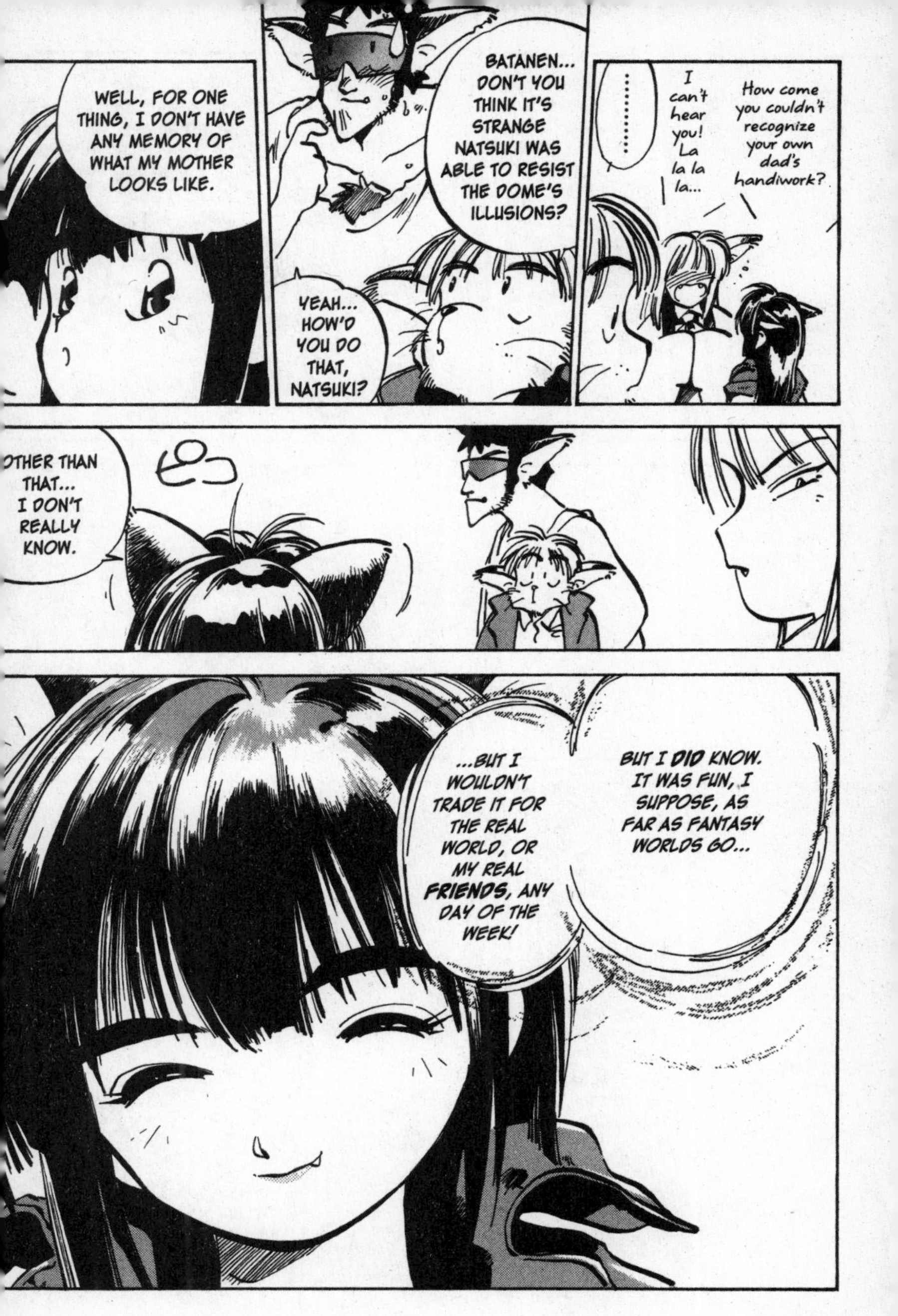
How come you couldn't recognize your own dad's handiwork?
I can't hear you! La la la la...
......
BATANEN... DON'T YOU THINK IT'S STRANGE NATSUKI WAS ABLE TO RESIST THE DOME'S ILLUSIONS?
YEAH... HOW'D YOU DO THAT, NATSUKI?
WELL, FOR ONE THING, I DON'T HAVE ANY MEMORY OF WHAT MY MOTHER LOOKS LIKE.
OTHER THAN THAT... I DON'T REALLY KNOW.
BUT I DID KNOW. IT WAS FUN, I SUPPOSE, AS FAR AS FANTASY WORLDS GO...
...BUT I WOULDN'T TRADE IT FOR THE REAL WORLD, OR MY REAL FRIENDS, ANY DAY OF THE WEEK!

Report #27
Rodent Problems

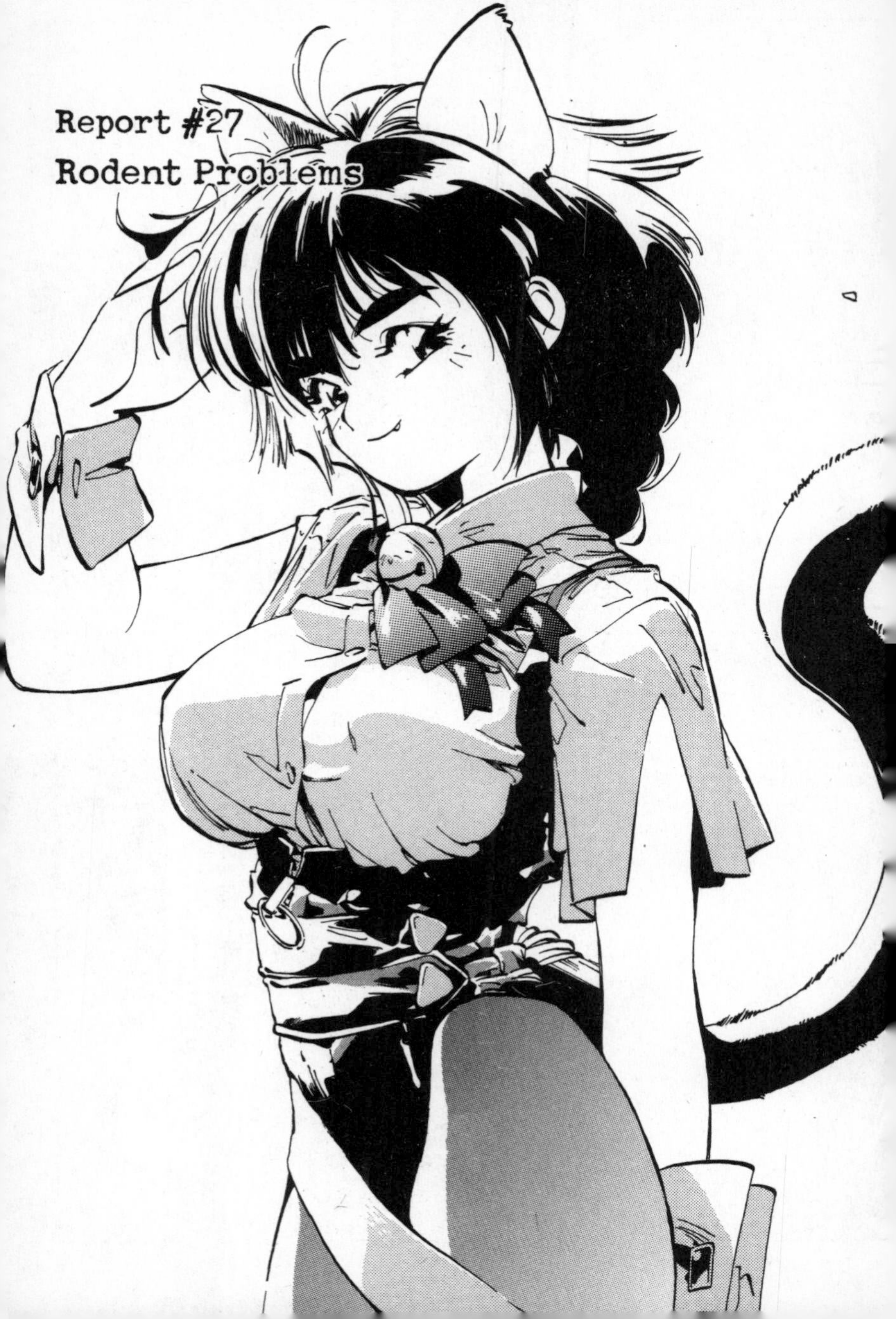

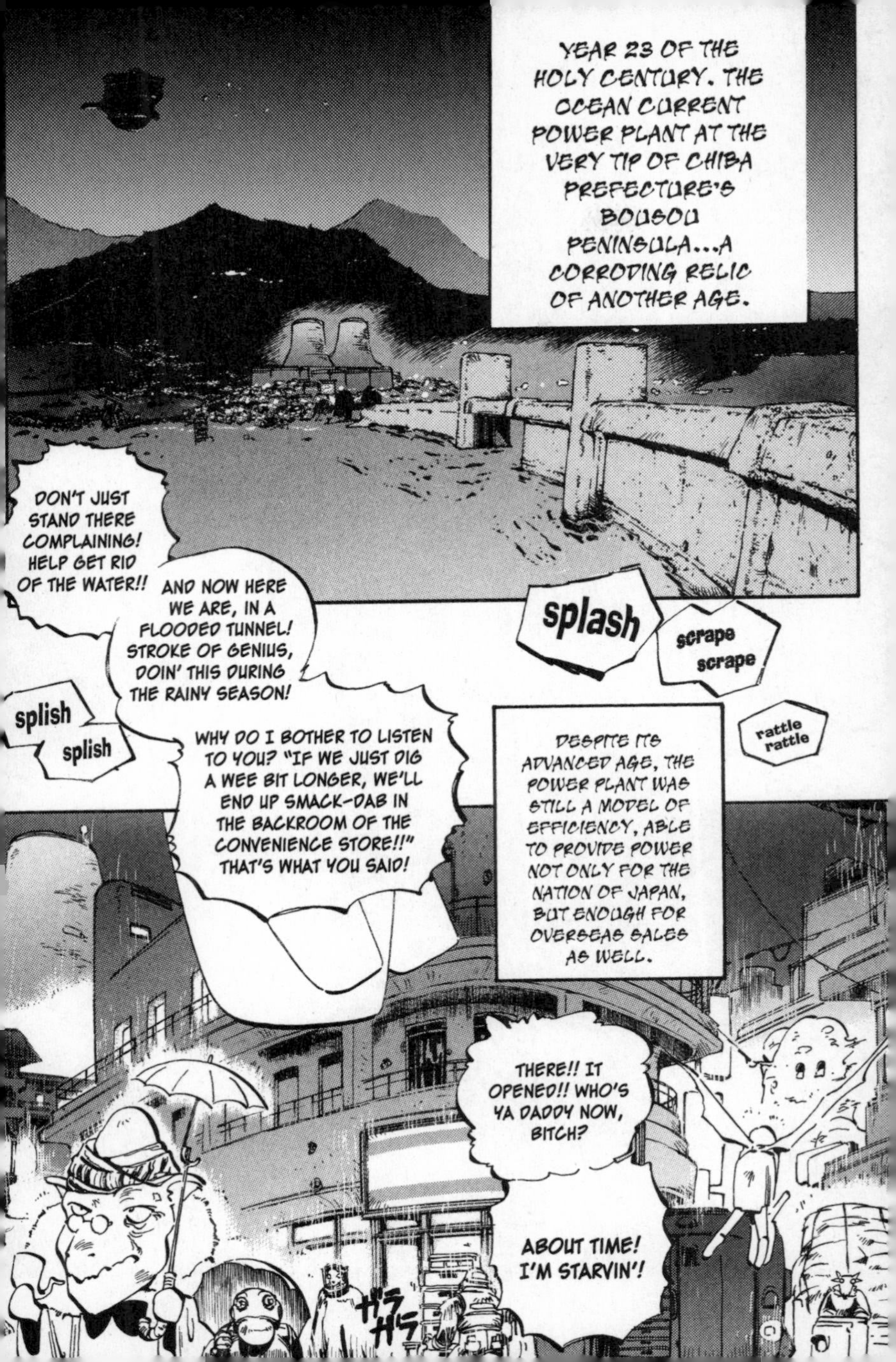
YEAR 23 OF THE HOLY CENTURY. THE OCEAN CURRENT POWER PLANT AT THE VERY TIP OF CHIBA PREFECTURE'S BOUSOU PENINSULA...A CORRODING RELIC OF ANOTHER AGE.
splash
scrape scrape
AND NOW HERE WE ARE, IN A FLOODED TUNNEL! STROKE OF GENIUS, DOIN' THIS DURING THE RAINY SEASON!
DON'T JUST STAND THERE COMPLAINING! HELP GET RID OF THE WATER!!
splish splish
WHY DO I BOTHER TO LISTEN TO YOU? "IF WE JUST DIG A WEE BIT LONGER, WE'LL END UP SMACK-DAB IN THE BACKROOM OF THE CONVENIENCE STORE!!" THAT'S WHAT YOU SAID!
rattle rattle
DESPITE ITS ADVANCED AGE, THE POWER PLANT WAS STILL A MODEL OF EFFICIENCY, ABLE TO PROVIDE POWER NOT ONLY FOR THE NATION OF JAPAN, BUT ENOUGH FOR OVERSEAS SALES AS WELL.
THERE!! IT OPENED!! WHO'S YA DADDY NOW, BITCH?
ABOUT TIME! I'M STARVIN'!
ガラガラ

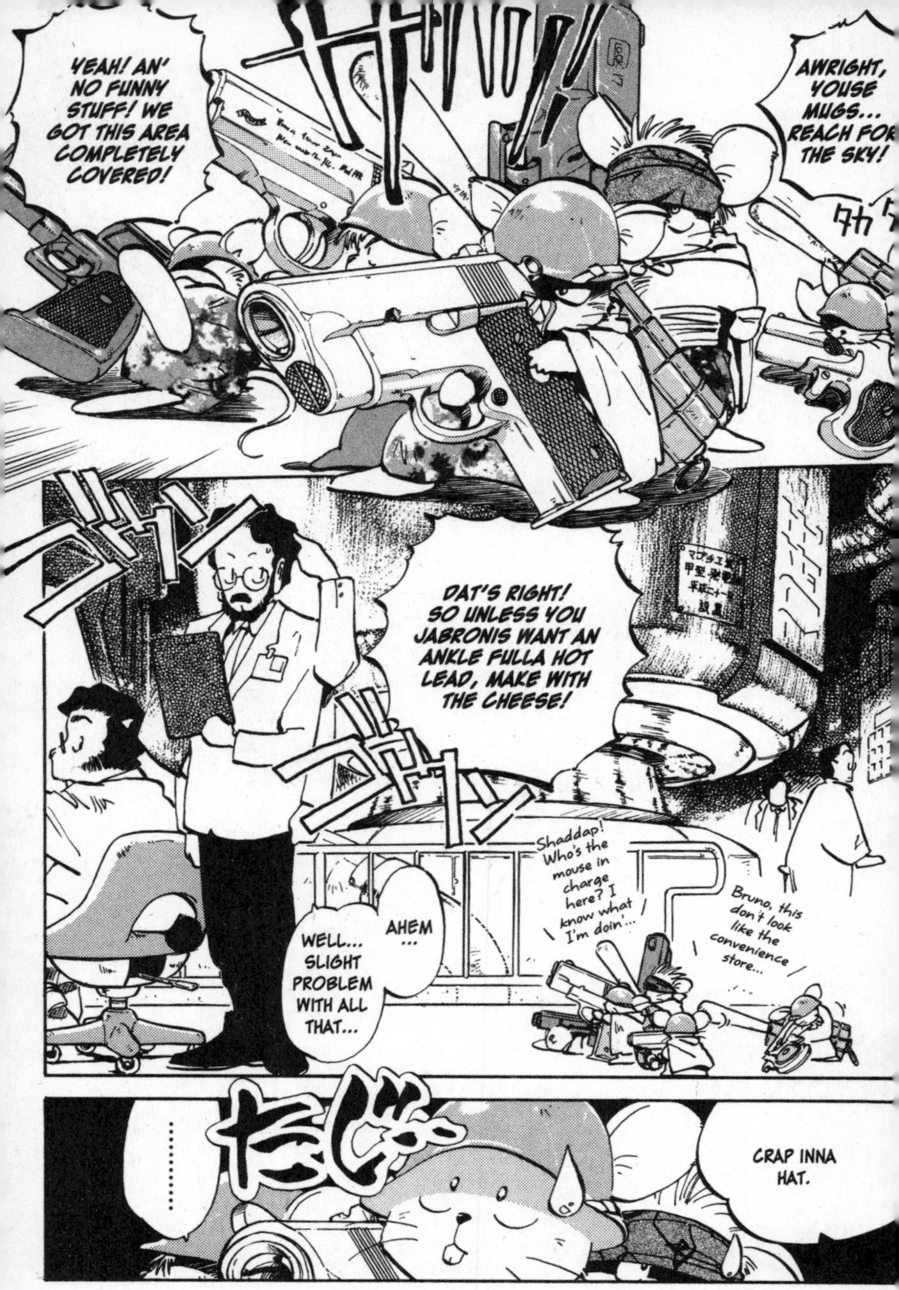
AWRIGHT, YOUSE MUGS... REACH FOR THE SKY!
YEAH! AN' NO FUNNY STUFF! WE GOT THIS AREA COMPLETELY COVERED!
DAT'S RIGHT! SO UNLESS YOU JABRONIS WANT AN ANKLE FULLA HOT LEAD, MAKE WITH THE CHEESE!
Bruno, this don't look like the convenience store...
Shaddap! Who's the mouse in charge here? I know what I'm doin'...
AHEM ...
WELL... SLIGHT PROBLEM WITH ALL THAT...
CRAP INNA HAT.
......

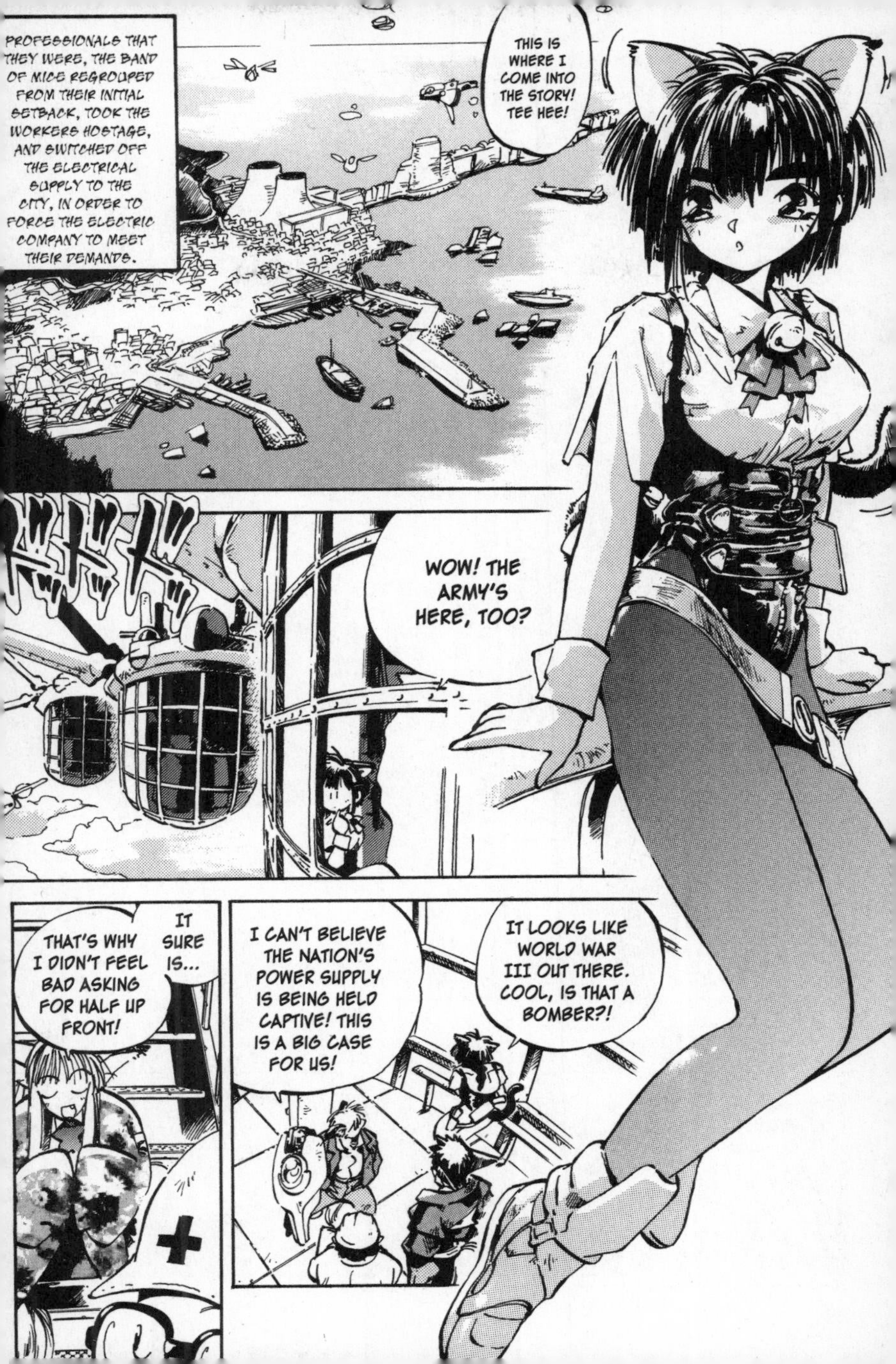
THIS IS WHERE I COME INTO THE STORY! TEE HEE!
PROFESSIONALS THAT THEY WERE, THE BAND OF MICE REGROUPED FROM THEIR INITIAL SETBACK, TOOK THE WORKERS HOSTAGE, AND SWITCHED OFF THE ELECTRICAL SUPPLY TO THE CITY, IN ORDER TO FORCE THE ELECTRIC COMPANY TO MEET THEIR DEMANDS.
WOW! THE ARMY'S HERE, TOO?
IT LOOKS LIKE WORLD WAR III OUT THERE. COOL, IS THAT A BOMBER?!
I CAN'T BELIEVE THE NATION'S POWER SUPPLY IS BEING HELD CAPTIVE! THIS IS A BIG CASE FOR US!
IT SURE IS...
THAT'S WHY I DIDN'T FEEL BAD ASKING FOR HALF UP FRONT!

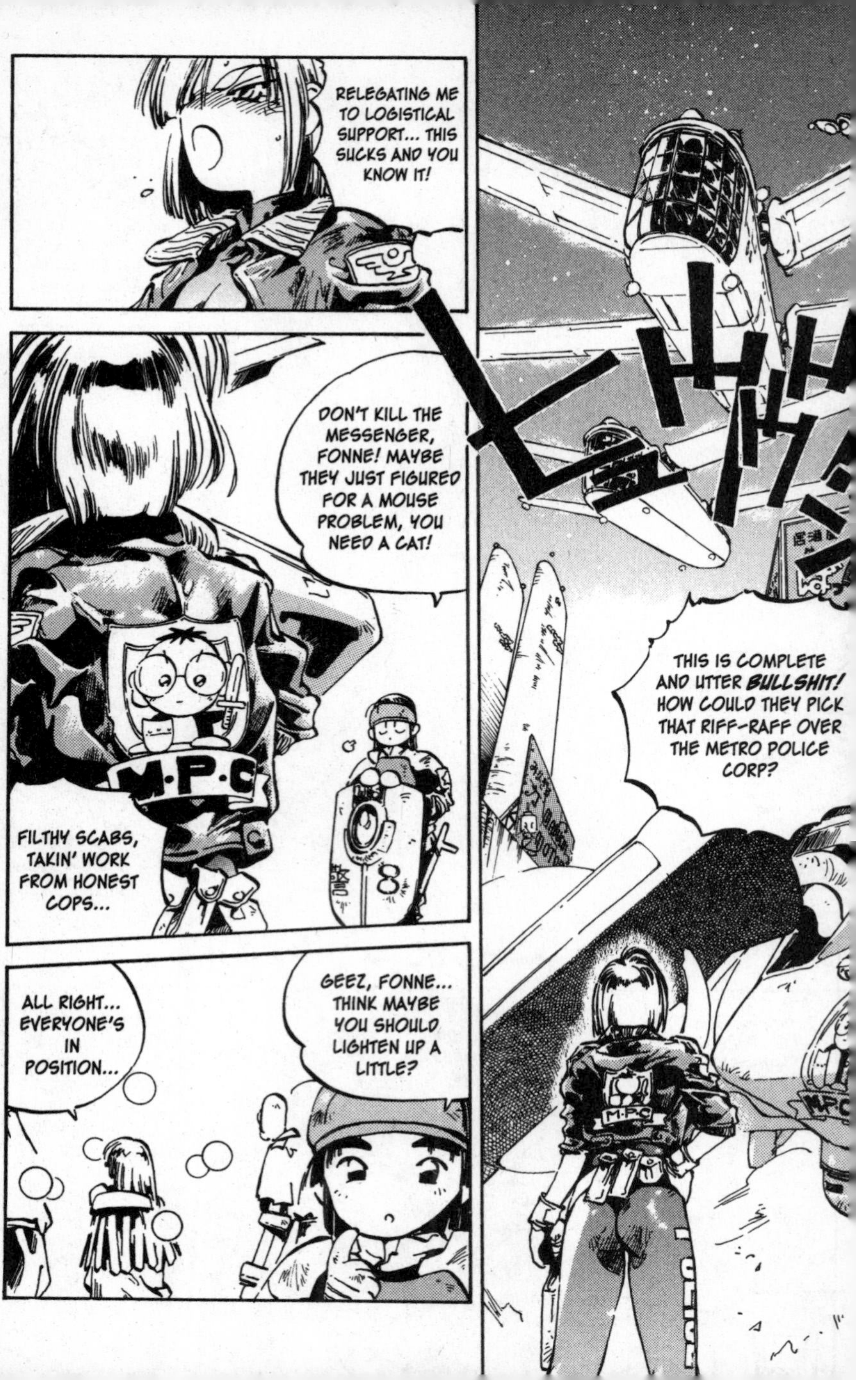
THIS IS COMPLETE AND UTTER **BULLSHIT!** HOW COULD THEY PICK THAT RIFF-RAFF OVER THE METRO POLICE CORP?
RELEGATING ME TO LOGISTICAL SUPPORT... THIS SUCKS AND YOU KNOW IT!
DON'T KILL THE MESSENGER, FONNE! MAYBE THEY JUST FIGURED FOR A MOUSE PROBLEM, YOU NEED A CAT!
FILTHY SCABS, TAKIN' WORK FROM HONEST COPS...
GEEZ, FONNE... THINK MAYBE YOU SHOULD LIGHTEN UP A LITTLE?
ALL RIGHT... EVERYONE'S IN POSITION...

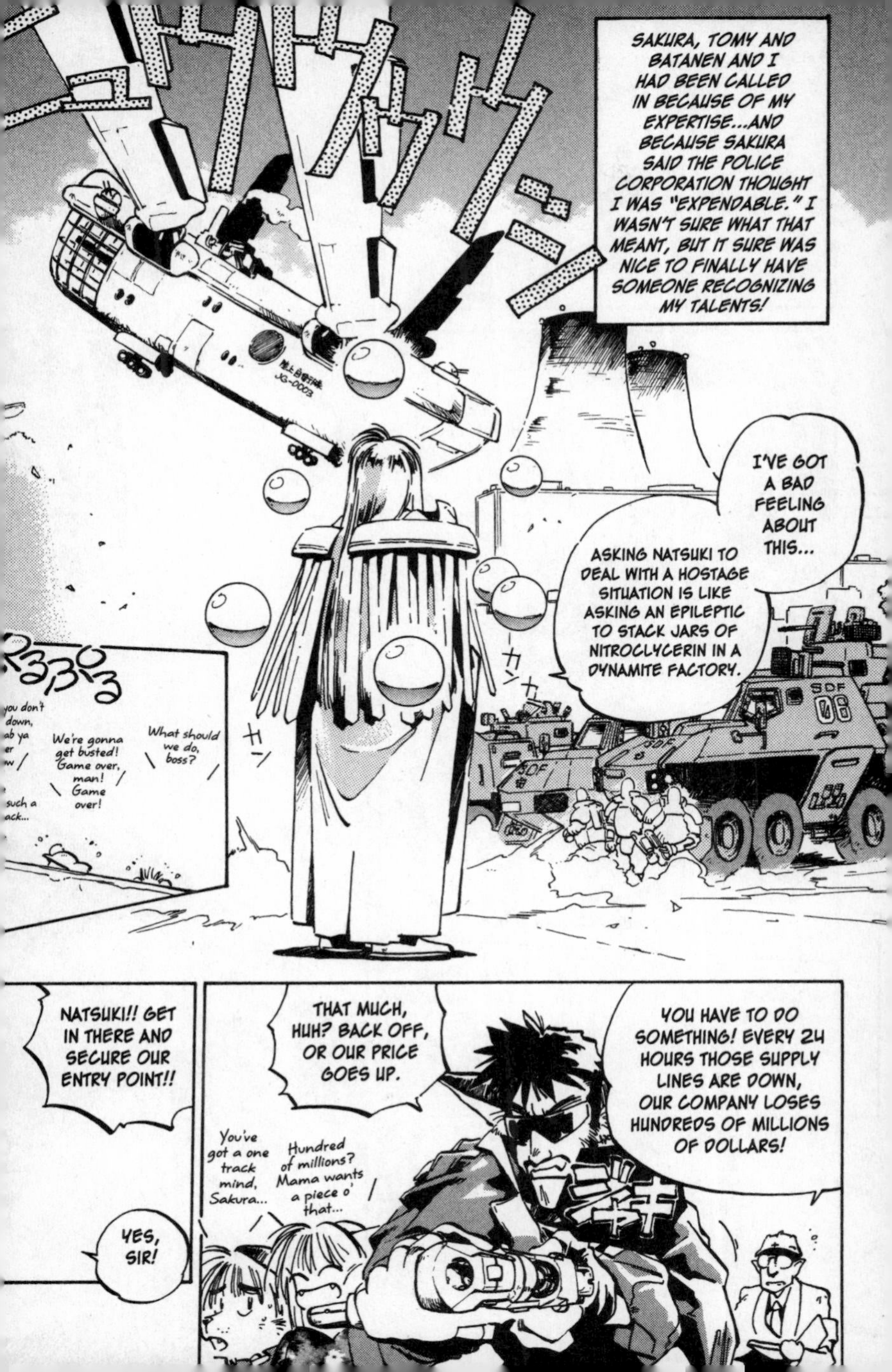
SAKURA, TOMY AND BATANEN AND I HAD BEEN CALLED IN BECAUSE OF MY EXPERTISE...AND BECAUSE SAKURA SAID THE POLICE CORPORATION THOUGHT I WAS "EXPENDABLE." I WASN'T SURE WHAT THAT MEANT, BUT IT SURE WAS NICE TO FINALLY HAVE SOMEONE RECOGNIZING MY TALENTS!
I'VE GOT A BAD FEELING ABOUT THIS...
ASKING NATSUKI TO DEAL WITH A HOSTAGE SITUATION IS LIKE ASKING AN EPILEPTIC TO STACK JARS OF NITROCLYCERIN IN A DYNAMITE FACTORY.
SDF
08
What should we do, boss?
We're gonna get busted! Game over, man! Game over!
YOU HAVE TO DO SOMETHING! EVERY 24 HOURS THOSE SUPPLY LINES ARE DOWN, OUR COMPANY LOSES HUNDREDS OF MILLIONS OF DOLLARS!
THAT MUCH, HUH? BACK OFF, OR OUR PRICE GOES UP.
Hundred of millions? Mama wants a piece o' that...
You've got a one track mind, Sakura...
NATSUKI!! GET IN THERE AND SECURE OUR ENTRY POINT!!
YES, SIR!

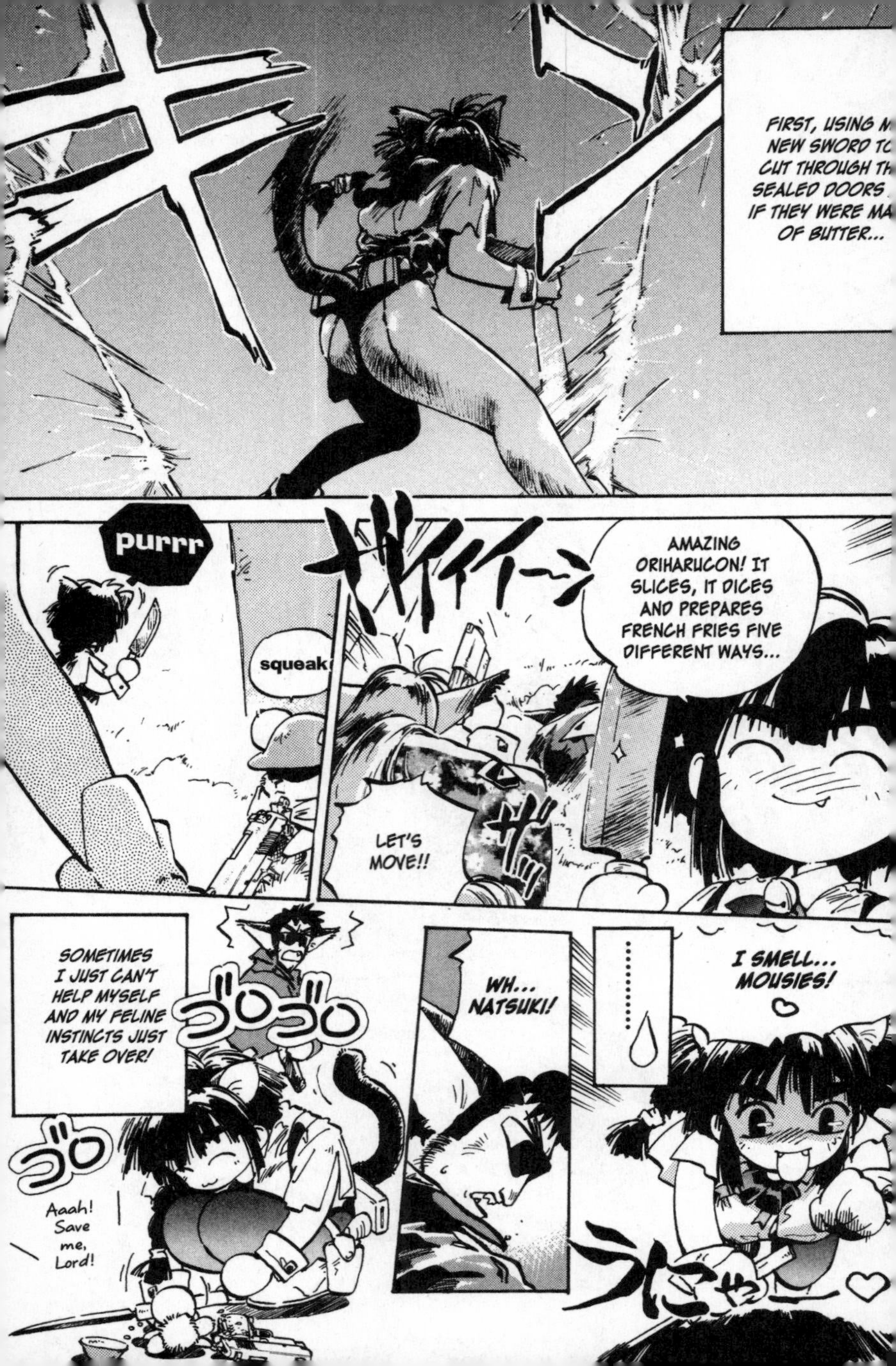
FIRST, USING M NEW SWORD TC CUT THROUGH TH SEALED DOORS IF THEY WERE MA OF BUTTER...
AMAZING ORIHARUCON! IT SLICES, IT DICES AND PREPARES FRENCH FRIES FIVE DIFFERENT WAYS...
LET'S MOVE!!
squeak!
purrr
I SMELL... MOUSIES!
....
WH... NATSUKI!
SOMETIMES I JUST CAN'T HELP MYSELF AND MY FELINE INSTINCTS JUST TAKE OVER!
Aaah! Save me, Lord!

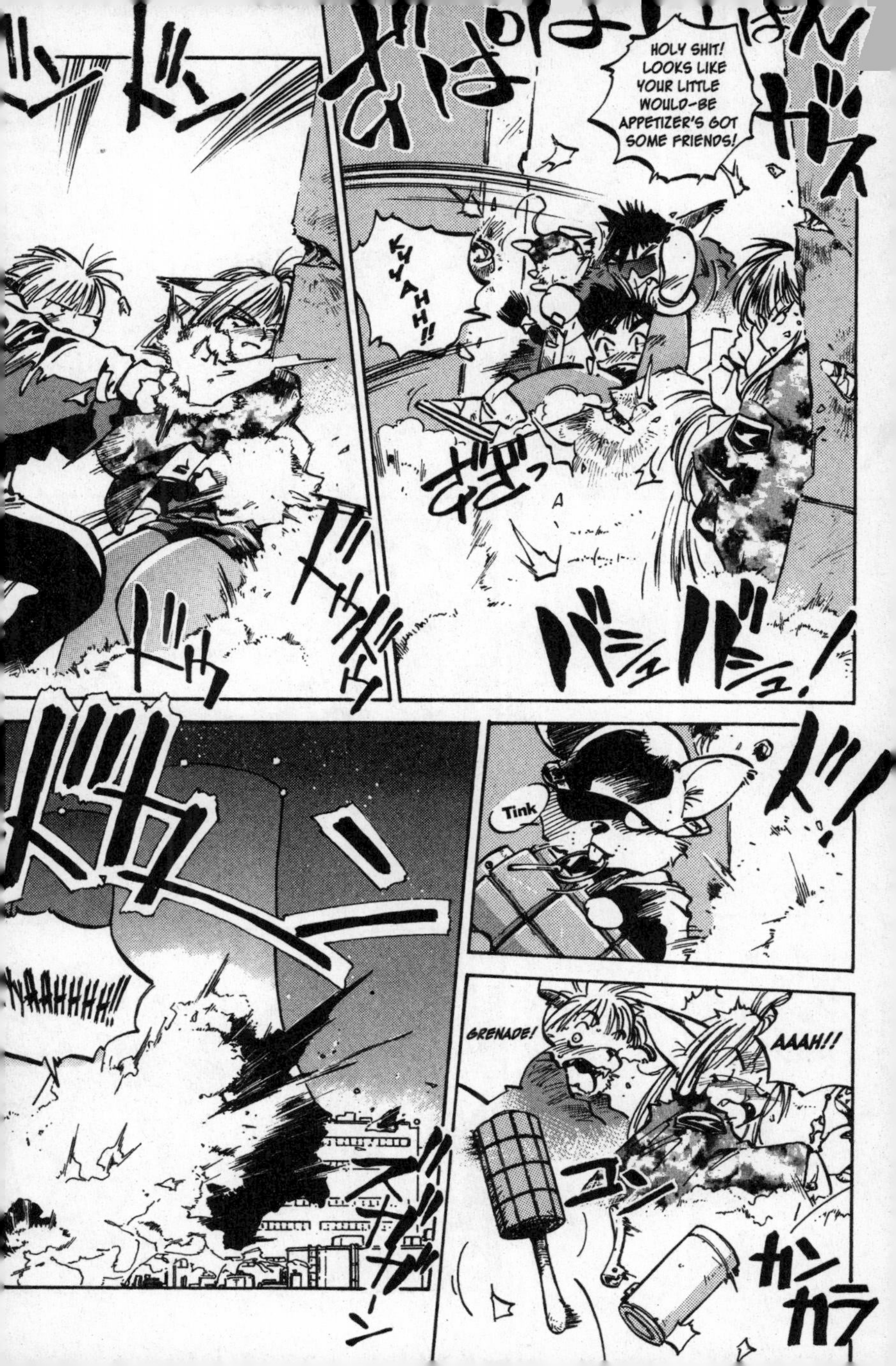

HOLY SHIT! LOOKS LIKE YOUR LITTLE WOULD-BE APPETIZER'S GOT SOME FRIENDS!
KYAAHH!!
Tink
GRENADE!
AAAH!!
カンカラ
yAAAHHHH!!

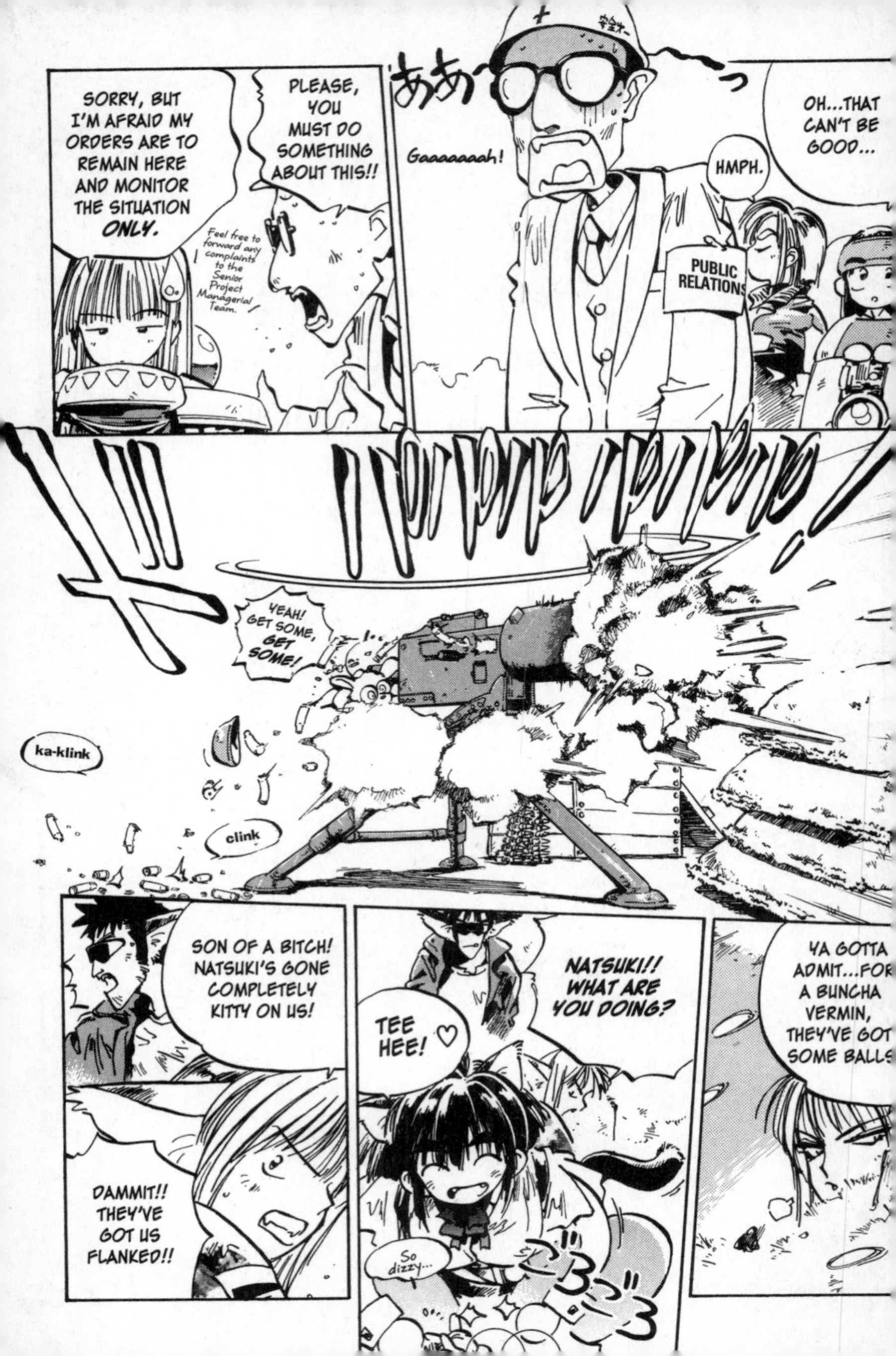
OH...THAT CAN'T BE GOOD...
HMPH.
PUBLIC RELATIONS
ああ〜っ
Gaaaaaaah!
PLEASE, YOU MUST DO SOMETHING ABOUT THIS!!
SORRY, BUT I'M AFRAID MY ORDERS ARE TO REMAIN HERE AND MONITOR THE SITUATION ONLY.
Feel free to forward any complaints to the Senior Project Managerial Team.
YEAH! GET SOME, GET SOME!
ka-klink
clink
YA GOTTA ADMIT...FOR A BUNCHA VERMIN, THEY'VE GOT SOME BALLS
NATSUKI!! WHAT ARE YOU DOING?
TEE HEE! ♡
So dizzy...
SON OF A BITCH! NATSUKI'S GONE COMPLETELY KITTY ON US!
DAMMIT!! THEY'VE GOT US FLANKED!!

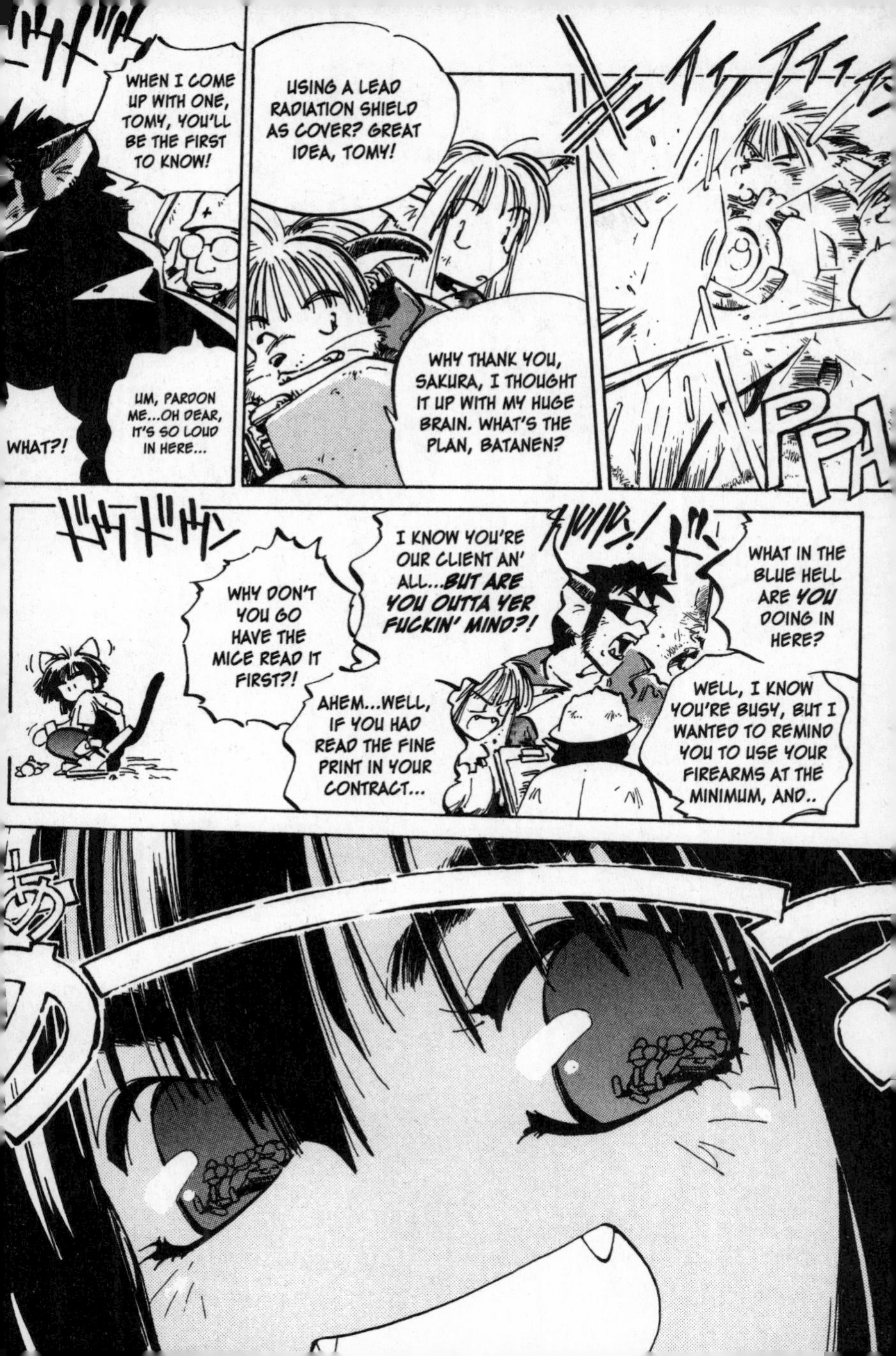
PPA
USING A LEAD RADIATION SHIELD AS COVER? GREAT IDEA, TOMY!
WHY THANK YOU, SAKURA, I THOUGHT IT UP WITH MY HUGE BRAIN. WHAT'S THE PLAN, BATANEN?
WHEN I COME UP WITH ONE, TOMY, YOU'LL BE THE FIRST TO KNOW!
UM, PARDON ME...OH DEAR, IT'S SO LOUD IN HERE...
WHAT?!
WHAT IN THE BLUE HELL ARE *YOU* DOING IN HERE?
WELL, I KNOW YOU'RE BUSY, BUT I WANTED TO REMIND YOU TO USE YOUR FIREARMS AT THE MINIMUM, AND..
I KNOW YOU'RE OUR CLIENT AN' ALL...*BUT ARE YOU OUTTA YER FUCKIN' MIND?!*
AHEM...WELL, IF YOU HAD READ THE FINE PRINT IN YOUR CONTRACT...
WHY DON'T YOU GO HAVE THE MICE READ IT FIRST?!
あ

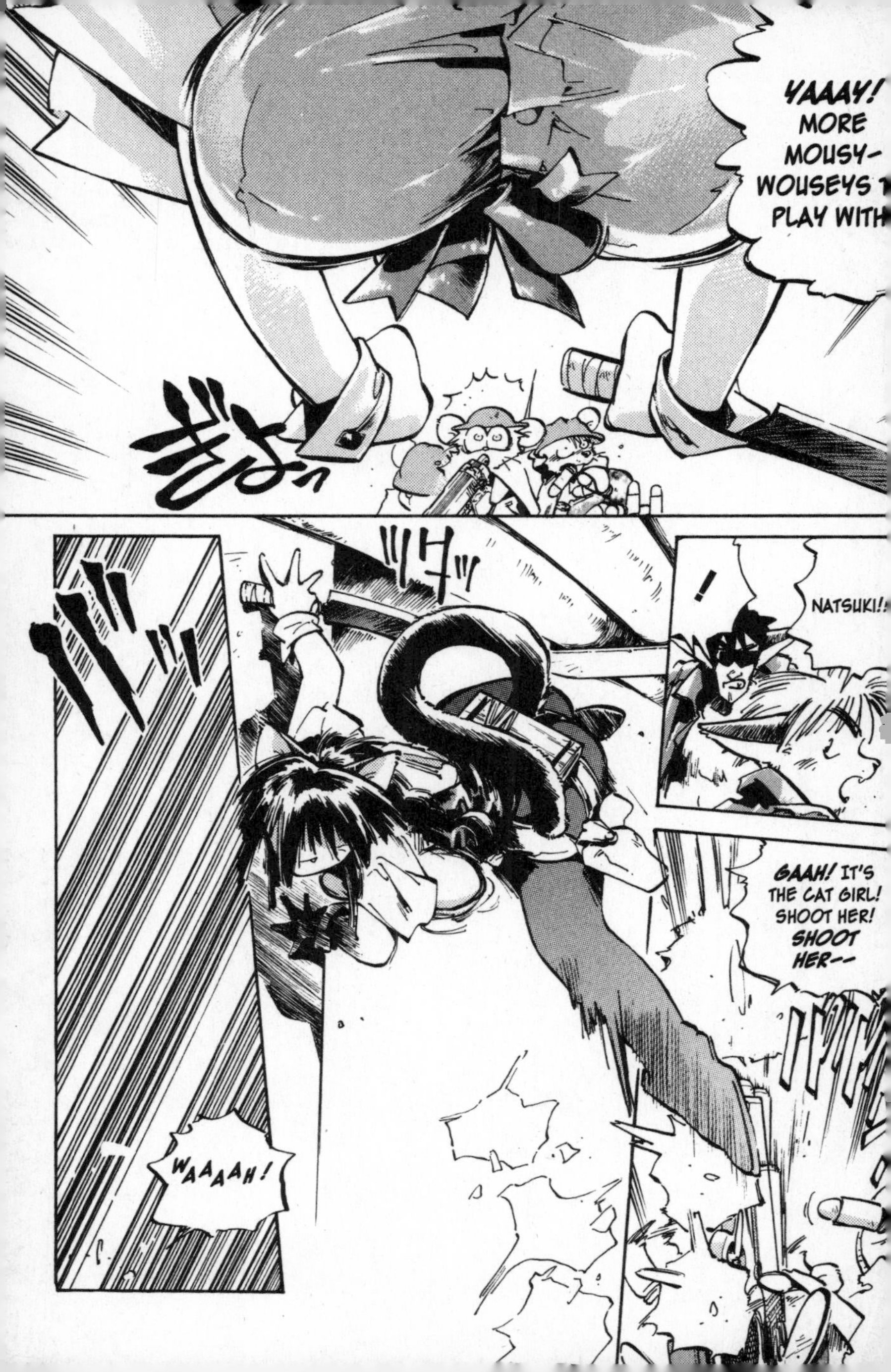
YAAAY! MORE MOUSY-WOUSEYS T PLAY WITH
!
NATSUKI!!
GAAH! IT'S THE CAT GIRL! SHOOT HER! SHOOT HER--
WAAAAH!

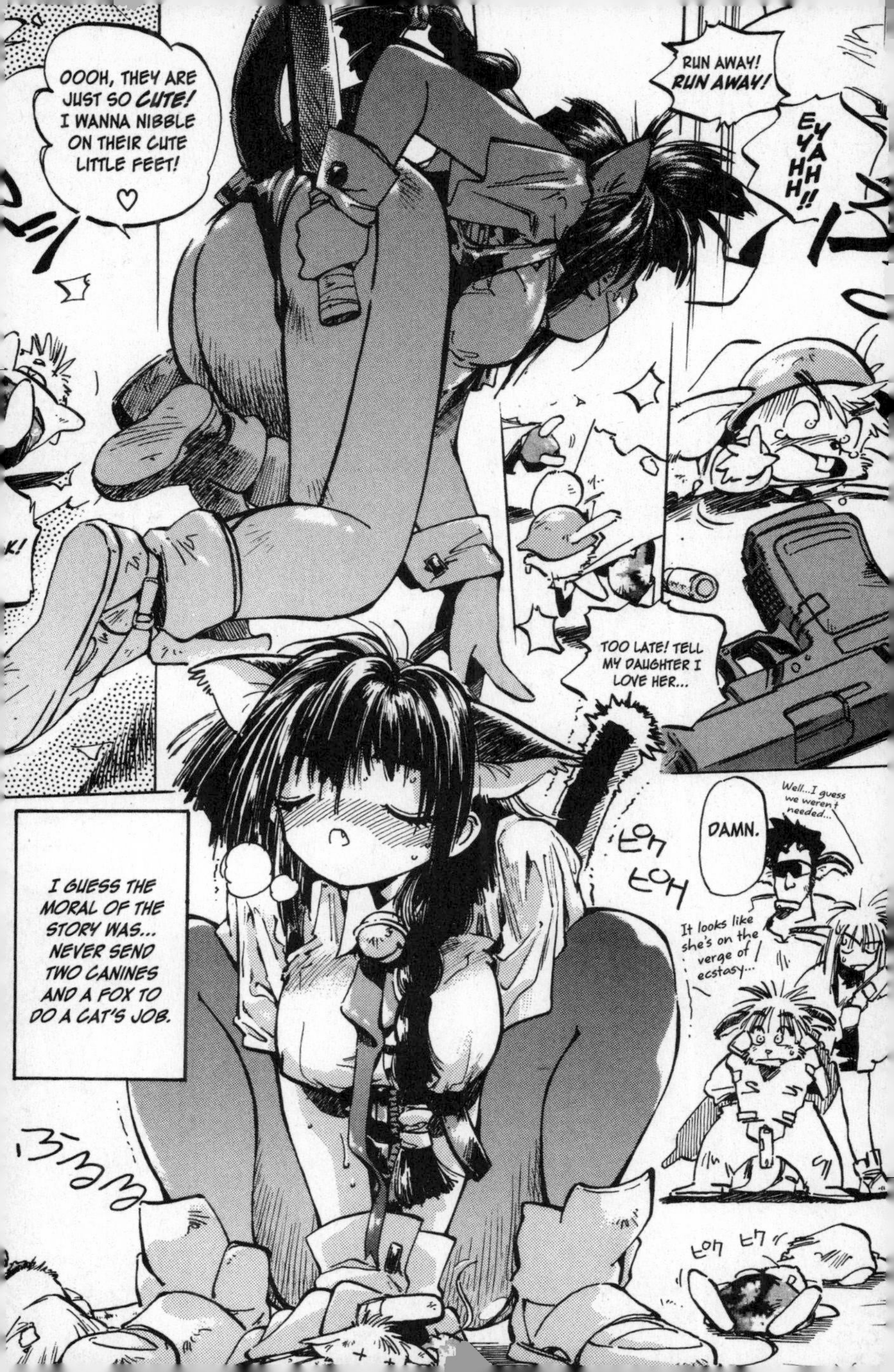

RUN AWAY! RUN AWAY!
EYYAHH!!
OOOH, THEY ARE JUST SO CUTE! I WANNA NIBBLE ON THEIR CUTE LITTLE FEET! ♡
TOO LATE! TELL MY DAUGHTER I LOVE HER...
DAMN.
Well...I guess we weren't needed...
It looks like she's on the verge of ecstasy...
ピク ヒク
ピクピク ピクピク
I GUESS THE MORAL OF THE STORY WAS... NEVER SEND TWO CANINES AND A FOX TO DO A CAT'S JOB.
ぶるるる

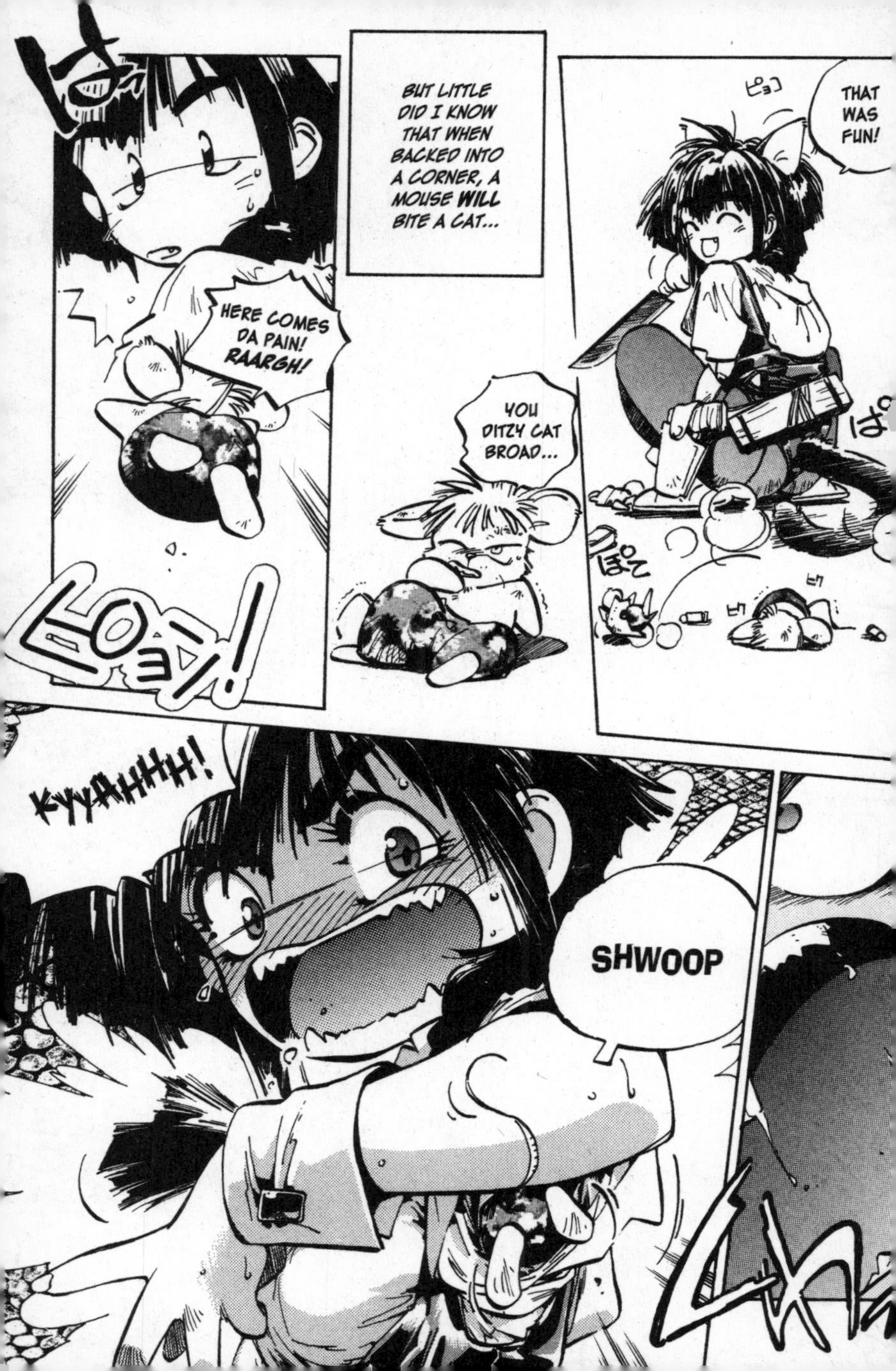
ピョコ
THAT WAS FUN!
ぱっ
ぽて
BUT LITTLE DID I KNOW THAT WHEN BACKED INTO A CORNER, A MOUSE **WILL** BITE A CAT...
YOU DITZY CAT BROAD...
HERE COMES DA PAIN! **RAARGH!**
SHWOOP
KYYAHHHH!

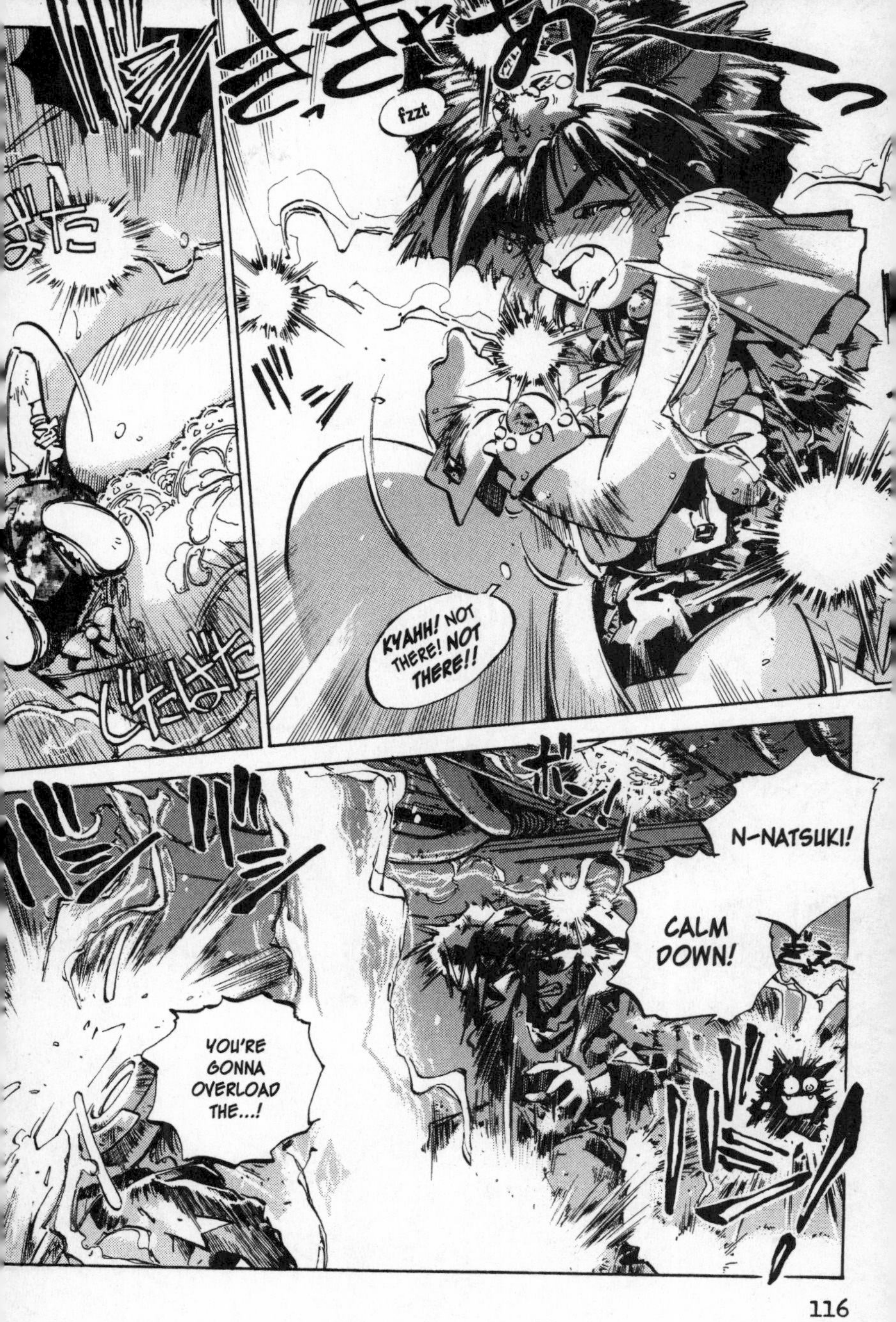
fzzt
KYAHH! NOT THERE! NOT THERE!!
N-NATSUKI!
CALM DOWN!
YOU'RE GONNA OVERLOAD THE...!

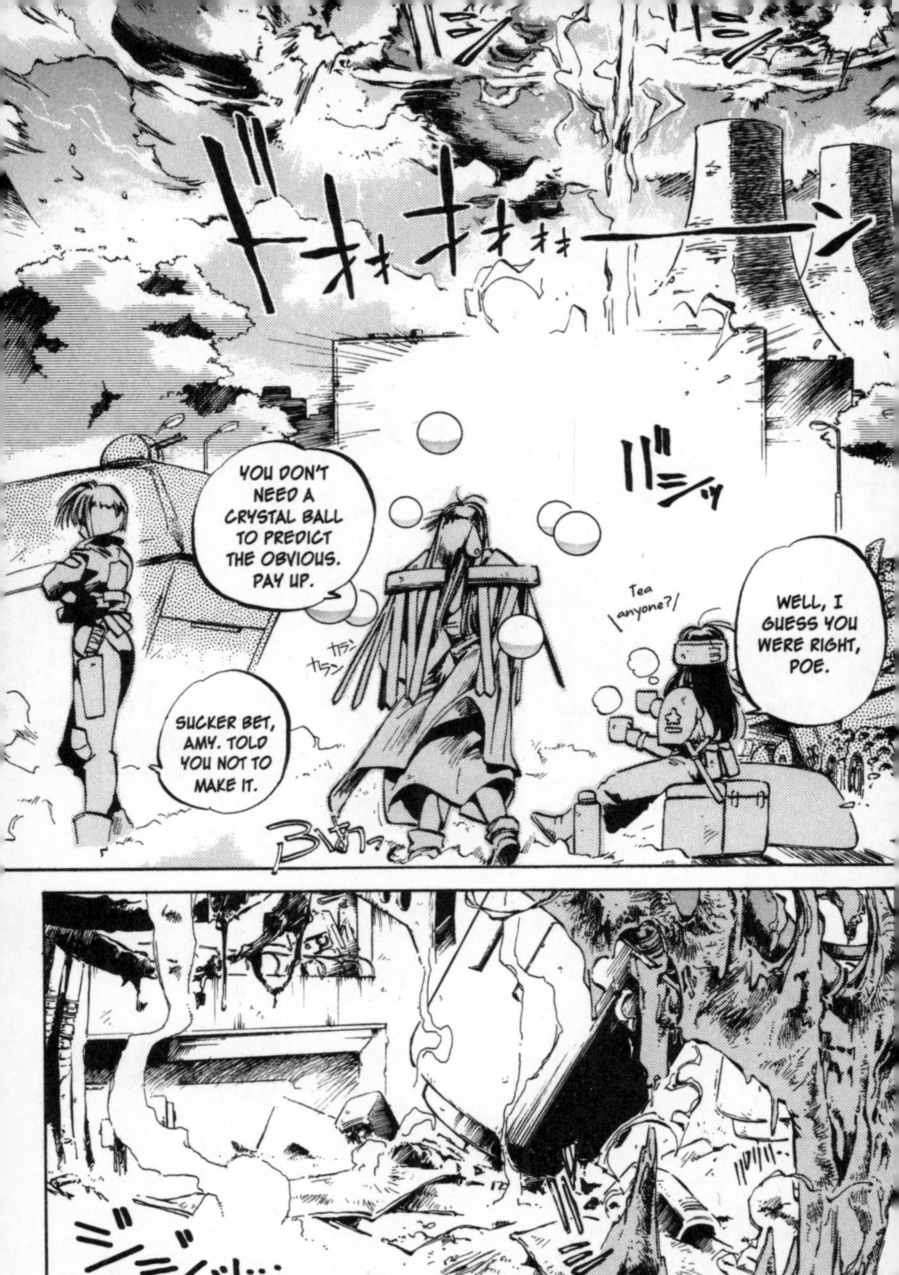
WELL, I GUESS YOU WERE RIGHT, POE.
Tea anyone?!
YOU DON'T NEED A CRYSTAL BALL TO PREDICT THE OBVIOUS. PAY UP.
SUCKER BET, AMY. TOLD YOU NOT TO MAKE IT.

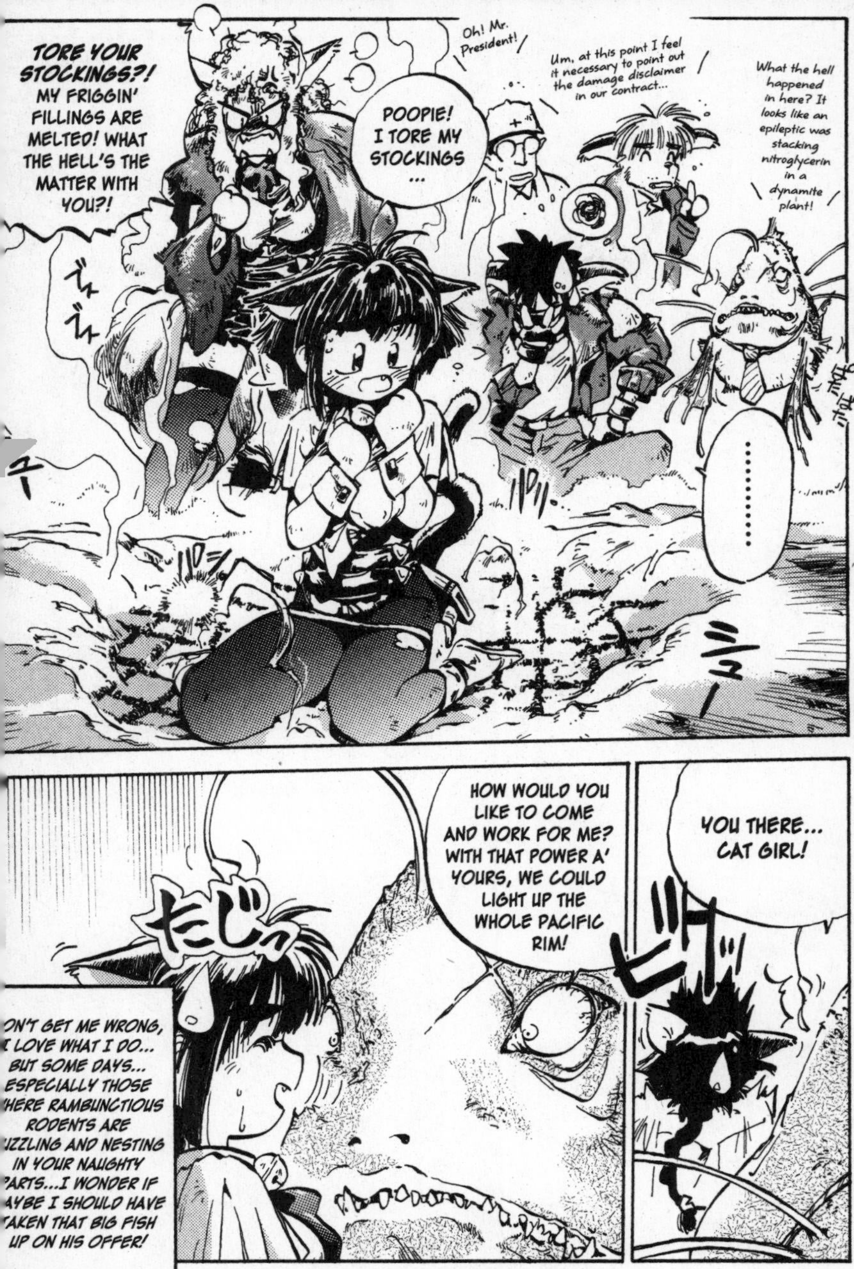
What the hell happened in here? It looks like an epileptic was stacking nitroglycerin in a dynamite plant!
Um, at this point I feel it necessary to point out the damage disclaimer in our contract...
Oh! Mr. President!
POOPIE! I TORE MY STOCKINGS ...
TORE YOUR STOCKINGS?! MY FRIGGIN' FILLINGS ARE MELTED! WHAT THE HELL'S THE MATTER WITH YOU?!
......
YOU THERE... CAT GIRL!
HOW WOULD YOU LIKE TO COME AND WORK FOR ME? WITH THAT POWER A' YOURS, WE COULD LIGHT UP THE WHOLE PACIFIC RIM!
ON'T GET ME WRONG, I LOVE WHAT I DO... BUT SOME DAYS... ESPECIALLY THOSE HERE RAMBUNCTIOUS RODENTS ARE UZZLING AND NESTING IN YOUR NAUGHTY ARTS...I WONDER IF AYBE I SHOULD HAVE AKEN THAT BIG FISH UP ON HIS OFFER!

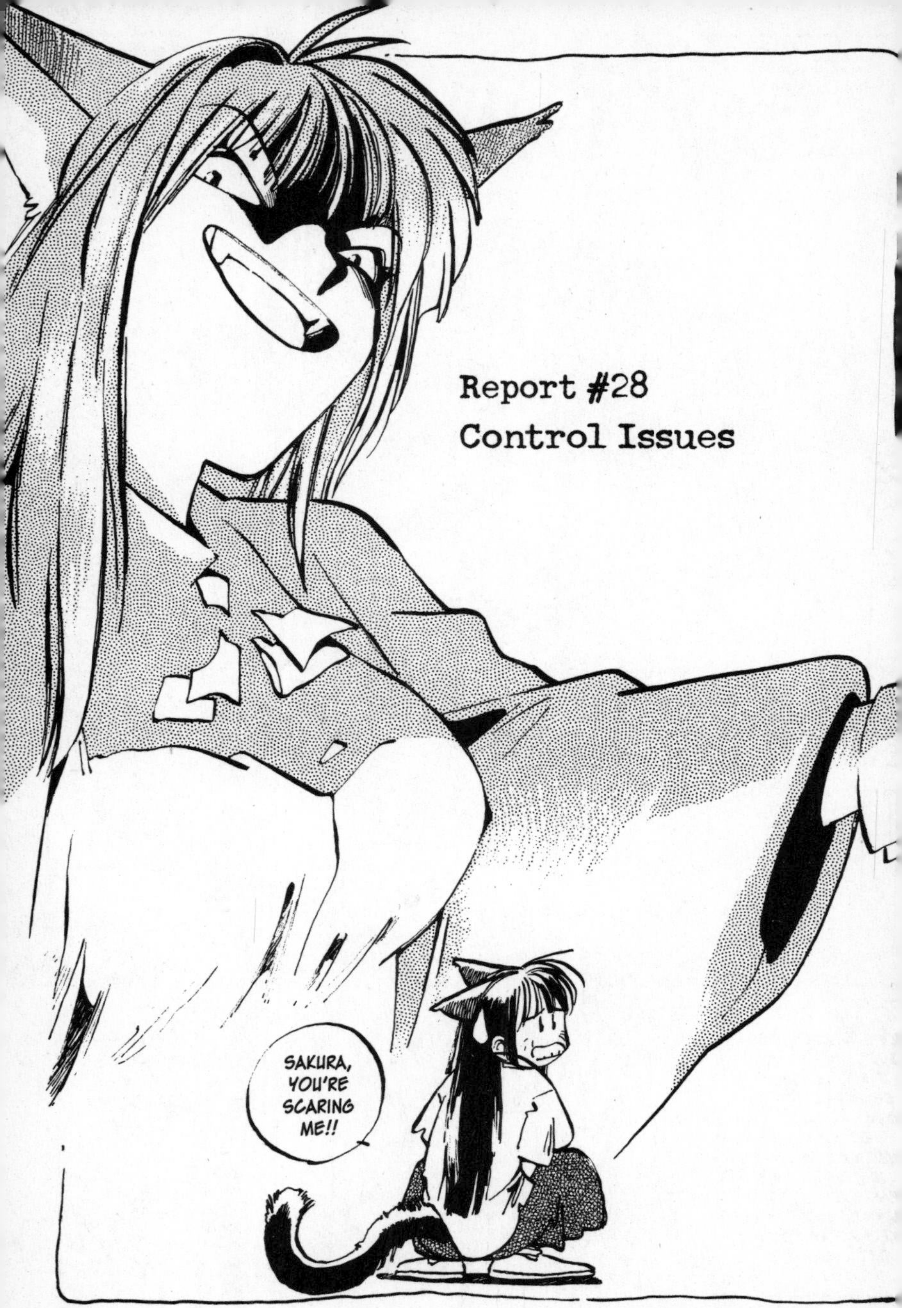
Report #28
Control Issues
SAKURA, YOU'RE SCARING ME!!

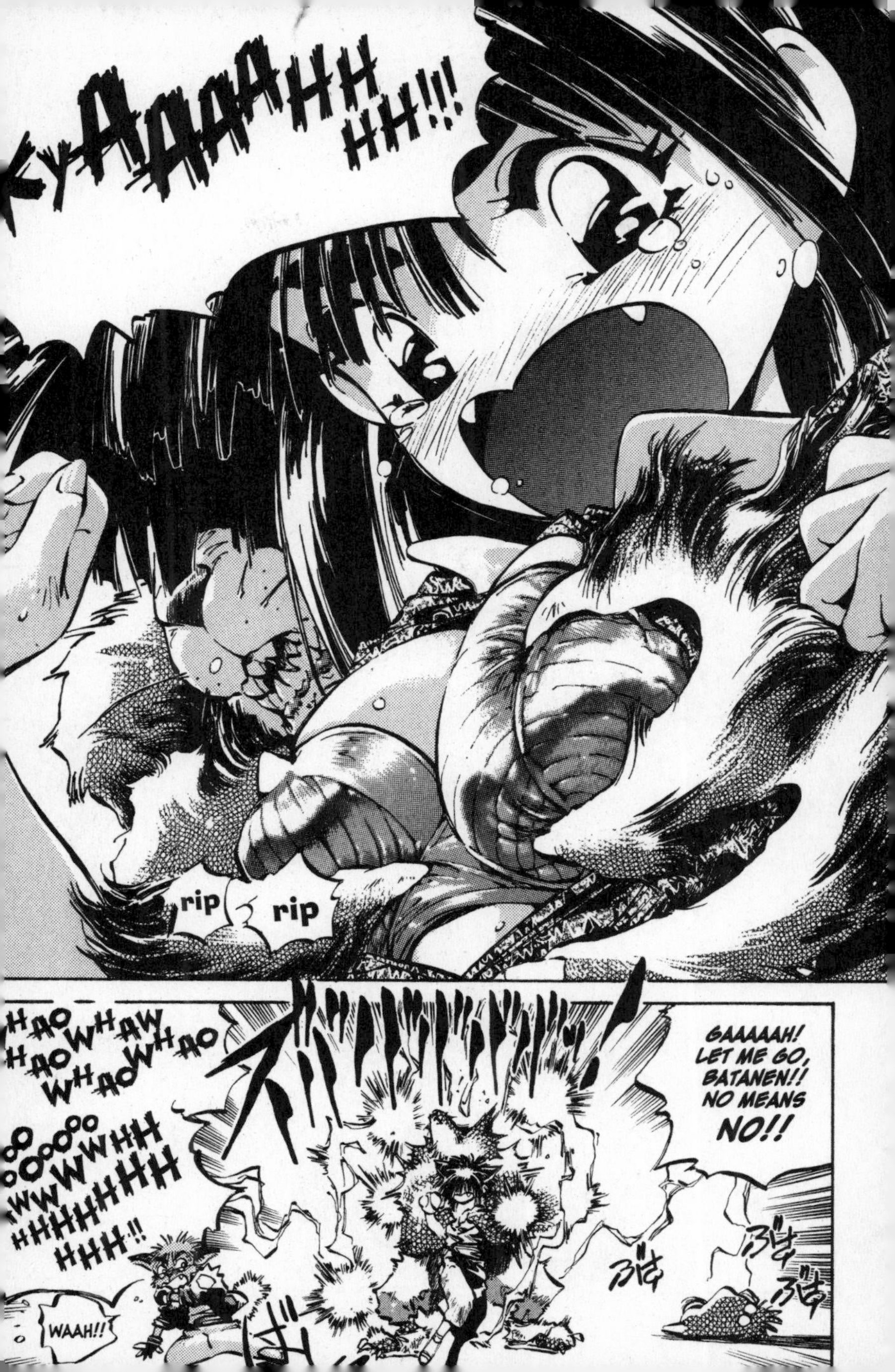
KYAAAAHH
HH!!!
rip
rip
GAAAAAH! LET ME GO, BATANEN!! NO MEANS NO!!
HAOWHAW
HAOWHAO
WHAO
OOOOOOO
OOOWWWHH
WWWHHHHHH
HHHHHHHHH
HHH!!
WAAH!!

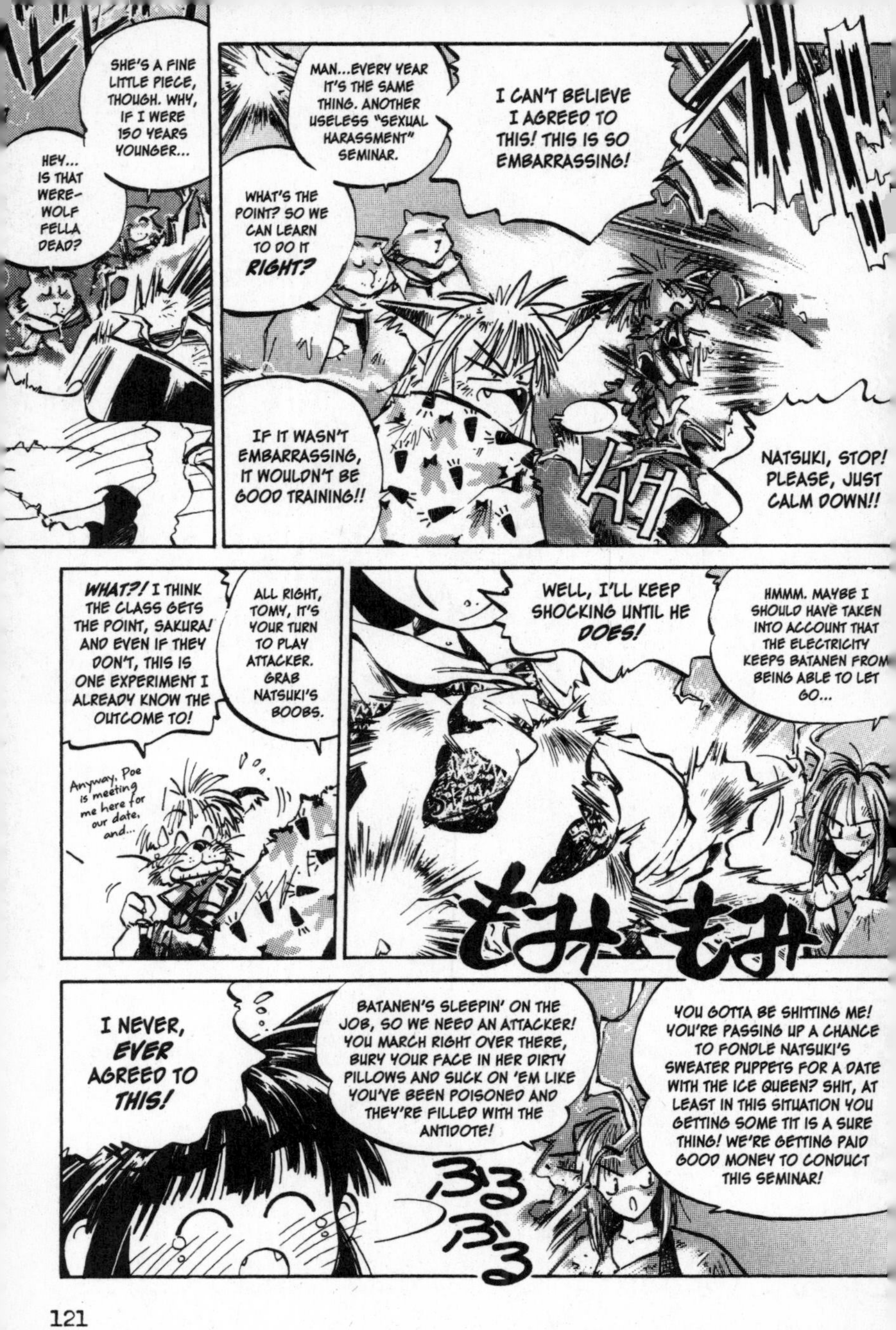
I CAN'T BELIEVE I AGREED TO THIS! THIS IS SO EMBARRASSING!
MAN...EVERY YEAR IT'S THE SAME THING. ANOTHER USELESS "SEXUAL HARASSMENT" SEMINAR.
WHAT'S THE POINT? SO WE CAN LEARN TO DO IT RIGHT?
NATSUKI, STOP! PLEASE, JUST CALM DOWN!!
IF IT WASN'T EMBARRASSING, IT WOULDN'T BE GOOD TRAINING!!
SHE'S A FINE LITTLE PIECE, THOUGH. WHY, IF I WERE 150 YEARS YOUNGER...
HEY... IS THAT WERE-WOLF FELLA DEAD?
HMMM. MAYBE I SHOULD HAVE TAKEN INTO ACCOUNT THAT THE ELECTRICITY KEEPS BATANEN FROM BEING ABLE TO LET GO...
WELL, I'LL KEEP SHOCKING UNTIL HE DOES!
もみもみ
ALL RIGHT, TOMY, IT'S YOUR TURN TO PLAY ATTACKER. GRAB NATSUKI'S BOOBS.
WHAT?! I THINK THE CLASS GETS THE POINT, SAKURA! AND EVEN IF THEY DON'T, THIS IS ONE EXPERIMENT I ALREADY KNOW THE OUTCOME TO!
Anyway, Poe is meeting me here for our date, and...
YOU GOTTA BE SHITTING ME! YOU'RE PASSING UP A CHANCE TO FONDLE NATSUKI'S SWEATER PUPPETS FOR A DATE WITH THE ICE QUEEN? SHIT, AT LEAST IN THIS SITUATION YOU GETTING SOME TIT IS A SURE THING! WE'RE GETTING PAID GOOD MONEY TO CONDUCT THIS SEMINAR!
BATANEN'S SLEEPIN' ON THE JOB, SO WE NEED AN ATTACKER! YOU MARCH RIGHT OVER THERE, BURY YOUR FACE IN HER DIRTY PILLOWS AND SUCK ON 'EM LIKE YOU'VE BEEN POISONED AND THEY'RE FILLED WITH THE ANTIDOTE!
ぷるぷる
I NEVER, EVER AGREED TO THIS!

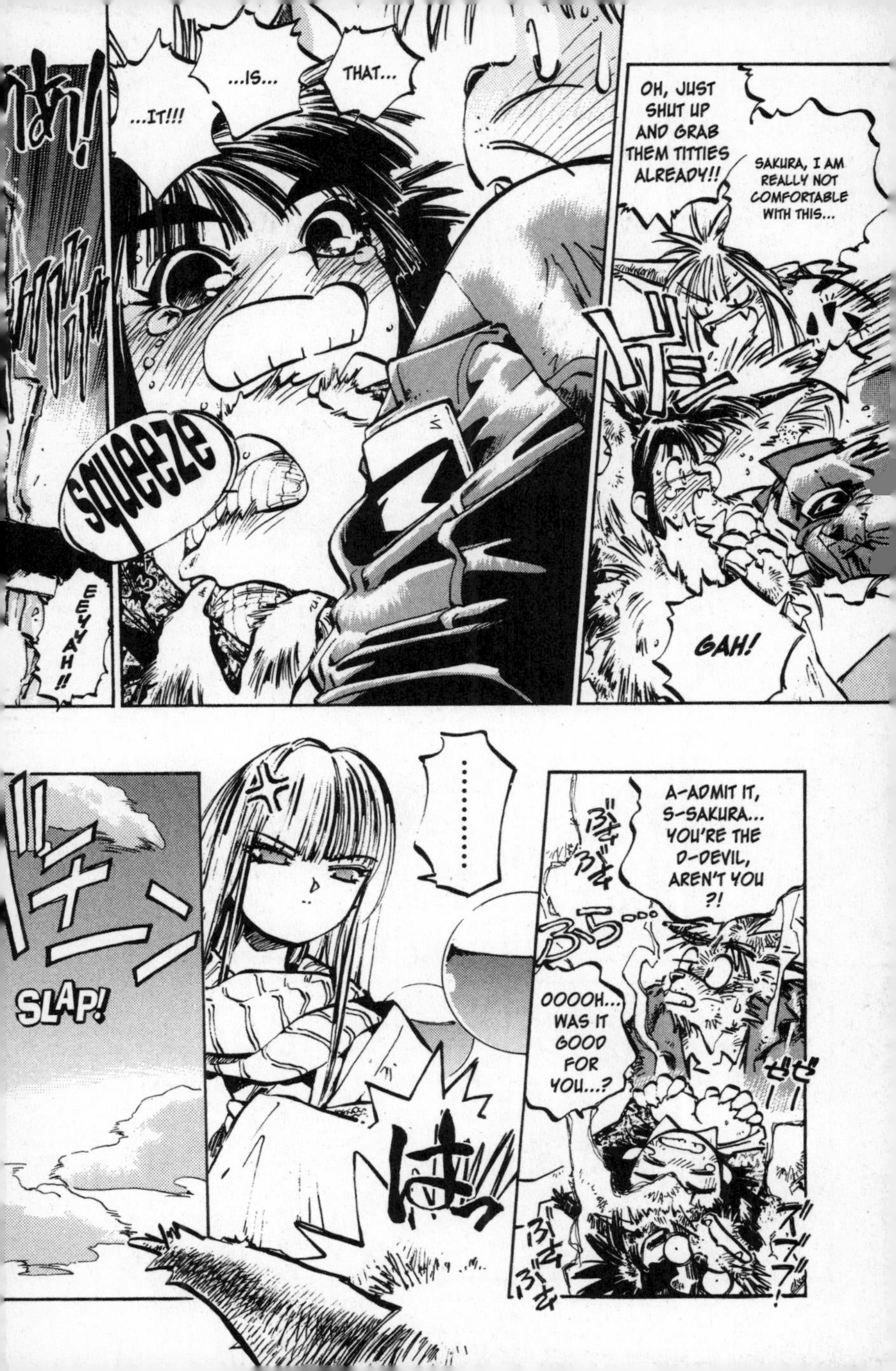
SAKURA, I AM REALLY NOT COMFORTABLE WITH THIS...
OH, JUST SHUT UP AND GRAB THEM TITTIES ALREADY!!
GAH!
THAT...
...IS...
...IT!!!
SQUEEZE
EEYYAH!!
A-ADMIT IT, S-SAKURA... YOU'RE THE D-DEVIL, AREN'T YOU?!
OOOOH... WAS IT GOOD FOR YOU...?
....
SLAP!

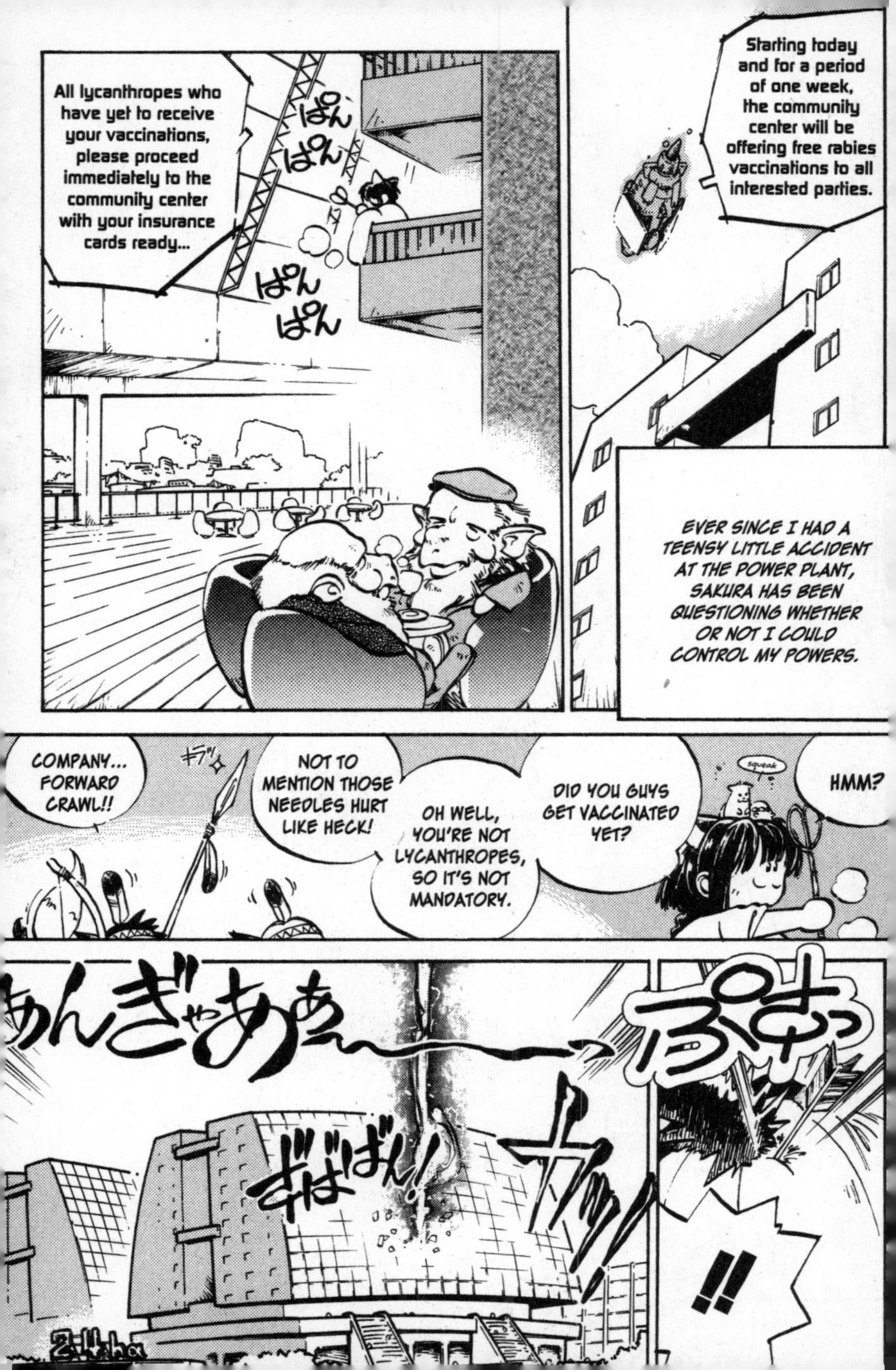

Starting today and for a period of one week, the community center will be offering free rabies vaccinations to all interested parties.
EVER SINCE I HAD A TEENSY LITTLE ACCIDENT AT THE POWER PLANT, SAKURA HAS BEEN QUESTIONING WHETHER OR NOT I COULD CONTROL MY POWERS.
All lycanthropes who have yet to receive your vaccinations, please proceed immediately to the community center with your insurance cards ready...
ぱん ぱん
ぱん ぱん
HMM?
squeak
DID YOU GUYS GET VACCINATED YET?
OH WELL, YOU'RE NOT LYCANTHROPES, SO IT'S NOT MANDATORY.
NOT TO MENTION THOSE NEEDLES HURT LIKE HECK!
キラッ
COMPANY... FORWARD CRAWL!!
ぷすっ
!!
あんぎゃああ〜
ずばばん!
ガッ!!

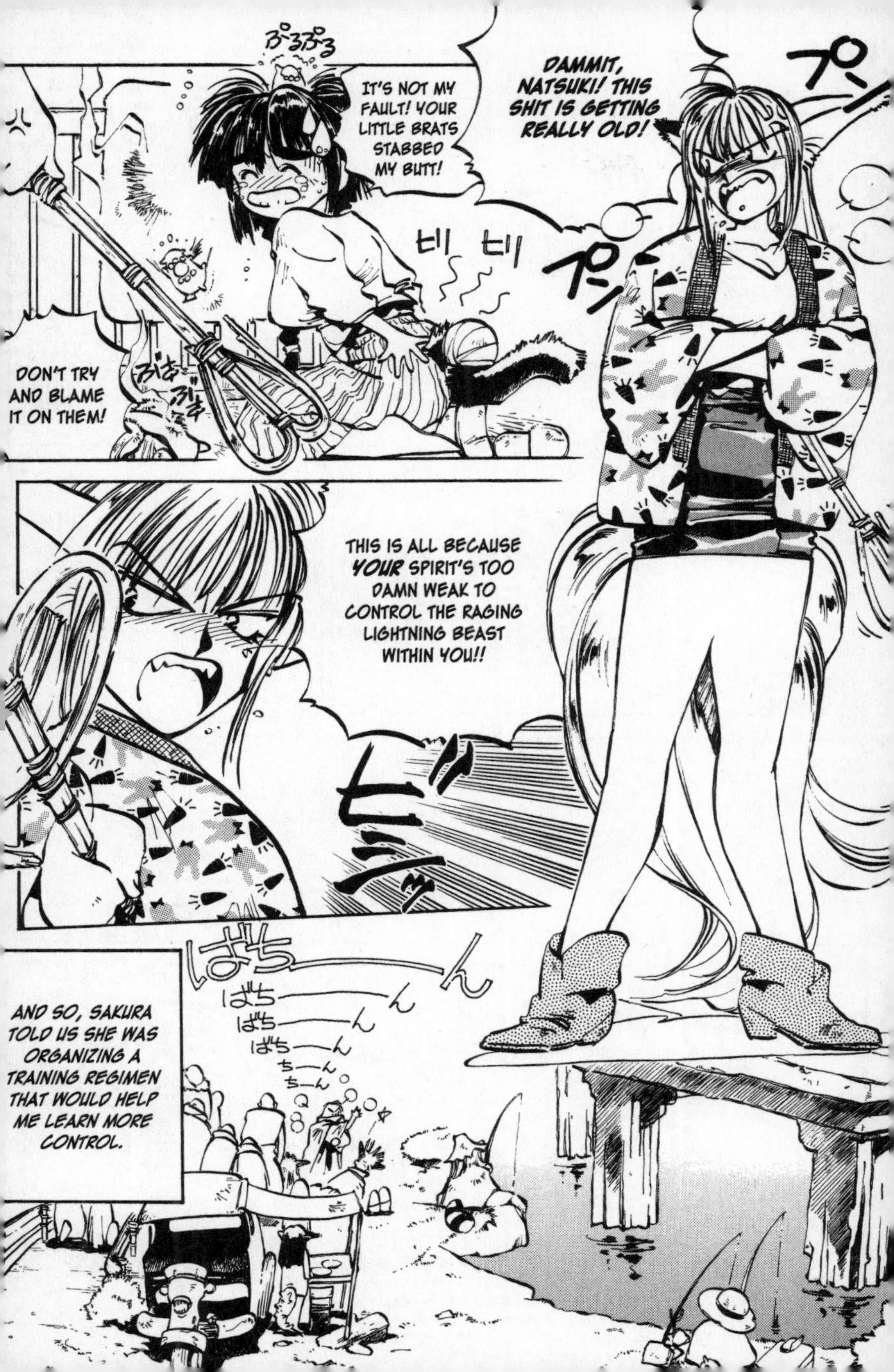

DAMMIT, NATSUKI! THIS SHIT IS GETTING REALLY OLD!
プン
ぷるぷる
IT'S NOT MY FAULT! YOUR LITTLE BRATS STABBED MY BUTT!
プン
ビリ ビリ
DON'T TRY AND BLAME IT ON THEM!
THIS IS ALL BECAUSE YOUR SPIRIT'S TOO DAMN WEAK TO CONTROL THE RAGING LIGHTNING BEAST WITHIN YOU!!
ぱち————ん
ぱち————ん
ぱち———ん
ぱち——ん
ち—ん
ち—ん
AND SO, SAKURA TOLD US SHE WAS ORGANIZING A TRAINING REGIMEN THAT WOULD HELP ME LEARN MORE CONTROL.

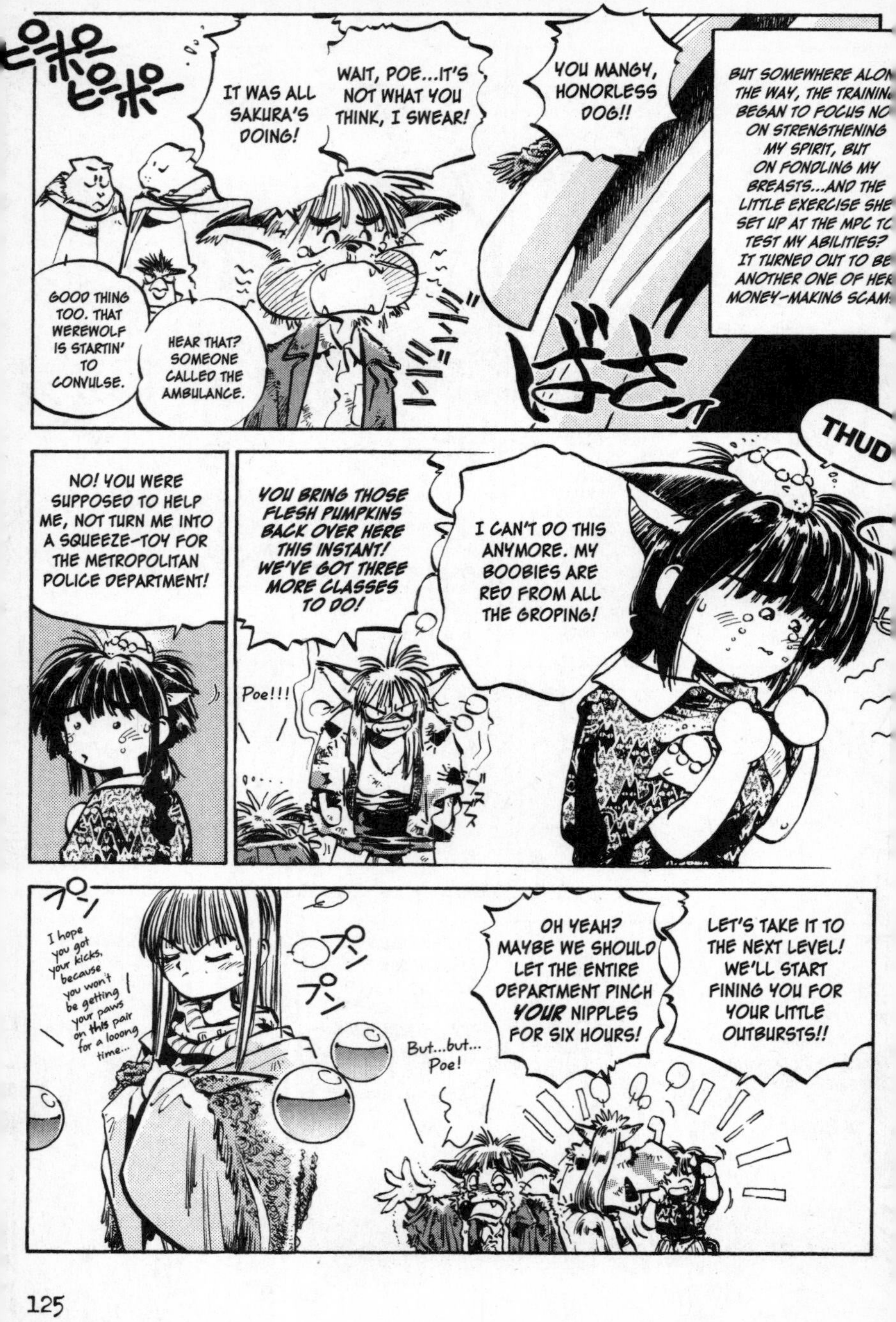

BUT SOMEWHERE ALON
THE WAY, THE TRAININ
BEGAN TO FOCUS NO
ON STRENGTHENING
MY SPIRIT, BUT
ON FONDLING MY
BREASTS...AND THE
LITTLE EXERCISE SHE
SET UP AT THE MPC TO
TEST MY ABILITIES?
IT TURNED OUT TO BE
ANOTHER ONE OF HER
MONEY-MAKING SCAMS
YOU MANGY, HONORLESS DOG!!
ばさっ
WAIT, POE...IT'S NOT WHAT YOU THINK, I SWEAR!
IT WAS ALL SAKURA'S DOING!
ピーポーピーポー
HEAR THAT? SOMEONE CALLED THE AMBULANCE.
GOOD THING TOO. THAT WEREWOLF IS STARTIN' TO CONVULSE.
THUD
I CAN'T DO THIS ANYMORE. MY BOOBIES ARE RED FROM ALL THE GROPING!
YOU BRING THOSE FLESH PUMPKINS BACK OVER HERE THIS INSTANT! WE'VE GOT THREE MORE CLASSES TO DO!
Poe!!!
NO! YOU WERE SUPPOSED TO HELP ME, NOT TURN ME INTO A SQUEEZE-TOY FOR THE METROPOLITAN POLICE DEPARTMENT!
LET'S TAKE IT TO THE NEXT LEVEL! WE'LL START FINING YOU FOR YOUR LITTLE OUTBURSTS!!
OH YEAH? MAYBE WE SHOULD LET THE ENTIRE DEPARTMENT PINCH YOUR NIPPLES FOR SIX HOURS!
But...but... Poe!
プンプン
プン
I hope you got your kicks, because you won't be getting your paws on this pair for a looong time...

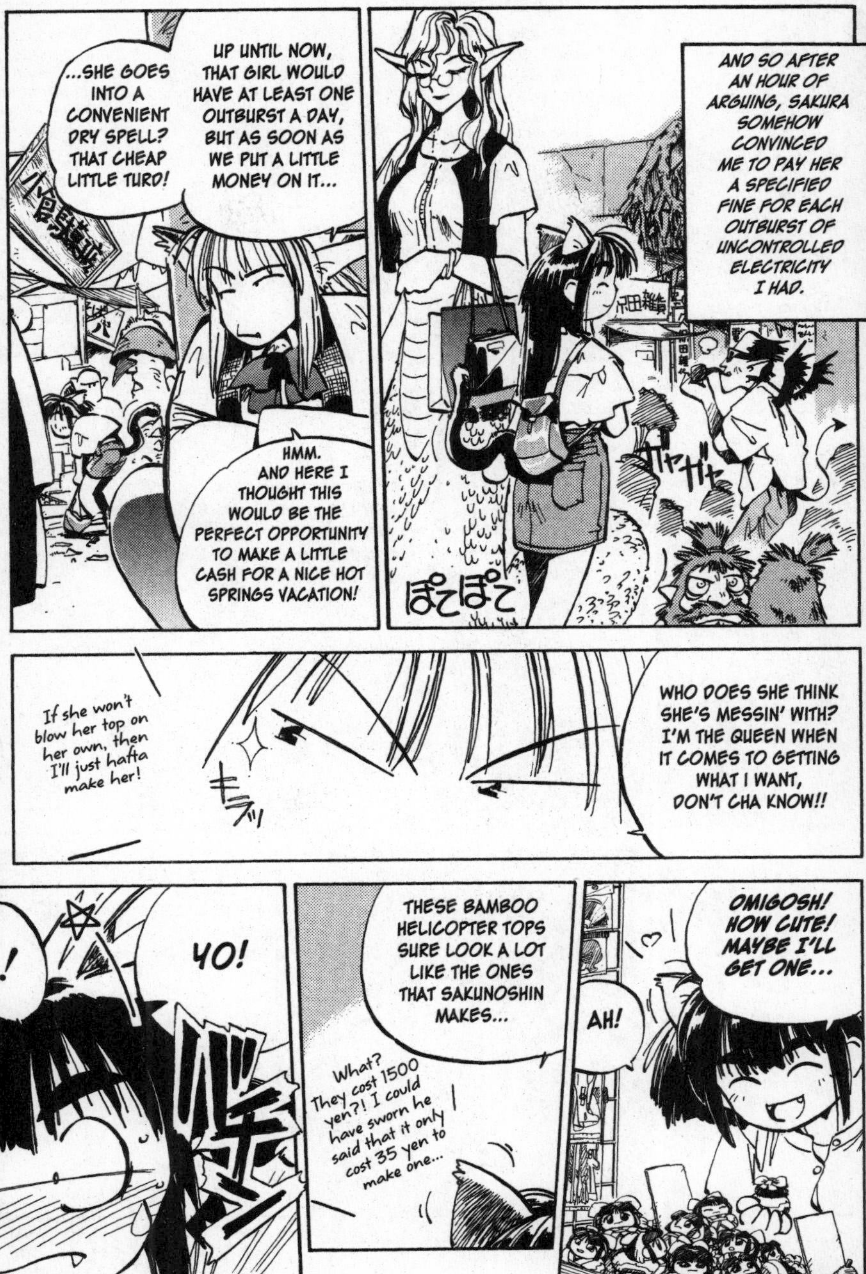
AND SO AFTER AN HOUR OF ARGUING, SAKURA SOMEHOW CONVINCED ME TO PAY HER A SPECIFIED FINE FOR EACH OUTBURST OF UNCONTROLLED ELECTRICITY I HAD.
ガヤガヤ
ぽてぽて
UP UNTIL NOW, THAT GIRL WOULD HAVE AT LEAST ONE OUTBURST A DAY, BUT AS SOON AS WE PUT A LITTLE MONEY ON IT...
...SHE GOES INTO A CONVENIENT DRY SPELL? THAT CHEAP LITTLE TURD!
HMM. AND HERE I THOUGHT THIS WOULD BE THE PERFECT OPPORTUNITY TO MAKE A LITTLE CASH FOR A NICE HOT SPRINGS VACATION!
WHO DOES SHE THINK SHE'S MESSIN' WITH? I'M THE QUEEN WHEN IT COMES TO GETTING WHAT I WANT, DON'T CHA KNOW!!
If she won't blow her top on her own, then I'll just hafta make her!
OMIGOSH! HOW CUTE! MAYBE I'LL GET ONE...
AH!
THESE BAMBOO HELICOPTER TOPS SURE LOOK A LOT LIKE THE ONES THAT SAKUNOSHIN MAKES...
What? They cost 1500 yen?! I could have sworn he said that it only cost 35 yen to make one...
YO!
!

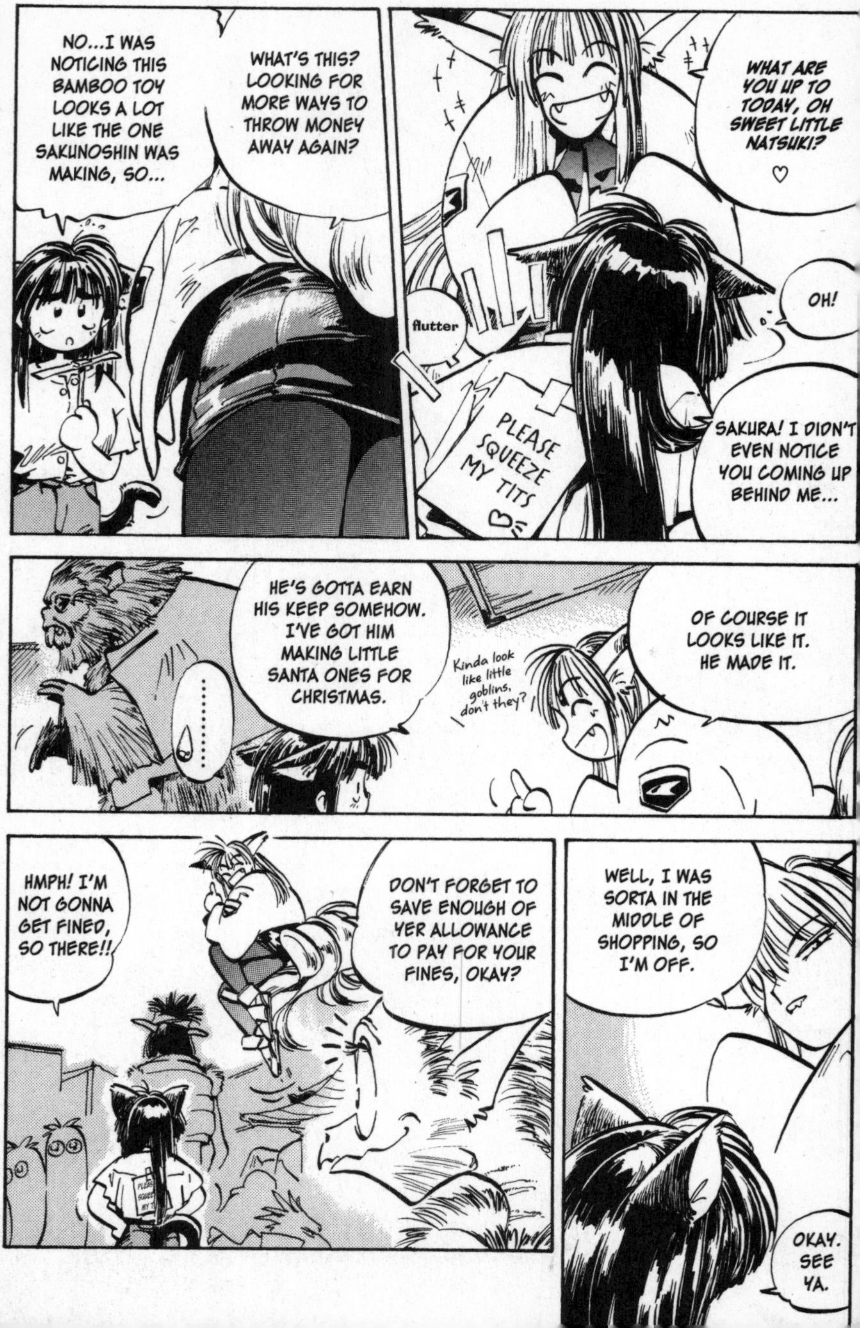

WHAT ARE YOU UP TO TODAY, OH SWEET LITTLE NATSUKI? ♡
OH!
SAKURA! I DIDN'T EVEN NOTICE YOU COMING UP BEHIND ME...
flutter
PLEASE SQUEEZE MY TITS ♡
WHAT'S THIS? LOOKING FOR MORE WAYS TO THROW MONEY AWAY AGAIN?
NO...I WAS NOTICING THIS BAMBOO TOY LOOKS A LOT LIKE THE ONE SAKUNOSHIN WAS MAKING, SO...
OF COURSE IT LOOKS LIKE IT. HE MADE IT.
Kinda look like little goblins, don't they?
HE'S GOTTA EARN HIS KEEP SOMEHOW. I'VE GOT HIM MAKING LITTLE SANTA ONES FOR CHRISTMAS.
......
WELL, I WAS SORTA IN THE MIDDLE OF SHOPPING, SO I'M OFF.
OKAY. SEE YA.
DON'T FORGET TO SAVE ENOUGH OF YER ALLOWANCE TO PAY FOR YOUR FINES, OKAY?
HMPH! I'M NOT GONNA GET FINED, SO THERE!!

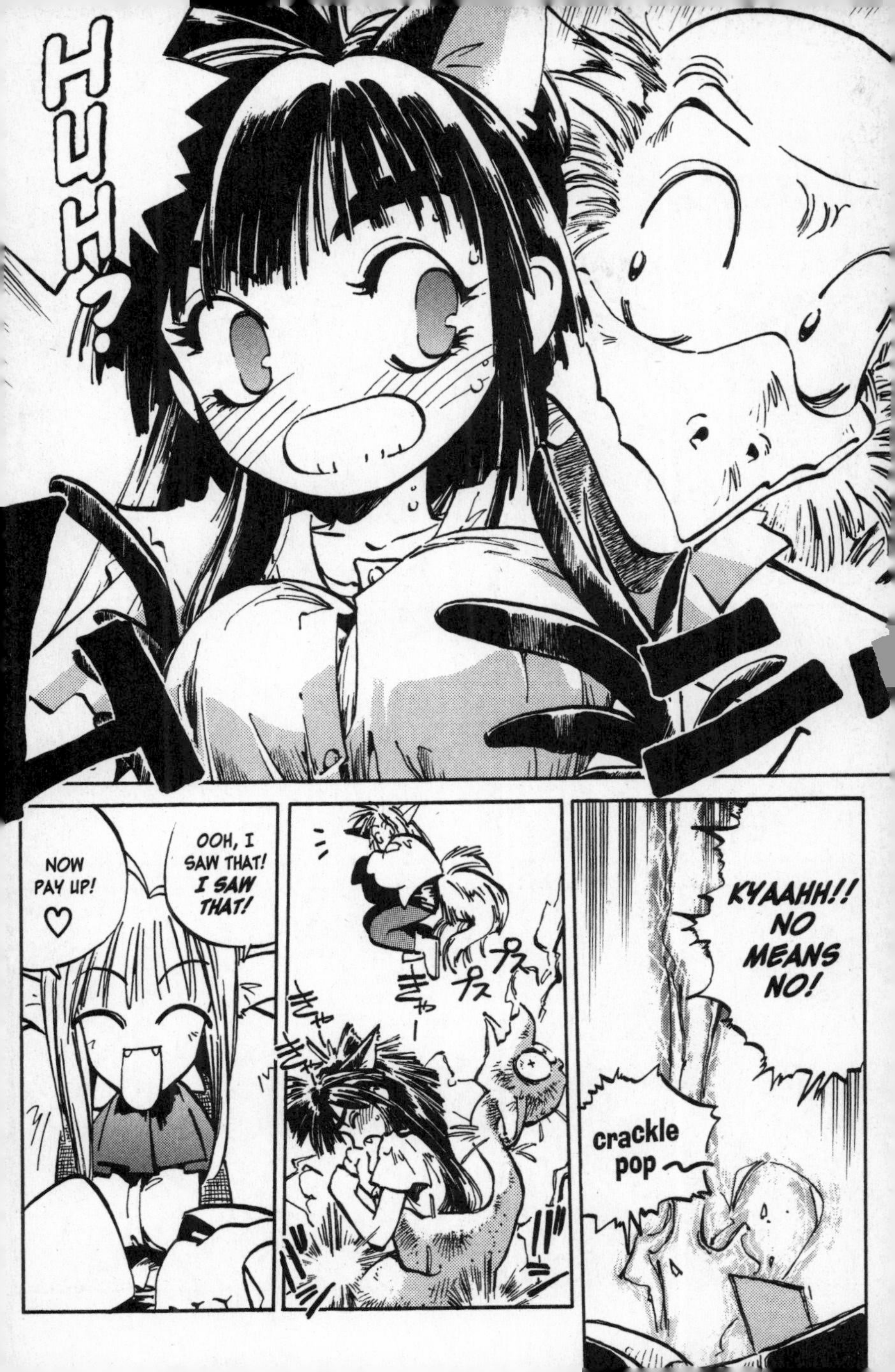
HUH?!
KYAAHH!! NO MEANS NO!
crackle pop~
きゃー
OOH, I SAW THAT! I SAW THAT!
NOW PAY UP! ♡

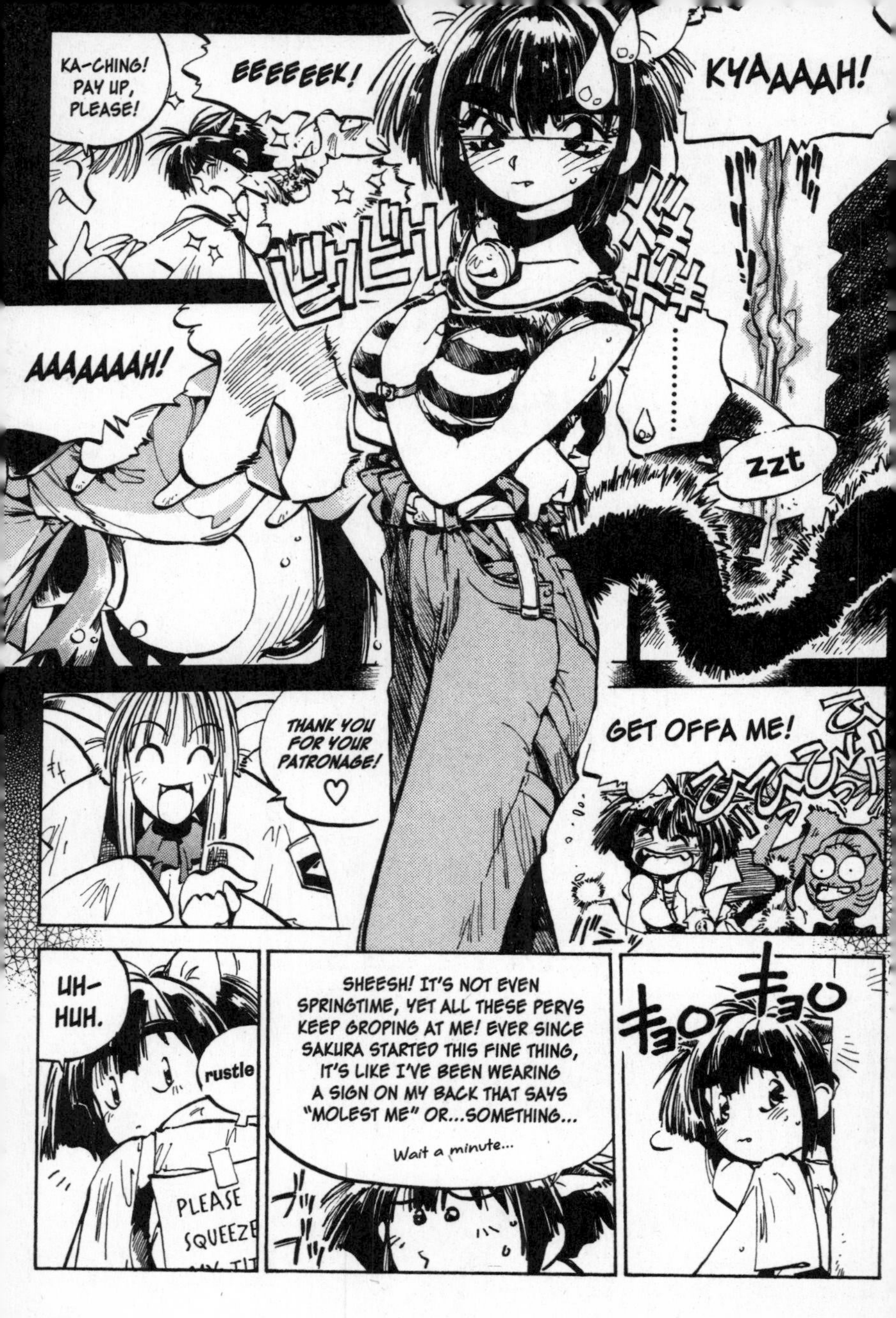
KYAAAAH!
zzt
EEEEEEK!
KA-CHING! PAY UP, PLEASE!
AAAAAAAH!
GET OFFA ME!
THANK YOU FOR YOUR PATRONAGE! ♡
キョロ キョロ
SHEESH! IT'S NOT EVEN SPRINGTIME, YET ALL THESE PERVS KEEP GROPING AT ME! EVER SINCE SAKURA STARTED THIS FINE THING, IT'S LIKE I'VE BEEN WEARING A SIGN ON MY BACK THAT SAYS "MOLEST ME" OR...SOMETHING...
Wait a minute...
UH-HUH.
rustle
PLEASE SQUEEZE

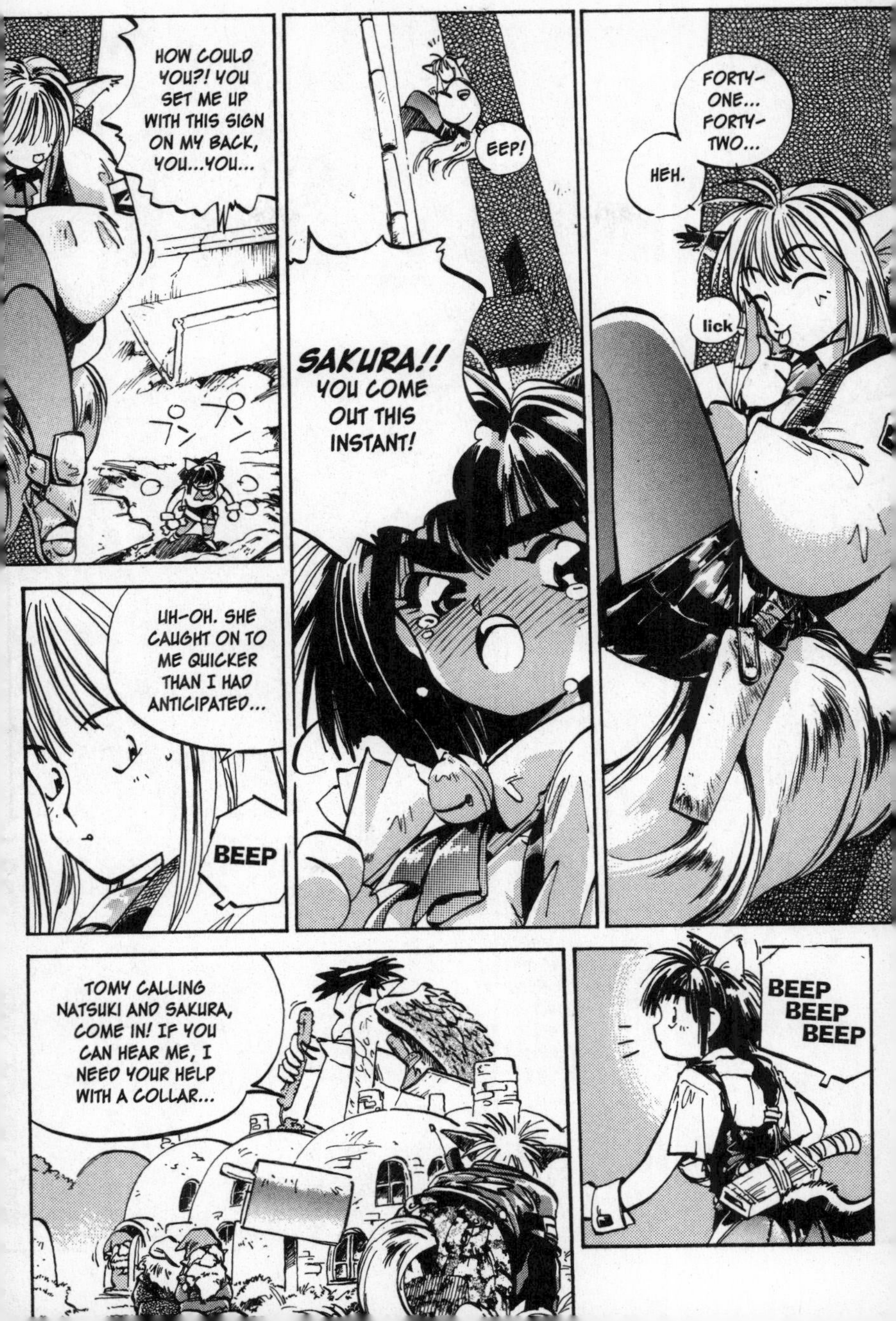
FORTY-ONE... FORTY-TWO...
HEH.
lick
EEP!
SAKURA!! YOU COME OUT THIS INSTANT!
HOW COULD YOU?! YOU SET ME UP WITH THIS SIGN ON MY BACK, YOU...YOU...
UH-OH. SHE CAUGHT ON TO ME QUICKER THAN I HAD ANTICIPATED...
BEEP
BEEP BEEP BEEP
TOMY CALLING NATSUKI AND SAKURA, COME IN! IF YOU CAN HEAR ME, I NEED YOUR HELP WITH A COLLAR...

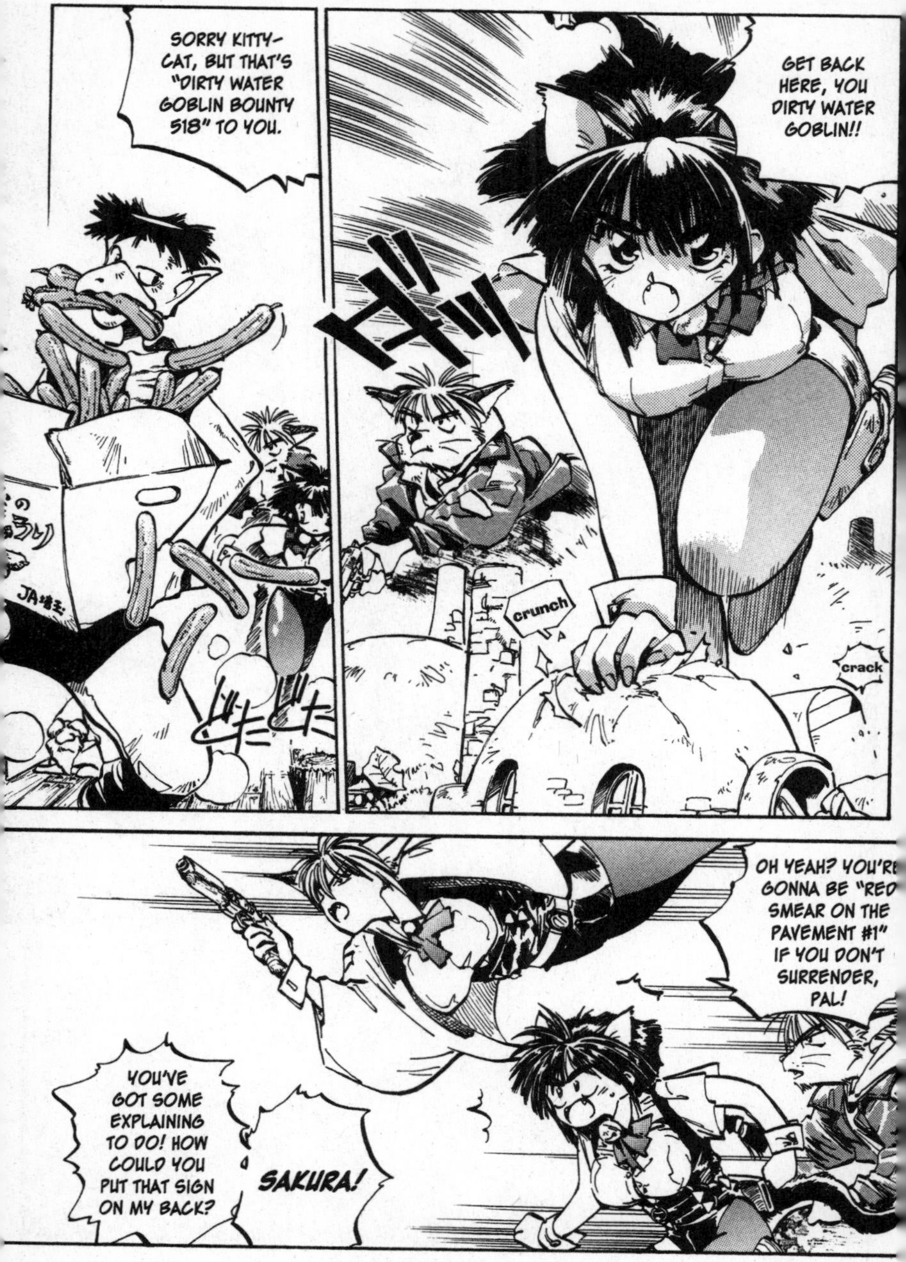
GET BACK HERE, YOU DIRTY WATER GOBLIN!!
crunch
crack
SORRY KITTY-CAT, BUT THAT'S "DIRTY WATER GOBLIN BOUNTY 518" TO YOU.
OH YEAH? YOU'RE GONNA BE "RED SMEAR ON THE PAVEMENT #1" IF YOU DON'T SURRENDER, PAL!
SAKURA!
YOU'VE GOT SOME EXPLAINING TO DO! HOW COULD YOU PUT THAT SIGN ON MY BACK?

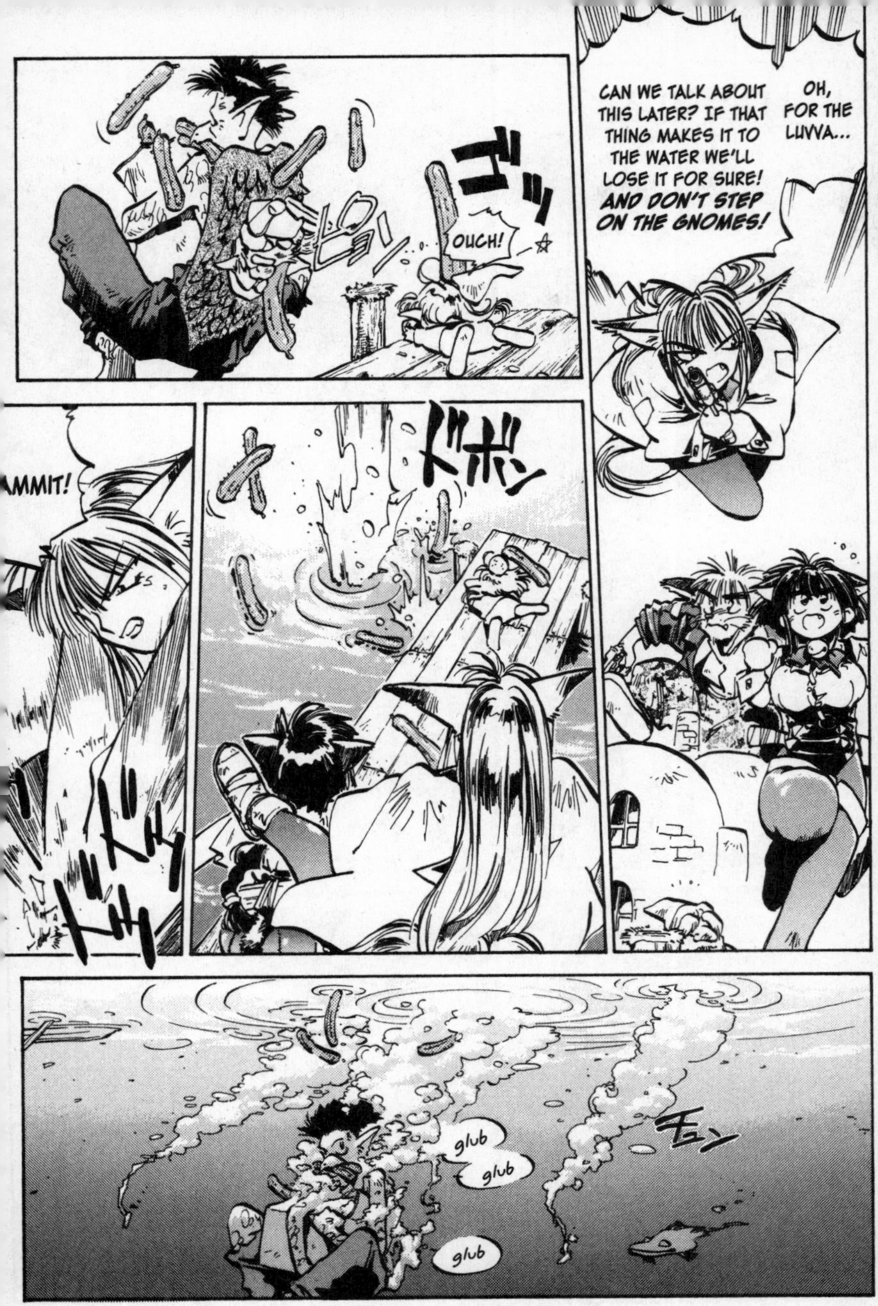

OH, FOR THE LUVVA...
CAN WE TALK ABOUT THIS LATER? IF THAT THING MAKES IT TO THE WATER WE'LL LOSE IT FOR SURE! ***AND DON'T STEP ON THE GNOMES!***
ゴッ
OUCH!
ドボン
AMMIT!
glub
glub
glub

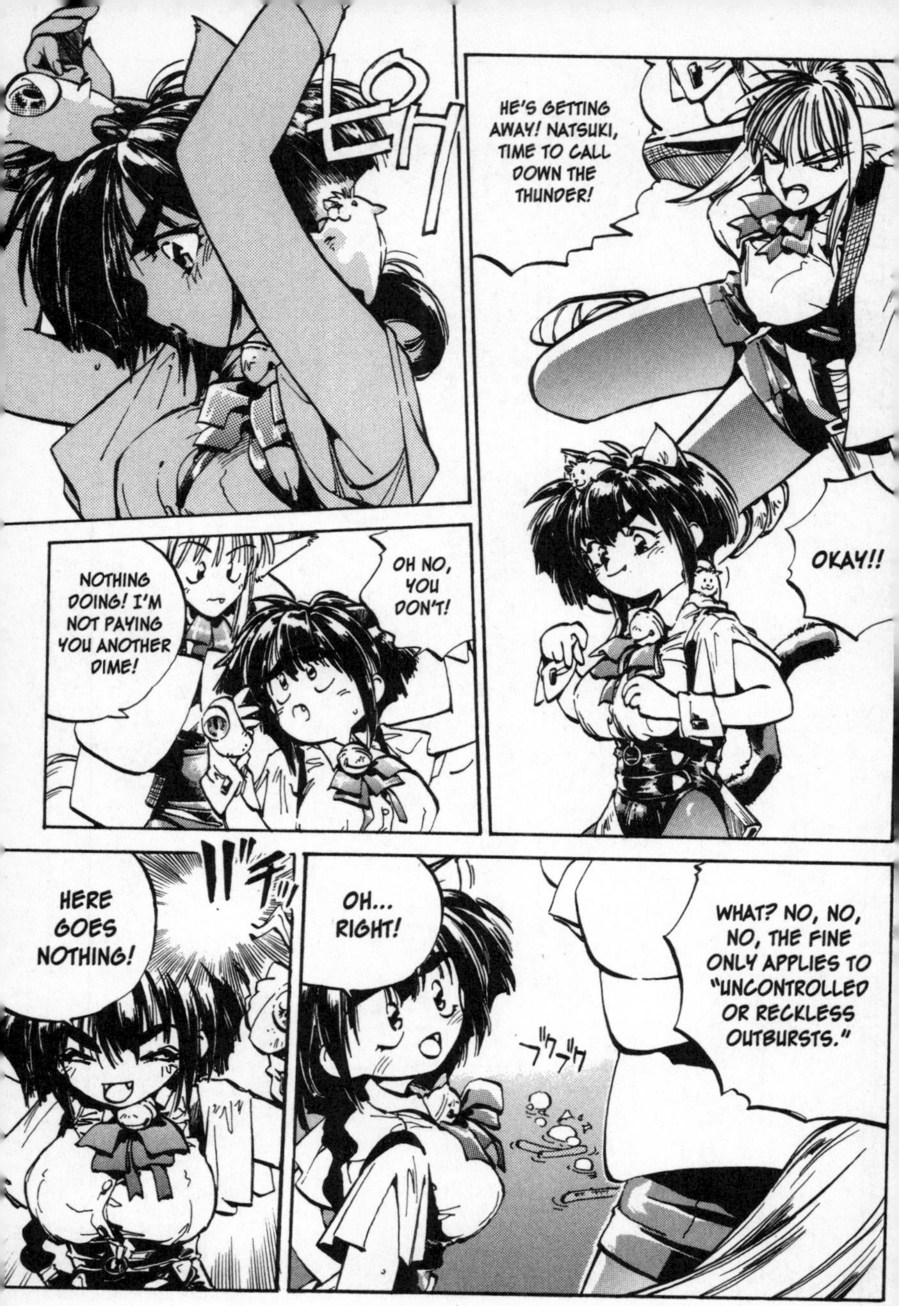
HE'S GETTING AWAY! NATSUKI, TIME TO CALL DOWN THE THUNDER!
OKAY!!
OH NO, YOU DON'T!
NOTHING DOING! I'M NOT PAYING YOU ANOTHER DIME!
WHAT? NO, NO, NO, THE FINE ONLY APPLIES TO "UNCONTROLLED OR RECKLESS OUTBURSTS."
OH... RIGHT!
HERE GOES NOTHING!

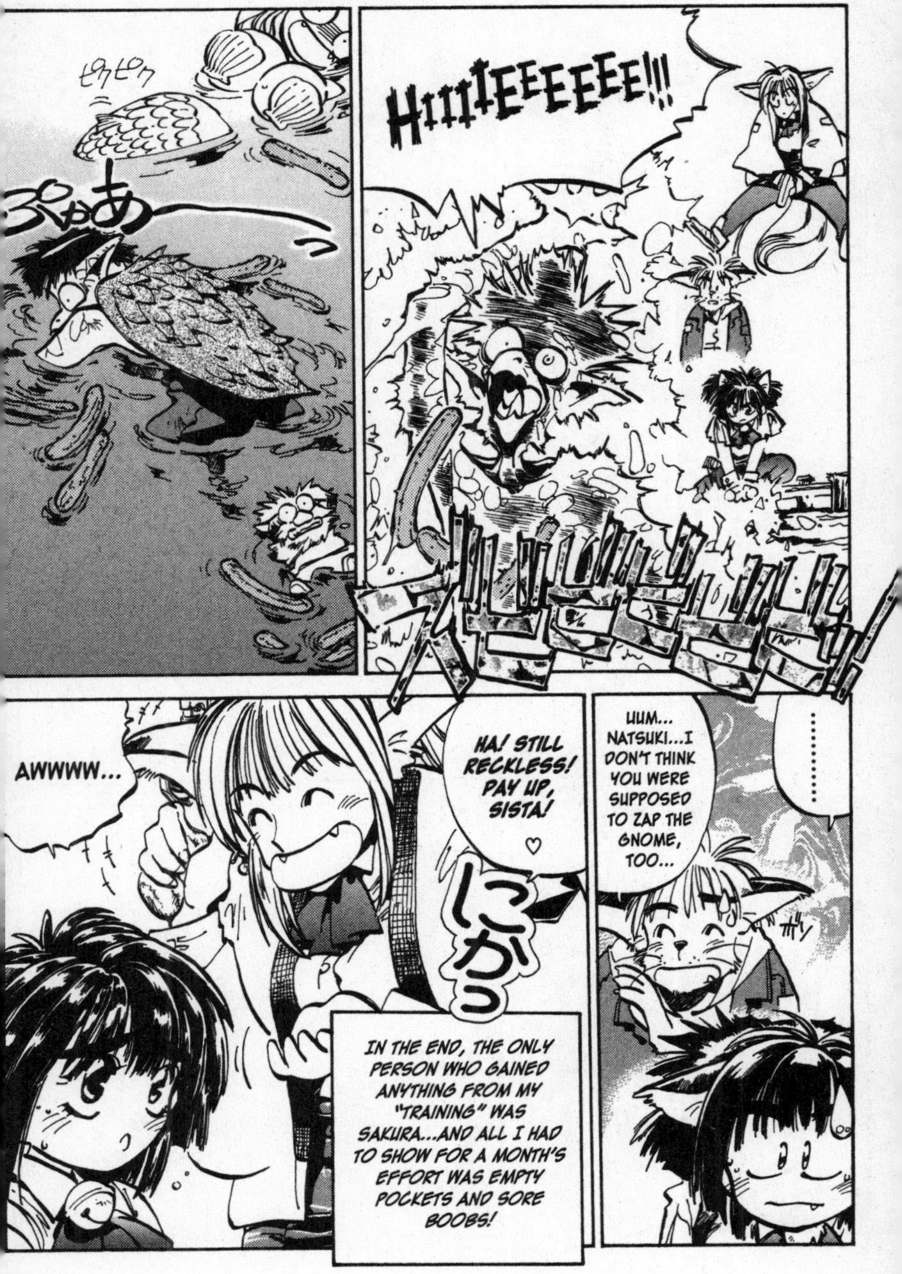
HIIIIEEEEEE!!!
ピクピク
......
UUM... NATSUKI...I DON'T THINK YOU WERE SUPPOSED TO ZAP THE GNOME, TOO...
HA! STILL RECKLESS! PAY UP, SISTA! ♡
にかっ
AWWWW...
IN THE END, THE ONLY PERSON WHO GAINED ANYTHING FROM MY "TRAINING" WAS SAKURA...AND ALL I HAD TO SHOW FOR A MONTH'S EFFORT WAS EMPTY POCKETS AND SORE BOOBS!

Report #29
The Green-Eyed Monster

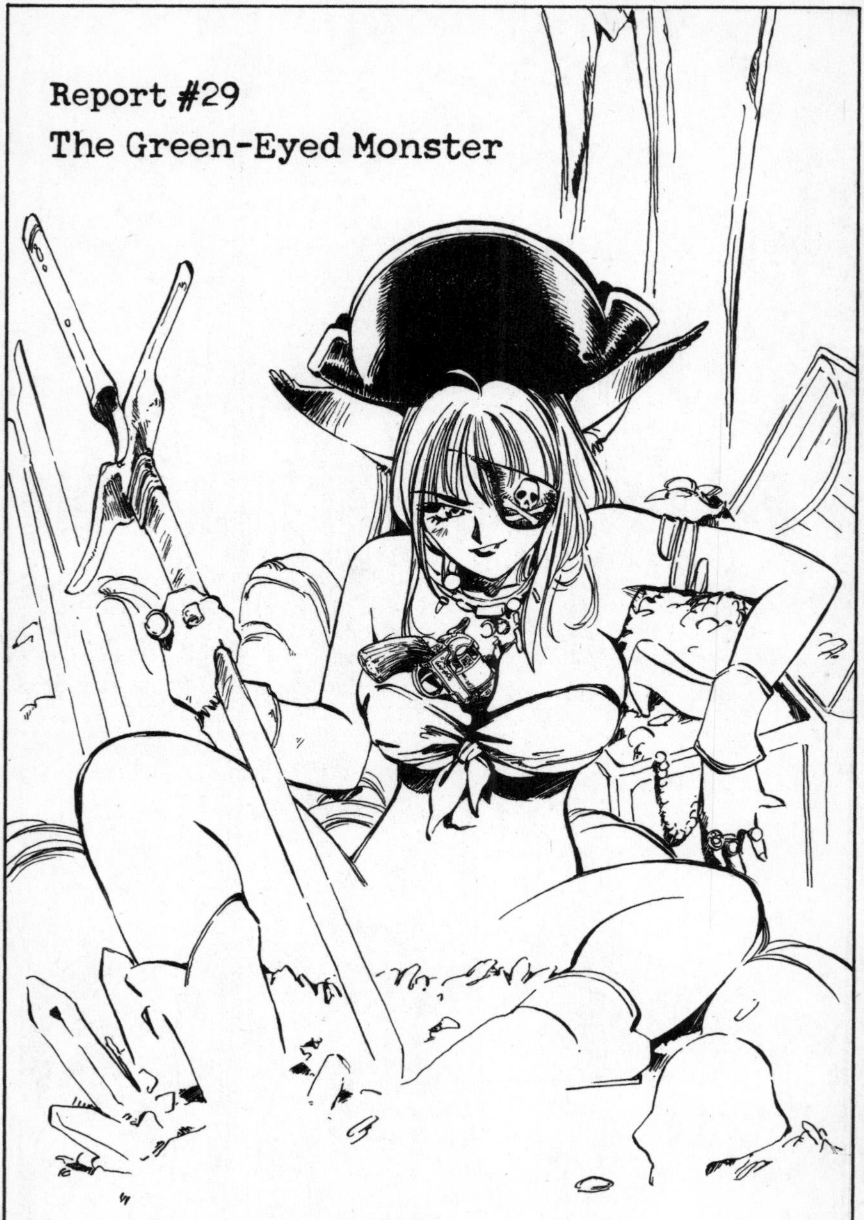

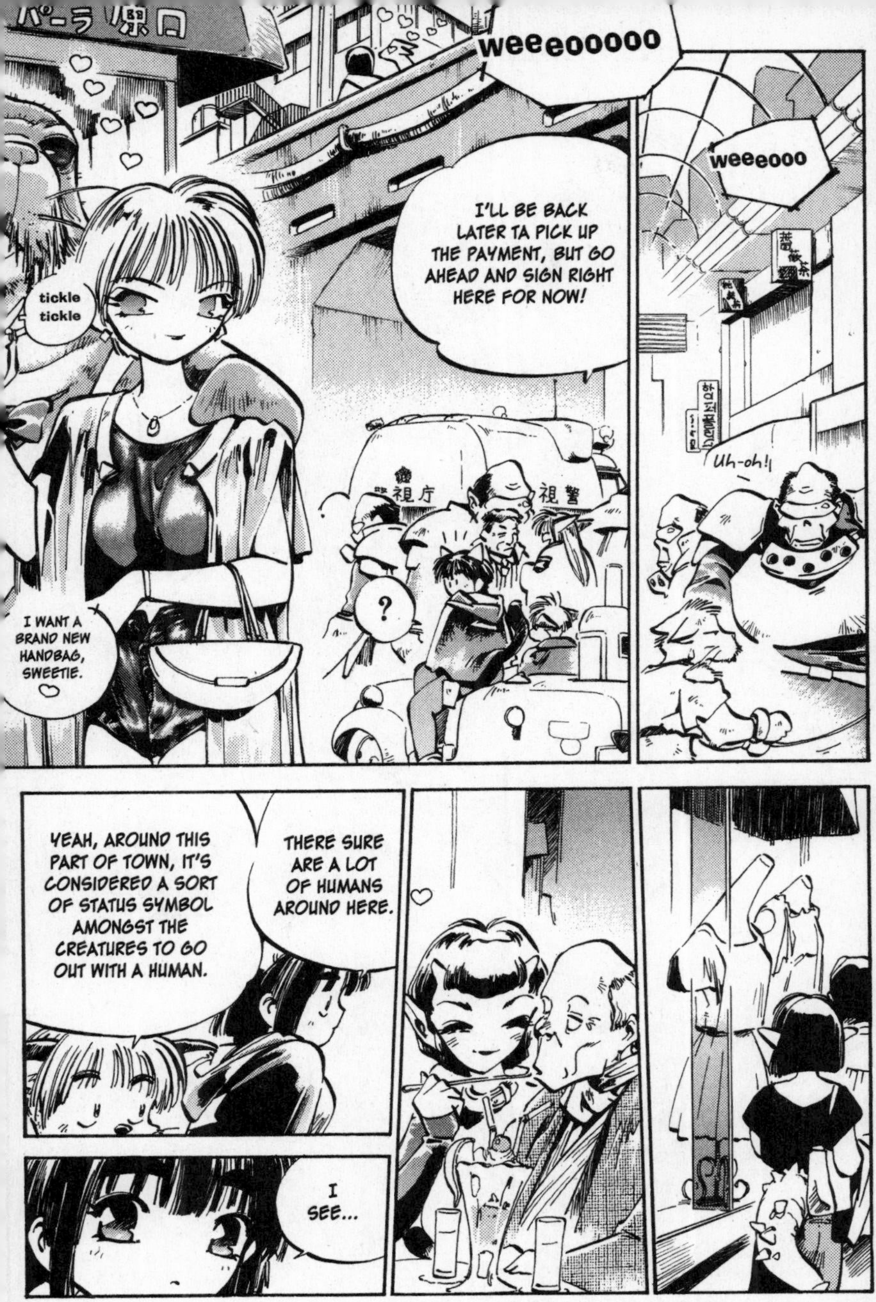
weeeooo
Uh-oh!
weeeoooooo
I'LL BE BACK LATER TA PICK UP THE PAYMENT, BUT GO AHEAD AND SIGN RIGHT HERE FOR NOW!
tickle tickle
?
I WANT A BRAND NEW HANDBAG, SWEETIE.
THERE SURE ARE A LOT OF HUMANS AROUND HERE.
YEAH, AROUND THIS PART OF TOWN, IT'S CONSIDERED A SORT OF STATUS SYMBOL AMONGST THE CREATURES TO GO OUT WITH A HUMAN.
I SEE...

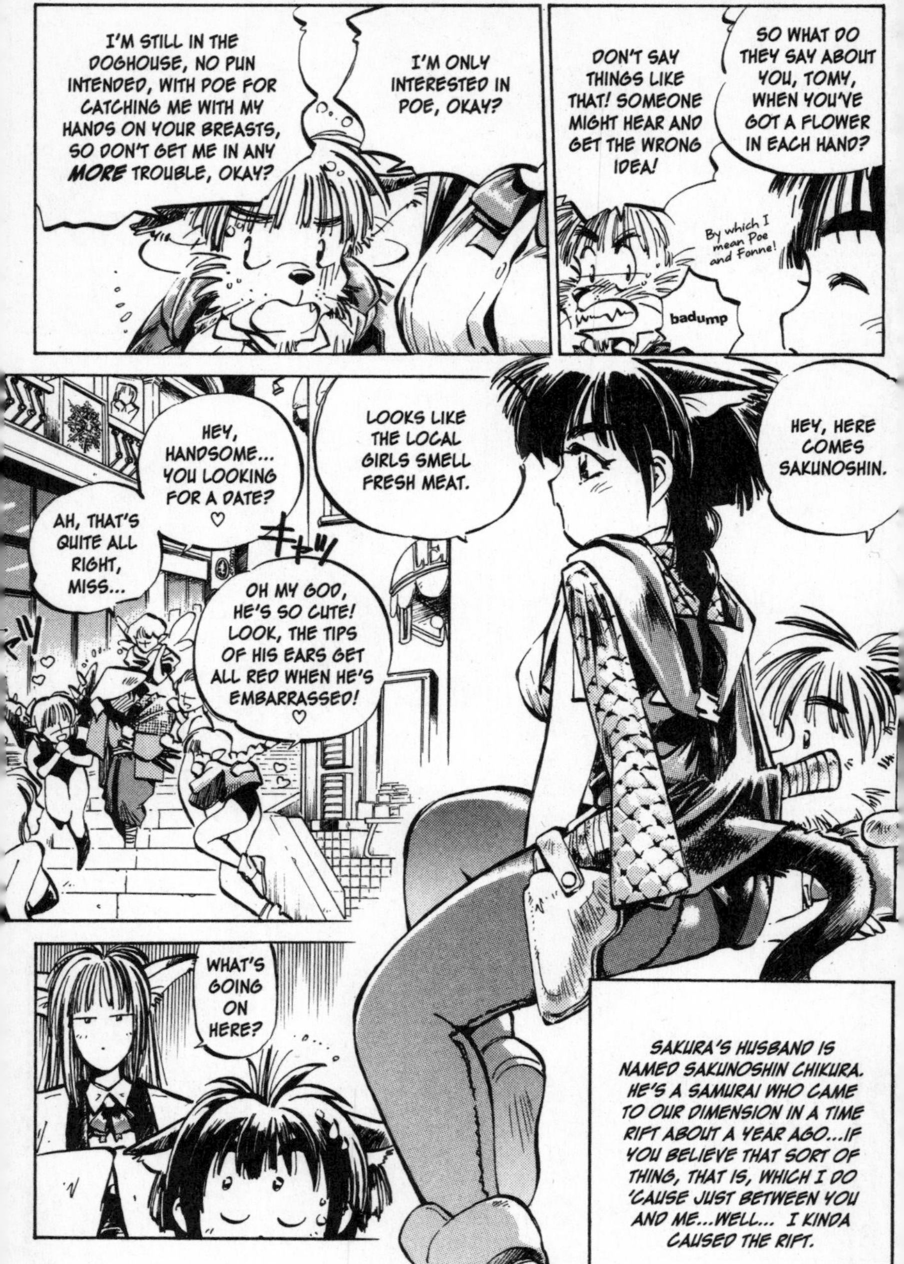
SO WHAT DO THEY SAY ABOUT YOU, TOMY, WHEN YOU'VE GOT A FLOWER IN EACH HAND?
DON'T SAY THINGS LIKE THAT! SOMEONE MIGHT HEAR AND GET THE WRONG IDEA!
By which I mean Poe and Fonne!
badump
I'M ONLY INTERESTED IN POE, OKAY?
I'M STILL IN THE DOGHOUSE, NO PUN INTENDED, WITH POE FOR CATCHING ME WITH MY HANDS ON YOUR BREASTS, SO DON'T GET ME IN ANY MORE TROUBLE, OKAY?
HEY, HERE COMES SAKUNOSHIN.
LOOKS LIKE THE LOCAL GIRLS SMELL FRESH MEAT.
HEY, HANDSOME... YOU LOOKING FOR A DATE? ♡
AH, THAT'S QUITE ALL RIGHT, MISS...
OH MY GOD, HE'S SO CUTE! LOOK, THE TIPS OF HIS EARS GET ALL RED WHEN HE'S EMBARRASSED! ♡
SAKURA'S HUSBAND IS NAMED SAKUNOSHIN CHIKURA. HE'S A SAMURAI WHO CAME TO OUR DIMENSION IN A TIME RIFT ABOUT A YEAR AGO...IF YOU BELIEVE THAT SORT OF THING, THAT IS, WHICH I DO 'CAUSE JUST BETWEEN YOU AND ME...WELL... I KINDA CAUSED THE RIFT.
WHAT'S GOING ON HERE?

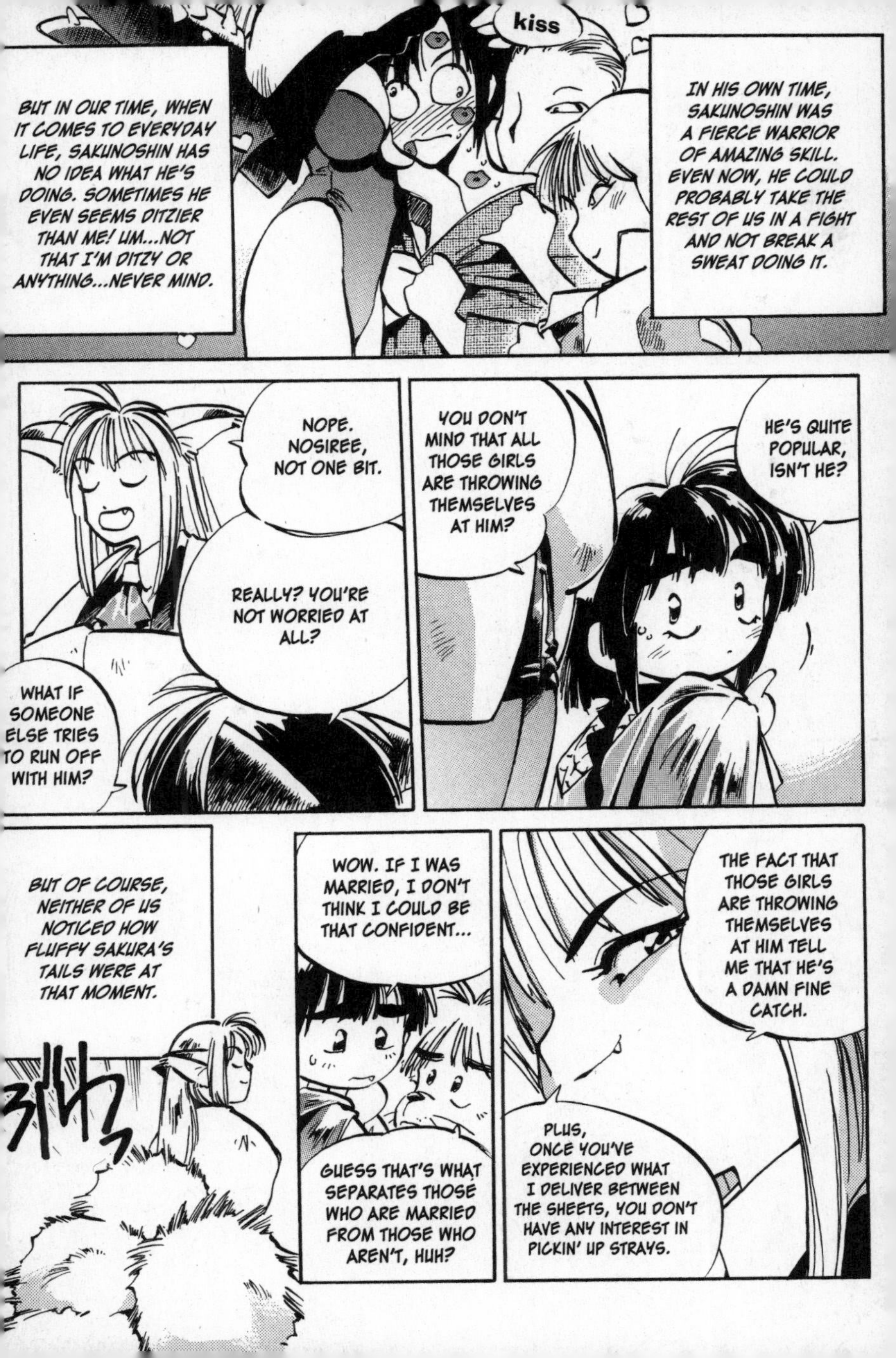
IN HIS OWN TIME, SAKUNOSHIN WAS A FIERCE WARRIOR OF AMAZING SKILL. EVEN NOW, HE COULD PROBABLY TAKE THE REST OF US IN A FIGHT AND NOT BREAK A SWEAT DOING IT.
kiss
BUT IN OUR TIME, WHEN IT COMES TO EVERYDAY LIFE, SAKUNOSHIN HAS NO IDEA WHAT HE'S DOING. SOMETIMES HE EVEN SEEMS DITZIER THAN ME! UM...NOT THAT I'M DITZY OR ANYTHING...NEVER MIND.
HE'S QUITE POPULAR, ISN'T HE?
YOU DON'T MIND THAT ALL THOSE GIRLS ARE THROWING THEMSELVES AT HIM?
NOPE. NOSIREE, NOT ONE BIT.
REALLY? YOU'RE NOT WORRIED AT ALL?
WHAT IF SOMEONE ELSE TRIES TO RUN OFF WITH HIM?
THE FACT THAT THOSE GIRLS ARE THROWING THEMSELVES AT HIM TELL ME THAT HE'S A DAMN FINE CATCH.
PLUS, ONCE YOU'VE EXPERIENCED WHAT I DELIVER BETWEEN THE SHEETS, YOU DON'T HAVE ANY INTEREST IN PICKIN' UP STRAYS.
WOW. IF I WAS MARRIED, I DON'T THINK I COULD BE THAT CONFIDENT...
GUESS THAT'S WHAT SEPARATES THOSE WHO ARE MARRIED FROM THOSE WHO AREN'T, HUH?
BUT OF COURSE, NEITHER OF US NOTICED HOW FLUFFY SAKURA'S TAILS WERE AT THAT MOMENT.

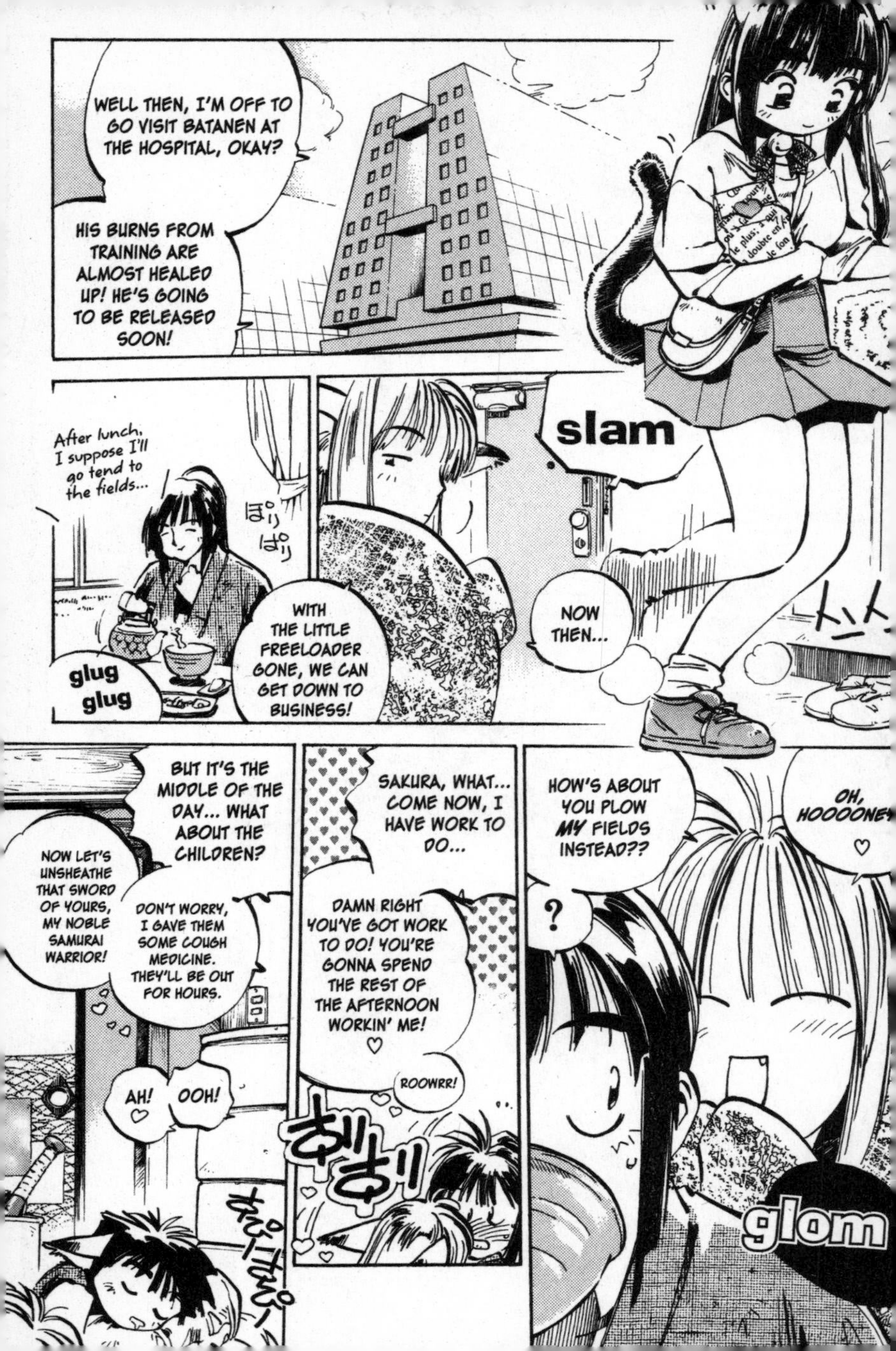
slam
NOW THEN...
WELL THEN, I'M OFF TO GO VISIT BATANEN AT THE HOSPITAL, OKAY?
HIS BURNS FROM TRAINING ARE ALMOST HEALED UP! HE'S GOING TO BE RELEASED SOON!
WITH THE LITTLE FREELOADER GONE, WE CAN GET DOWN TO BUSINESS!
After lunch, I suppose I'll go tend to the fields...
ぽりぽり
glug glug
OH, HOOOONEY ♡
?
HOW'S ABOUT YOU PLOW MY FIELDS INSTEAD??
glom
SAKURA, WHAT... COME NOW, I HAVE WORK TO DO...
DAMN RIGHT YOU'VE GOT WORK TO DO! YOU'RE GONNA SPEND THE REST OF THE AFTERNOON WORKIN' ME! ♡
ROOWRR!
BUT IT'S THE MIDDLE OF THE DAY... WHAT ABOUT THE CHILDREN?
DON'T WORRY, I GAVE THEM SOME COUGH MEDICINE. THEY'LL BE OUT FOR HOURS.
NOW LET'S UNSHEATHE THAT SWORD OF YOURS, MY NOBLE SAMURAI WARRIOR!
OOH!
AH! ♡

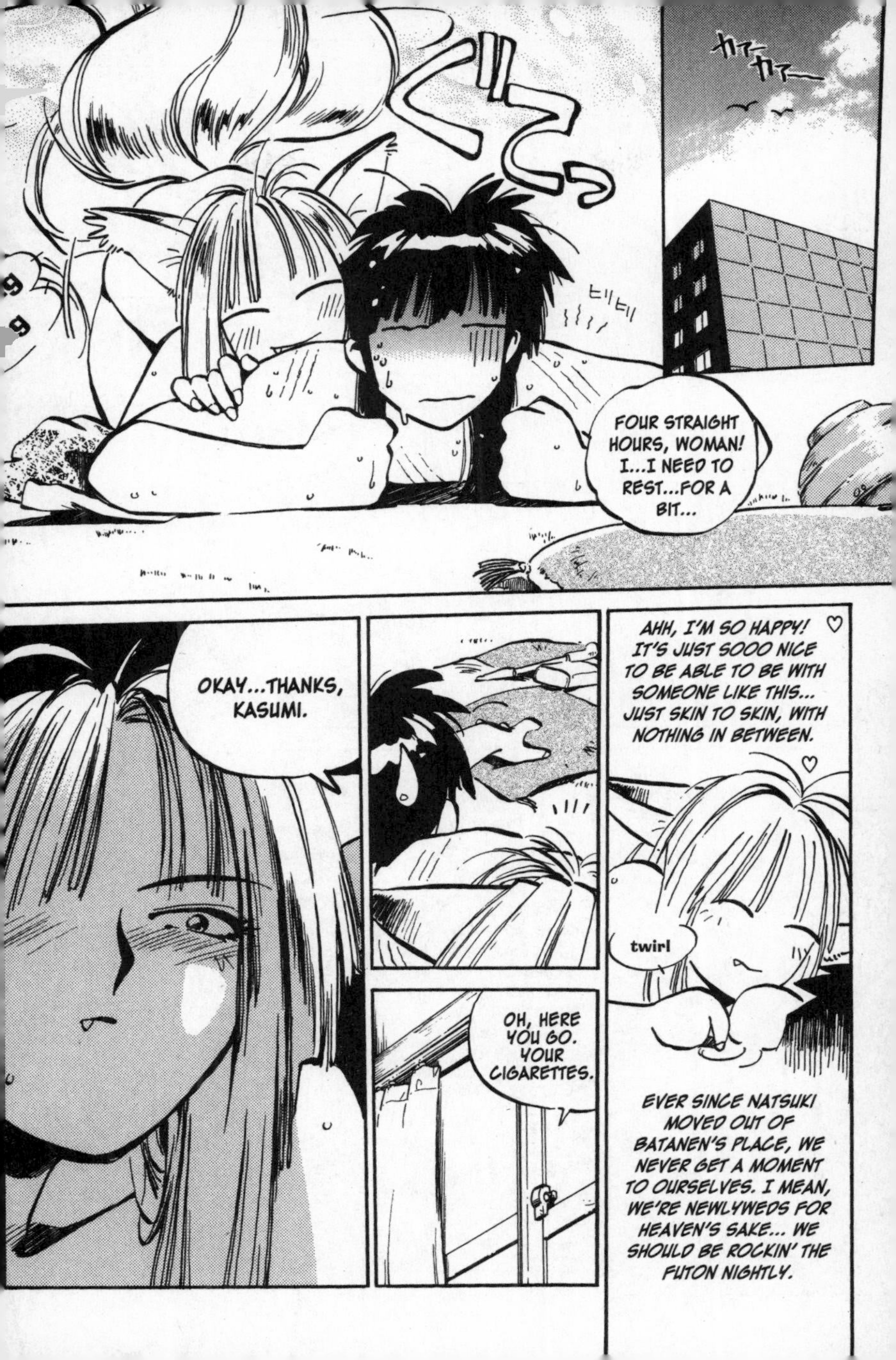
カァーカァー
ぐでっ
ヒリヒリ
FOUR STRAIGHT HOURS, WOMAN! I...I NEED TO REST...FOR A BIT...
AHH, I'M SO HAPPY! IT'S JUST SOOO NICE TO BE ABLE TO BE WITH SOMEONE LIKE THIS... JUST SKIN TO SKIN, WITH NOTHING IN BETWEEN.
twirl
EVER SINCE NATSUKI MOVED OUT OF BATANEN'S PLACE, WE NEVER GET A MOMENT TO OURSELVES. I MEAN, WE'RE NEWLYWEDS FOR HEAVEN'S SAKE... WE SHOULD BE ROCKIN' THE FUTON NIGHTLY.
OH, HERE YOU GO. YOUR CIGARETTES.
OKAY...THANKS, KASUMI.

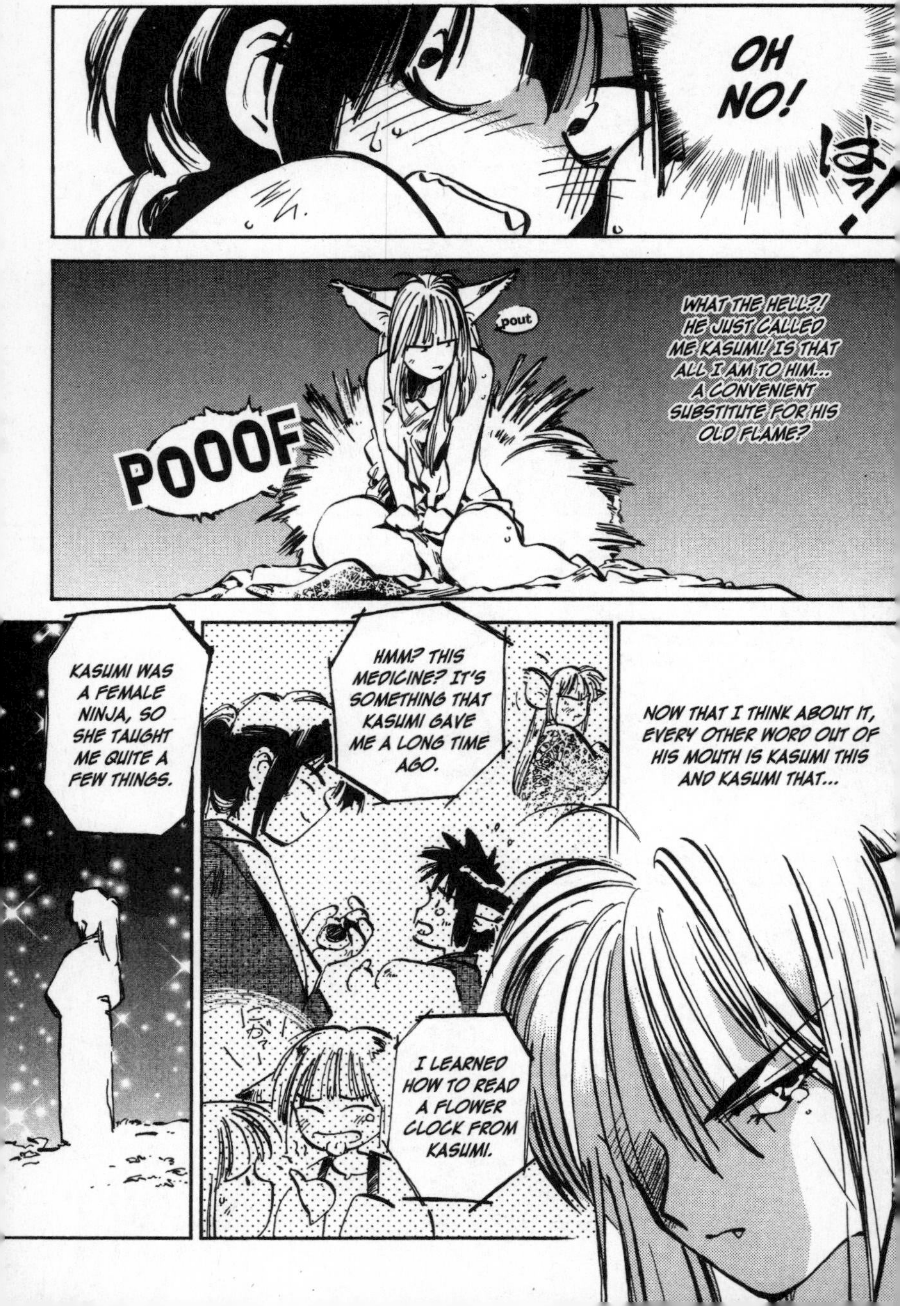
OH NO!
はっ!
pout
POOOF
WHAT THE HELL?! HE JUST CALLED ME KASUMI! IS THAT ALL I AM TO HIM... A CONVENIENT SUBSTITUTE FOR HIS OLD FLAME?
NOW THAT I THINK ABOUT IT, EVERY OTHER WORD OUT OF HIS MOUTH IS KASUMI THIS AND KASUMI THAT...
HMM? THIS MEDICINE? IT'S SOMETHING THAT KASUMI GAVE ME A LONG TIME AGO.
I LEARNED HOW TO READ A FLOWER CLOCK FROM KASUMI.
KASUMI WAS A FEMALE NINJA, SO SHE TAUGHT ME QUITE A FEW THINGS.

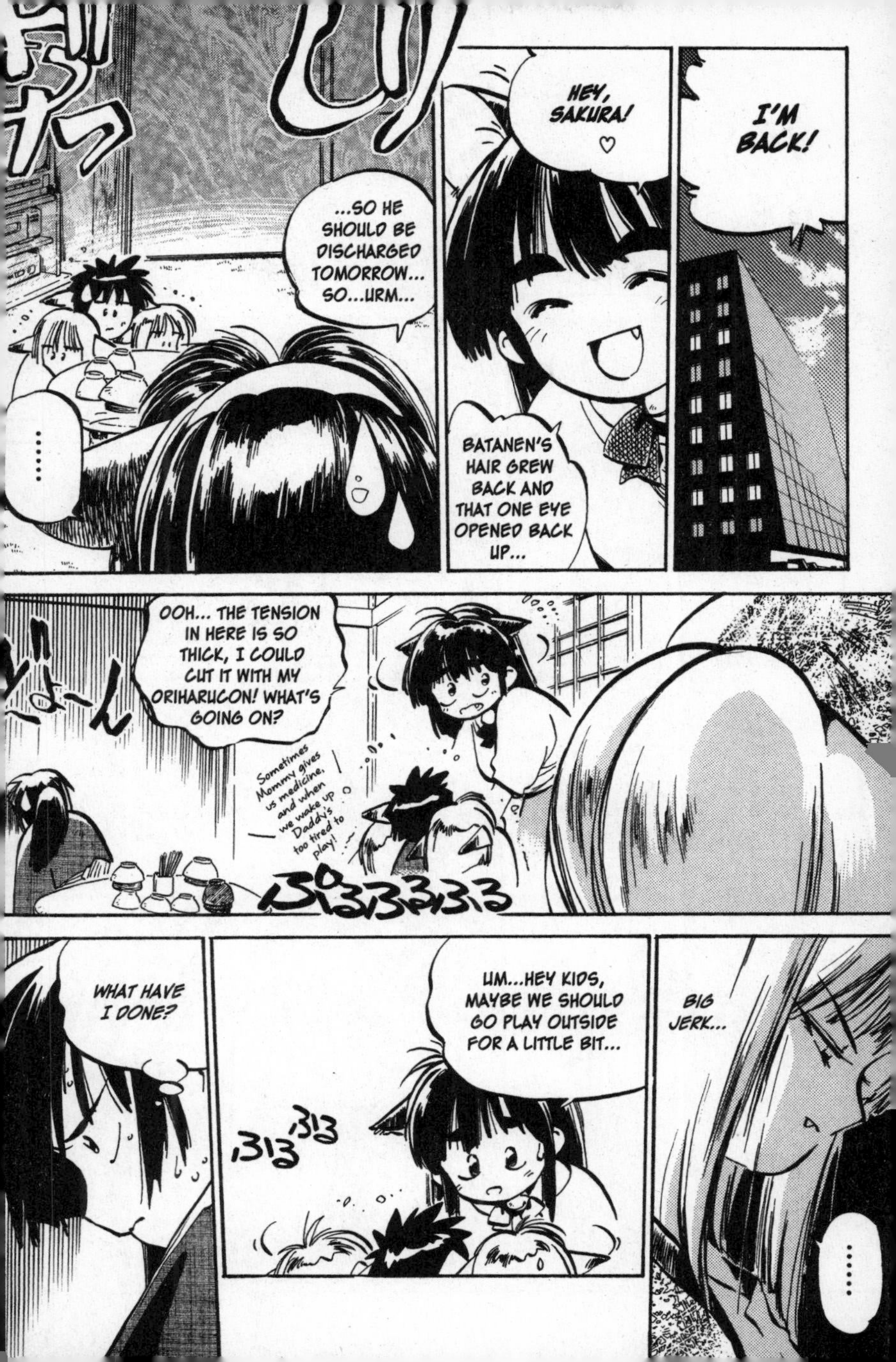
I'M BACK!
HEY, SAKURA! ♡
BATANEN'S HAIR GREW BACK AND THAT ONE EYE OPENED BACK UP...
...SO HE SHOULD BE DISCHARGED TOMORROW... SO...URM...
......
OOH... THE TENSION IN HERE IS SO THICK, I COULD CUT IT WITH MY ORIHARUCON! WHAT'S GOING ON?
Sometimes Mommy gives us medicine, and when we wake up Daddy's too tired to play!
BIG JERK...
......
UM...HEY KIDS, MAYBE WE SHOULD GO PLAY OUTSIDE FOR A LITTLE BIT...
WHAT HAVE I DONE?

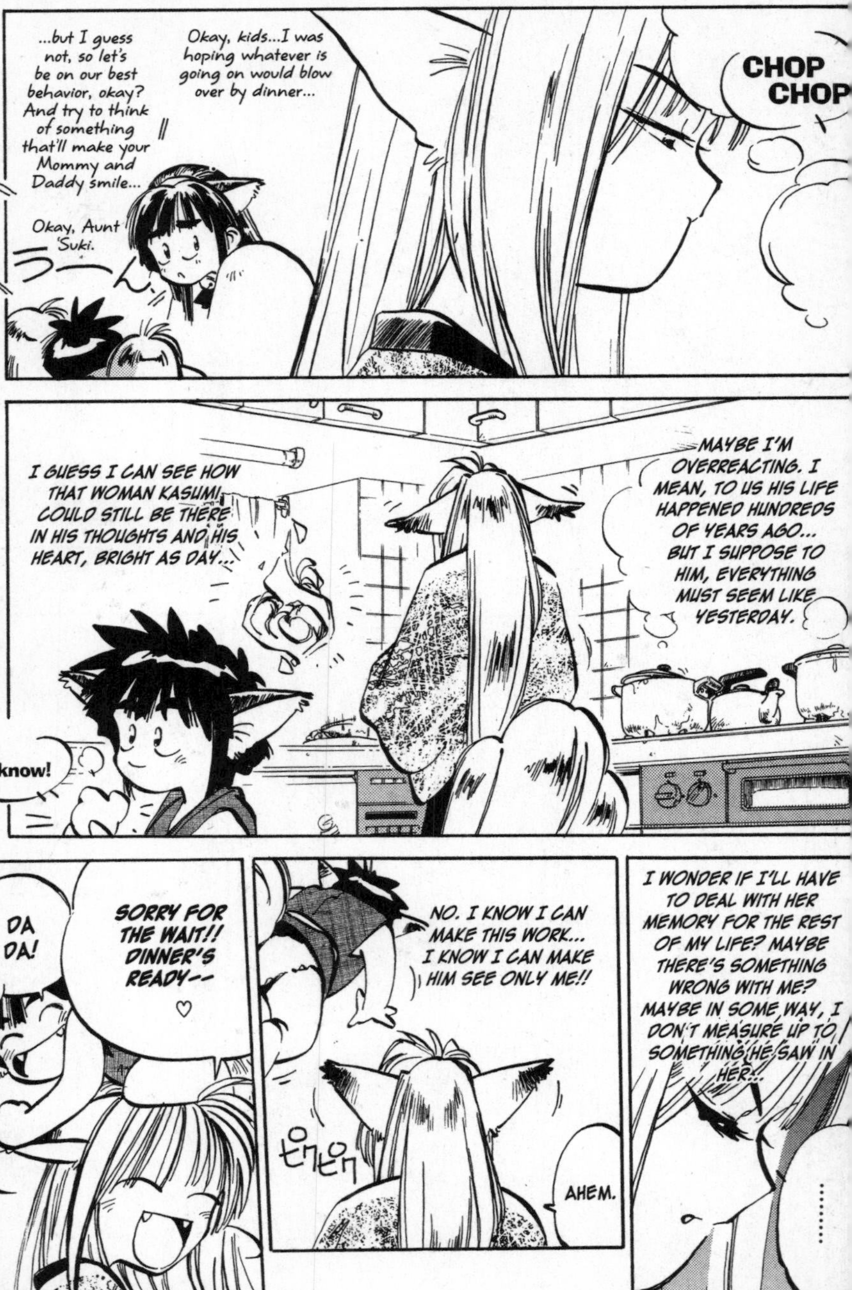
CHOP CHOP
Okay, kids...I was hoping whatever is going on would blow over by dinner...
...but I guess not, so let's be on our best behavior, okay? And try to think of something that'll make your Mommy and Daddy smile...
Okay, Aunt 'Suki.
MAYBE I'M OVERREACTING. I MEAN, TO US HIS LIFE HAPPENED HUNDREDS OF YEARS AGO... BUT I SUPPOSE TO HIM, EVERYTHING MUST SEEM LIKE YESTERDAY.
I GUESS I CAN SEE HOW THAT WOMAN KASUMI COULD STILL BE THERE IN HIS THOUGHTS AND HIS HEART, BRIGHT AS DAY...
I know!
I WONDER IF I'LL HAVE TO DEAL WITH HER MEMORY FOR THE REST OF MY LIFE? MAYBE THERE'S SOMETHING WRONG WITH ME? MAYBE IN SOME WAY, I DON'T MEASURE UP TO SOMETHING HE SAW IN HER...
......
NO. I KNOW I CAN MAKE THIS WORK... I KNOW I CAN MAKE HIM SEE ONLY ME!!
AHEM.
ピクピク
SORRY FOR THE WAIT!! DINNER'S READY--♡
DA DA!

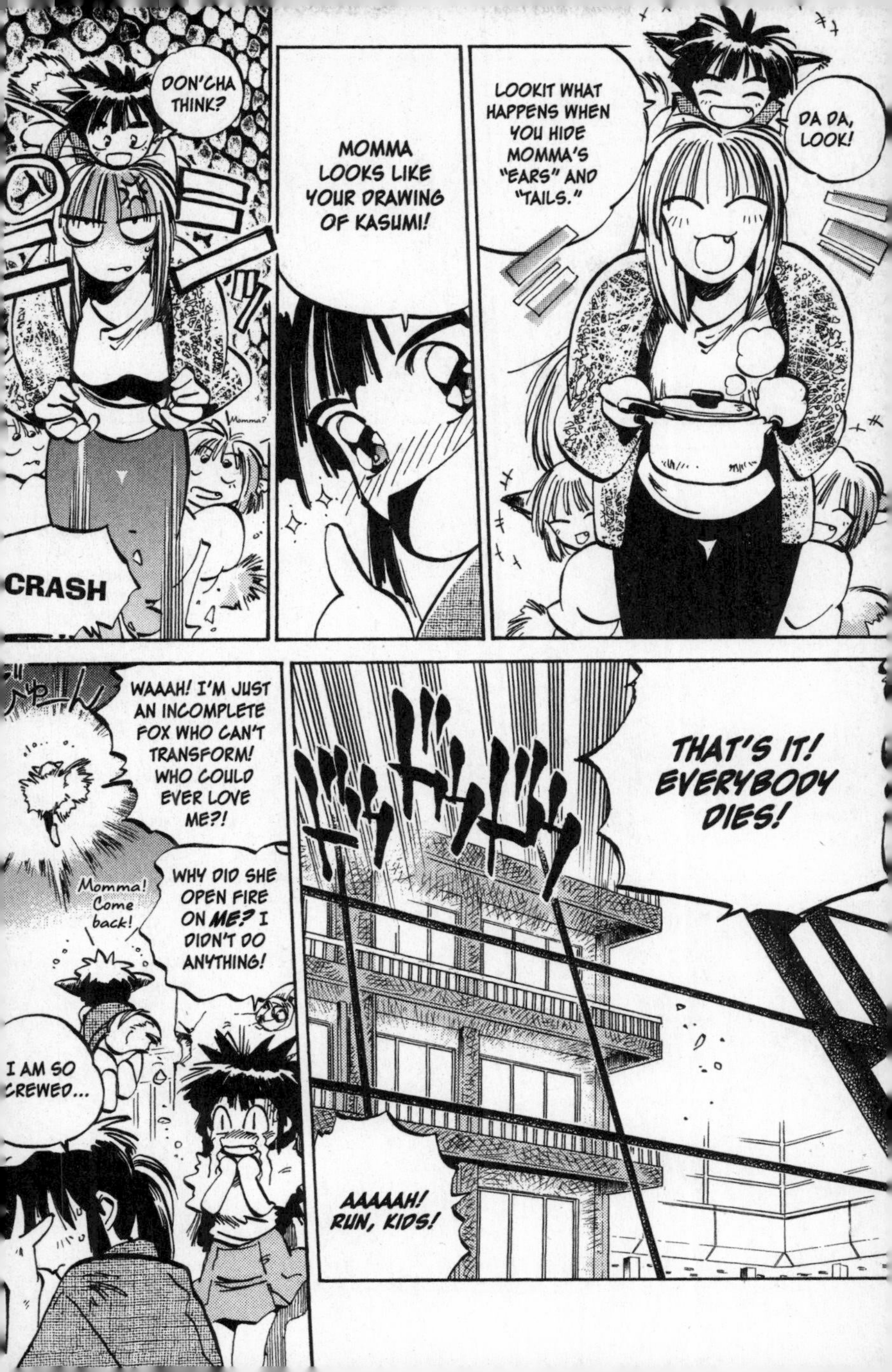
DA DA, LOOK!
LOOKIT WHAT HAPPENS WHEN YOU HIDE MOMMA'S "EARS" AND "TAILS."
MOMMA LOOKS LIKE YOUR DRAWING OF KASUMI!
DON'CHA THINK?
Momma?
CRASH
THAT'S IT! EVERYBODY DIES!
AAAAAH! RUN, KIDS!
WAAAH! I'M JUST AN INCOMPLETE FOX WHO CAN'T TRANSFORM! WHO COULD EVER LOVE ME?!
WHY DID SHE OPEN FIRE ON ME? I DIDN'T DO ANYTHING!
Momma! Come back!
I AM SO CREWED...

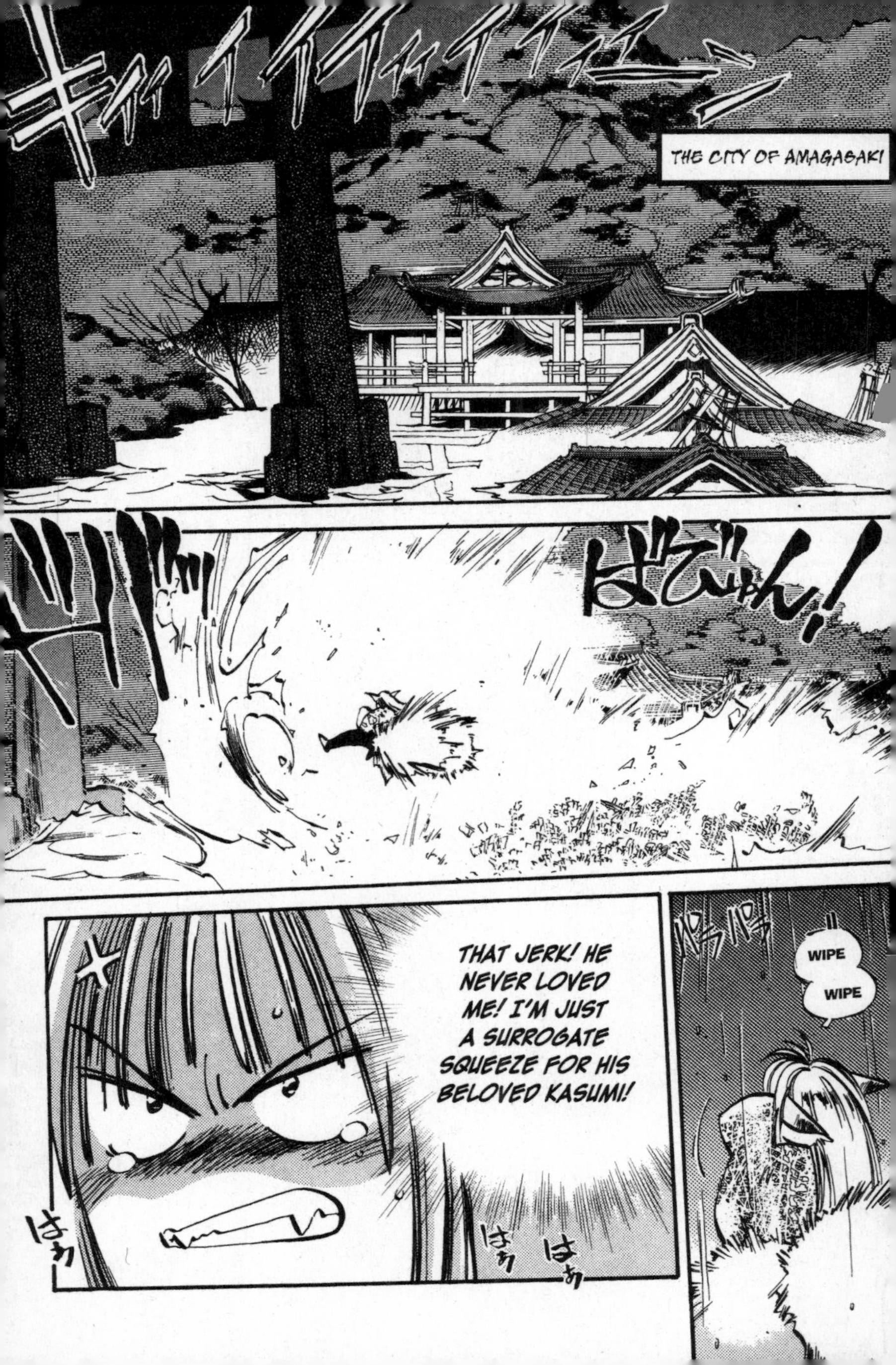
THE CITY OF AMAGASAKI
WIPE
WIPE
THAT JERK! HE NEVER LOVED ME! I'M JUST A SURROGATE SQUEEZE FOR HIS BELOVED KASUMI!

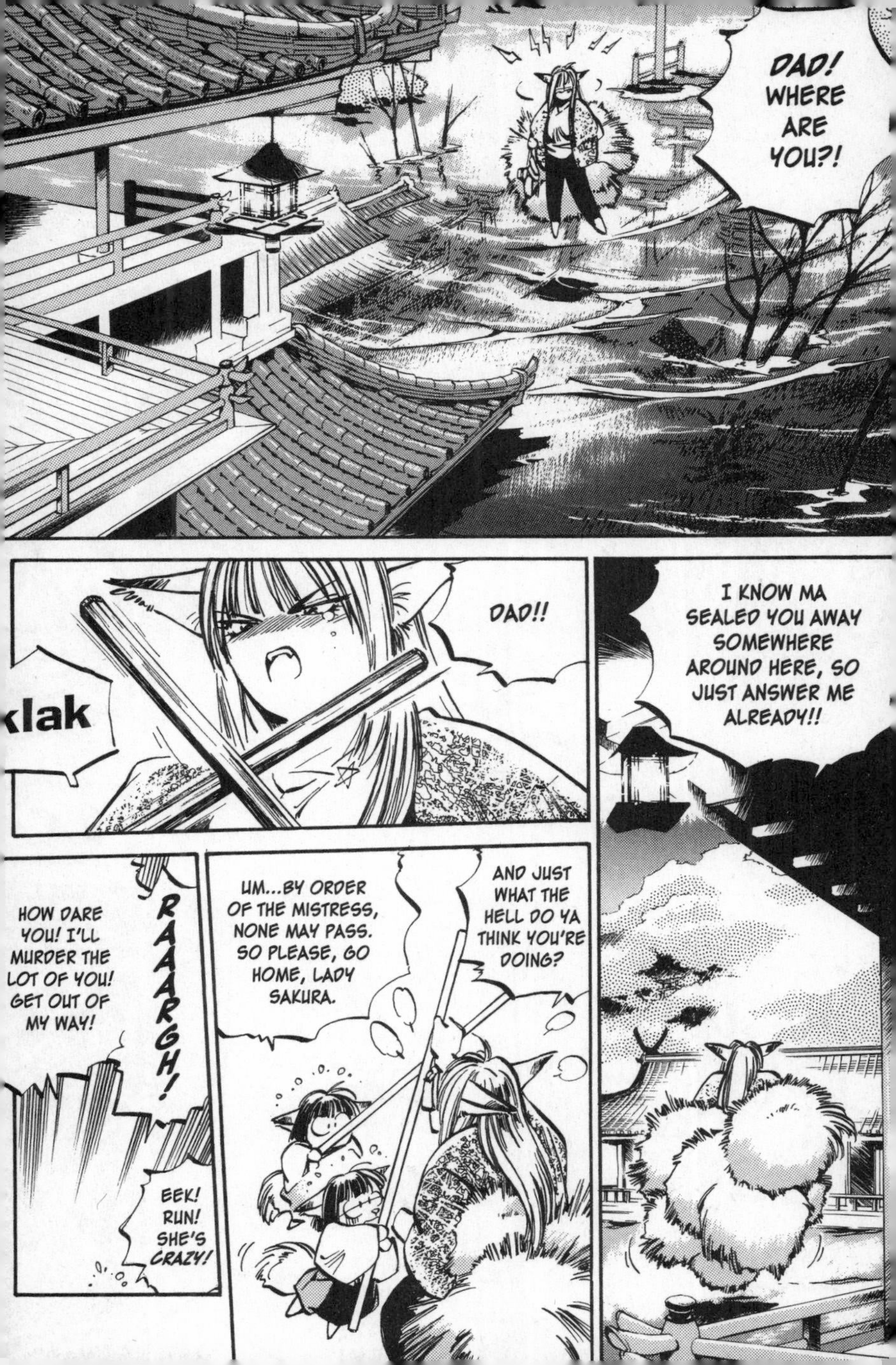
DAD! WHERE ARE YOU?!
I KNOW MA SEALED YOU AWAY SOMEWHERE AROUND HERE, SO JUST ANSWER ME ALREADY!!
DAD!!
klak
AND JUST WHAT THE HELL DO YA THINK YOU'RE DOING?
UM...BY ORDER OF THE MISTRESS, NONE MAY PASS. SO PLEASE, GO HOME, LADY SAKURA.
RAAARGH!
HOW DARE YOU! I'LL MURDER THE LOT OF YOU! GET OUT OF MY WAY!
EEK! RUN! SHE'S CRAZY!

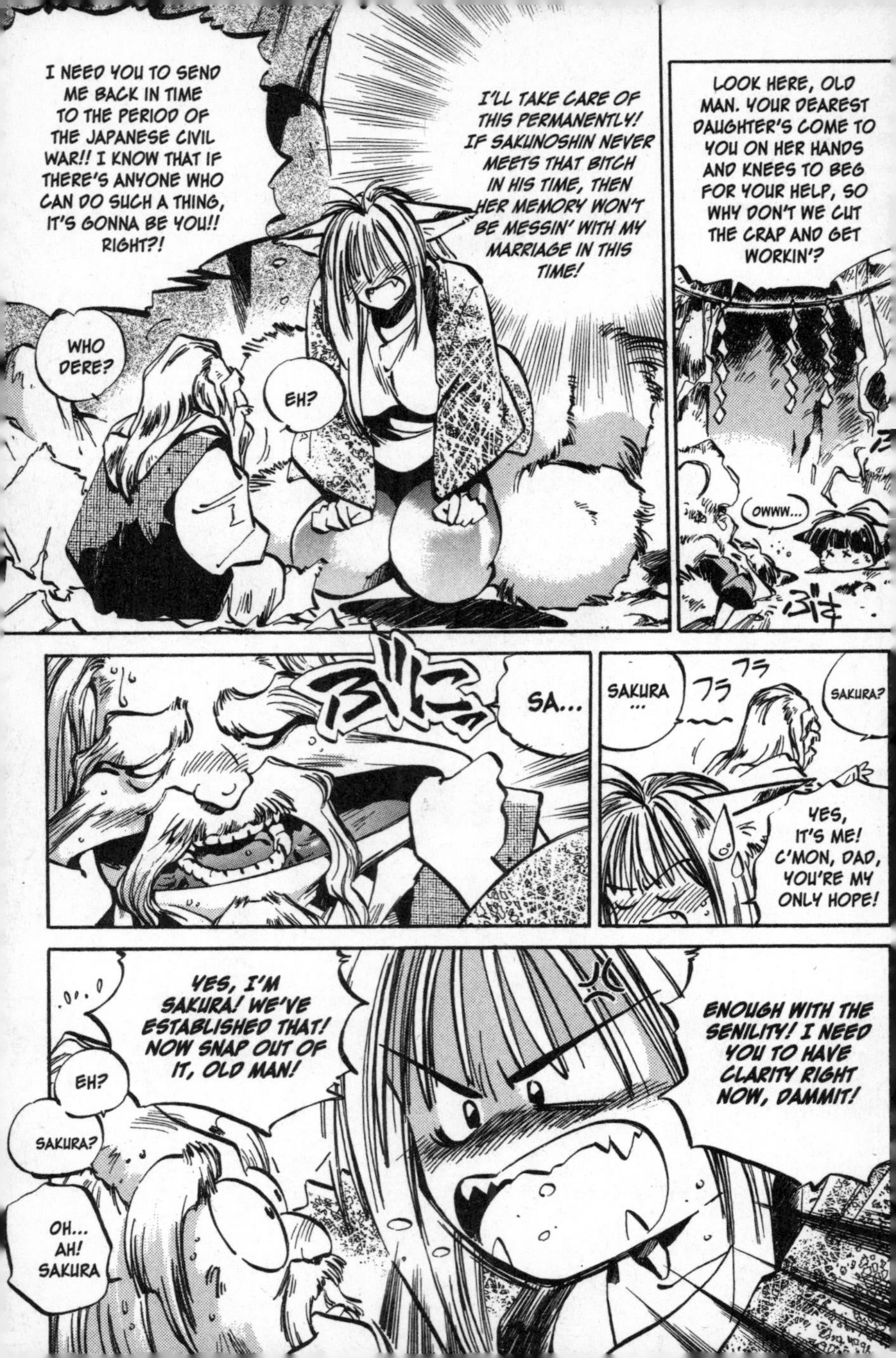
LOOK HERE, OLD MAN. YOUR DEAREST DAUGHTER'S COME TO YOU ON HER HANDS AND KNEES TO BEG FOR YOUR HELP, SO WHY DON'T WE CUT THE CRAP AND GET WORKIN'?
OWWW...
I'LL TAKE CARE OF THIS PERMANENTLY! IF SAKUNOSHIN NEVER MEETS THAT BITCH IN HIS TIME, THEN HER MEMORY WON'T BE MESSIN' WITH MY MARRIAGE IN THIS TIME!
I NEED YOU TO SEND ME BACK IN TIME TO THE PERIOD OF THE JAPANESE CIVIL WAR!! I KNOW THAT IF THERE'S ANYONE WHO CAN DO SUCH A THING, IT'S GONNA BE YOU!! RIGHT?!
EH?
WHO DERE?
SAKURA?
フラ
フラ
SAKURA ...
YES, IT'S ME! C'MON, DAD, YOU'RE MY ONLY HOPE!
SA...
ENOUGH WITH THE SENILITY! I NEED YOU TO HAVE CLARITY RIGHT NOW, DAMMIT!
YES, I'M SAKURA! WE'VE ESTABLISHED THAT! NOW SNAP OUT OF IT, OLD MAN!
...
EH?
SAKURA?
OH... AH! SAKURA

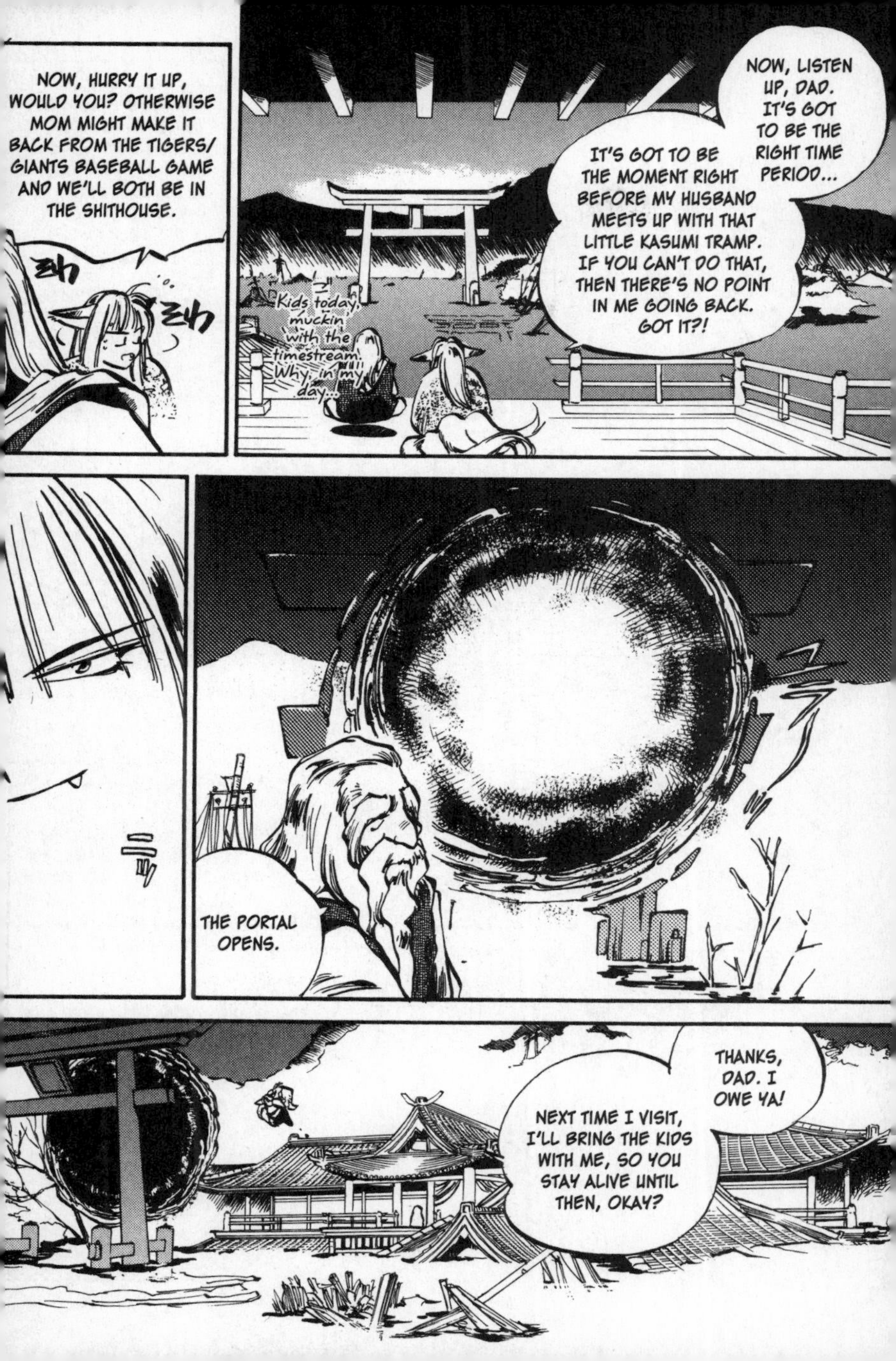
NOW, LISTEN UP, DAD. IT'S GOT TO BE THE RIGHT TIME PERIOD...
IT'S GOT TO BE THE MOMENT RIGHT BEFORE MY HUSBAND MEETS UP WITH THAT LITTLE KASUMI TRAMP. IF YOU CAN'T DO THAT, THEN THERE'S NO POINT IN ME GOING BACK. GOT IT?!
Kids today, muckin' with the timestream. Why, in my day...
NOW, HURRY IT UP, WOULD YOU? OTHERWISE MOM MIGHT MAKE IT BACK FROM THE TIGERS/GIANTS BASEBALL GAME AND WE'LL BOTH BE IN THE SHITHOUSE.
THE PORTAL OPENS.
THANKS, DAD. I OWE YA!
NEXT TIME I VISIT, I'LL BRING THE KIDS WITH ME, SO YOU STAY ALIVE UNTIL THEN, OKAY?

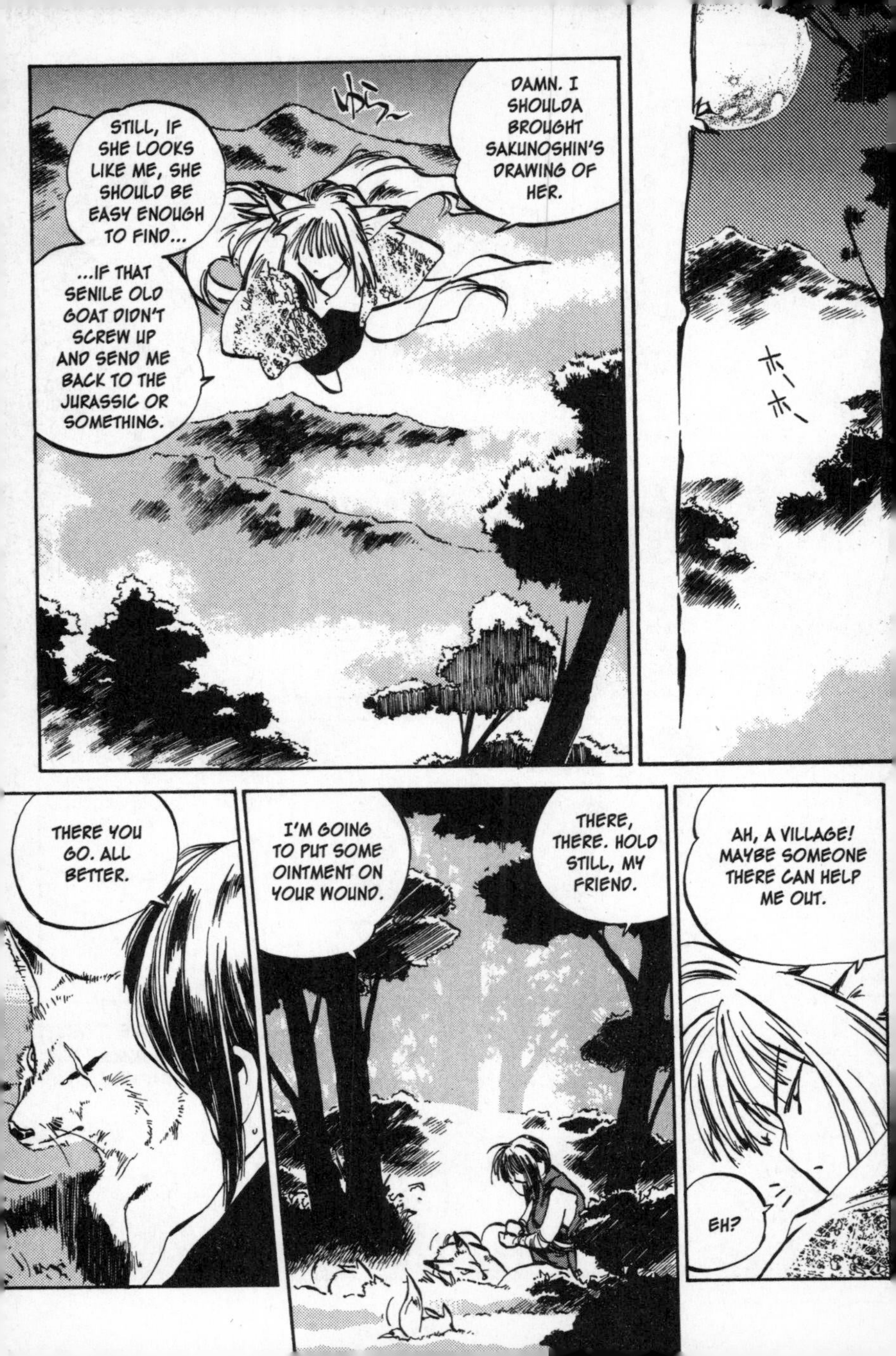
ホーホー
DAMN. I SHOULDA BROUGHT SAKUNOSHIN'S DRAWING OF HER.
STILL, IF SHE LOOKS LIKE ME, SHE SHOULD BE EASY ENOUGH TO FIND...
...IF THAT SENILE OLD GOAT DIDN'T SCREW UP AND SEND ME BACK TO THE JURASSIC OR SOMETHING.
AH, A VILLAGE! MAYBE SOMEONE THERE CAN HELP ME OUT.
EH?
THERE, THERE. HOLD STILL, MY FRIEND.
I'M GOING TO PUT SOME OINTMENT ON YOUR WOUND.
THERE YOU GO. ALL BETTER.

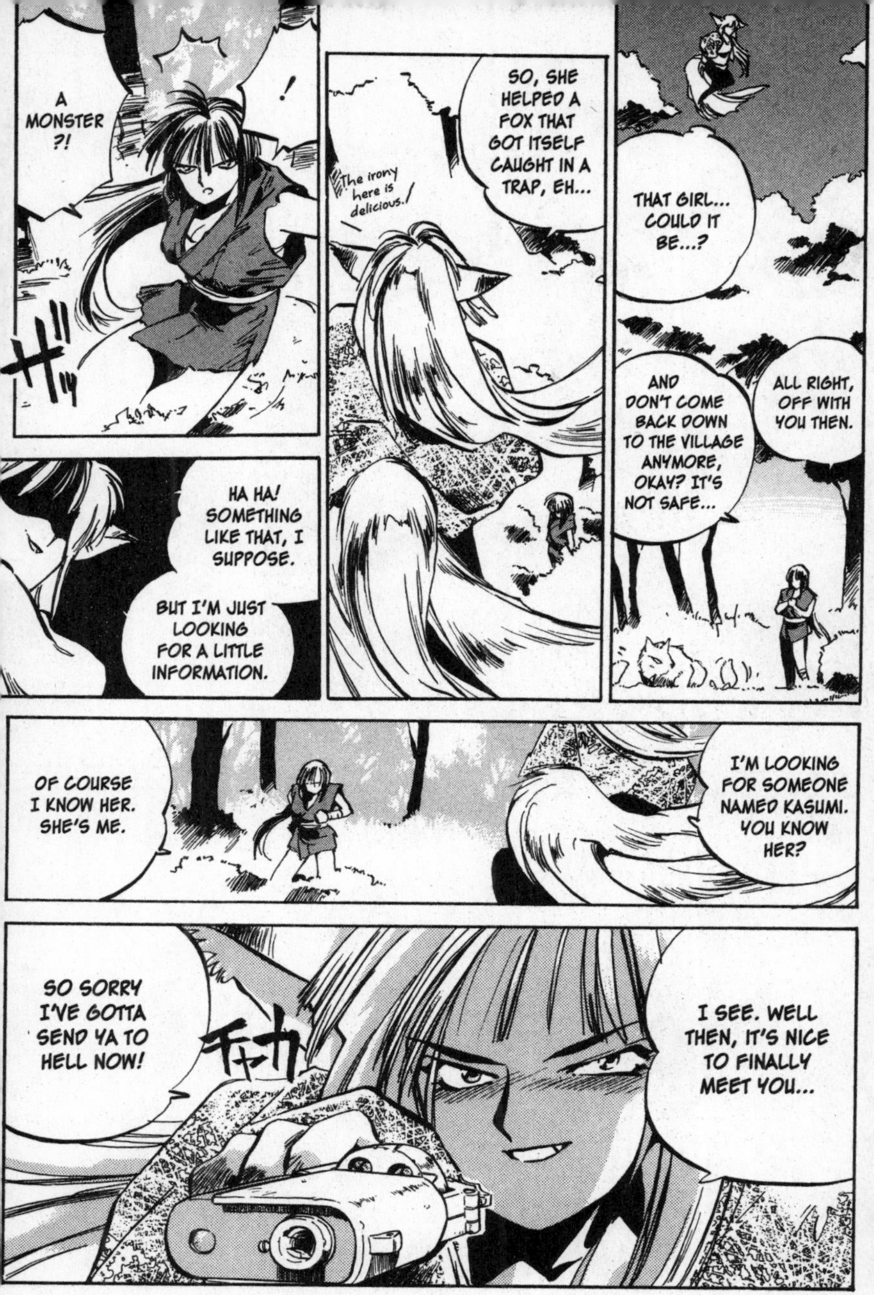
THAT GIRL... COULD IT BE...?
ALL RIGHT, OFF WITH YOU THEN.
AND DON'T COME BACK DOWN TO THE VILLAGE ANYMORE, OKAY? IT'S NOT SAFE...
SO, SHE HELPED A FOX THAT GOT ITSELF CAUGHT IN A TRAP, EH...
The irony here is delicious.
!
A MONSTER ?!
ガッ
HA HA! SOMETHING LIKE THAT, I SUPPOSE.
BUT I'M JUST LOOKING FOR A LITTLE INFORMATION.
I'M LOOKING FOR SOMEONE NAMED KASUMI. YOU KNOW HER?
OF COURSE I KNOW HER. SHE'S ME.
I SEE. WELL THEN, IT'S NICE TO FINALLY MEET YOU...
チャカ
SO SORRY I'VE GOTTA SEND YA TO HELL NOW!

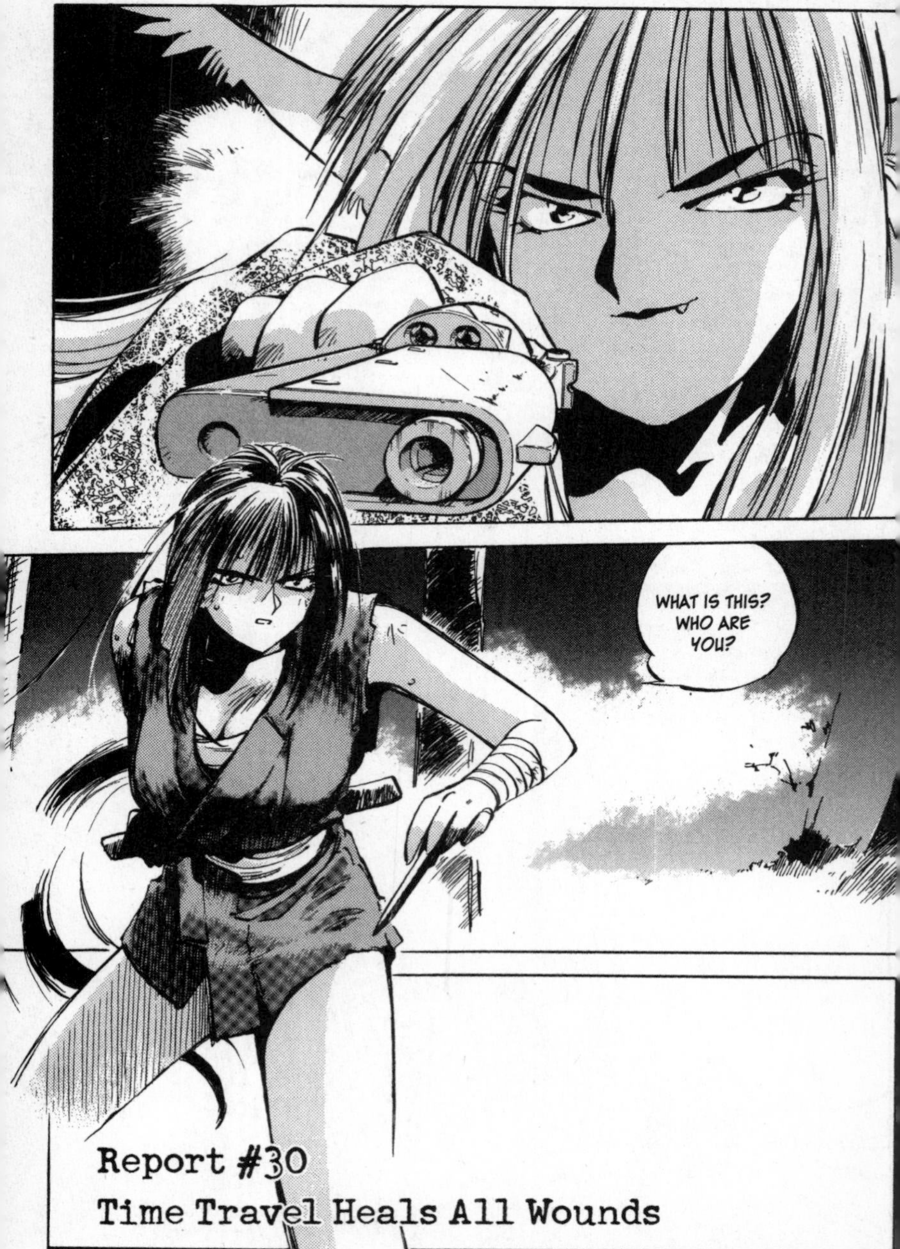
WHAT IS THIS?
WHO ARE
YOU?

Report #30
Time Travel Heals All Wounds

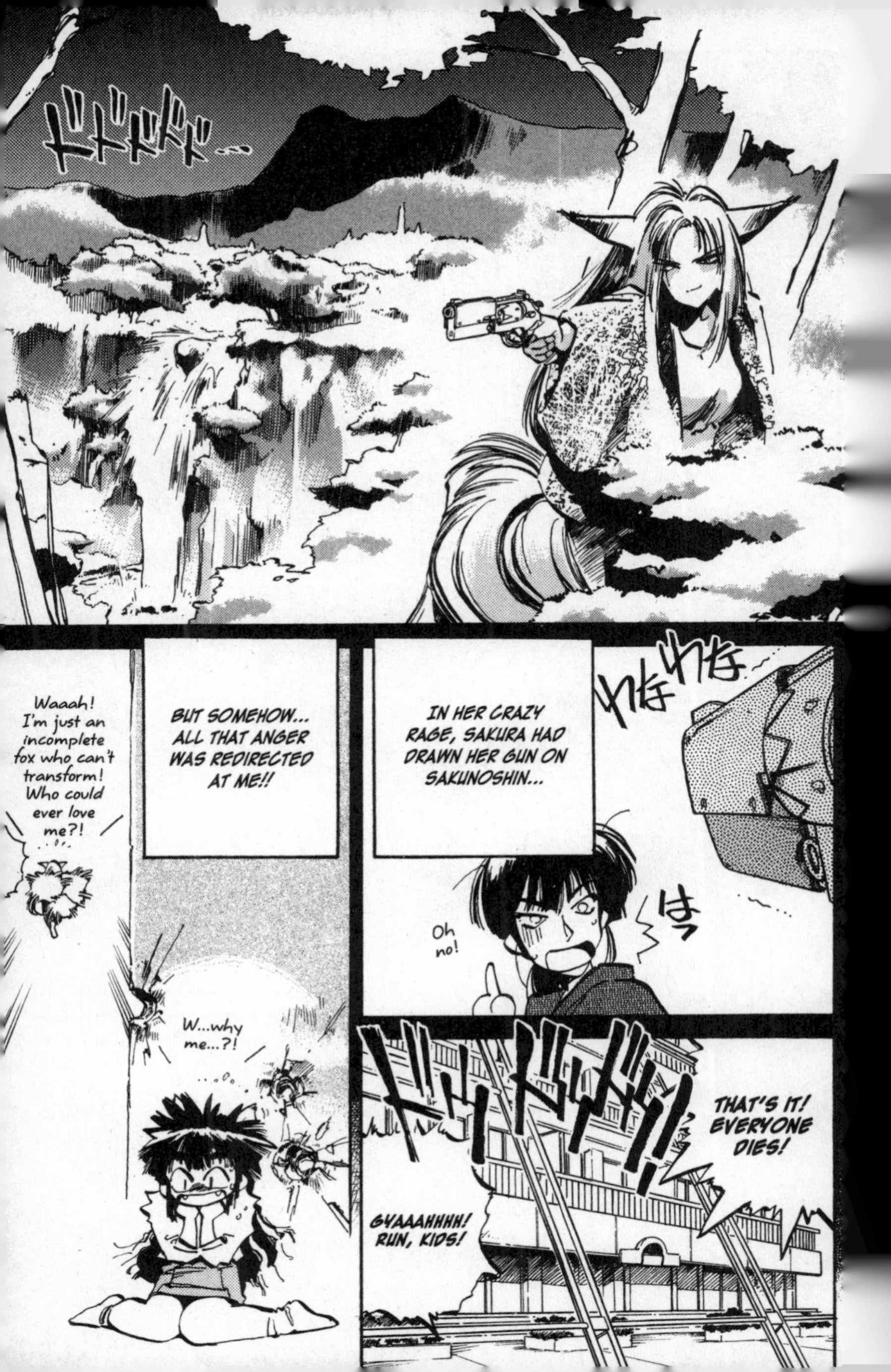
ドドドドド…
わなわな
IN HER CRAZY RAGE, SAKURA HAD DRAWN HER GUN ON SAKUNOSHIN...
はっ
Oh no!
THAT'S IT! EVERYONE DIES!
GYAAAHHHH! RUN, KIDS!
BUT SOMEHOW... ALL THAT ANGER WAS REDIRECTED AT ME!!
Waaah! I'm just an incomplete fox who can't transform! Who could ever love me?!
W...why me...?!

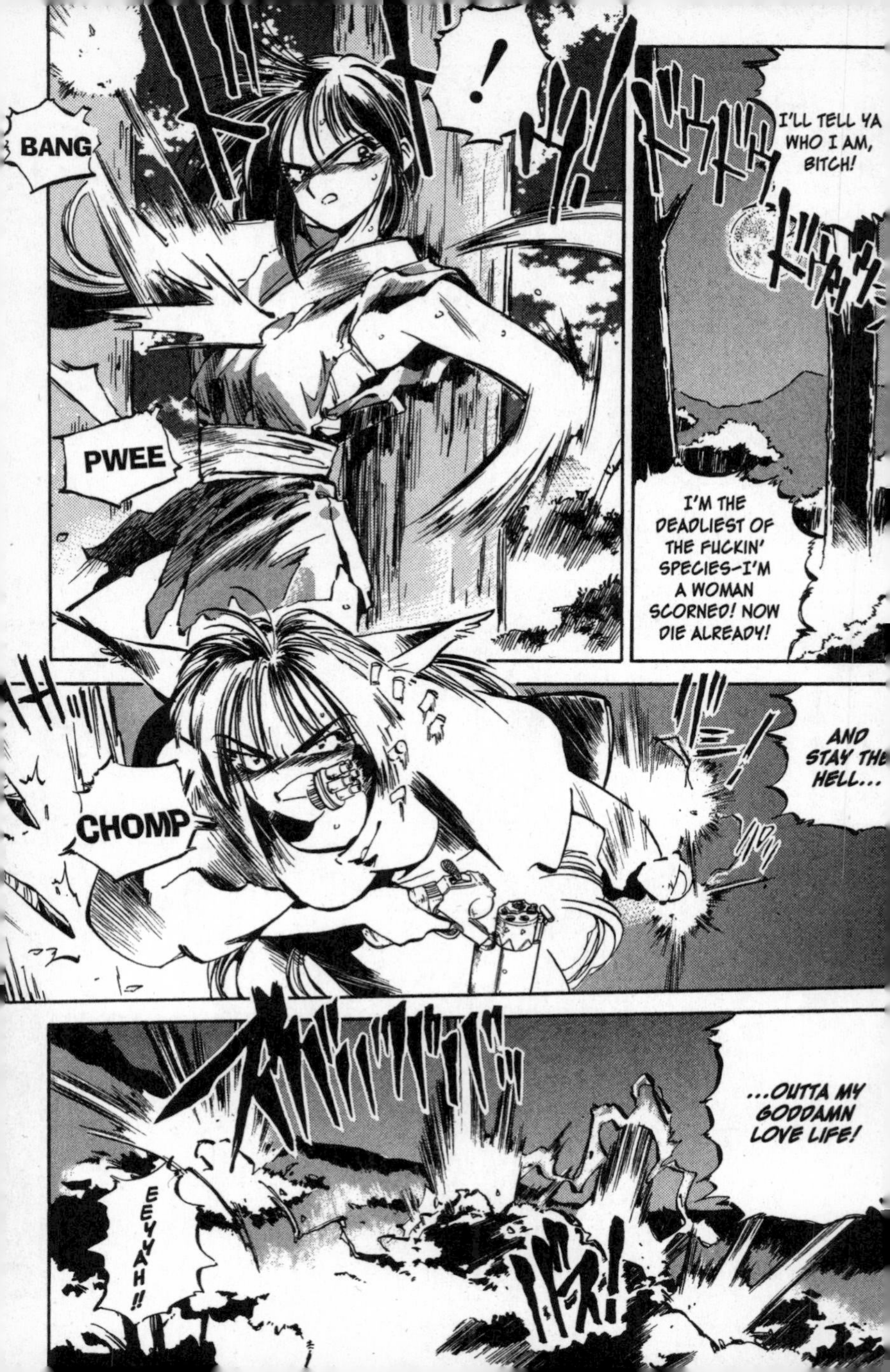
I'LL TELL YA WHO I AM, BITCH!
I'M THE DEADLIEST OF THE FUCKIN' SPECIES–I'M A WOMAN SCORNED! NOW DIE ALREADY!
BANG
PWEE
AND STAY THE HELL...
CHOMP
...OUTTA MY GODDAMN LOVE LIFE!
EEYAH!!

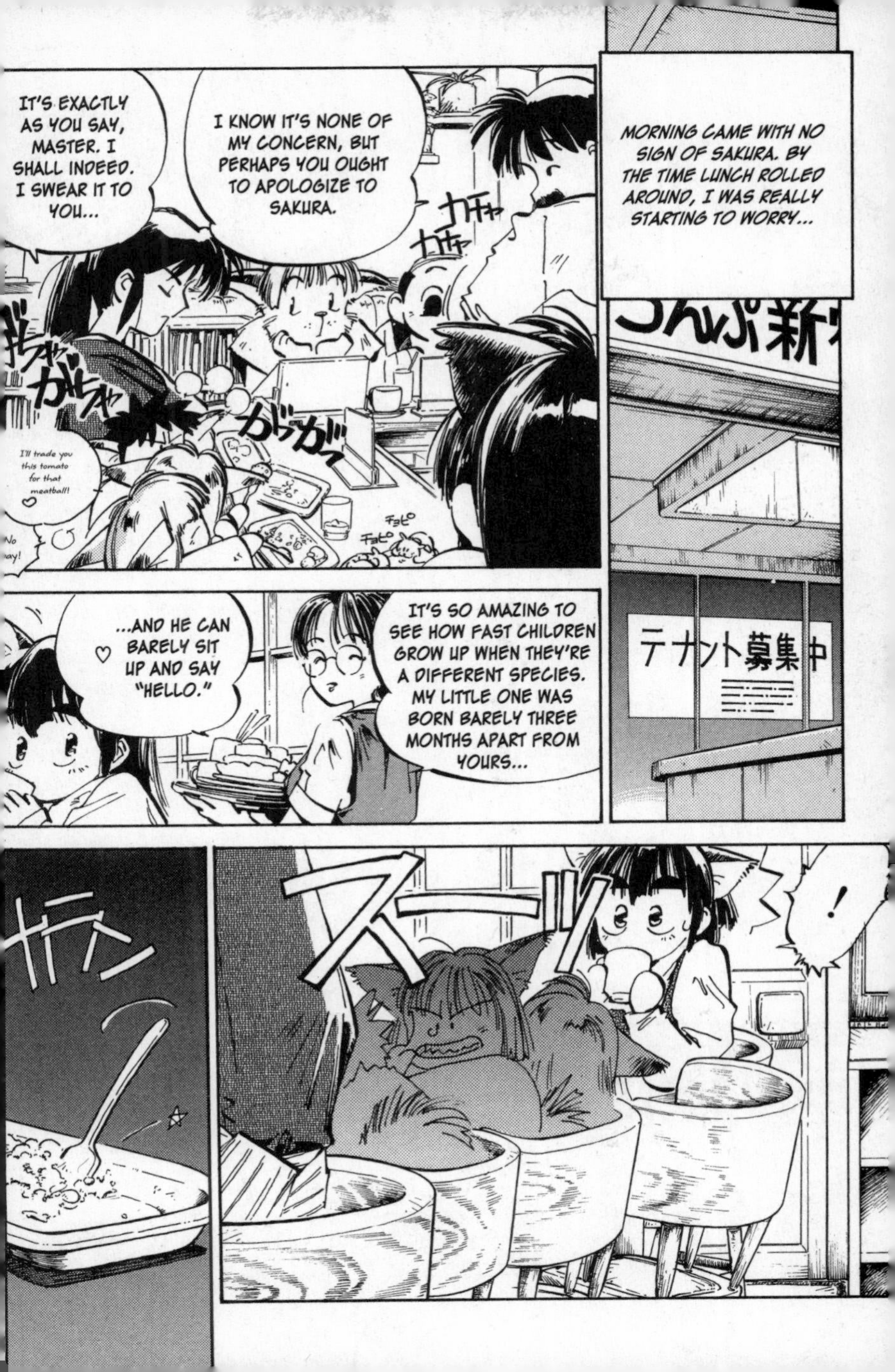
MORNING CAME WITH NO SIGN OF SAKURA. BY THE TIME LUNCH ROLLED AROUND, I WAS REALLY STARTING TO WORRY...
I KNOW IT'S NONE OF MY CONCERN, BUT PERHAPS YOU OUGHT TO APOLOGIZE TO SAKURA.
IT'S EXACTLY AS YOU SAY, MASTER. I SHALL INDEED. I SWEAR IT TO YOU...
カチャ カチャ
がちゃ がちゃ
がつがつ
I'll trade you this tomato for that meatball!
No way!
チョピ チョピ
テナント募集中
IT'S SO AMAZING TO SEE HOW FAST CHILDREN GROW UP WHEN THEY'RE A DIFFERENT SPECIES. MY LITTLE ONE WAS BORN BARELY THREE MONTHS APART FROM YOURS...
...AND HE CAN BARELY SIT UP AND SAY "HELLO."
!
スーッ

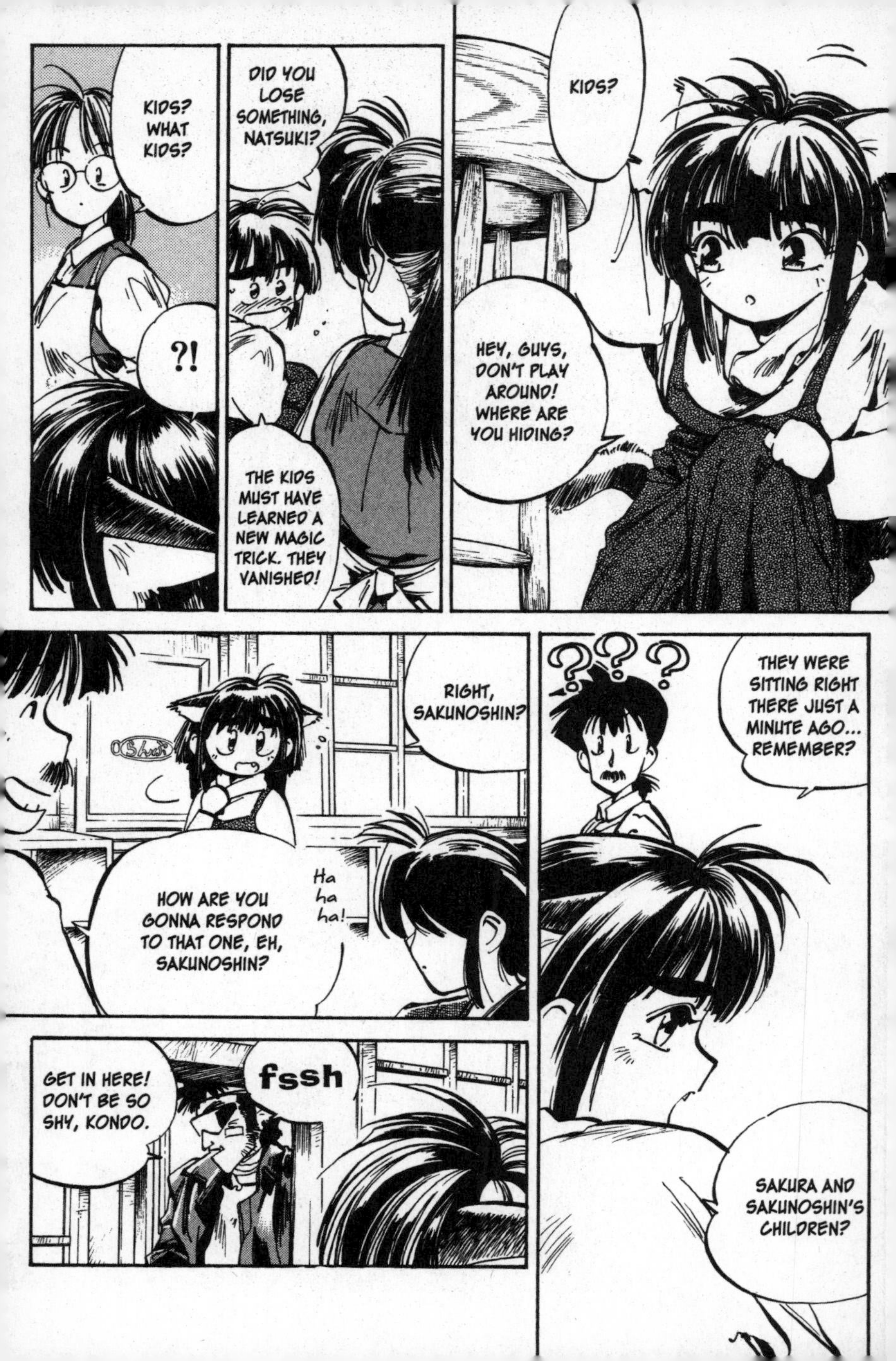
KIDS?
HEY, GUYS, DON'T PLAY AROUND! WHERE ARE YOU HIDING?
DID YOU LOSE SOMETHING, NATSUKI?
THE KIDS MUST HAVE LEARNED A NEW MAGIC TRICK. THEY VANISHED!
KIDS? WHAT KIDS?
?!
THEY WERE SITTING RIGHT THERE JUST A MINUTE AGO... REMEMBER?
SAKURA AND SAKUNOSHIN'S CHILDREN?
RIGHT, SAKUNOSHIN?
Ha ha ha!
HOW ARE YOU GONNA RESPOND TO THAT ONE, EH, SAKUNOSHIN?
fssh
GET IN HERE! DON'T BE SO SHY, KONDO.

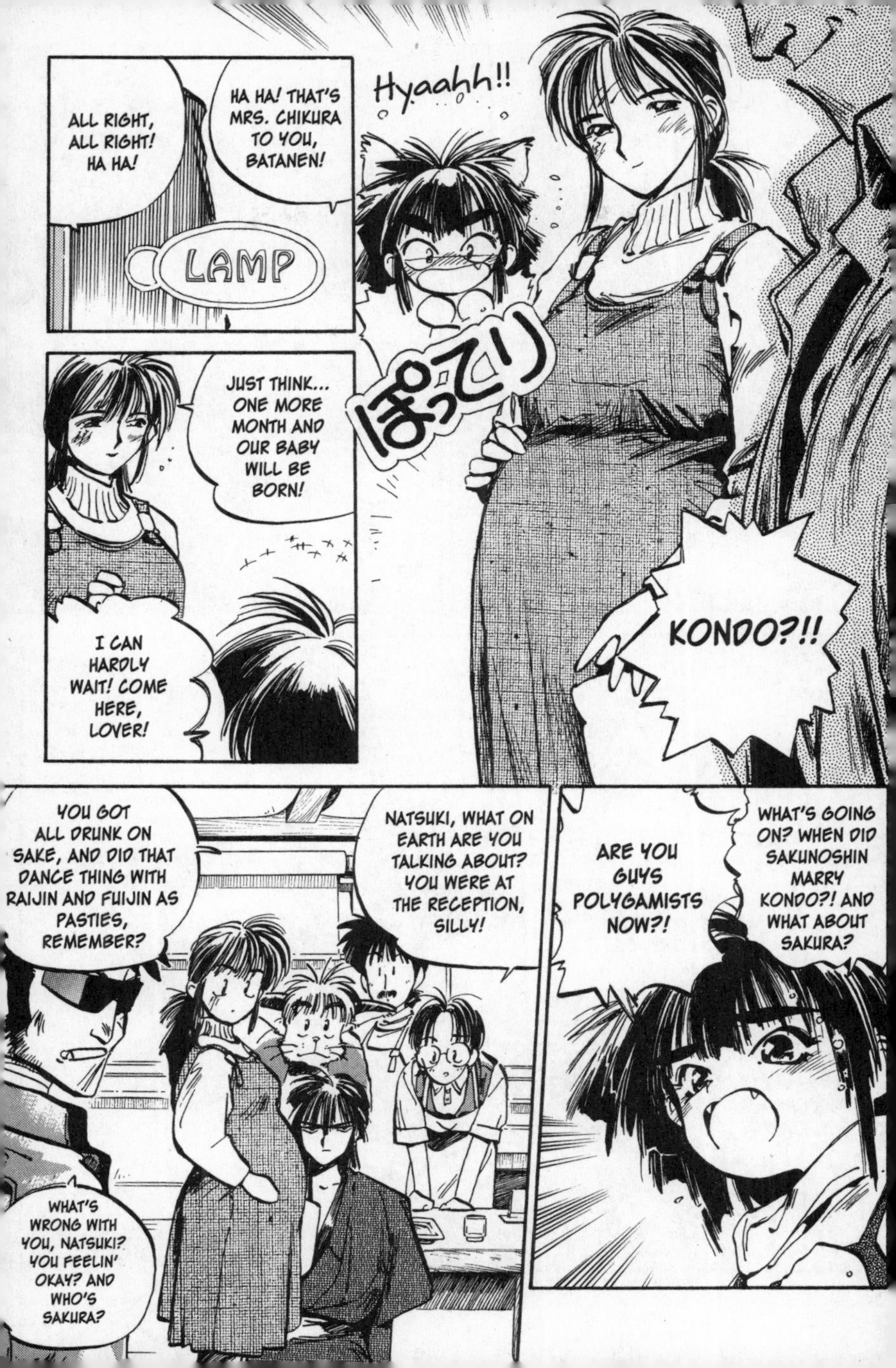
Hyaahh!!
ぽってり
KONDO?!!
HA HA! THAT'S MRS. CHIKURA TO YOU, BATANEN!
ALL RIGHT, ALL RIGHT! HA HA!
LAMP
JUST THINK... ONE MORE MONTH AND OUR BABY WILL BE BORN!
I CAN HARDLY WAIT! COME HERE, LOVER!
WHAT'S GOING ON? WHEN DID SAKUNOSHIN MARRY KONDO?! AND WHAT ABOUT SAKURA?
ARE YOU GUYS POLYGAMISTS NOW?!
NATSUKI, WHAT ON EARTH ARE YOU TALKING ABOUT? YOU WERE AT THE RECEPTION, SILLY!
YOU GOT ALL DRUNK ON SAKE, AND DID THAT DANCE THING WITH RAIJIN AND FUIJIN AS PASTIES, REMEMBER?
WHAT'S WRONG WITH YOU, NATSUKI? YOU FEELIN' OKAY? AND WHO'S SAKURA?

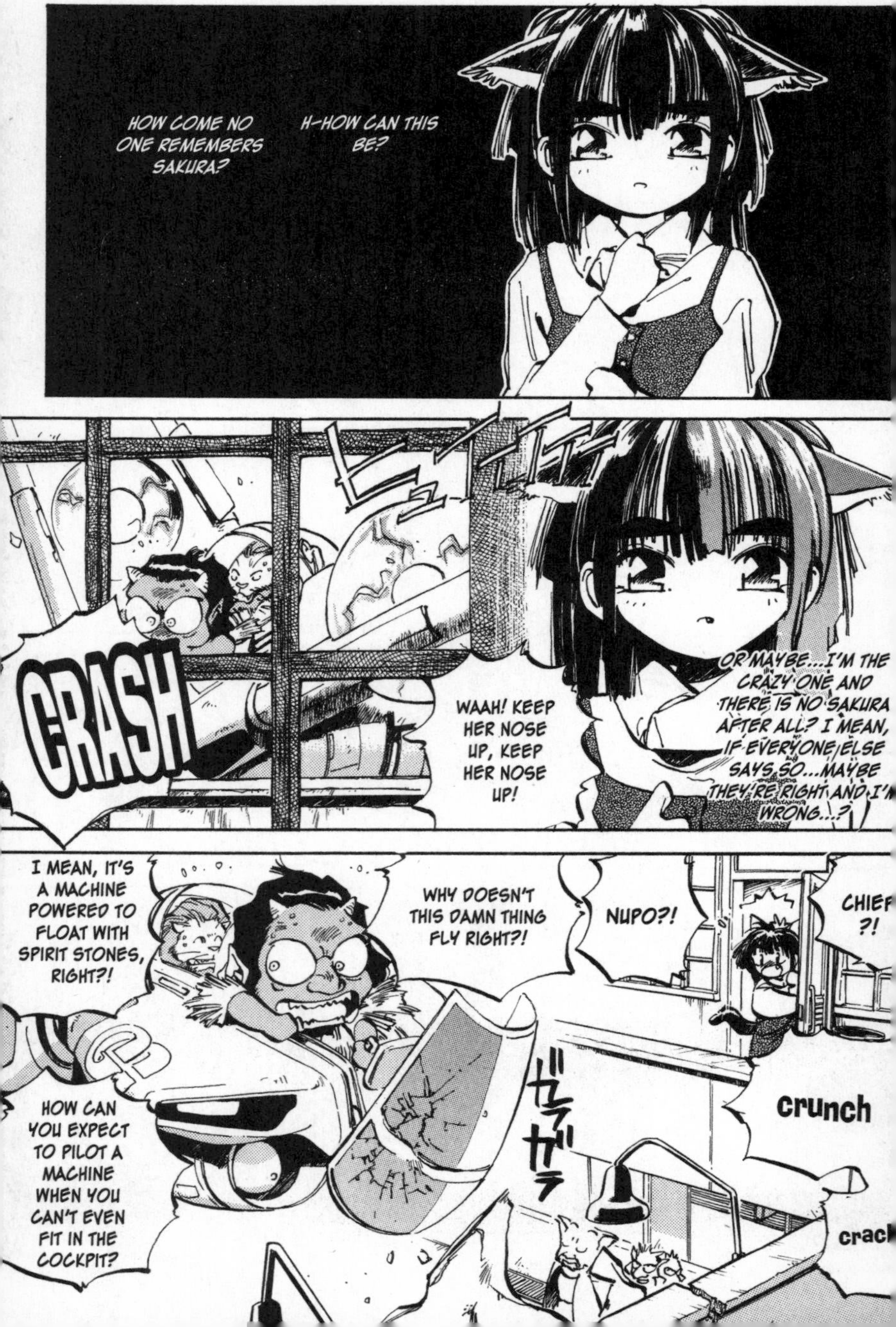
H-HOW CAN THIS BE?
HOW COME NO ONE REMEMBERS SAKURA?
OR MAYBE...I'M THE CRAZY ONE AND THERE IS NO SAKURA AFTER ALL? I MEAN, IF EVERYONE ELSE SAYS SO...MAYBE THEY'RE RIGHT AND I'M WRONG...?
WAAH! KEEP HER NOSE UP, KEEP HER NOSE UP!
CRASH
CHIEF?!
NUPO?!
WHY DOESN'T THIS DAMN THING FLY RIGHT?!
I MEAN, IT'S A MACHINE POWERED TO FLOAT WITH SPIRIT STONES, RIGHT?!
crunch
crack
HOW CAN YOU EXPECT TO PILOT A MACHINE WHEN YOU CAN'T EVEN FIT IN THE COCKPIT?

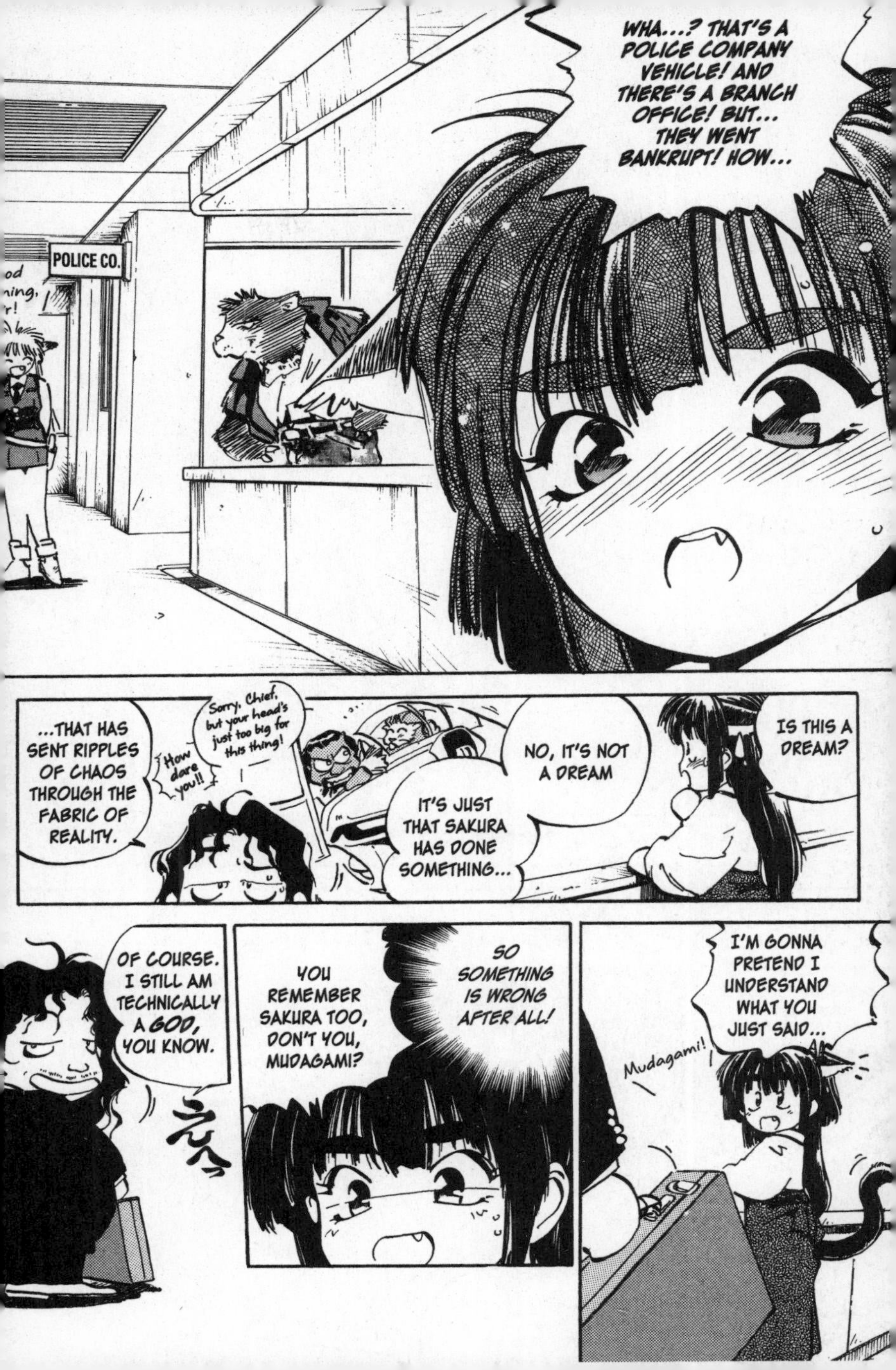
WHA...? THAT'S A POLICE COMPANY VEHICLE! AND THERE'S A BRANCH OFFICE! BUT... THEY WENT BANKRUPT! HOW...
POLICE CO.
IS THIS A DREAM?
NO, IT'S NOT A DREAM
IT'S JUST THAT SAKURA HAS DONE SOMETHING...
Sorry, Chief, but your head's just too big for this thing!
How dare you!!
...THAT HAS SENT RIPPLES OF CHAOS THROUGH THE FABRIC OF REALITY.
I'M GONNA PRETEND I UNDERSTAND WHAT YOU JUST SAID...
Mudagami!
SO SOMETHING IS WRONG AFTER ALL!
YOU REMEMBER SAKURA TOO, DON'T YOU, MUDAGAMI?
OF COURSE. I STILL AM TECHNICALLY A *GOD*, YOU KNOW.

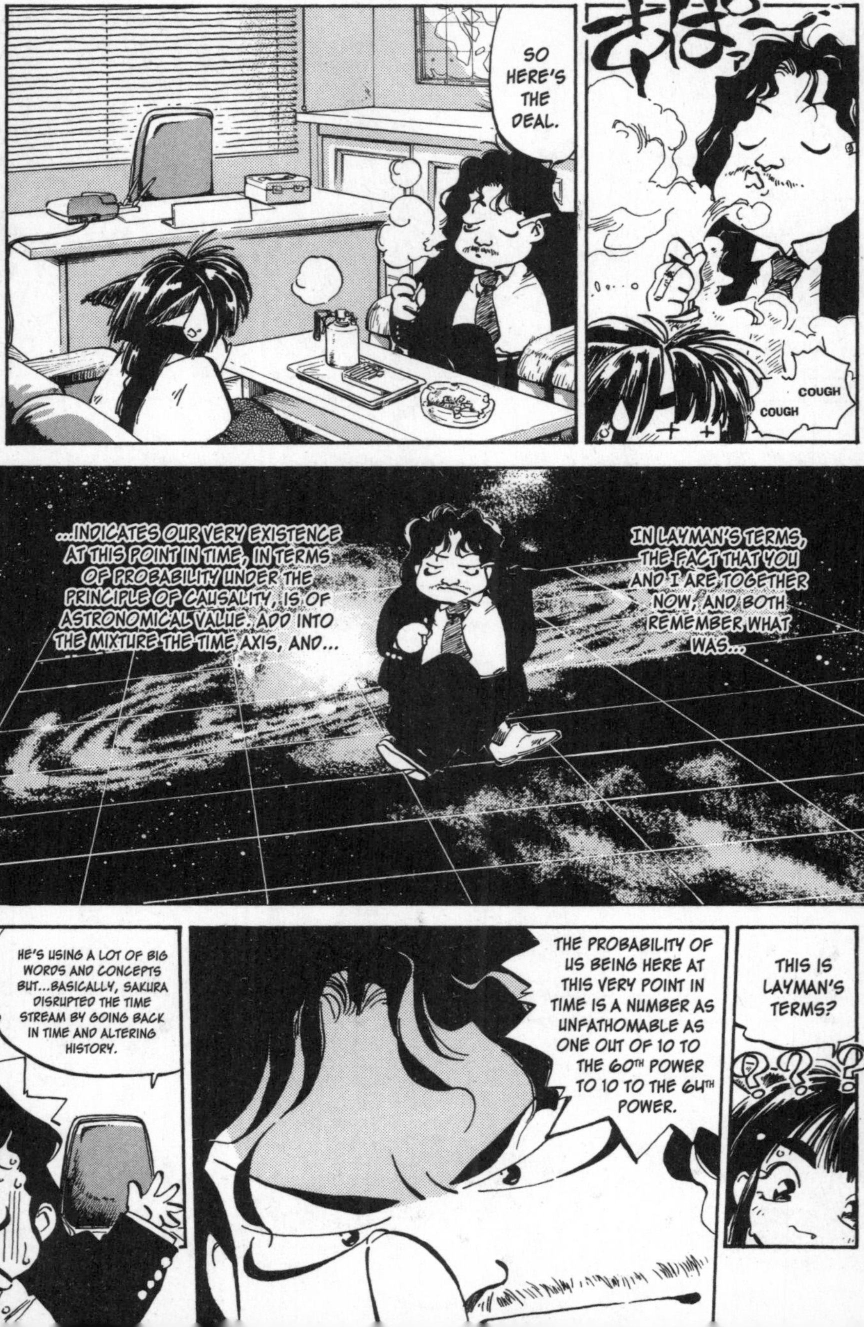

COUGH
COUGH
SO HERE'S THE DEAL.
IN LAYMAN'S TERMS, THE FACT THAT YOU AND I ARE TOGETHER NOW, AND BOTH REMEMBER WHAT WAS...
...INDICATES OUR VERY EXISTENCE AT THIS POINT IN TIME, IN TERMS OF PROBABILITY UNDER THE PRINCIPLE OF CAUSALITY, IS OF ASTRONOMICAL VALUE. ADD INTO THE MIXTURE THE TIME AXIS, AND...
THIS IS LAYMAN'S TERMS?
THE PROBABILITY OF US BEING HERE AT THIS VERY POINT IN TIME IS A NUMBER AS UNFATHOMABLE AS ONE OUT OF 10 TO THE 60TH POWER TO 10 TO THE 64TH POWER.
HE'S USING A LOT OF BIG WORDS AND CONCEPTS BUT...BASICALLY, SAKURA DISRUPTED THE TIME STREAM BY GOING BACK IN TIME AND ALTERING HISTORY.

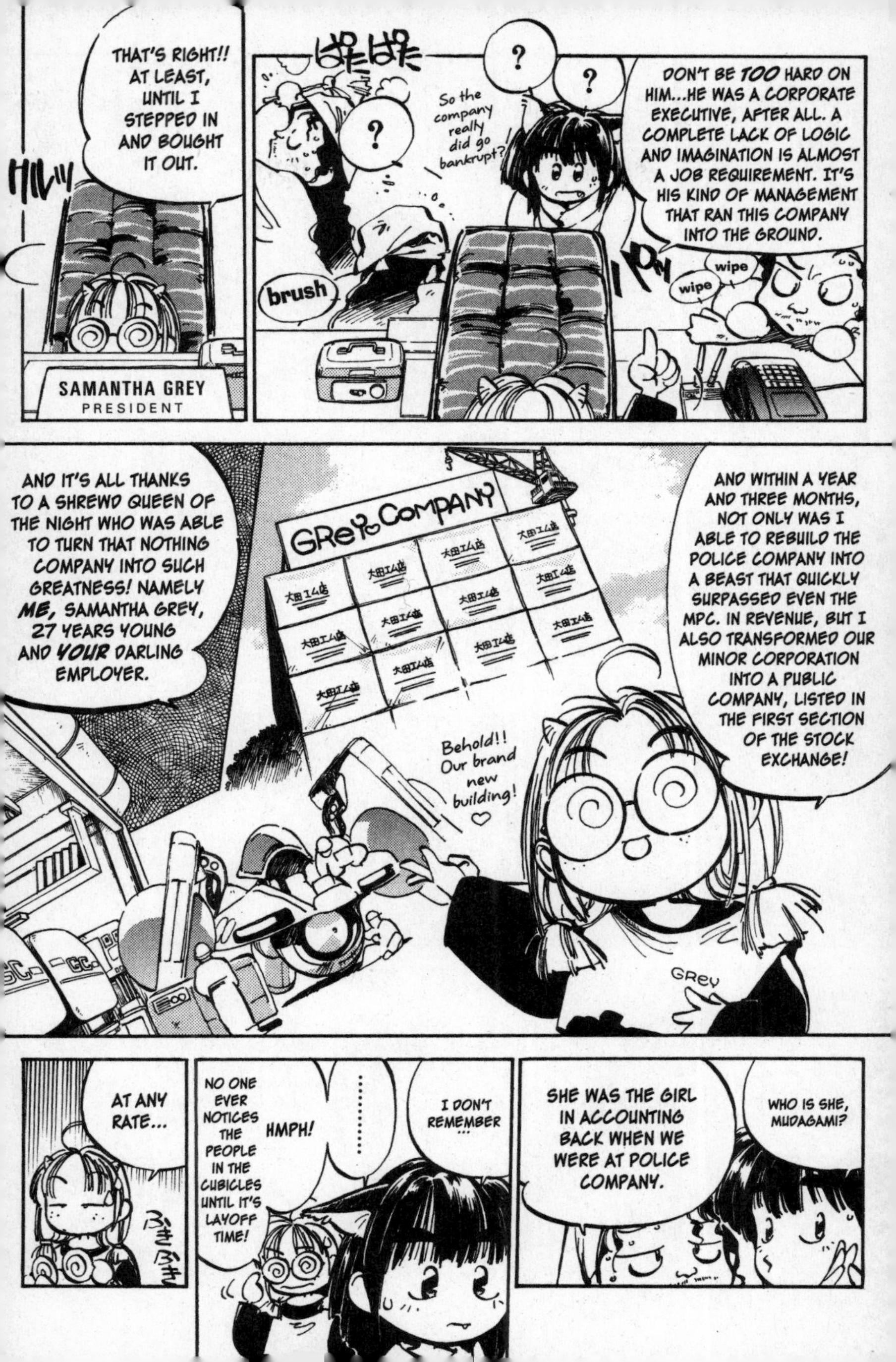

ぱたぱた
?
?
DON'T BE TOO HARD ON HIM...HE WAS A CORPORATE EXECUTIVE, AFTER ALL. A COMPLETE LACK OF LOGIC AND IMAGINATION IS ALMOST A JOB REQUIREMENT. IT'S HIS KIND OF MANAGEMENT THAT RAN THIS COMPANY INTO THE GROUND.
So the company really did go bankrupt?
?
brush
wipe
wipe
THAT'S RIGHT!! AT LEAST, UNTIL I STEPPED IN AND BOUGHT IT OUT.
SAMANTHA GREY
PRESIDENT
AND WITHIN A YEAR AND THREE MONTHS, NOT ONLY WAS I ABLE TO REBUILD THE POLICE COMPANY INTO A BEAST THAT QUICKLY SURPASSED EVEN THE MPC. IN REVENUE, BUT I ALSO TRANSFORMED OUR MINOR CORPORATION INTO A PUBLIC COMPANY, LISTED IN THE FIRST SECTION OF THE STOCK EXCHANGE!
GRey COMPANY
AND IT'S ALL THANKS TO A SHREWD QUEEN OF THE NIGHT WHO WAS ABLE TO TURN THAT NOTHING COMPANY INTO SUCH GREATNESS! NAMELY ME, SAMANTHA GREY, 27 YEARS YOUNG AND YOUR DARLING EMPLOYER.
Behold!! Our brand new building!
GRey
WHO IS SHE, MUDAGAMI?
SHE WAS THE GIRL IN ACCOUNTING BACK WHEN WE WERE AT POLICE COMPANY.
I DON'T REMEMBER...
......
HMPH!
NO ONE EVER NOTICES THE PEOPLE IN THE CUBICLES UNTIL IT'S LAYOFF TIME!
AT ANY RATE...

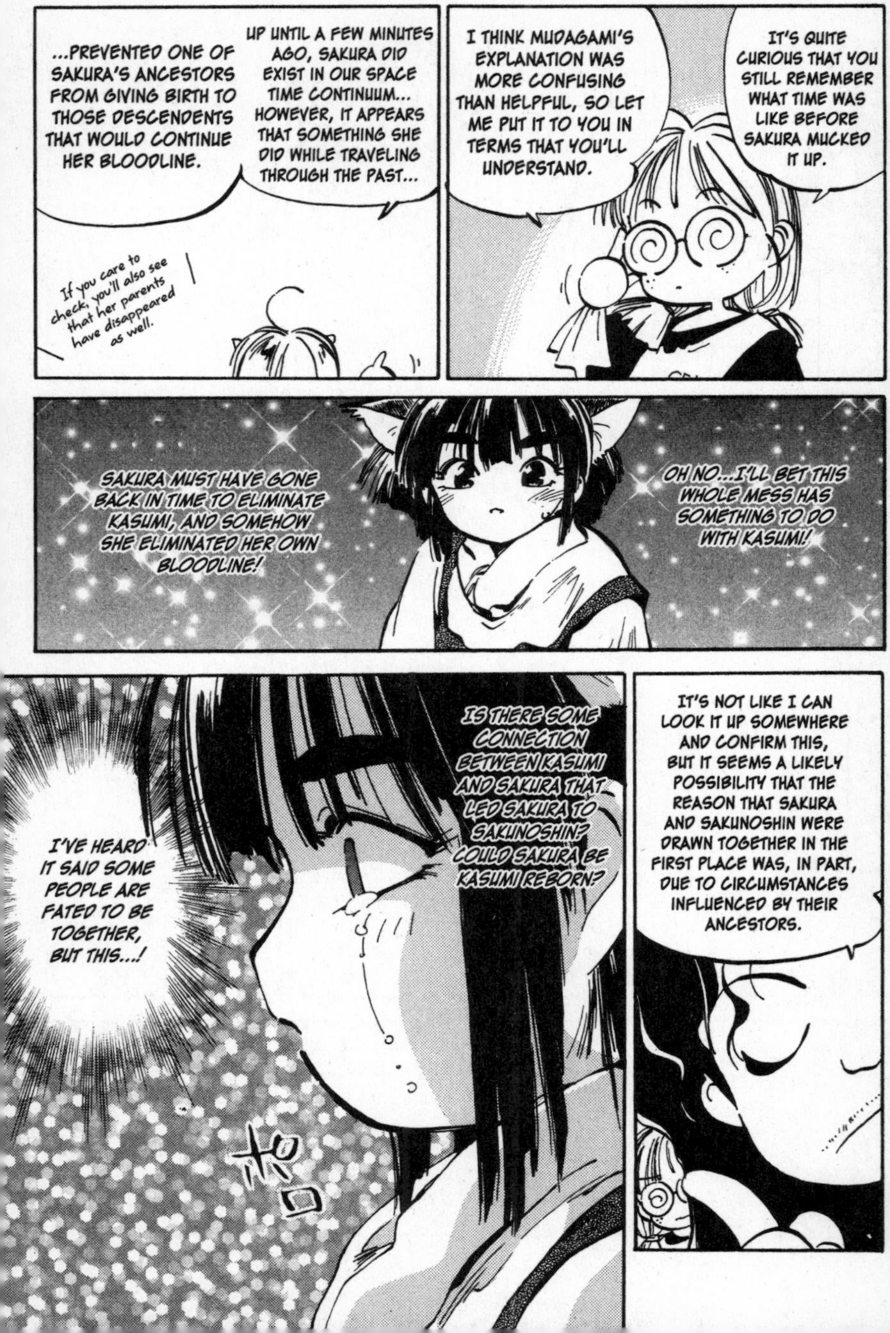
IT'S QUITE CURIOUS THAT YOU STILL REMEMBER WHAT TIME WAS LIKE BEFORE SAKURA MUCKED IT UP.
I THINK MUDAGAMI'S EXPLANATION WAS MORE CONFUSING THAN HELPFUL, SO LET ME PUT IT TO YOU IN TERMS THAT YOU'LL UNDERSTAND.
UP UNTIL A FEW MINUTES AGO, SAKURA DID EXIST IN OUR SPACE TIME CONTINUUM... HOWEVER, IT APPEARS THAT SOMETHING SHE DID WHILE TRAVELING THROUGH THE PAST...
...PREVENTED ONE OF SAKURA'S ANCESTORS FROM GIVING BIRTH TO THOSE DESCENDENTS THAT WOULD CONTINUE HER BLOODLINE.
If you care to check, you'll also see that her parents have disappeared as well.
OH NO...I'LL BET THIS WHOLE MESS HAS SOMETHING TO DO WITH KASUMI!
SAKURA MUST HAVE GONE BACK IN TIME TO ELIMINATE KASUMI, AND SOMEHOW SHE ELIMINATED HER OWN BLOODLINE!
IT'S NOT LIKE I CAN LOOK IT UP SOMEWHERE AND CONFIRM THIS, BUT IT SEEMS A LIKELY POSSIBILITY THAT THE REASON THAT SAKURA AND SAKUNOSHIN WERE DRAWN TOGETHER IN THE FIRST PLACE WAS, IN PART, DUE TO CIRCUMSTANCES INFLUENCED BY THEIR ANCESTORS.
IS THERE SOME CONNECTION BETWEEN KASUMI AND SAKURA THAT LED SAKURA TO SAKUNOSHIN? COULD SAKURA BE KASUMI REBORN?
I'VE HEARD IT SAID SOME PEOPLE ARE FATED TO BE TOGETHER, BUT THIS...!

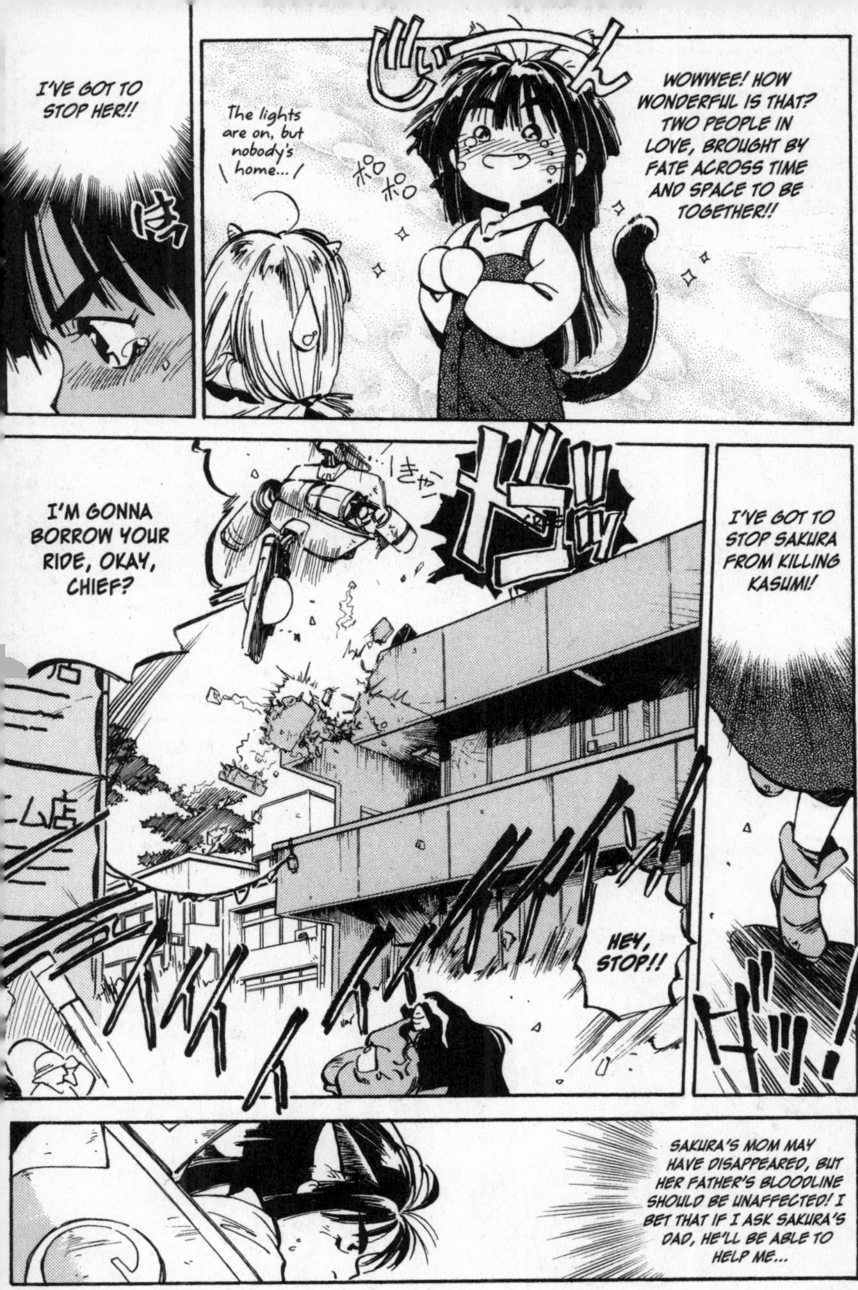
WOWWEE! HOW WONDERFUL IS THAT? TWO PEOPLE IN LOVE, BROUGHT BY FATE ACROSS TIME AND SPACE TO BE TOGETHER!!
The lights are on, but nobody's home...
ポロ ポロ
I'VE GOT TO STOP HER!!
I'VE GOT TO STOP SAKURA FROM KILLING KASUMI!
I'M GONNA BORROW YOUR RIDE, OKAY, CHIEF?
HEY, STOP!!
SAKURA'S MOM MAY HAVE DISAPPEARED, BUT HER FATHER'S BLOODLINE SHOULD BE UNAFFECTED! I BET THAT IF I ASK SAKURA'S DAD, HE'LL BE ABLE TO HELP ME...

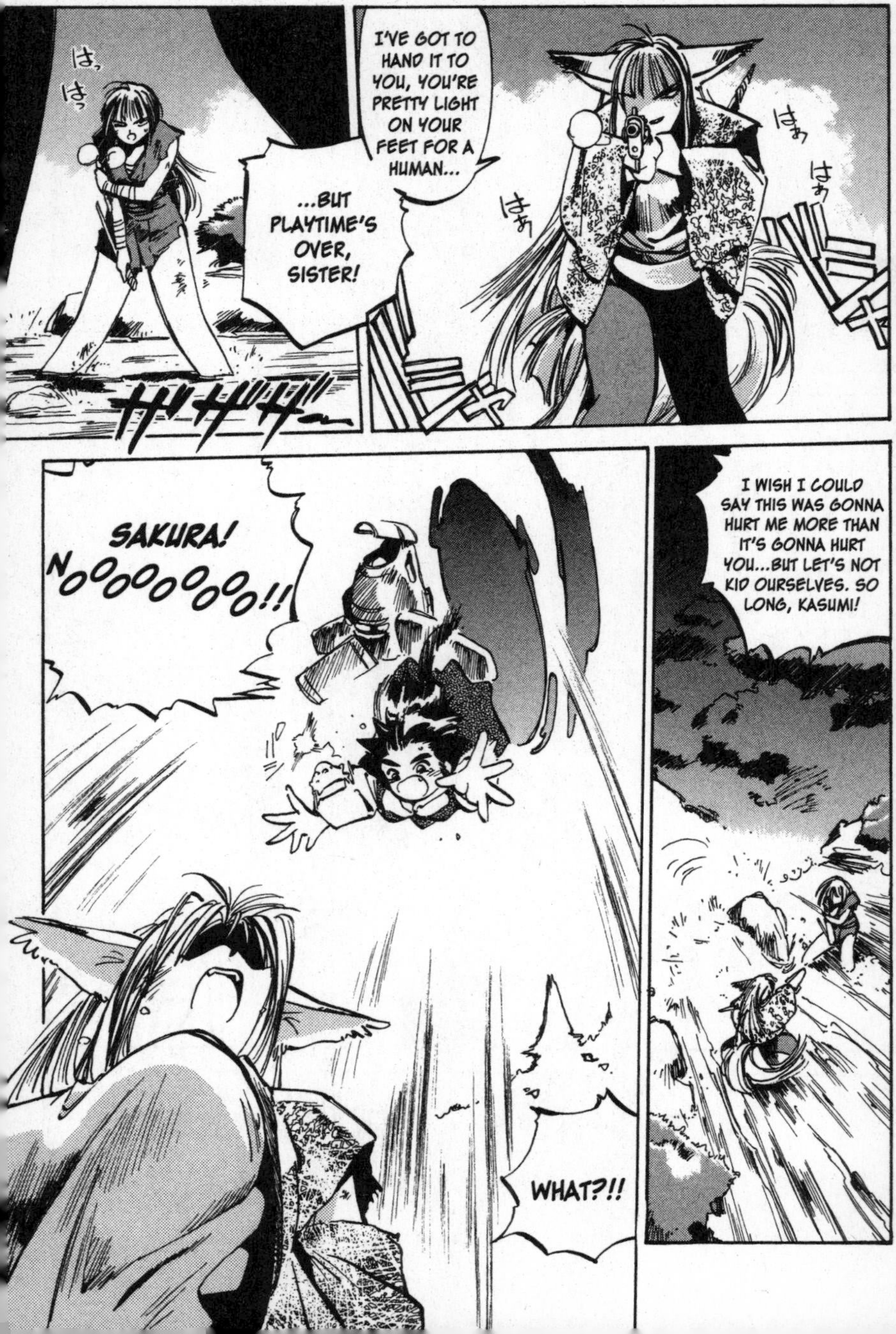

I'VE GOT TO HAND IT TO YOU, YOU'RE PRETTY LIGHT ON YOUR FEET FOR A HUMAN...
...BUT PLAYTIME'S OVER, SISTER!
I WISH I COULD SAY THIS WAS GONNA HURT ME MORE THAN IT'S GONNA HURT YOU...BUT LET'S NOT KID OURSELVES. SO LONG, KASUMI!
SAKURA!
NOOOOOOOOOO!!
WHAT?!!

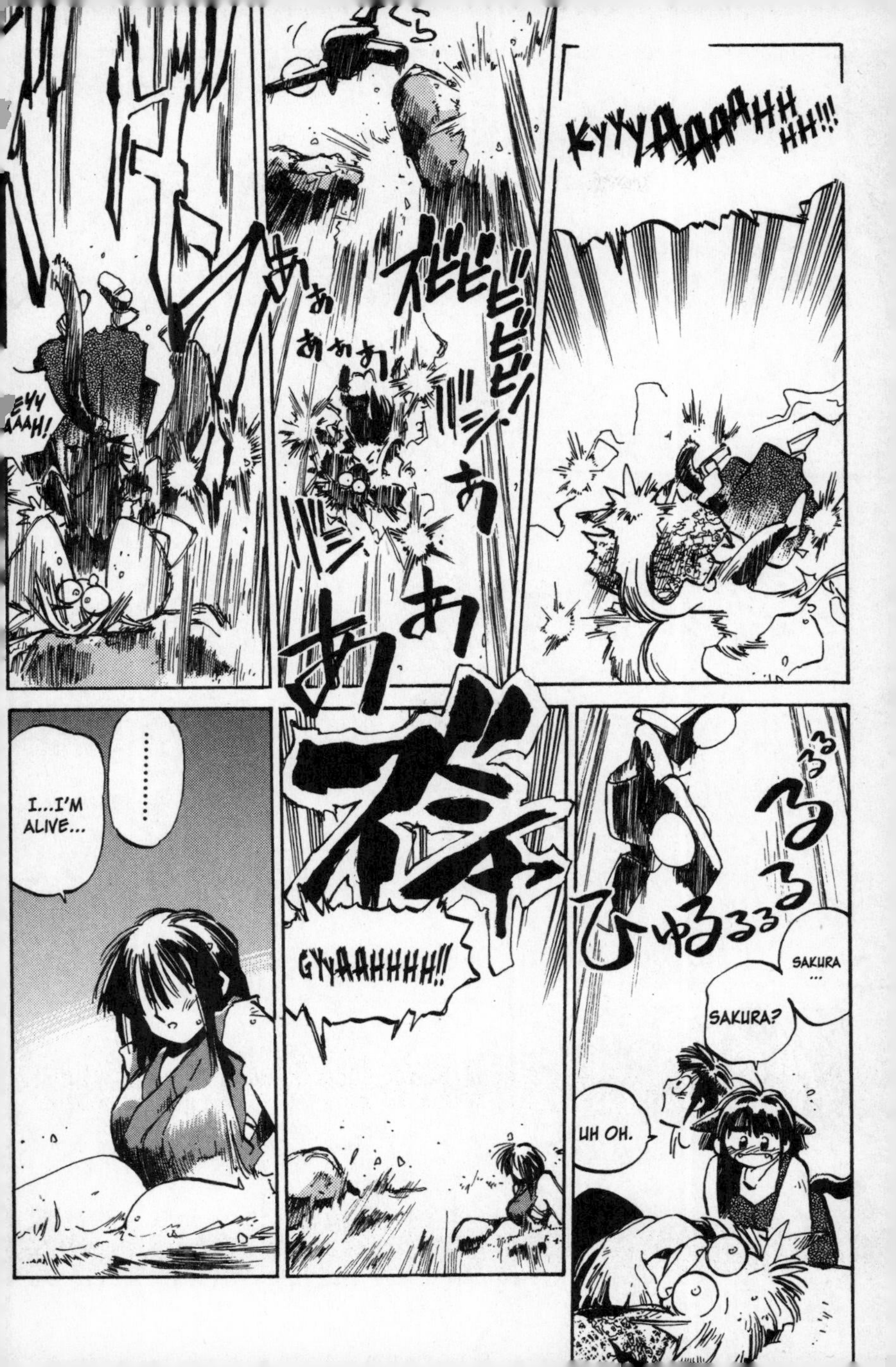

KYYAAAAHH HH!!!
EYY AAAH!
SAKURA ...
SAKURA?
UH OH.
GYAAHHHH!!
......
I...I'M ALIVE...

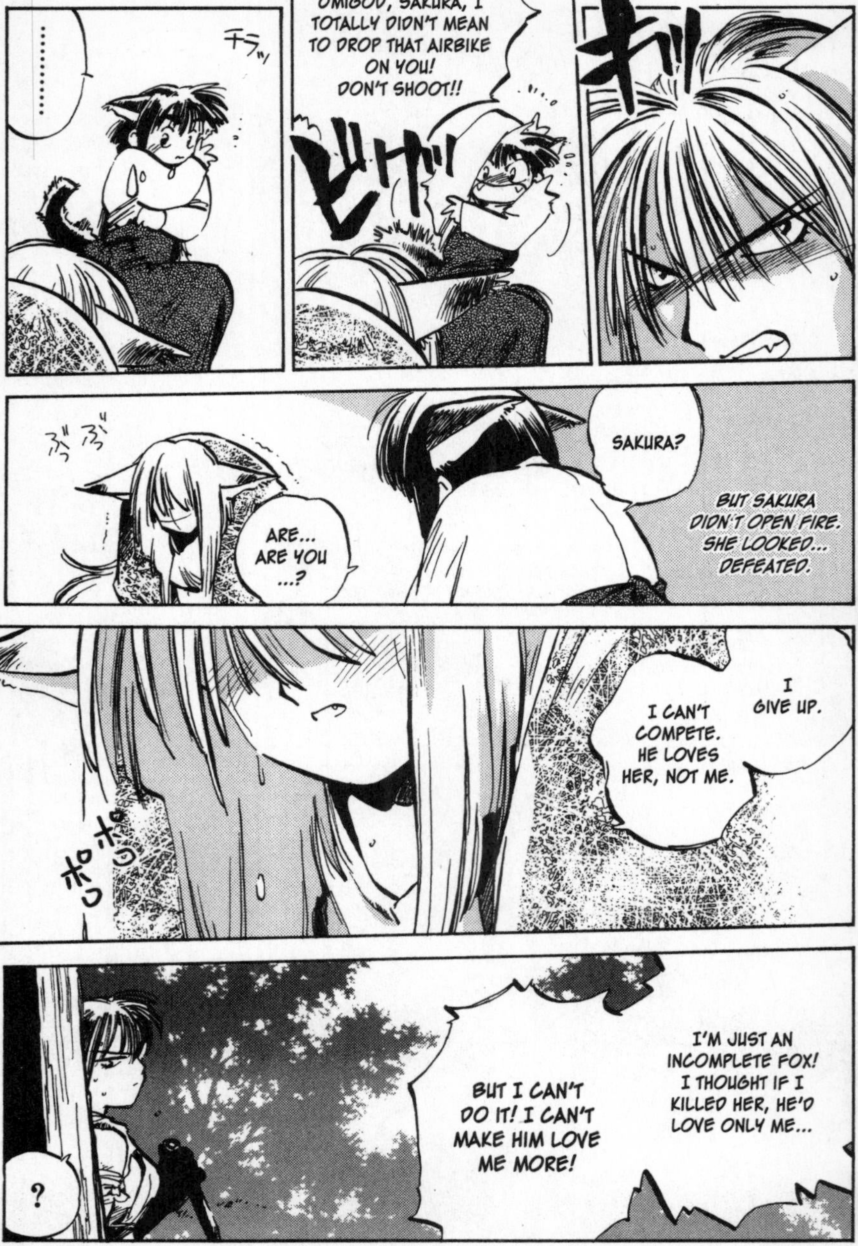
OMIGOD, SAKURA, I TOTALLY DIDN'T MEAN TO DROP THAT AIRBIKE ON YOU! DON'T SHOOT!!
……
チラッ
BUT SAKURA DIDN'T OPEN FIRE. SHE LOOKED... DEFEATED.
SAKURA?
ARE... ARE YOU ...?
I GIVE UP.
I CAN'T COMPETE. HE LOVES HER, NOT ME.
ポロ ポロ
I'M JUST AN INCOMPLETE FOX! I THOUGHT IF I KILLED HER, HE'D LOVE ONLY ME...
BUT I CAN'T DO IT! I CAN'T MAKE HIM LOVE ME MORE!
?

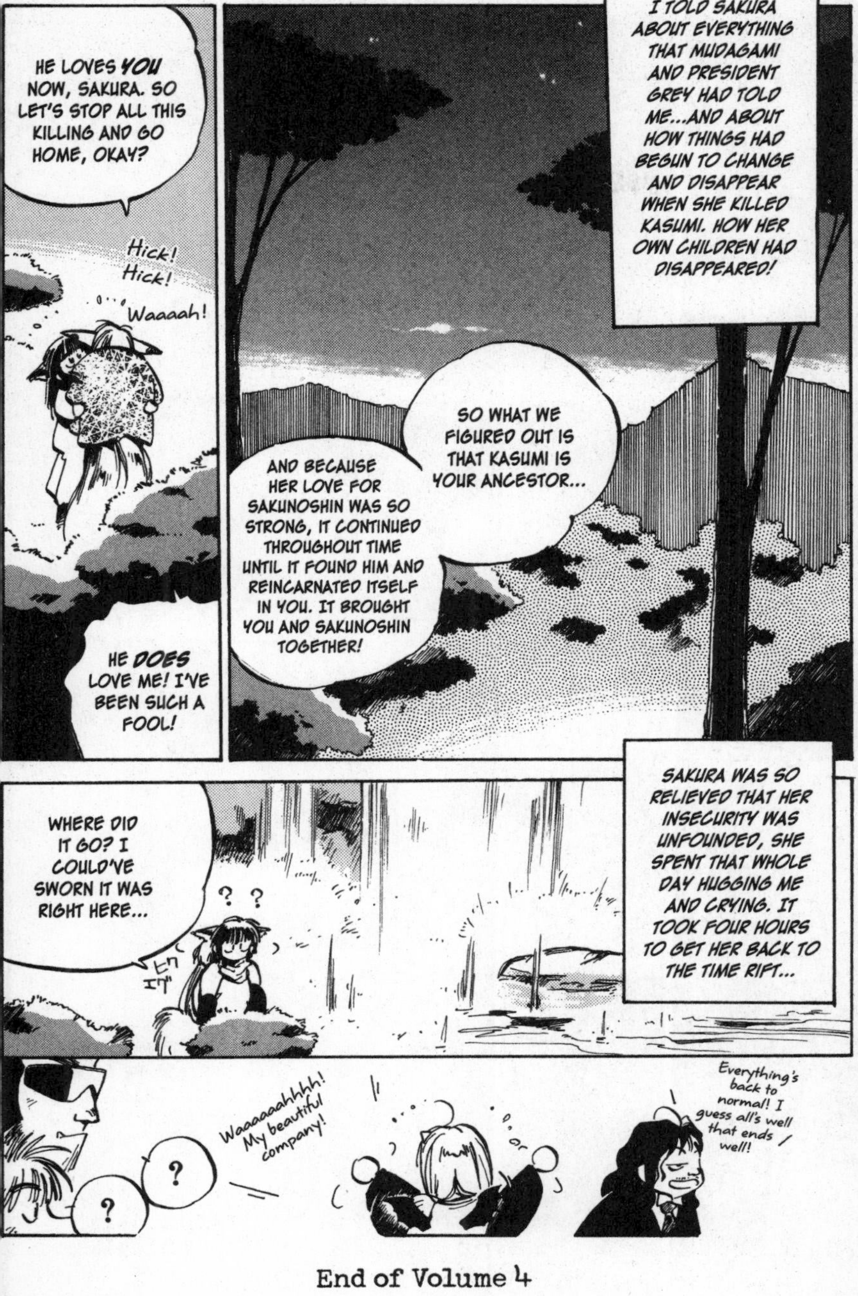

I TOLD SAKURA ABOUT EVERYTHING THAT MUDAGAMI AND PRESIDENT GREY HAD TOLD ME...AND ABOUT HOW THINGS HAD BEGUN TO CHANGE AND DISAPPEAR WHEN SHE KILLED KASUMI. HOW HER OWN CHILDREN HAD DISAPPEARED!
SO WHAT WE FIGURED OUT IS THAT KASUMI IS YOUR ANCESTOR...
AND BECAUSE HER LOVE FOR SAKUNOSHIN WAS SO STRONG, IT CONTINUED THROUGHOUT TIME UNTIL IT FOUND HIM AND REINCARNATED ITSELF IN YOU. IT BROUGHT YOU AND SAKUNOSHIN TOGETHER!
HE LOVES ***YOU*** NOW, SAKURA. SO LET'S STOP ALL THIS KILLING AND GO HOME, OKAY?
Hick! Hick!
Waaaah!
HE ***DOES*** LOVE ME! I'VE BEEN SUCH A FOOL!
SAKURA WAS SO RELIEVED THAT HER INSECURITY WAS UNFOUNDED, SHE SPENT THAT WHOLE DAY HUGGING ME AND CRYING. IT TOOK FOUR HOURS TO GET HER BACK TO THE TIME RIFT...
? ?
WHERE DID IT GO? I COULD'VE SWORN IT WAS RIGHT HERE...
ヒク エグ
Everything's back to normal! I guess all's well that ends well!
Waaaaaahhhh! My beautiful company!
?
?

End of Volume 4

POLICE COMPANY

UNSOLVED CASE REPORT

GENERAL INFORMATION	
Case file number: TJB-2854477-HF	

Investigation status:

Attention All Units: We've received notice of a kidnapping. Victim is one Natsuki Sasahara, a former Police Company bounty hunter. Suspect's name is Fujioka—Batanen Fujioka. Yes, THE Batanen Fujioka. A sizeable reward has been offered for Sasahara's safe return by the victim's father. All interested hunters are warned to proceed with caution and advised to invest in a pair of insulated rubber gloves.

The Shinjuku Police Department has requested assistance in protecting the honor of one of their own. Officer Poe responded to a report of Goblin trouble downtown and is reportedly now in some sort of danger. Details are sketchy, but private hunters Tomy and Sakura have already responded and are presumably on their way. Any other hunters looking to earn a few brownie points with the feds should consider joining them.

This concludes our report. However, we've obtained an additional bit of information that—while not pertaining to any active crimes—may be of interest to any unemployed or freelance bounty hunters operating in the vicinity. A new private police operation, Grey Company, has been established and is currently hiring new officers. All interested parties should get in touch with the company's owner, Samantha Grey...

PD-292 (Rev. 2-89) This information is available in alternative formats upon request. Printed on Recycled Paper

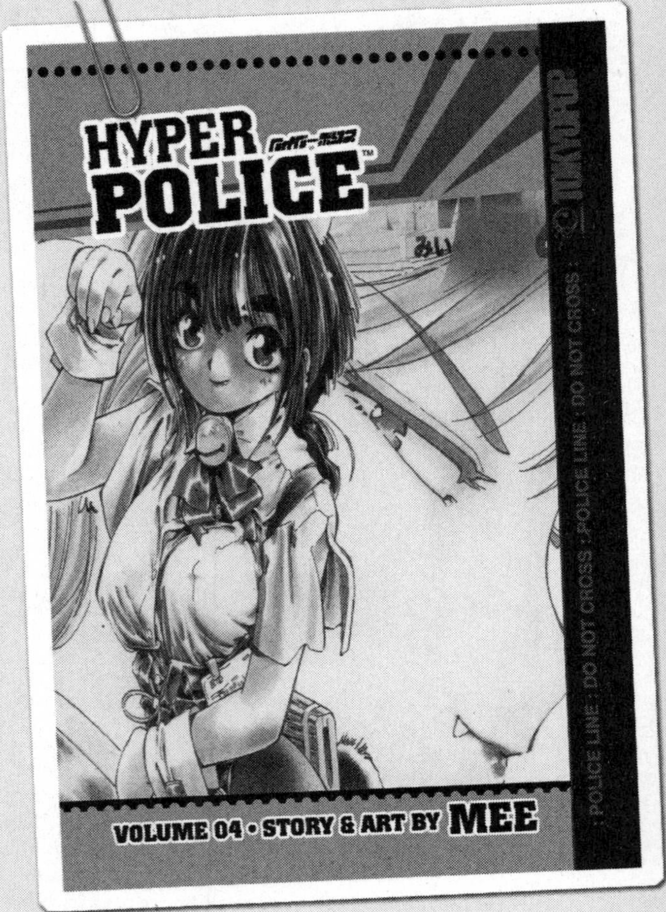
HYPER POLICE™
VOLUME 04 • STORY & ART BY MEE
POLICE LINE : DO NOT CROSS : POLICE LINE : DO NOT CROSS : DO NOT CROSS :

WANTED

MEE

FOR THE PERPETRATION AND SALE OF TRULY TWISTED MANGA FEATURING FURRY FEMME FATALES.

A PRODUCT OF YANAGAWA IN THE FUKUOKA PREFECTURE, MEE WAS BORN ON JUNE 24 IN 1963. PAST ACTIVITY HAS INCLUDED WRITING AND ILLUSTRATING KOTETSU NO DAIBOKEN (KOTETETSU'S GREAT ADVENTURES) FOR WANI MAGAZINE COMICS. CURRENTLY BELIEVED TO BE WORKING ON THE HYPER POLICE MANGA (THOUGH THIS INFORMATION MAY BE OUT OF DATE).

SUSPECT HAS ISSUED THE FOLLOWING STATEMENT TO POLICE COMPANY: "I WOULD LIKE TO HOOK SAKURA UP WITH A BOYFRIEND AND NATSUKI WITH A FIANCE, BUT IT LOOKS LIKE THIS MAY TAKE A WHILE. NEVERTHELESS, I THANK YOU FOR YOUR SUPPORT."

TOKYOPOP SHOP

SCRAPPED PRINCESS

BY GO YABUKI, ICHIRO SAKAKI, AND YUKINOBU AZUMI

HER BIRTH FORETOLD THE DESTRUCTION OF THE WORLD!

Fifteen years ago, a set of twins—a girl and a boy—was born to the king of Linevan. Shortly after their birth, a prophecy foretold that when the girl turned 16, she would bring about the end of humanity. To avoid this terrible fate, the king ordered the girl disposed of—scrapped! She miraculously survived and was raised away from the kingdom that would kill her. But now she has turned 15, the king's guards have caught wind that she's still alive...and they set out to finish the job!

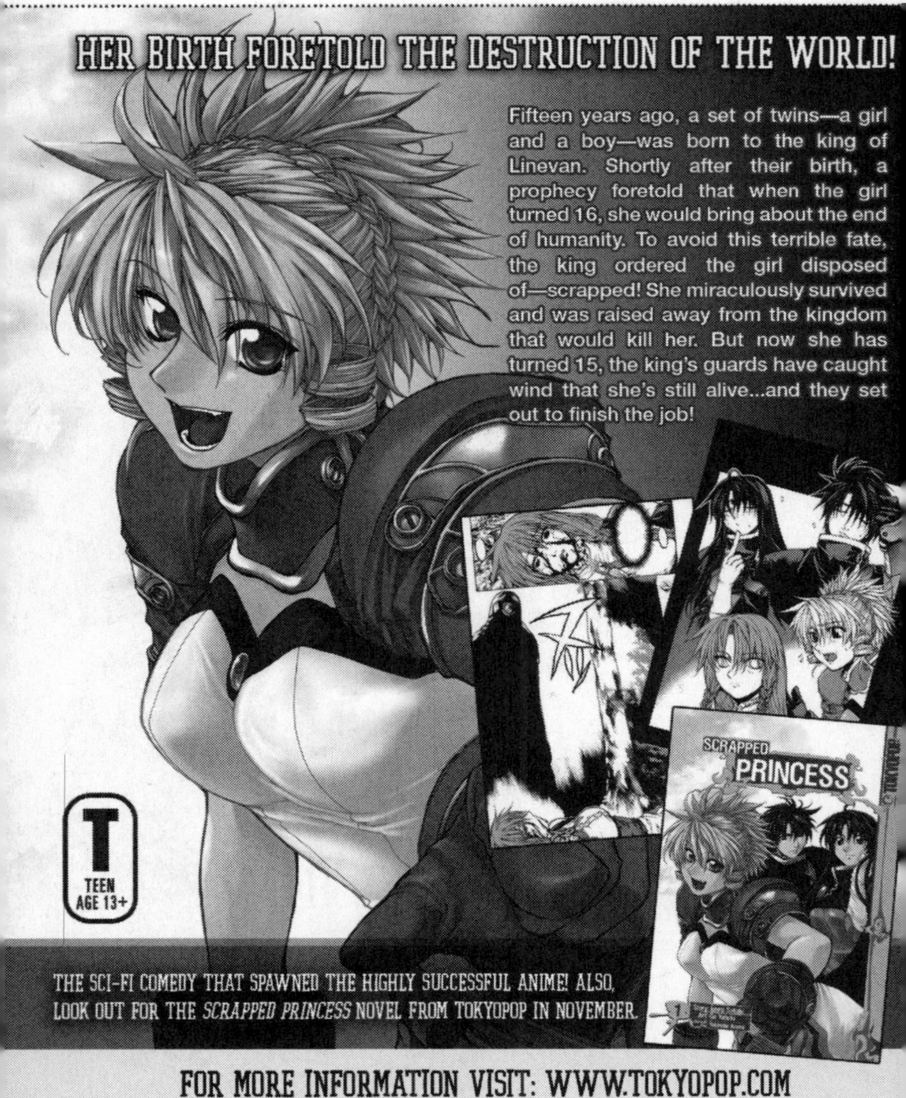
SCRAPPED PRINCESS
TOKYOPOP

T TEEN AGE 13+

THE SCI-FI COMEDY THAT SPAWNED THE HIGHLY SUCCESSFUL ANIME! ALSO, LOOK OUT FOR THE *SCRAPPED PRINCESS* NOVEL FROM TOKYOPOP IN NOVEMBER.

FOR MORE INFORMATION VISIT: WWW.TOKYOPOP.COM

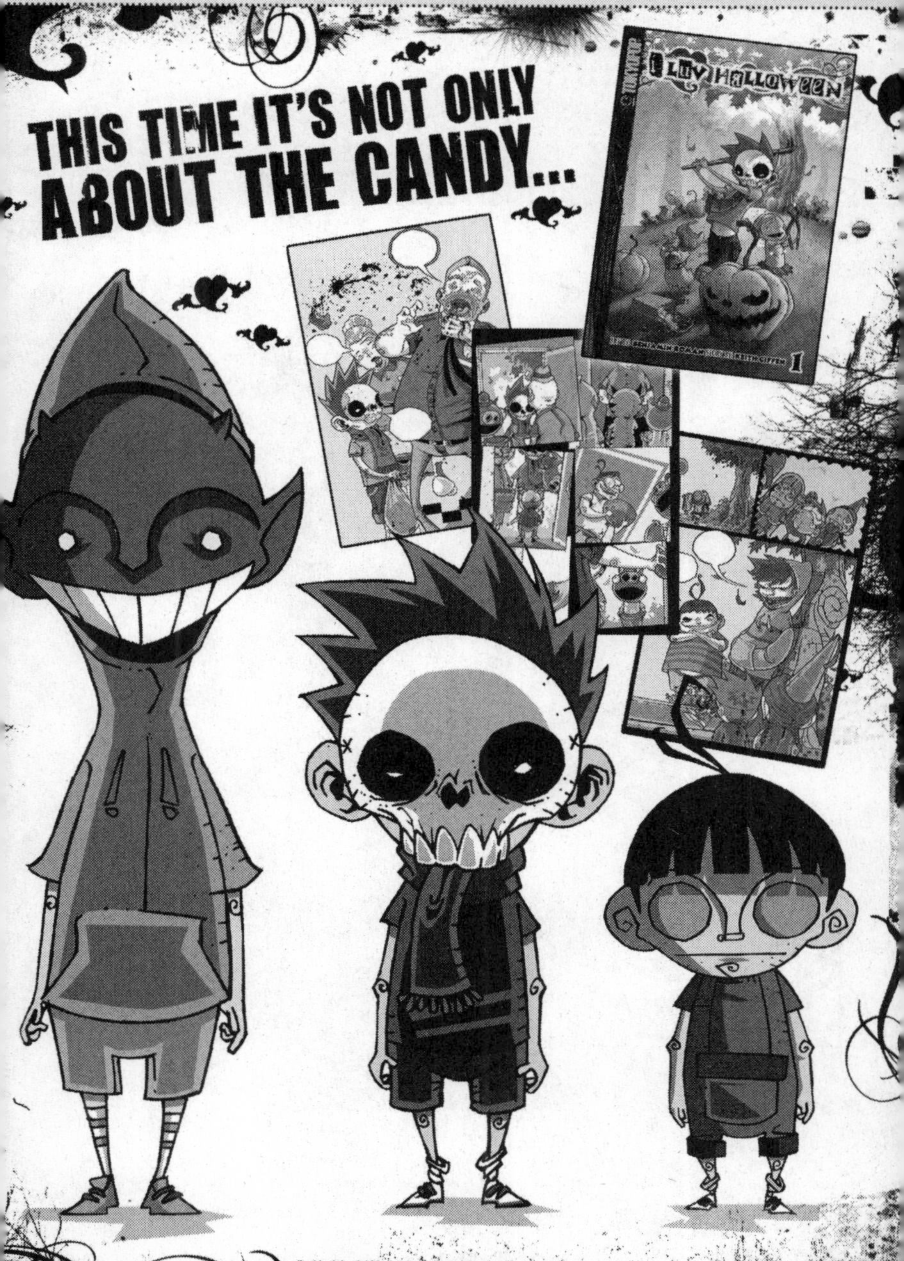
THIS TIME IT'S NOT ONLY ABOUT THE CANDY...
I LUV HALLOWEEN
1

Written by Keith Giffen, comic book pro and English language adapter of *Battle Royale* and *Battle Vixens*.

Join the misadventures of a group of particularly disturbing trick-or-treaters as they go about their macabre business on Halloween night. Blaming the apples they got from the first house of the evening for the bad candy they've been receiving all night, the kids plot revenge on the old bag who handed out the funky fruit. Riotously funny and always wickedly shocking— who doesn't *love* Halloween?

OT
OLDER TEEN
AGE 16+

Y0-BEC-551

STOP!

This is the back of the book.
You wouldn't want to spoil a great ending!

This book is printed "manga-style," in the authentic Japanese right-to-left format. Since none of the artwork has been flipped or altered, readers get to experience the story just as the creator intended. You've been asking for it, so TOKYOPOP® delivered: authentic, hot-off-the-press, and far more fun!

DIRECTIONS

If this is your first time reading manga-style, here's a quick guide to help you understand how it works.

It's easy... just start in the top right panel and follow the numbers. Have fun, and look for more 100% authentic manga from TOKYOPOP®!

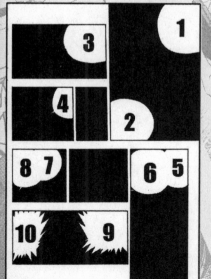